Data for Learning

DIRECTIONS IN DEVELOPMENT
Human Development

Data for Learning

Building a Smart Education Data System

Husein Abdul-Hamid

 **WORLD BANK GROUP**

Contents

Boxes

Figures

Maps

Tables

Foreword

Providing quality education is an extremely complex task. It requires getting millions of students to school every single day, guaranteeing continuous effective interactions between them and thousands of teachers, and ensuring that basic inputs and materials reach classrooms in even the most remote locations. Countless decisions regarding teacher deployment, training, promotion, and salaries must be made. Judgments on school maintenance, construction, and the location of new campuses are also regularly required.

National data systems that inform decision-making and strategic-planning processes of government bureaucrats and school administrators are the backbone of the efficient delivery of this vastly intricate educational service. Data on inputs, processes, finances, and educational outcomes can be used to monitor the effectiveness of service delivery, increase accountability, and engage in cycles of continuous improvement. The School Performance Data Program in the United Kingdom has enhanced efficiency and accountability by maintaining and using school spending, performance, and pupil cohort data. At the classroom level, data can benefit instruction by providing inputs for teachers to guide students and teach at the right level. The United States has made substantial progress in using a data-driven culture in teaching and learning processes. Finally, data can help parents make informed schooling decisions and, by making the lack of learning apparent, increase their demand for quality. The National System for Measuring the Quality of Education in Chile and the My School system in Australia allow parents, schools, and the community to compare school performance nationwide.

However, building and sustaining a data system are complicated tasks, and despite significant investments many countries struggle to have a functional Education Management and Information System (EMIS). *Data for Learning: Building a Smart Education Data System* provides practical strategies to navigate this complex challenge. After outlining the foundations of a successful data system, the book provides tips for harnessing it to maximize learning outcomes. Furthermore, it provides guidance on how to avoid common implementation mistakes when developing such a system and provides examples of countries that have been successful in doing so. The author argues that a successful EMIS requires robust software (with a solid system architecture, serviceability, data coverage, and system dynamics), a sound policy framework, strong organizational structure, physical infrastructure, human capital, and appropriate funding streams.

I hope that this publication helps policy makers worldwide improve their EMIS and, through this, contribute to the provision of the educational systems that our children deserve.

Jaime Saavedra Chanduvi
Senior Director
Education Global Practice
The World Bank Group

Preface

An education data system is expensive and complex. It requires an institutionalized information architecture that understands and engages with the whole education system in a comprehensive, structured, and systematic manner. Many governments suffer from a lack of information about their education systems, leaving them to grapple with demands for information about learning outcomes and the effectiveness and efficiency of policies and programs. Whether too costly to maintain, unable to promote efficiency, riddled with unreliable data, or simply not contributing to effectiveness and equality across the education system, information systems remain an area of confusion, inaccuracy, and misuse in many countries. These issues result in data gaps, hampering the ability of countries to conduct data-driven decision making. Data gaps are global issues that limit the ability of governments and the international community to monitor progress toward achievement of global development goals such as those outlined in Education for All (EFA) and the Sustainable Development Goals (SDGs). An Education Management Information System (EMIS) at the country level should be a primary choice for systematically monitoring progress and fostering accountability for local, national, and international education goals. When effectively institutionalized, an EMIS is also a tool that teachers, principals, and administrators can use to improve learning opportunities for students.

In some countries, information systems do not exist, and important education indicators related to the SDGs and other educational goals are not tracked systematically. For the period 2009–13, only 71 percent of developing countries reported the necessary data for four Millennium Development Goal (MDG) indicators[1] (figure P.1). In recent years, governments have realized the importance of data, and trends toward increased education data collection and performance monitoring have emerged (Bruns, Filmer, and Patrinos 2011). Ultimately, reforming a country's education data system moves well beyond a technology platform. It entails a shift in the way that education professionals think about and value information, toward a strategic mindset around data. *Data for Learning: Building a Smart Education Data System* and its forthcoming companion volume support governments in designing and using a data system that effectively monitors learning outcomes and improves educational performance.

These titles serve as a guide to policy makers wishing to establish, implement or improve, and use an education data system. *Data for Learning* focuses on

Figure P.1 Low and Stagnant Reporting of Indicators

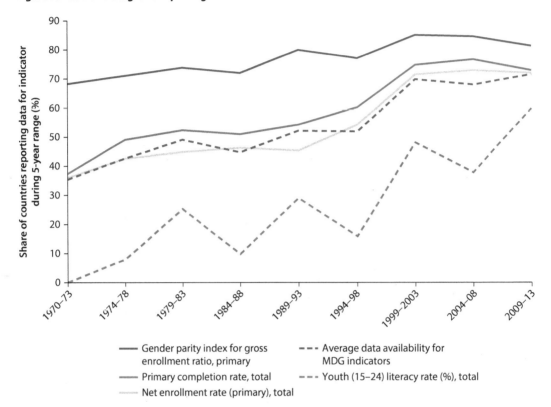

Source: World Bank EdStats calculations based on UNESCO Institute for Statistics data, May 2014.

providing governments with a how-to manual and a road map toward an efficient, effective EMIS that produces high-quality and useable data; a forthcoming second volume highlights education data use. This first volume introduces the basics of any EMIS and guides the reader through common challenges and pitfalls. Data systems should be used to improve efficiency of resources, make smart investments, and improve learning outcomes for all students. An EMIS should be accessible to all stakeholder groups so that they can make informed decisions. Both volumes magnify the importance of institutionalized data systems, as well as the leadership and additional key components required to make these data systems a reality. The key points raised in these titles are applicable to governments aiming to introduce a new EMIS as well as to those wishing to upgrade an existing one.

Data for Learning: Building a Smart Education Data System commences by reviewing the ingredients that are necessary in building this strategic mindset. It defines EMISs, examines the importance of data within an education system, and identifies what matters most in the journey to an effective EMIS. After guiding the reader through the key aspects of an education data system and how its strength should be assessed, it thoroughly discusses crucial EMIS elements. The school census provides a snapshot of the education system, which can be compared on a year-to-year basis, and allows policy makers to track education progress toward national goals. Unique identifiers for schools, teachers, and students enable longitudinal studies and provide important insights. In today's digitalized world, selecting the appropriate software solution for the national EMIS is a decisive factor in the system's effectiveness and success. Finally, this volume presents case studies from all over the world, each offering a wide array of lessons learned that are applicable to many other countries. For instance, the case of the United States illustrates how advanced systems use data for classroom instruction and focus on learning outcomes. The Chilean case demonstrates how strong institutionalization ensures a functioning EMIS in a highly centralized education system. Similarly, the Australian case focuses on how national policies and institutionalization are the foundation of an operational EMIS and enable stakeholders to compare schools across the country. The experience of Fiji illustrates how affordable EMIS solutions are possible and acts as a role model for other education data systems in the region. The establishment of a functioning EMIS in Afghanistan demonstrates that education data systems can work even in fragile environments. Overall, this first volume provides a comprehensive and detailed description of key aspects of the EMIS supported by key country examples. The forthcoming second volume will dig deeper into EMIS uses and applications.

Note

1. MDG indicators included (1) primary completion rate, (2) net enrollment rate, (3) gender parity index primary, and (4) youth literacy rate (15–24 years). The MDGs can be considered the "predecessors" of the SDGs. Data are from the Education Projects Database, World Bank, Washington, DC (accessed September 7, 2016), http://datatopics.worldbank.org/education/wDataQuery/QProjects.aspx.

Reference

Bruns, Barbara, Deon Filmer, and Harry Anthony Patrinos. 2011. *Making Schools Work: New Evidence on Accountability Reforms*. Washington, DC: World Bank.

Acknowledgments

Many individuals provided valuable inputs and suggestions for this work. Particular thanks to the peer reviewers: Fred Brooker, Thomas Cassidy, Dingyong Hou, Lindsay Read, and Lianqin Wang. Guidance and support were provided by Luis Benveniste, Director of the Education Global Practice. Special thanks to Colin Connelly, Christine Joo, Diana Katharina Mayrhofer, Sarah M. Mintz, Namrata Saraogi, and Wouter Takkenberg for the literature reviews and edits. Thanks to Cassia Miranda, who provided the logistics support, and to Jung-Hwan Choi, Jessica Cross, and Tara Siegel for their edits and support.

The document also benefited from discussions and guidance from colleagues at the Global Engagement and Knowledge Unit and the Education Global Practice at the World Bank Group. Finally, special thanks to the publishing team's Stephen Pazdan and Jewel McFadden.

This work was made possible by financial support from the Australian Department of Foreign Affairs and Trade (DFAT) and the United Kingdom's Department for International Development (DfID).

About the Author

Husein Abdul-Hamid is a Senior Education Specialist and the Education Statistics Coordinator at the World Bank. Dr. Abdul-Hamid works on global engagements such as data for learning and the education flagship initiative, "Systems Approach for Better Education Results." He manages education lending operations in the Middle East and North Africa, Sub-Saharan Africa, Eastern Europe and Central Asia, Latin America, the Pacific Islands, and North America, with a focus on education system reform, education in fragile contexts, and learning in the face of adversity.

His professional career includes international development, academia, and government. He has more than 25 years of experience in the following areas of education: teaching, education system reform, data analytics and strategic planning, system intelligence, institutional effectiveness and system accountability, equality in education, and analysis of learning outcomes.

Before joining the World Bank Group, Dr. Abdul-Hamid was a Senior Administrator and Professor of Management at the University of Maryland, College Park. During his tenure at Maryland, he pioneered research on instructions and policies in relation to e-learning and adult education. He holds a PhD in statistics.

His recent publications include *Lessons Learned from World Bank Education Management Information System Operations, From Compliance to Learning, Learning in the Face of Adversity,* and "What Matters Most for Education Management Information Systems."

Abbreviations

ABS	Australian Bureau of Statistics
ACARA	Australian Curriculum, Assessment and Reporting Authority
AFIS	Automated Fingerprint Identification System
AGE	*Apoyo a la Gestión Escolar*
AITSL	Australian Institute for Teaching and School Leadership
ALS	Alternative Learning System
API	application programming interface
AQEP	Access to Quality Education Program
ARRA	American Recovery and Reinvestment Act
ARTF	Afghanistan Reconstruction Trust Fund
ARTS	Afghanistan Reliable Technology Services
ASC	annual school census
AYP	adequate yearly progress
BI	business intelligence
BISP	Benazir Income Support Program
CAPI	Computer-Assisted Personal Interview
CEDS	Common Education Data Standards
CHESSN	Commonwealth Higher Education Student Support Number
CNED	Chilean National Education Council (*Consejo Nacional de Educación*)
COAG	Council of Australian Governments
COMAR	Code of Maryland Regulations
COPPA	Children's Online Privacy Protection Act
CRC	Child Registration Certificates
DATA	Direct Access to Achievement
DBMS	database management system
DCAA	Division of Curriculum, Assessment, and Accountability
DEO	district education office

DER	Digital Education Revolution
DFAT	Department of Foreign Affairs and Trade, Australia
DfID	Department for International Development, U.K.
DHS	Demographic and Health Surveys
DLI	delivery-linked indicator
DLLR	Department of Labor, Licensing, and Regulation
DLT	delivery-linked target
DQAF	Data Quality Assessment Framework
DQC	Data Quality Campaign
DSS	Data Science Studio
EAU	Examination and Assessment Unit
ECE	early childhood education
ECS	Education Commission of the States
EFA	Education for All
EIS	Executive Information System
EMIS	Education Management Information System
EQUIP	Education Quality Improvement Project
ESEA	Elementary and Secondary Education Act
ESRA	Education Sciences Reform Act
ETEB	Enhancing Teacher Effectiveness in Bihar
FDOE	Florida Department of Education
FEMIS	Fiji Education Management Information System
FERPA	Family Educational Rights and Privacy Act
GER	gross enrollment rate
HEIMS	Higher Education Information Management System
HELP	Higher Education Loan Program
HEPCAT	Higher Education Provider Client Assistance Tool
HP	Hewlett Packard
ICR	intelligent character recognition
ICSEA	Index of Community Socio-Educational Advantage
ICT	information and communication technology
IDB	Inter-American Development Bank
IMF	International Monetary Fund
IOS	International Organization for Standardization
ISCA	Independent School Council of Australia
ISDP	Information Systems Development Policy
LANA	Literacy and Numeracy Assessment
LDS	Longitudinal Data System
LEA	local education agency

LGE	Chilean Law of General Education (*Ley General de Educación*, 2009)
LIS	Learner Information System
LSMS	Living Standards Measurement Study
M&E	monitoring and evaluation
MLDS	Maryland Longitudinal Data System
MoE	Ministry of Education
MoEHA	Ministry of Education, Heritage and Arts
MoH	Ministry of Health
MoI	Ministry of Interior
MoNE	Ministry of National Education
MSAD	Ministry of State for Administrative Development
MSDE	Maryland State Department of Education
MSPAP	Maryland School Performance Assessment Program
NAP	National Assessment Programme
NCEC	National Catholic Education Commission
NCES	National Center for Education Statistics
NCLB	No Child Left Behind
NER	net enrollment rate
NGO	nongovernmental organization
NIA	National Identification Authority
NSIP	National Schools Interoperability Program
OCMIS	Oversight Committee on Management Information System
ODK	Open Data Kit
OMR	optical mark recognition
PC	personal computer
PED	Provincial Education Department
PER	Chilean Educational Achievement Evaluation Program
PHP	Personal Home Page
PLC	professional learning community
PTUZ	Progressive Teachers' Union of Zimbabwe
QA	quality assurance
RBF	results-based financing
RDBMS	relational database management system
RENIEC	Registered in the National Registry of Identification and Civil Status
RFP	request for proposal
RTTT	Race to the Top
SaaS	Software as a Service

SABER	Systems Approach for Better Education Results
SBP	System Baseline Profile
SDG	Sustainable Development Goals
SIES	Chilean National Higher Education Information System
SIF	Systems Interoperability Framework
SIGE	*Système d'Information pour la Gestion de l'Education*
SIMS	School Information Management System
SLDS	Statewide Longitudinal Data Systems
SLO	Student Learning Objectives
SPC	Secretariat of the Pacific Community
SPI	School Progress Index
SQL	Structured Query Language
STR	student–teacher ratio
SWYP	*Soluciones Web Y Portales*
TA	Technical Advisor
TEAMS	The Evaluation & Assets Management System
TED	Teacher Education Department
TEMIS	Teacher Education Management Information System
TIMSS	Trends in International Mathematics and Science Study
UFE	Utilization-Focused Evaluation
UID	unique identification
UIDAI	Unique Identification Authority of India
UIS	UNESCO Institute for Statistics
UNESCO	United Nations Educational, Scientific, and Cultural Organization
USAID	U.S. Agency for International Development
USI	unique student identifier
VET	vocational education training
VPN	virtual private network

Executive Summary

Data are an important ingredient in any successful education system, the provision of which rests on the development of an Education Management Information System (EMIS). However, building and sustaining a data system are challenging tasks. Many countries around the world have spent significant resources but still struggle to accomplish a functioning EMIS. On the other hand, countries that have created successful systems are harnessing the power of data to improve education outcomes. Increasingly, the focus of EMISs is moving away from using data narrowly for counting students and schools. Instead they are using data to drive system-wide innovations, accountability, professionalization, and, most important, quality and learning. Data can play an important role to inform decision making, effectiveness of delivery, and strategic planning. Data can also benefit classroom instruction and support at schools. A data system can ensure that education cycles, from preschool to tertiary, are aligned and the education system is monitored so that it will achieve the ultimate goals of producing graduates who are able to successfully transition into the labor market and contribute to the overall national economy.

Overall, education data systems empower data users at the central, regional, and local levels. An EMIS extends far beyond a mere monitoring tool and should be used for education decisions by policy makers, school staff, parents, and students. An EMIS enables smart investments, evidence-based decision making, and effective resource allocation and guides education policy to foster learning at all levels of the education system. Information also fosters efficiency, sustainability, and accountability to all stakeholder groups and provides links across education and related sectors to improve learning outcomes of all students.

The motivation of *Data for Learning: Building a Smart Education Data System* and its forthcoming companion volume is to focus on the common implementation challenges in building a data system and provide actionable direction on how to navigate the complex issues associated with education data for better learning outcomes and beyond. Their intent is to guide education stakeholders in collecting, managing, and using data to improve efficiency and quality in the education system. The first volume, *Data for Learning*, delineates the building blocks of a successful data system and provides a toolkit on how to avoid common implementation mistakes while developing sustainable systems through including tangible examples and best practices. Engineers define a *smart system* as one that incorporates functions of sensing, actuation, and control in order to describe and analyze a situation, and make decisions on the basis of the available data in a predictive or adaptive manner. In the EMIS context, smart means a system that functions in the same way by contributing to smart actions toward student learning and system improvement. The forthcoming second volume will dig deeper into the practical applications of EMIS by various user groups. It will focus on how the framework and building blocks developed in the first volume can be used to address the lack of data-driven culture in different countries with different capabilities, context, and issues.

This volume is organized in the following manner. It begins with providing a framework to assist countries in understanding the current status of their EMIS operations. The framework categorizes the issues related to EMIS development into four areas: (1) political support and stakeholder buy-in (chapters 1, 2, and 3); (2) data collection and school census (chapter 4); (3) management of the collected data and issues related to software and hardware (chapter 5); and (4) integration of the different databases for decision making to improve learning outcomes (chapter 6). It then provides some examples of countries that have been successful in moving from a rudimentary or nonexistent data-driven system to one that is able to monitor the progress of their education system, overcoming some of the abovementioned four issue areas.

The motivation behind these sections is to provide a "how-to" guide for countries that are currently at different stages of EMIS deployment, so they can look at specific sections relevant to their purpose. For example, a country at the procurement stage for software could refer to chapter 5 to understand the step-by-step process of moving forward, whereas another country looking for examples of good practices in developing or upgrading a school census can navigate through chapter 4. It is also a resource for policy makers working to craft the vision and strategic road map of an EMIS as well as a handbook to assist teams and decision makers in avoiding common mistakes.

In a successful EMIS an array of factors—such as vision, policies, leadership, processes, and resources, to name a few—must be aligned in order to effectively harness data in such a way that they support the education mission and drive strong outcomes. Some of the key ingredients of success include the following.

It begins with assessing the current state of the data system in a country before embarking on system improvement. Improvements need to be phased out into steps; doing the whole system at once is not recommended. The chances of success depend on thorough planning and on having all steps aligned to produce a sustainable system with a clear value. In this process, coordination between EMIS stakeholders is important, especially among data-providing units to ensure proper and timely data flows, eliminate duplications, and reduce cost. Engaging with units outside of the ministry of education (such as national statistics bureau, ministry of finance, and so on) is also crucial. Roles and responsibilities should be clearly assigned so that all stakeholders are able to fulfill their unique purpose. Moreover, if data access and/or ownership resides with data users, this is likely to increase data use and consequently data quality as well as stakeholder buy-in. The framework paper, "What Matters Most for Education Management Information Systems" (Abdul-Hamid 2014), is a useful resource, as is the Systems Approach for Better Education Results (SABER)–EMIS Rubric and Data Collection Instrument.

A successful EMIS is embedded in a strong enabling environment supported by a well-defined policy framework, organizational structure, infrastructure capacity, human resources, and budget with a sound EMIS system (system architecture, serviceability, data coverage, and system dynamics) that produces high-quality data. An operational EMIS should empower all data users such as government officials, external users (for example, independent researchers and nongovernmental organizations), and local users (for example, school staff, parents, and the community) to make informed decisions to produce effective student learning outcomes.

A successful EMIS also relies on the buy-in of and the collaboration between stakeholders within the ministry of education and with other relevant agencies across the education system. It is important that data stakeholders are empowered at the central, regional, and local levels to effectively do their share to gather all relevant data. A culture of data enables education stakeholders to realize the value of data. A culture of data means that education decisions at all levels of the education structure are based on data and evidence. Data provide policy makers with the opportunity to implement cost-efficient, smart, and effective investments focusing on outcomes. Overall, an EMIS should be embedded into the country-specific context and be sustainable, efficient, and accountable to all stakeholders.

Education indicators, often compiled using annual school census forms, provide a snapshot of the education system, which is comparable over time and should be integrated into the EMIS. It should include accurate and detailed administrative data on schools, students, human resources, and other resources and should be directly aligned with national education goals. Before implementing a school census, the legal, financial, technological, roles and responsibilities, and administrative capacities need to be assessed. Then, the census processes, system architecture, timelines, budget, and necessary trainings should be planned carefully. Before national implementation of a school census, a comprehensive review of the prior school censuses needs to take place. Once completed, the school census is generally initiated with proper communication activities at the central level, local authorities, and schools. Regional offices collect the school census data (digitally or on paper), which are later internally and externally verified. Timely completion is crucial, and penalties should be enforced in case of noncompliance. Data need to be analyzed and disseminated within no more than four to six months of data collection. The school census has to be fully institutionalized and annually reviewed to identify cost-saving measures, better compliance, overcome challenges, and introduce innovations. Schools need to receive individual reports so that they can compare the school census data with that of other schools, which will ensure relevance of the census and will help in school improvement.

EMIS software solutions need to be carefully selected, keeping in mind affordability, sustainability, usability, interoperability with existing systems, and customizability for future expansions. The process of acquiring an EMIS software solution requires the following steps:

- Assessing the country-specific education needs
- Deciding on the required education modules (for example, attendance, finance, textbook, enrollment, teacher, and staff modules)
- Designing the system architecture (for example, client–server vs. cloud-based options)
- Choosing between self-developed or off-the-shelf software
- Weighing proprietary ("self-coded") and open-source codes
- Considering short- and long-term required resources
- Ensuring data quality

While considering the options, it is important to think of future sustainability of the system at all levels of procurement and development processes, taking into consideration short- and long-term cost commitments. A proper procurement process needs to be carefully designed with the following in consideration: clear process for request for proposals documents and for evaluating tender proposals, ensuring efficient sequencing of functions based on priorities, and affordability. A software solution needs to fulfill certain minimum requirements. Open-source customizable options are recommended specifically when local talent is available. However, it is important to ensure compatibility, integrability, and security of information. Training is crucial to ensure mastery among relevant staff to customize and update the system. Some open-source applications have hidden costs associated with them and need to be selected with care. Applications should comply with legal policies in relation to security, protection, privacy, and confidentiality of data.

Core enablers need to exist to make data links possible. Unique identification systems for schools, teachers, and students should be based on (existing) national identification systems. These enable governments to track progress of individuals throughout their academic experience and allow for tracer studies, which may reap substantial insights into policy making. The unique identifiers in education should be fully integrated into national identification policies spanning different sectors and ministries. In order to do so, the government needs to decide which methodology/technology—paper-based, digital, or biometric unique identification—is the most appropriate and effective given the individual country context. This should be institutionalized through a strong legal framework and national policies on the division of responsibilities, budget, and data privacy protection to ensure sustainability, efficiency, and accountability. Data protection, security, and privacy provisions include a modern cybersecurity architecture, security training for employees, appropriate data collection, and storage rules.

Country context is important, and examples from different countries provide many valuable lessons for other countries aiming at establishing, improving, or expanding their existing EMIS. The cases of the United States, Chile and Australia, and Fiji and Afghanistan are all unique in their context and each offers special insights into different aspects of EMIS structures and purposes. All these cases have a strong legal framework at the center, which is linked directly to schools and their success in improving student learning. They have ensured that their respective EMIS is adaptable to change and improvements. In addition, introducing a culture of data at all levels and ensuring political buy-in at the central level were key for the successful implementation of the EMIS.

The United States has a highly decentralized EMIS structure, where the strong legal framework at both the state and federal levels ensures that education data are captured and used. Some states like Maryland have made substantial progress in establishing a data-driven culture at every level of the education system. The new EMIS in Maryland was procured through a competitive process at a reasonable cost by taking advantage of public-private partnerships. The EMIS introduced education data directly to the classroom, where teachers use academic indexing tools to identify students at risk and tailor their teaching accordingly. Schools receive feedback from the central level through the School Progress Index, which is publicly accessible. Longitudinal tracking has been effectively established in both Maryland and Florida, where students are tracked throughout their entire academic experience leading up to college graduation. This allows for longitudinal studies and can guide policy makers toward a closer alignment of education and labor market needs. One of the many strengths of the decentralized EMIS structure in the United States centers on the fact that states can learn from each other, and the system is conducive to continuous improvements and adaptable to change.

The Chilean and Australian EMISs are supported by strong leadership at the central level, which in Australia is embedded in a highly decentralized education structure. In Chile the EMIS is highly centralized, whereas Australia illustrates a hybrid option between decentralized and centralized systems with powerful national policies. Both countries incentivize national data reporting by linking it directly to funding disbursements. Chile has long established centralized education data agencies such as the National System for Measuring the Quality of Education (*Sistema de Medición de la Calidad de la Educación*, SIMCE), which analyzes and disseminates education data by providing a unique school index as well as school rankings. Australia has lately introduced the My School website, which allows parents, schools, and the community to compare school performance nationwide. Both of these initiatives ensure that schools receive feedback for the data they provide and that data are widely accessible to the public. Australia and Chile continuously seek to expand, innovate, and upgrade their education data systems to adapt to the needs of the education system.

The EMIS experience in Fiji provides insights on how to establish an affordable EMIS in the context of a small country with a challenging island geography and can act as a role model for other countries with a similar context. Early ministry buy-in and effective communication strategies to all education stakeholders were instrumental in the success of the Fiji EMIS (FEMIS). Data entry responsibility and data ownership were closely aligned, which in combination with quality training ensured the availability of high-quality data in FEMIS. FEMIS is a real-time monitoring tool and at the center of daily school usage because schools use FEMIS to compile individual reports such as attendance, financial, and enrollment reports. Unique identifiers of students enable a smooth process when students transfer between schools and allow for longitudinal tracking. The system is regularly reviewed and new modules, features, and processes are constantly added as required.

The case of Afghanistan clearly demonstrates that it is possible to establish a functional EMIS in a fragile environment. One of the key factors was prioritizing education data and designing an EMIS structure specifically tailored to a fragile country context. Decentralization of the data collection process and increased usage of modern information and communication technologies decreased safety concerns to data collectors, who previously had been required to travel long distances through fragile territory. Constant reviews, feedback, and improvements in combination with staff training in all aspects of data collection, entry, verification, and analysis ensured the functionality of the Afghan EMIS. The EMIS has proved to be instrumental at tracking teacher payroll and student attendance, especially for girls. Data use now also expands beyond education monitoring, and EMIS information is now used for policy making.

Reference

Abdul-Hamid, Husein. 2014. "What Matters Most for Education Management Information Systems: A Framework Paper." SABER Working Paper Series No. 7, World Bank, Washington, DC.

CHAPTER 1

What Is an Education Management Information System, and Who Uses It?

Key Takeaways

- An Education Management Information System (EMIS) is a data system that collects, monitors, manages, analyzes, and disseminates information about education inputs, processes, and outcomes—in particular student learning.
- A successful EMIS is based on the interplay of appropriate policies, budget, human resources, organizational structure, and institutions to produce valid education data.
- An EMIS should empower all data users to benefit from the data and foster data-driven decision making, transparency, and accountability.
- Data users are central and local authorities, schools, teachers, parents, and the broader community including, for example, media, researchers, and nongovernmental organizations (NGOs).

Definition

An EMIS is a multifaceted structure, comprising institutional arrangements for collecting, processing, and disseminating data (Abdul-Hamid 2014). An EMIS is based on the interplay of appropriate policies, budget, and institutions that function together in a system to produce and use valid and reliable education data. The continuity of operation in a data system is also dependent on the manpower and the infrastructure. An effective data system provides solutions of value to multiple stakeholders to make evidence-based choices. The stakeholders include policy makers, school administrators, teachers, parents, researchers, and the community at large.

An EMIS, in engineering terms, is defined as a *smart system* that incorporates functions of sensing, actuation, and control in order to describe and analyze a situation and to make decisions on the basis of available data in a predictive or adaptive manner (see Akhras 1997; Culshaw 1996; Bank, Smith, and Wang 1996; Buckley 1985; Desilva 1989). In this context, *smart* means a system that functions in the same way by contributing to smart actions toward student learning and system improvements. A smart system requires the following:

- A high degree of reliability, efficiency, and sustainability—not only of the structure but also of the whole system
- Full integration of all functions of the system
- High security of the infrastructure, particularly when subjected to extreme and unconventional conditions
- Continuous health and integrity monitoring
- Damage detection and self-recovery
- An intelligent operational and management system

The basis of an EMIS should be school and student data because those data link measures of education inputs to outputs, particularly learning, from which important education analysis and conclusions can be derived. Therefore, a complete EMIS includes data on enrollments, attendance, graduation rates, learning assessments, student health, and administrative statistics. In addition, student demographics, teachers, support services, and the learning materials and environment are equally important (figure 1.1). A complete EMIS integrates data from human resources, finances, school facilities and resources, local population, and labor market. An EMIS should be a credible source for all relevant education data so that it can be used as an effective tool to foster student learning. The EMIS's effectiveness depends upon its sustainability, its accessibility, and the efficiency of its operation.

Figure 1.1 Components and Inputs of an EMIS

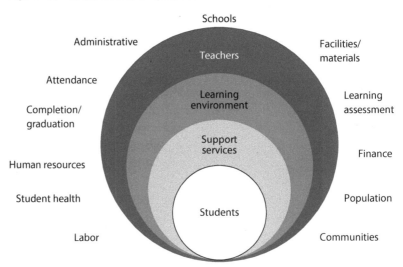

Source: World Bank.
Note: EMIS = Education Management Information System.

What Does a Data System Look Like?

An EMIS platform consists of four core components:

1. Data collection to gather information
2. A database and a data warehouse to host and secure the data
3. Analytics to slice and dice the data and create evidence
4. A front-end portal with reporting and navigation features as well as a summary dashboard

Data systems might vary in design and scope. In fact, countries' different needs and contexts make it unlikely that one single model of EMIS will ever exist. An EMIS in a small country context is likely to look different from one in a country with a large student population. An EMIS needs to take into account the general audience, the government structure (for example, centralized vs. decentralized), and the education financing mechanisms. Operations in a data system should follow a defined organizational structure (figure 1.2), which also determines how and at which level data are collected, validated, analyzed, and disseminated.

Data collection efforts can be manual or technology-based. Because education data are collected at the school level, it is important to provide the school staff with clear instructions on what data should be collected, and when, how, and why. Increasingly, countries have started to move toward technological means of data collection as an effort to simplify this process. However, such automation would only be possible with the appropriate technology. A functioning Internet connection in schools may not pose any issues in advanced economies, but it does in some developing nations. Some countries, such as Nigeria, have even made use of tablet technology in order to collect school data with increased efficiency and cost reduction.

Figure 1.2 Data Coverage, Sharing, and Analysis

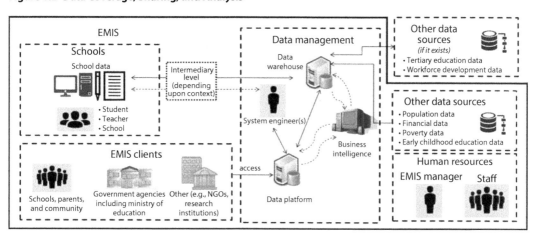

Source: Abdul-Hamid 2014.
Note: EMIS = Education Management Information System.

An EMIS can be a centralized or decentralized system. Many countries collect data locally from schools, and then compile and analyze the information at a central location, very often within the ministry of education (MoE) (box 1.1). However, in some countries, data collection is a more decentralized process with the data entry and collection taking place at the schools, with information fed directly into the EMIS. In Fiji, for example, an EMIS administrator sits at every school entering all the individual student, teacher, and financial information into the system, which the MoE or any district office can access by logging into the system. Whatever the type of system, training of staff at different levels is essential for its successful execution. Only by providing appropriate training on how to input data into the EMIS system is it possible to ensure that the data are of high quality.

Analysis of data produces information in an accessible manner, useful for decision making at different levels of the education system. Some countries use comprehensive analytic toolkits to perform projects and statistical analysis to understand and predict the performance of the system. Others use basic Excel to compute statistics, depending on the capabilities and capacity of governments. Whatever the kind of analysis done, it is important that schools and local authorities understand the usefulness and application of the data they collect. In addition, they should be able to read analysis results from the EMIS and make use of them in their operations and decision making. This could, for instance, be by identifying schools and students at risk, or for using learning materials online for classroom instruction.

Front-end portals and dashboards allow education stakeholders to use data in an easy manner. At every level of the education structure, stakeholders use pieces of an EMIS. An effective data system produces accessible education statistics that are both easily digestible and useful for a variety of purposes. Often, data users access education statistics via designated platforms and/or dashboards that are standardized across the system or are customized depending upon the need. Information on education sector performance enables informed policies and programs, as well as enhanced management, planning, and instruction at the school level.

Box 1.1 Example of an Organizational Structure in Maryland (United States)

Clear organizational structures and roles and responsibilities are a central component of institutionalization. At the state level in the United States, Maryland's Division of Curriculum, Assessment, and Accountability maintains the Education Data Warehouse. It is responsible for the collection of data from local school systems and other entities as well as the validation, definition, and maintenance of multiyear data in accordance with documented policies and procedures to assure data quality and accessibility (MSDE 2003). The Office of Accountability consists of an Analysis and Data Systems branch, an Accountability Support Services branch, and a Research and Evaluation branch. Each branch is staffed with technical experts.

Beneficiaries of a Data System

Governments (national, provincial, and district) use education data for decision making within and outside of the education system. Below are some of the examples of data use by governments:

- *Ministries of education*: The government clearly is the main user of education data. It uses the information obtained through education data in its decision-making process. In a successful educational environment, data form the basis for designing and implementing new policies. Data are also crucial for tracking schools and students and for longitudinally monitoring their outcomes. Using longitudinal data allows governments to more effectively design and implement beneficial policies that promote students' progress throughout their academic journey. Every country exhibits different MoE structures, which may use different types of data.
- *Other ministries and government entities*: Even within the central government there may be a variety of education data users. Naturally, the MoE is the main government education data user, but information usage may extend to other government entities. These entities combine, link, and integrate the data to internal and external reports of the particular department, unit, or ministry. For instance, ministries concerned with employment may use education data to assess the youth labor market. Because the education system intersects with the youth labor market, both the education and labor ministries may use education statistics to track students' skill level and preparedness for work. In addition, education data systems may also be used to compile poverty, population, administrative, human resources, and financial data.
- *Local governments (district, provincial)*: Local government offices use data to manage schools within their region, district, or province. For example, they use data to allocate resources strategically, make projections, and monitor the implementation of education strategies and objectives.

Schools, teachers, and parents are the primary owners and beneficiaries of data. Schools and teachers not only provide data but also use EMIS data. There are two categories of data: raw information and aggregate figures. A data system maintains raw information on the education system, such as payroll, teacher qualifications, human resources, and finance. It also contains aggregate figures derived from data, such as enrollment rates and completion rates. Parents make use of both types of data to track their child's performance, compare, and make school choices. For example, data on student absenteeism, classroom behavior, test scores by subject over time, and so on would allow parents to track student progress. By gaining access to individual student data, parents are able to supervise performance of their own children and, as a result, may be able to offer additional support. By tracking the academic performance of their children throughout the year, parents will become aware of any potential challenges and red flags early on. Through parent-teacher conferences and committees these challenges may be directly addressed.

In addition, access to education data may provide parents with the opportunity to compare schools across a country. With a modern EMIS, most users can access education data online and base their decisions on the data they see. For instance, in Australia, the My School platform publishes scores on average school performance, enabling parents to select schools on the basis of performance. Also, students' ability to track their academic performance and measure it against that of their peers may lead to higher levels of motivation. The community at large uses data to compare the academic performance of neighborhood schools to that of others in the country. In some countries, the quality of education in schools is linked to property prices, so the community has a direct incentive to keep education standards high. A community that sees a decline in its schools' academic performance may also intervene by petitioning the regional school offices for additional resources to improve learning standards and counterbalance the decline.

External agencies are also direct EMIS data users. Some of the examples include:

- *International agencies, universities, and researchers* use EMIS aggregated statistics to offer an outside perspective on education policy. In most countries a variety of researchers in the form of academic institutions (for example, universities), think tanks, or research institutes analyze and disseminate results. Their activities increase internal dialogue as well as accountability. In addition, international organizations such as the United Nations use EMIS administrative data to track global education statistics. Their tracking adds value to the discussion surrounding education, promotes best practices, and can help introduce new innovative ideas.
- *National NGOs* are also key users of education data. An EMIS is used as a reporting tool to external agencies for monitoring and analysis purposes. NGOs bring civil society into the discussion surrounding education policy. In order to foster an informed and high-level political dialogue, NGOs must be allowed access to relevant education data (box 1.2). On the basis of the information provided by the education data, civil society may organize conferences and institute a culture of education dialogue.

To empower the beneficiaries with the right information, data must be made available and tailored to the country-specific context. This includes a data dissemination strategy based on the needs of the country. For example, disseminating data on the MoE website may work very well in countries with high levels of Internet connectivity, but other data dissemination strategies may be necessary in countries without Internet connection because of lack of accessibility.

Some examples of dissemination strategies include publicizing education statistics results through television, radio, local newspapers, and pamphlets to using online channels (box 1.3).

Box 1.2 Research, Analysis, and Dissemination of Data by Nonprofits Such as EdBuild

Public access to data has encouraged NGOs and nonprofit organizations to become more active in terms of research, data analysis, and dissemination. In the United States, the nonprofit EdBuild has been providing education data for free and now has added FundED, a tool that offers easily digested information on education funding in all U.S. states. The website uses education data to produce smart graphics and compare funding practices across the states. Initiatives like EdBuild ensure that the public has easy access to education data delivered in a simple and effective manner. Moreover, EdBuild complements the information provided by the government, which often is not easily accessible or is very spread out over different sources. This is particularly true with regard to education financing. FundED could serve as a role model for similar initiatives in other countries.

Source: EdBuild, http://funded.edbuild.org/.

Box 1.3 Channels for Reaching Data Users in Cameroon

In 2012, the majority of education data in Cameroon had not yet been published online but were available instead through a variety of other channels. The MoE published education data on the radio, in the local press, and on television. These are highly effective channels of publication that have a deep reach within the population. Many other countries do not make sufficient use of non-Internet channels of communication and, therefore, potentially forgo the chance of reaching some prospective data users. Making data available is a crucial aspect of data usage, but just as important is communicating the findings to the general population even if they may not be actively looking for the information.

Source: UNESCO 2012.

Figure 1.3 illustrates how and if data are available on the websites of the MoEs in developing countries. In total, Read and Atinc (2017) investigate 133 developing countries and their education-related ministries. Almost half had no data available or the data were too difficult to find on their websites. This does not mean that these countries do not collect the data, but it indicates the immense need for accessible, publicly available, relevant, and useful data.

The data in the EMIS collected by the school census should be available in a usable format. Many ministries now base at least part of their data dissemination strategy on the Internet and publish annual school census reports online, which can be effective if the majority of stakeholders are connected to the Internet. For example, allowing data users to download data in an Excel format will enable further analysis and more meaning. This may be particularly helpful to schools as well as to NGOs and researchers. Publishing reports only in Portable Document Format (PDF) files makes data analysis and projections more difficult. Figure 1.4 illustrates the most popular publishing formats of developing countries.[1]

Finally, data availability, access, and use foster data-driven decision making, transparency, and accountability. Making data available to the public enables data users to make more informed decisions. The improved transparency and accountability can directly affect user actions (table 1.1).

Figure 1.3   Data Available on Ministry of Education Websites

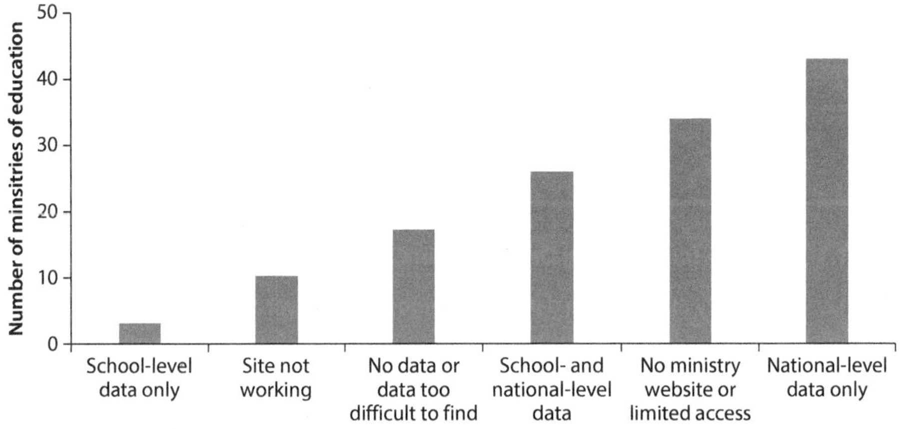

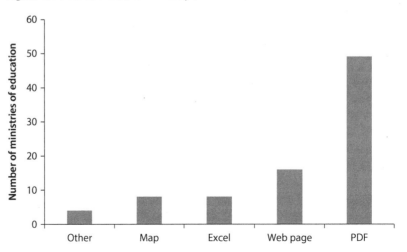

Source: Read and Atinc 2017.

Figure 1.4   Format of Data on Ministry of Education Websites

Source: Read and Atinc 2017.

Table 1.1 Improvements of Service Delivery through Accountability Policies at the School Level

Agent	Target group	Effect
Service providers and local officials	Teachers, school administrators, and local officials	Incentivizing monitoring and data collection through rewards or sanctions can improve accountability and allocation of responsibility. By using the available data, teachers and school administrators are able to set individual school achievement goals by benchmarking their performance to top-performing schools. In this process, data collection on teaching quality through classroom observation or student performance may be instrumental. Teaching quality should be linked to identifying the need and finally providing teacher support. This could occur in the form of additional training and collaboration. School administrators will also be able to identify continuously low-performing teachers. If the provision of additional support does not improve their teaching quality, then school administrators may need to prepare the teachers' exit. In addition, school administrators and local officials can respond to outside pressure and adjust school management accordingly by improving education practices and performance or by adjusting tuition fees.
	School-based management organizations	Data collection at the school level enables school-based management organizations to develop an improved understanding of school and learning processes. This will increase confidence by the organization and potentially enable it to suggest reforms based on the information obtained.
Citizens and the community	Parents and students	They are able to react to their own individual performance and intervene if necessary. Such an intervention could be in the school by directly engaging with teachers and school administrators to receive additional support or increase academic out-of-school activities. Data comparing schools across the nation can also provide parents with information on which school to choose for their children.
	Communities	Communities can become data collectors, verifiers, and data users. Through data collection and verification, communities may be able to identify failures in education service delivery and can correct for these. This would drive demand for improvements and may even reduce corruption, if applicable. In general, comparative indicators (for example, student assessment scores or funding allocation) across different communities may trigger collective action if discrepancies in treatment between similar communities are uncovered.
	Civil society	Information on education can motivate actions from civil society within a country that goes beyond single communities. Civil society can use the information for education advocacy campaigns. One outlet of such a campaign could be popular media to draw attention to service delivery failures such as inadequate school funding allocation or corruption.

Source: Adapted from Read and Atinc 2017.

Note

1. Read and Atinc (2017) assessed 133 developing countries in total, but not all had data available or accessible.

References

Abdul-Hamid, Husein. 2014. "What Matters Most for Education Management Information Systems: A Framework Paper." SABER Working Paper Series No. 7, World Bank, Washington, DC.

Akhras, Georges. 1997. "Smart Structures and Their Applications in Civil Engineering." Civil Engineering Report CE97-2, Royal Military College of Canada, Kingston, Ontario.

Bank, H. Thomas, Ralph Charles Smith, and Yun Wang. 1996. *Smart Material Structures: Modeling, Estimation, and Control.* John Wiley and Sons.

Buckley, S. 1985. "Automation Sensing Mimics Organisms." *Sensors*, June.

Culshaw, Brian. 1996. *Smart Structures and Materials.* Norwood, MA: Artech House, Inc.

Desilva, C. W. 1989. *Control Sensors and Actuators.* Englewood Cliffs, NJ: Prentice- Hall, Inc.

MSDE (Maryland State Department of Education). 2003. "Divisions: Curriculum, Assessment & Accountability." http://www.marylandpublicschools.org/MsDE /divisions/instruction/index.html.

Read, Lindsay, and Tamar Manuelyan Atinc. 2017. "Education Data in Four Charts." Education Plus Development (blog), March 24. https://www.brookings.edu/blog /education-plus-development/2017/03/24/education-data-in-four-charts/.

UNESCO (United Nations Educational, Scientific and Cultural Organization). 2012. "Rapport Diagnostique du Sytème d'Information pour la Gestion de l'Education (SIGE) au Cameroun (Data Quality Assessment Framework)." UNESCO, Paris.

CHAPTER 2

Value of Data: Better Data, Better Education

Key Takeaways

- Information plays a crucial role in helping an education system achieve high returns. Promoting a culture that recognizes the value of data promises economic benefits for the individual and the nation as a whole.
- High-quality, accurate, and useful data allow stakeholders to make informed decisions and overcome challenges, ensuring that learning stays at the forefront of the education system.
- Many countries are experiencing cost-efficient, smart, and effective resource allocation and governance by using data systems.
- Data systems support school leadership, teaching, and learning and engage the community to achieve better education results.
- Only actionable integrated interventions with data lead to improved outcomes.

Education Data Improve Learning

Education data and improved learning can quantify and reap economic benefits. Research clearly shows that education has a direct impact on gross domestic product (GDP) per capita. It is estimated that a year of additional schooling in a country could lead to an increase of more than 10 percent in GDP per capita (Patrinos and Psacharopoulos 2013; Thomas and Burnett 2013). Quality of education, and its ability to produce positive learning outcomes, is a priority across global development agendas such as the Sustainable Development Goals (SDGs) and the World Bank's Learning for All Education Strategy 2020. There are many reasons to focus on learning: growth, development, and poverty reduction depend on the knowledge and skills that people acquire (Currie and Thomas 1999; Hanushek and Kimko 2000; Hanushek and Wößmann 2007, 2015). System-level interventions provide data that can influence accountability and learning (Alvarez, Garcia-Moreno, and Patrinos 2007; Bruns, Filmer, and Patrinos 2011;

Jimenez and Sawada 1999; King, Orazem, and Gunnarsson 2003; Pradhan et al. 2011). Also, details of implementation hold many promises for education systems in developing countries (Glewwe and Kremer 2006).

The Value of Data to Strengthen the Whole System

In an adaptive education delivery system, information permeates the entire environment. There, standards (learning attainment goals, national education objectives, equity, and access to education benchmarks) are linked to resource allocation (financial, human resources, facilities, and infrastructure provisions), leading to education service delivery operation, which yields learning outcomes. All over the system, information guides and monitors each of the stages in this cycle and feeds into governance and accountability. Comprehensive and quality education data hold high value, and if used well are proven to improve learning, teaching quality, and planning, and to help overcome education challenges.

Establishing a data-driven culture is a key ingredient in the evolution to a learning orientation. A culture of data means that data are expected, valued, and used by various stakeholders across the education system. It also means that data are part of the fabric of daily operations, processes, and decision making. Specifically, data play an essential role at each step in the process: (1) designing and evaluating policies and standards, (2) communicating and facilitating resource allocation, (3) enabling active real-time use in classroom instruction, and (4) strengthening school management and planning (figure 2.1). The aim is to rethink the compliance-driven education model and induce a shift to continuous improvements and learning for all, with data playing a significant role.

A learning-focused approach uses data to support and improve a shared accountability model in which all stakeholders—policy makers, principals, teachers, school administrators, parents, and students—are responsible for student learning (Linn 2003). In a learning-based education system, information is an essential element used across the education system by everyone from teachers to policy makers. Personalized learning analytics are used in the classroom.

Figure 2.1 EMIS and Learning-Centered Approach

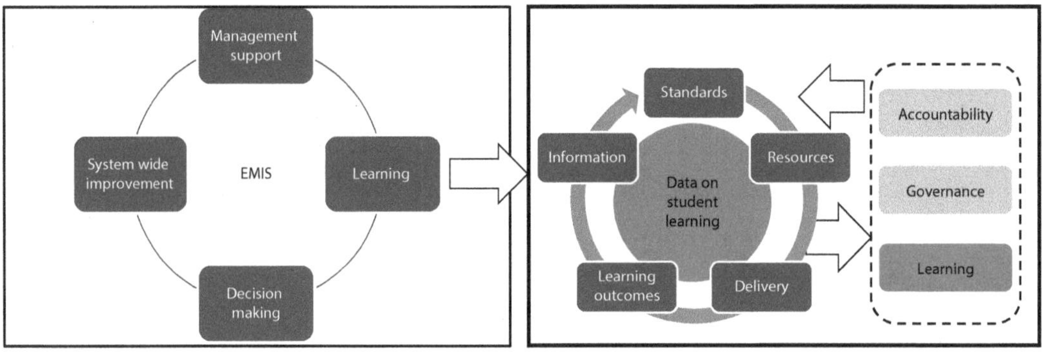

Note: EMIS = Education Management Information System.

Decision makers bring data into a myriad of conversations, not just to evaluate the efficacy of programs but to monitor them in real time. Simply put, data are a constant guide, providing greater insight into student learning outcomes and strengthening the system as a whole.

Compliance with standard, accountability, and government requirements is not sufficient any more. Using data as an enforcement tool with negative repercussions will only cultivate more defensiveness and opposition from stakeholders across the education system. Instead, successful leaders and practitioners tactfully use data to drive curiosity and wonder, to spark meaningful dialogue, and to draw people in instead of pushing them away.

Nongovernmental organizations (NGOs) and the private sector often push for a data-driven culture, supplying the government with additional information. Many NGOs and private sector companies focus on education through research or other means. Providing researchers with the opportunity to assess and analyze education data could bring new and innovative insights into the education system and learning (box 2.1). The government could substantially benefit from the additional input provided by internal and external analysts. The goal would be to design an access tool for different stakeholders with a reasonable level of automation and use of data. Researchers can aid legislators in deciphering and presenting data in a more easily understandable manner.

Box 2.1 Private Sector and NGOs Pushing for a Learning Focus within a Data-Driven Culture

Data-driven culture can also stem from nongovernmental entities. For instance, the private sector in the United States has pushed for more data-based decision making and resource allocation in the education sector. The Sunlight Foundation—a national, nonpartisan, nonprofit organization that uses the tools of civic tech, open data, policy analysis, and journalism to make government and politics more accountable and transparent to all—maintains an open data map that tracks policies at the state and local levels, as well as best-practice resources. EdBuild is an independent website focusing on education data in the United States. EdBuild has recently extended its repertoire to include FundED, which provides free and easily digestible information on school funding across the United States. Its presentation of school financial data is innovative and tailored to the needs of data users with little statistical expertise. In addition, it combines a considerable variety of data sources scattered across different departments and states in the United States.

By highlighting best practices and sharing innovative policies, the private sector may contribute to a data-driven culture. It may help build consensus and collaboration for the effective use of data to improve education outcomes as well as build knowledge and create evidence-based recommendations and resources for the field. Moreover, the nongovernmental sector may also advocate for and support changes in policy and practice to ensure that data effectively and securely follow and serve the individuals.

Data Guide Policy Makers and Ensure Efficient Resource Allocation and Management

Data help policy makers in the design and implementation of policies that are based on evidence and proven to reach intended outcomes. "The achievement of good-quality education is dependent on the quality of statistics which inform the policy formulation, educational planning, management and monitoring processes" (Makwati, Audinos, and Lairez 2003, 9). After all, data guide education system improvements. Wößmann (2000) uses a large, international student-level micro database grounded on the Trends in International Mathematics and Science Study (TIMSS) to explore educational inputs as well as institutional arrangements within an education system. Student-level research shows that international differences in student performance are not influenced by inputs but are considerably related to institutional differences. These include (1) centralized examinations and control mechanisms, (2) school autonomy in personnel and process decisions, (3) individual teacher influence over teaching methods, (4) limits to teacher unions' influence on curriculum scope, (5) scrutiny of students' achievement, and (6) competition from private schools. This cannot be achieved without a functioning information system.

Information systems enable policy makers to be cost-efficient and effective in education planning and allocation of scarce resources. High levels of expenditure do not necessarily translate into high-quality education. One of the recommendations made by the World Bank's Education 2020 Strategy is to invest smartly. A value-added dimension of an education data system is that it empowers decision makers to make smart spending decisions, based on data and analytics proven to contribute to learning (World Bank 2011). An education data management system is certainly a smart investment because it provides information and feedback on the education system. One of the motivations for governments to create an EMIS is to improve the internal efficiency of the education system, that is, to "address issues of redundancy or improved targeting of resources [that] typically require a greater degree of data accuracy and precision" (Crouch, Enache, and Supanc 2001, 46). Cost-efficiency in an EMIS ensures its sustainability. Using existing databases and data collection processes that are familiar to users, while reducing redundancies, enhances cost-efficiency in the long term (Crouch, Enache, and Supanc 2001).

Data are needed to ensure that smart financial investments are made. Smart education investments should be made where they have a true impact on learning outcomes. A recent study by the World Bank has compared education expenditure as percent of GDP with the quality of education. For instance, Ghana and Slovenia spend almost 6 percent of GDP each, yet Ghana lacks quality of education in comparison.[1] This illustrates the importance of data on efficient education expenditure. Collecting, analyzing, and using the information provided by the data allow important resource allocation decisions to be made.

Data Help Schools, Teachers, and the Community to Improve Learning

Collection and dissemination of data should follow predetermined plans to influence schools, students, parents, and teachers to guarantee positive outcomes. Data need to be actionable and require plans, analysis discussions, explanation, and training on use in order for the data to be effective. It is important to provide the necessary support and skill to work with school administrators and stakeholders to improve outcomes. Research demonstrates that the way in which data are presented and communicated has an important effect on intermediate variables and learning outcomes. Mere data collection is not sufficient to improve learning outcomes and may even have adverse learning effects. For instance, in India students taking pictures to verify teacher attendance had a negative impact on intermediate variables and student learning (Duflo, Hanna, and Ryan 2012). In Uganda, reports from head teachers verifying teacher attendance using mobile technology had a negative effect on intermediate variables (Cilliers et al. 2016). In those cases, teachers may have felt overly supervised, causing their teaching quality to decrease. In Brazil, school "shaming" proved ineffective, given that the dissemination of education output data online and in newspapers generally worsened intermediate variables and learning indicator performance (Camargo et al. 2014; Lepine 2015).

Engagement of parents and the community with schools via data supplied by an EMIS provides an opportunity to improve learning. In Argentina, a diagnostic report was produced to support and design the implementation of a school improvement plan involving both school management and teachers. This contributed to direct improvements in student learning outcomes (de Hoyos, Ganimian, and Holland, forthcoming). In Mexico, disseminating education input and output data through websites has shown to improve awareness by different education stakeholders. Moreover, it seems that some stakeholders have used the site to combat corruption (Clare et al. 2016). The type of intervention and the intervening agents are similarly important for a positive impact on intermediate variables and learning outcomes. Box 2.2 highlights three examples of data engagement interventions using similar strategies, but with contrasting results.

Data improve schools and learning outcomes. The increased use of data and information is part of a shift from summative to formative data use; it depends on the data systems to create feedback loops built on evidence that guides teachers and school leaders (Halverson 2010). Evidence-based school leadership has been found to substantially influence learning outcomes (box 2.3). Branch, Hanushek, and Rivkin (2013) contend that highly effective school management raises the achievement of a typical student between two to seven months of learning in a single school year, and ineffective school leadership lowers achievement by the same amount. Box 2.4 provides an example of how school management and data intervention have raised student learning and improved intermediate variables. Glewwe, Kremer, and Moulin (2009) demonstrate that the provision of official government textbooks in Kenya raised test scores for the top two quintiles of students (measured by initial academic achievement)

Box 2.2 Data Intervention—Similar Strategy, Contrasting Outcomes

In Uganda two interventions, both involving school scorecards, were conducted with opposite effects. The first intervention involved the introduction of a scorecard on school inputs by the school management. The collecting agents were parents and students, but no further action other than mere data collection was taken, resulting in a negative effect on intermediate variables as well as student learning. In contrast, another intervention used scorecards to inform education stakeholders about their rights and responsibilities in addition to school inputs. The aim of the second intervention was to facilitate meetings between parents, teachers, and the school administration to define objects, roles, and indicators of school progress. This participatory approach not only collected information but also immediately translated data into use. This had a positive effect on intermediate variables and student learning (Barr et al. 2012).

In India, comparing different studies showed that the communication channel and the involved stakeholder groups determined the success or failure of an intervention. Banerjee et al. (2010) find that informing parents and teachers about their roles and responsibilities through pamphlets or school scorecards negatively affected intermediate variables and student learning. Pandey, Goyal, and Sundararaman (2011), however, find that communicating rights and responsibilities of parents through film, posters, calendars, and booklets improved intermediate variables and student learning.

Another experience also shows that the channel of communication is instrumental to the success of the intervention. In Indonesia, two different channels were used to communicate the rights and responsibilities to parents: pamphlets and text messages. The intervention using pamphlets was highly unsuccessful and negatively affected intermediate variables. However, text messages were well received and contributed to a raised awareness by stakeholders and improved intermediate variables (Cerdan-Infantes and Filmer 2015).

Box 2.3 Impact of Performance Data at the School Level

Rockoff et al. (2010) use a pilot program conducted by the New York City Department of Education in which principals were randomly selected to receive performance measures (estimates of "value added") for teachers at their schools and training on the methodology used to construct the estimates. In the context of this paper and relevance to student learning, the most compelling finding was that, after the provision of performance data, the probability of job separation increases for low-performing teachers, and that following the attrition student achievement exhibits small improvements the following year. Finally, the Oregon Direct Access to Achievement (DATA) Project provided evidence linking data use to student learning outcomes.

Source: Next Level Evaluation, Incorporated 2011.

Box 2.4 Informing Stakeholders of Rights and Responsibilities Improves Learning

In India, school management received training on effective school management and monitoring. This enabled the school management to plan more effectively and lead the schools. The new management strategy included a scorecard informing education stakeholders of their rights and responsibilities. One key component of the intervention was the focus on participatory meetings between all local stakeholder groups to foster a dialogue and to support school management. This ensured that school management, teachers, and parents were informed about the school's needs and priorities as well as the different responsibilities of each stakeholder group. These measures directly improved intermediate variables and student learning (Galab, Latham, and Churches 2013).

---

but had no effect on either the test scores or the dropout and repetition rates of average and below average students. Various reports have also found that paying for school uniforms increased test scores and decreased dropout rates, teen marriage, and childbearing (Duflo et al. 2006; Evans, Kremer, and Ngatia 2009). With these sorts of data results, decision makers are in a substantially better position to make informed decisions.

Data on teaching quality can help improve teacher effectiveness and, thus, student learning. Many researchers examining the impact of school-level inputs on student learning find that teacher effectiveness is a key predictor of student learning (Hanushek and Rivkin 2006; Rockoff 2004). Inputs such as, for instance, the quality of teachers, curriculum design, school resources, and family characteristics will have an impact on learning outcomes of individual students. In terms of school resources, this is easily quantified by looking at the available technology, schoolbooks, classrooms, and so forth. What is certainly more difficult to measure is quality of teaching. Teachers are crucial in the learning process of their students, but there is no one single measure of teaching quality. The Education Commission of the States (ECS) has identified six indicators for teaching quality: (1) lesson objective, (2) instructional delivery mechanisms, (3) teacher questioning strategies, (4) clarity of presentation of concepts, (5) time on task, and (6) level of student understanding (Gargani and Strong 2014). These are complementary indicators to measure teaching quality and require substantial data collection as well as analysis. The analysis can then be used to develop best-practice standards as well as identify high and low achievers in teaching quality.

Data literacy enables stakeholders to use a variety of tools, such as academic indexing, to identify students at risk and improve learning. If teachers have access to data on student learning in real time, this can substantially improve teaching quality because teachers will be able to provide targeted support to students. By comparing student records against their classmates, also longitudinally, teachers can provide support in a more targeted, efficient, and effective manner. These factors make data literacy training for teachers imperative. Principals and school administrators actively use data to evaluate teachers, monitor school progress, and manage school plans. Policy makers use data to monitor education quality and equity, improve accountability, and gauge effectiveness of policies and programs (see chapter 8 for further discussion). Box 2.5 illustrates the direct effects of data literacy on student learning outcomes.

Data can help mitigate the cycle of student underachievement by counteracting the potential problem of low parental education. On a broader scale, Aturupane, Glewwe, and Wisniewski (2013) examine three different sources of data from Sri Lanka to investigate the determinants of reading and math skills among fourth-grade students. Findings show that parents' education plays a large role in student learning as do early childhood nutrition, measured by height-for-age; principals' and teachers' years of experience; grouping schools into "school families"; and parent–teacher meetings. In order to establish a learning environment that is conducive to success, data can help identify neighborhoods at risk, where parents' education is already below average, and intervene with special policies, subsidies, or trainings. Such interventions could potentially break the cycle of student underachievement and instead promote across-the-board success. In fact, data suggest that community and family settings exert considerable influence on learning outcomes. Data also underscore the importance of new ways of understanding the learning environment and how data can aid policy makers in creating that environment, such as with cash subsidies. A handful of studies have examined the impact of information on student learning (box 2.6).

Box 2.5 Training Teachers in Data Literacy Improves Student Learning

In the United States, the Oregon DATA Project linked data use to student learning results, which were applied to classroom instruction. The three-year, US$4.7 million initiative sought to increase data use in the classroom and worked from the premise that effective training is essential for helping educators employ data effectively to strengthen student achievement. In 2007, the Oregon DATA Project set out to train teachers on the value and use of data to enhance classroom practice and improve student learning by giving them the resources to collect, analyze, and use longitudinal data. DATA changed the way teachers valued and used data. This was essential and had positive outcomes for student achievement. As early as two years into the project, the difference in learning improvements between participatory and nonparticipatory schools was clearly visible. At the beginning of the project, schools that participated in the Oregon DATA Project had lower achievement numbers than nonparticipating schools. At the evaluation after two years, the percentage of students at or above proficient on the state test grew at a significantly higher rate in participating schools than for students in schools whose teachers did not receive training. This meant that the achievement gap between the two groups of schools decreased in reading and closed in math.

Sources: DQC 2015; Next Level Evaluation, Incorporated 2011.

Box 2.6 Informing Parents to Improve Student Learning

In a large-scale study conducted in Punjab Province, Pakistan, Andrabi, Das, and Khwaja (2015) examine how information provision to parents and schools affects learning outcomes. The study provided simple, accurate report cards to households and schools in treatment villages, sharing test scores for their own children and all schools in the village. Average test scores increased by 0.10 to 0.15 of a standard deviation in the villages where report cards were distributed. With regard to the study, Bruns, Filmer, and Patrinos (2011, 71) note that the education data provided to parents are most effective when they are simple: "The priority should be on simple indicators that parents care about, that they understand, and that are likely to motivate them to action."

A variety of reports explore interventions that aim to improve learning by informing families and communities. Gertler, Rubio-Codina, and Patrinos (2006) examine a federal government initiative in Mexico, *Apoyo a la Gestión Escolar* (AGE), which provided small grants to parent associations to invest in school infrastructure or materials. In addition to financial funds, parents also received training in financial management and participatory skills. Using a combination of quantitative and qualitative methods, the authors find that the initiative reduced grade repetition and grade failure by 4 to 5 percent, controlling for the presence of a conditional cash transfer program and other educational interventions. This supports the argument that a hospitable environment matters for learning.

Note

1. For more information, see the Identification for Development web page of the World Bank, Washington, DC (accessed November 04, 2016), http://www.worldbank.org /en/topic/governance/brief/identification-for-development.

References

Alvarez, Jesús, Vicente Garcia-Moreno, and Harry Anthony Patrinos. 2007. "Institutional Effects as Determinants of Learning Outcomes: Exploring State Variations in Mexico." Policy Research Working Paper 4286, World Bank, Washington, DC. http://ssrn.com /abstract=1004200.

Andrabi, Tahir, Jishnu Das, and Asim Khwaja. 2015. "Report Cards: The Impact of Providing School and Child Test Scores on Educational Markets." Policy Research Working Paper 7226, World Bank, Washington, DC. https://www.openknowledge .worldbank.org/handle/10986/21670.

Aturupane, Harsha, Paul Glewwe, and Suzanne Wisniewski. 2013. "The Impact of School Quality, Socioeconomic Factors, and Child Health on Students' Academic Performance: Evidence from Sri Lankan Primary Schools." *Education Economics* 21 (1): 2–37. doi:10.1080/09645292.2010.511852.

Barr, Abigail, Frederick Mugisha, Pieter Serneels, and Andrew Zeitlin. 2012. "Information and Collective Action in Community-Based Monitoring of Schools: Field and Lab Experimental Evidence from Uganda." Preliminary Draft.

Banerjee, Abhijit, Rukmini Banerji, Esther Duflo, Rachel Glennester, and Stuti Khemani. 2010. "Pitfalls of Participatory Programs: Evidence from a Randomized Evaluation of Education in India." *American Economic Journal: Economic Policy* 2 (1): 1–30.

Branch, Gregory, Eric Hanushek, and Steven Rivkin. 2013. "School Leaders Matter." *Education Next* 13 (1): 62–69. http://hanushek.stanford.edu/publications/school -leaders-matter-measuring-impact-effective-principals.

Bruns, Barbara, Deon Filmer, and Harry Anthony Patrinos. 2011. *Making Schools Work: New Evidence on Accountability Reforms*. Washington, DC: World Bank.

Camargo, Braz, Rafael Camelo, Sergio Firpo, and Vladimir Ponczek. 2014. "Information, Market Incentives, and Student Performance." IZA Discussion Paper 7941, Institute for the Study of Labor (IZA), Bonn, Germany.

Cerdan-Infantes, Pedro, and Deon Filmer. 2015. "Information, Knowledge and Behavior: Evaluating Alternative Methods of Delivering School Information to Parents." Policy Research Working Paper 7233, World Bank, Washington, DC.

Cilliers, Jacobus, Ibrahim Kasirye, Clare Leaver, Pieter Serneels, and Andrew Zeitlin. 2016. "Pay for Locally Monitored Teacher Attendance? A Welfare Analysis for Ugandan Primary Schools." IZA Discussion Paper 10118, Institute for the Study of Labor, Bonn, August.

Clare, Ali, David Sangokoya, Stefan Verhulst, and Andrew Young. 2016. "Open Contracting and Procurement in Slovakia." Open Data's Impact, New York.

Crouch, Luis, Mircea Enache, and Patrick Supanc. 2001. "Education Management Information Systems (EMIS): Guidelines for Design and Implementation." *Techknowlogia: International Journal of Technology for the Advancement of Knowledge and Learning* 3 (1): 46–9.

Currie, Janet, and Duncan Thomas. 1999. "Early Test Scores, Socioeconomic Status and Future Outcomes." NBER Working Paper 6943, National Bureau of Economic Research.

de Hoyos, Rafael, Alejandro Ganimian, and Peter Holland. Forthcoming. "Two to Tango? Combining Diagnostic Feedback and Capacity-Building for Schools in Argentina." World Bank, Washington, DC.

DQC (Data Quality Campaign). 2014. "Teacher Data Literacy: It's About Time." DQC, Washington, DC.

———. 2015. "EMIS in Different Country Contexts." Presented by Paige Kowalski at the World Bank Education Staff Development Program, Washington, DC.

Duflo, Esther, Pascaline Dupas, Michael Kremer, and Samuel Sinei. 2006. "Education and HIV/AIDS Prevention: Evidence from a Randomized Evaluation in Western Kenya." Policy Research Working Paper 4024, World Bank, Washington, DC.

Duflo, Esther, Rema Hanna, and Stephen Ryan. 2012. "Incentives Work: Getting Teachers to Come to School." *American Economic Review* 102 (4): 1241–78.

Evans, David, Michael Kremer, and Mūthoni Ngatia. 2009. "The Impact of Distributing School Uniforms on Children's Education in Kenya." Poverty Action Lab Working Paper 169, Abdul Latif Jameel Poverty Action Lab, Cambridge, MA.

Galab, S., C. Jones, M. Latham, and R. Churches. 2013. "Community-Based Accountability for School Improvement: A Case Study for Rural India." Center for Education Innovations, Washington, DC.

Gargani, John, and Michael Strong. 2014. "Can We Identify a Successful Teacher Better, Faster, and Cheaper? Evidence for Innovating Teacher Observation Systems." *Journal of Teacher Education* 65 (5): 389–401.

Gertler, Paul, Marta Rubio-Codina, and Harry Patrinos. 2006. "Empowering Parents to Improve Education: Evidence from Rural Mexico." Policy Research Working Paper 3935, World Bank, Washington, DC.

Glewwe, Paul, and Michael Kremer. 2006. "Schools, Teachers, and Education Outcomes in Developing Countries." In *Handbook of the Economics of Education*, edited by Eric A. Hanushek and Finis Welch, 945–1017. Amsterdam: North Holland. doi:10.1016/s1574-0692(06)02016-2.

Glewwe, Paul, Michael Kremer, and Sylvie Moulin. 2009. "Many Children Left Behind? Textbooks and Test Scores in Kenya." *American Economic Journal: Applied Economics* 1 (January): 112–35. doi:10.3386/w13300.

Hanushek, Eric, and Dennis Kimko. 2000. "Schooling, Labor Force Quality, and the Growth of Nations." *American Economic Review* 90 (5): 1184–208.

Hanushek, Eric, and Ludger Wößmann. 2007. *Education Quality and Economic Growth.* Washington, DC: World Bank.

———. 2015. *The Knowledge Capital of Nations.* CESifo Book Series. Boston, MA: The MIT Press.

Hanushek, Eric, and Steven Rivkin. 2006. "Teacher Quality." In *Handbook of the Economics of Education*, edited by Eric A. Hanushek and Finis Welch. Amsterdam: North Holland.

Halverson, Richard. 2010. "School Formative Feedback Systems." *Peabody Journal of Education* 85 (2); 130–46. doi:10.1080/01619561003685270.

Jimenez, Emmanuel, and Yasuyuki Sawada. 1999. "Do Community Managed Schools Work? An Evaluation of El Salvador's EDUCO Program." *The World Bank Economic Review* 13: 415–41.

King, E., P. F. Orazem, and V. Gunnarsson. 2003. "Decentralization and Student Achievement: International Evidence on the Roles of School Autonomy and Community Participation." Paper presented to the Fourth Annual Global Development Conference on Globalization and Equity, Cairo, Egypt, January 19–21.

Lepine, Andrea. 2015. "School Reputation and School Choice in Brazil: A Regression Discontinuity Design." Working Paper Series 2015-38, University of Sao Paulo, Brazil.

Linn, Robert. 2003. "Accountability: Responsibility and Reasonable Expectations." *Educational Researcher* 32 (7): 3–13.

Makwati, Glory, Bernard Audinos, and Thierry Lairez. 2003. "The Role of Statistics in Improving the Quality of Basic Education in Sub-Saharan Africa." Working Document, Association for the Development of Education in Africa, African Development Bank, Tunis, Tunisia.

Mills, Lane. 2011. "Creating a Data-Driven Culture: Leadership Matters." SAS White Paper, Statistical Analysis System (SAS), Cary, NC.

Next Level Evaluation, Incorporated. 2011. *Oregon DATA Project Final Evaluation Report.* Oregon Department of Education, Salem.

Pandey, Priyanka, Sangeeta Goyal, and Venkatesh Sundararaman. 2011. "Does Information Improve School Accountability? Results of a Large Randomized Trial." Discussion Paper Series 49, World Bank, Washington, DC.

Patrinos, Harry, and Georg Psacharopoulos. 2013. "Education: The Income and Equity Loss of Not Having a Faster Rate of Human Capital Accumulation." In *How Much Have Global Problems Cost the World? A Scorecard from 1900 to 2050*, edited by Bjørn Lomborg, 170–191. Cambridge University Press.

Pradhan, Menno, Daniel Suryadarma, Amanda Beatty, Maisy Wong, Arya Gaduh, Armida Alisjahbana, and Rima Prama Artha. 2011. "Improving Educational Quality through Enhancing Community Participation: Results from a Randomized Field Experiment in Indonesia." Policy Research Working Paper 5795, World Bank, Washington, DC.

Rockoff, J. E. 2004. "The Impact of Individual Teachers on Student Achievement: Evidence from Panel Data." *The American Economic Review* 94 (2): 247–52.

Rockoff, Jonah, Douglas Staiger, Thomas Kane, and Eric Taylor. 2010. "Information and Employee Evaluation: Evidence from a Randomized Intervention in Public Schools." NBER Working Paper 16240, National Bureau of Economic Research, Cambridge, MA.

Thomas, Milan, and Nicholas Burnett. 2013. "Exclusion from Education: The Economic Cost of Out of School Children in 20 Countries." Results for Development, Washington, DC.

World Bank. 2011. *Learning for All: Investing in People's Knowledge and Skills to Promote Development; World Bank Group Education Strategy 2020.* Washington, DC: World Bank.

Wößmann. 2000. "Schooling Resources, Educational Institutions, and Student Performance: The International Evidence." Kiel Working Paper 983, Kiel Institute of World Economics, Kiel, Germany.

CHAPTER 3

Understanding Where You Are Today: Assessing the Current State of Education Management Information Systems

Key Takeaways

- A successful Education Management Information System (EMIS) is supported by an enabling environment (legal framework, organizational structure, infrastructural capacity, personnel, and budget); system soundness (system architecture, dynamics, serviceability, and data coverage); quality data (methodology, accuracy, integrity, and periodicity); and data use (operational use, openness, accessibility, and data dissemination).
- An information cycle ensures system feedback loops between data input and output levels, adjusting to the needs of the education system.
- The country context drives the choice between options such as decentralized and centralized data systems. Roles and responsibilities, financing structure, data privacy, and staffing need to be clearly determined.
- The assessment and benchmarking of an EMIS should be used to determine the state of the current data management system and, thus, guide policy changes that improve the quality of data and learning outcomes. As the managing authority, the government should continuously assess the data system and look toward examples of best practices from other countries.
- The Systems Approach for Better Education Results (SABER)–EMIS tool provides a structured methodology to assess and benchmark the enabling environment, system soundness, data quality, and utilization for decision making. Such assessment should guide the planning, design, and implementation of any EMIS-related investments because it could reduce cost, eliminate redundancies, identify priorities, highlight what to do and not to do, and help in the sustainability of investment in data systems.

- Designers of EMIS activities need to account for all stages of the EMIS value chain: pre-start, input, operation, output, and long-term sustainability.
- A results-based financing approach can be an effective option to ensure returns on investment and increase the chances of success in EMIS activities.

Characteristics of a Successful Data System

For a data system to fully function, appropriate principles and standards need to be in place. An examination of data systems and utilization practices worldwide reveals a set of key characteristics. These drivers are shared by advanced systems and provide a road map to those looking to strengthen and upgrade their systems. These guiding principles and functionalities make up the bundle of what matters most to an effective EMIS given the specific needs and context. Key policy actions are required to set the foundations of the system (figure 3.1).

- *A strong enabling environment* lays the foundation for an effective system. The enabling environment refers to the laws, policies, structure, processes, resources, and data-driven culture surrounding an EMIS that make data collection, management, use, and access possible.
- *System soundness* encompasses the processes, structures, and integration capabilities that bring data together within the data system. Education data are sourced from different institutions, but all data feed into and make up an overarching data system. Databases within an EMIS are viewed not as separate databases but as part of the whole system. Key aspects of system soundness include what data are covered in the EMIS and how they come together in the overarching system.

Figure 3.1 SABER–EMIS Policy Areas and Levers

Policy areas

Enabling environment	*Policy levers:* Legal framework, organizational structure and institutionalized processes, human resources, infrastructural capacity, budget, data-driven culture
System soundness	*Policy levers:* Data architecture, data coverage, data analytics, dynamic system, serviceability
Quality data	*Policy levers:* Methodological soundness, accuracy and reliability, integrity, periodicity, timeliness
Utilization for decision making	*Policy levers:* Openness to EMIS users, operational use, accessibility, effectiveness in disseminating findings

Source: Abdul-Hamid 2014.
Note: EMIS = Education Management Information System; SABER = Systems Approach for Better Education Results.

- *Quality data* establish the mechanisms required to collect, save, produce, and use information in an accurate, secure, and timely manner. Data quality is a multidimensional concept that encompasses more than just the underlying accuracy of the statistics produced. It means not only that the data are accurate but also that the data address specific needs in a timely fashion. Quality data lay the groundwork for utilization.
- An effective *data system is used* in decision making by all stakeholders (parents, students, teachers, principals, and policy makers) across the education system. An EMIS informs stakeholders so that measures can be taken to improve educational quality. Accurate information on education sector performance enables more informed policies and programs, as well as enhanced management, planning, and instruction at the school level. To assess utilization, it is imperative to understand where decision making occurs, if the capacity to analyze and interpret education data exists, and if specific data are available to inform decisions.

The EMIS shall follow a policy pathway to ensure proper outcome cycles. Policy needs first to be crafted to lay out how an EMIS and its overarching purpose are articulated by decision makers and documented in policies and legislation, as well as standards and strategy documents. Yet policy intent reveals only part of the picture. The means for the intended policies to be communicated, implemented, and understood by stakeholders (for example, policy makers, county administrators, principals, teachers, students, and so forth) are just as important. Implementation can be observed and influenced through use of the EMIS in the day-to-day activities of stakeholders, budget allocation, distribution of human resources, professional development activities, communication and dissemination of information, and the extent of institutionalization across the system (figure 3.2).

Functionalities and characteristics of an effective data system include an information cycle, a multifaceted system, and data coverage, use, and effectiveness (Abdul-Hamid 2014). These characteristics are increasingly important in the era of open and integrated data. Without them, an education data system cannot be fully effective. The collection, maintenance, analysis, dissemination, and use of education data in an information system occur in a cyclical manner, referred to as the *information cycle* (Abdul-Hamid 2014) (figure 3.3). The system tracks inputs and helps assess the quality of policies and institutions, ultimately informing decision makers on student learning and other outcomes and policy actions. Information produced by the system is provided back to the data provider (for example, schools) to be reviewed, acted on, and improved. This also includes feedback on improving the effectiveness of the information cycle itself. Feedback about the collection and analysis process then informs the next information cycle (Al Koofi 2007). Without such a feedback loop, it is considerably more difficult to flag potential deficiencies within the system and thus correct them. Any EMIS should be monitored and assessed at regular intervals so that its efficiency can be ensured. In addition, EMIS leadership should constantly be on the lookout for

Figure 3.2 Policy Intent, Implementation, and Outcomes Cycle

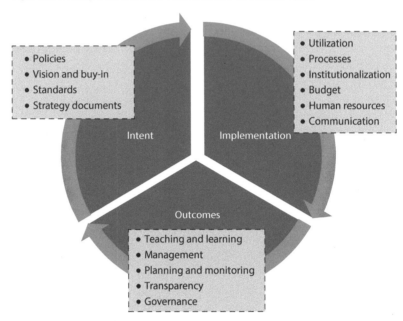

Figure 3.3 Education Data System—Information Cycle

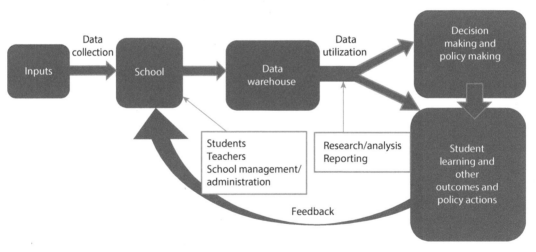

Source: Abdul-Hamid 2014.

new and innovative EMIS practices. Countries should benchmark their EMIS and cooperate to achieve system improvements, where necessary. Users of an EMIS are generally schools, parents, and the broader community.

An EMIS is a dynamic system that is elastic and easily adaptable to allow for changes and advancements in data needs (Abdul-Hamid 2014).

- *Quality assurance measures*: Systems should follow and implement an internationally accepted quality assurance management approach (for example, the International Organization for Standards [IOS] Series ISO 9000, Total Quality Management).[1] In order to maintain quality, internal and external reviews are performed and processes are in place to ensure data quality, validation, monitoring, processing, and dissemination of education statistics.
- *Data requirements and considerations*: There must be mechanisms for addressing new and emerging data requirements. Agile processes need to be in place to deal with quality considerations in planning and expanding EMIS activities. EMIS stakeholders and other data users periodically review the existing portfolio of education statistics and reports and identify any emerging data requirements. Data in the system can be aggregated or disaggregated without difficulty. The system is able to adapt to new or emerging data requirements.
- *System adaptability* to changes and/or advancements in the education system: The system needs to be adaptable to changes and advancements in the education structure, operations, or focus, including advances in technology. These changes and/or advancements include new arrangements in schools, added functionalities (for example, new reported data for a specific school), and new technologies. For instance, if a new category of students needs to be included in the data warehouse, this category can be easily created and integrated within the existing system. The system is also able to work with preexisting components (for example, legacy systems), as needed. Data collected by other agencies outside of the EMIS (for example, administrative data, population data, socio-demographic data, and, sometimes, geographic information systems data) should be easily integrated into the EMIS data warehouse; application programming interfaces (APIs) are important for this integration.

The Country-Specific Context Matters

The system architecture needs to be practical, catering to the specific financial and technological capabilities, a country's size, and the needs of the education system. Education systems of large countries may function better when decentralized, whereas the opposite may be true for small countries. There is generally less scatter in a small-country education system, so that the subsystems are primarily responsible for data collection and quality assurance while the system as a whole remains decentralized. Greater access and levels of participation are strong advantages of decentralized systems but can be expensive at the same time. The following factors need to be included in the system structure and each of these factors should be tailored to the unique country context.

- *Roles and responsibilities* within the country need to be specified and data flow mechanisms as well as data access points identified. This is crucial in order to assign the specific roles and responsibilities between the government and local authorities.
- *Financing structures* need to be clarified. This includes the distribution, allocation, and reporting of school funds. This, for instance, includes determining

who is responsible for raising school funds, how they will be distributed, and where the allocation will be recorded.

- **School staff** recruitment and professional development processes should be clearly specified according to the unique education structure.
- **Data privacy** has become increasingly important. Some data systems (for example, decentralized ones) exhibit a high number of access points. This calls for individual privacy allowances.

Tailoring EMIS to the Country's Capabilities and Education Priorities

Education data systems are highly complex, and their architecture should be tailored according to the country's capabilities and available budget. Introducing and maintaining an EMIS comes with associated costs. Policy makers need to carefully assess the financial requirements of an EMIS in the long and short terms. This will enable policy makers to design a designated EMIS budget and ensure financial sustainability. Otherwise, the entire EMIS may be jeopardized if the life cycle cost of the project is not accounted for. A common error is to account solely for the initial expenditure but neglect the long-term costs of sustaining an EMIS. This is particularly often the case with donor-funded projects in developing countries. The donor is generally willing to fund the inception and design stage of an EMIS, but the reoccurring costs such as licensing agreements with external vendors are often the burden of the EMIS country. Important financial commitments are often overlooked in the initial budgeting of EMIS projects. The lack of financial resources can thus limit sustainability and the overall success of the EMIS.

The size of the country and education system is important to consider when deciding on the system. It is only natural that countries with a small population make different EMIS choices than those with a substantially larger population. For instance, the EMIS structure in the United States, a country with a population over 300 million, exhibits a different system structure (more decentralized) than that of Samoa with a population of 100,000 people.

Current and future requirements of the EMIS are also important to consider while making decisions on the type of system. In many countries, the focus still remains on providing education for all and enforcing minimum learning standards. However, some jurisdictions like the State of Maryland in the United States have already surpassed compliance and have introduced a learning focus (see chapter 7 for more information on the education data system in Maryland). When designing an EMIS, flexibility and adaptability for future education needs are important and should be considered.

Technology is different in every country; and, in order to properly institutionalize an EMIS, the existing technological capabilities in the country need to be taken into consideration. For instance, some developing nations struggle with Internet and electricity connectivity in school, whereas advanced economies are less likely to face this challenge. Decisions on data collection, analysis, and procurement of necessary software and hardware need to take into account all of this information. Some countries have been able to leverage the use of

---

Box 3.1 Efficiency in Data Collection, Processing, and Reporting

The ED*ASSIST data collection tool developed by FHI 360 (formerly the Academy for Education Development, or AED) is being adapted from paper form for use on a tablet. The tablet application will collect information for budget development and effective resource allocation in the education sector. In Benin and Nicaragua, ED*ASSIST increased efficiency in their respective EMISs. The tool is currently being used in Djibouti, Equatorial Guinea, Liberia, Malawi, South Sudan, Uganda, and Zambia. As part of FHI 360's Liberia Teacher Training Program II (LTTP II), which aims to address the shortage of qualified teachers and the capacity to produce new teachers, ED*ASSIST is also being introduced for biometric teacher attendance monitoring.

Sources: Sampson 2000; Bernbaum and Moses 2011; FHI 360, http://www.fhi360.org/projects/liberia-teacher-training -program-ii-lttp-ii.

---

technology to meet EMIS needs for data gathering and management. Certain preexisting tools are now being updated and/or borrowed from other sectors to advance the collection and use of data by such technological means as mobile phones and tablets. These means have been proven to increase efficiency in some countries (box 3.1).

Deciding between Centralized and Decentralized EMIS Structures
Decentralized Systems
Architects of education systems and policy makers are often faced with the question of centralization vs. decentralization (figure 3.4). Decentralization is defined as surrendering authority from the central government to local entities. This decentralization may present itself in many different forms such as financial, administrative, and strategic. Centralization is when the design, supervision, and execution of the data management system remain with the central authority.

Decentralized data systems surrender certain decision-making power to local authorities. The federal level allows provinces or states to implement their own education data system while the central government acts as the main oversight authority. In many cases, the federal authorities collect only very minimal aggregate information on the education data and delegate education data management to the state level. There are different types of decentralization: delegation, deconcentration, or devolution. In the first scenario, *delegation*, local entities are solely responsible for implementing the policies designed by the central government. In the *deconcentration* phase, the system is officially decentralized, but in reality the local authorities act as agents of the central government without true decision-making power. In the final stage of *devolution*, actual authority and responsibility are transferred to the local authorities. At this stage, the local entities have decision-making power over many aspects of the education data system.

Recently, many countries have chosen to implement a more decentralized approach in their education systems (boxes 3.2 and 3.3). This is particularly true for many large and populous countries, where a fully centralized education data system may be more difficult to implement (Benete 2014). Table 3.1 provides an overview of advantages and disadvantages of decentralized systems, and box 3.4 illustrates countries that have established decentralized data systems.

Figure 3.4 Centralized and Decentralized Data Systems

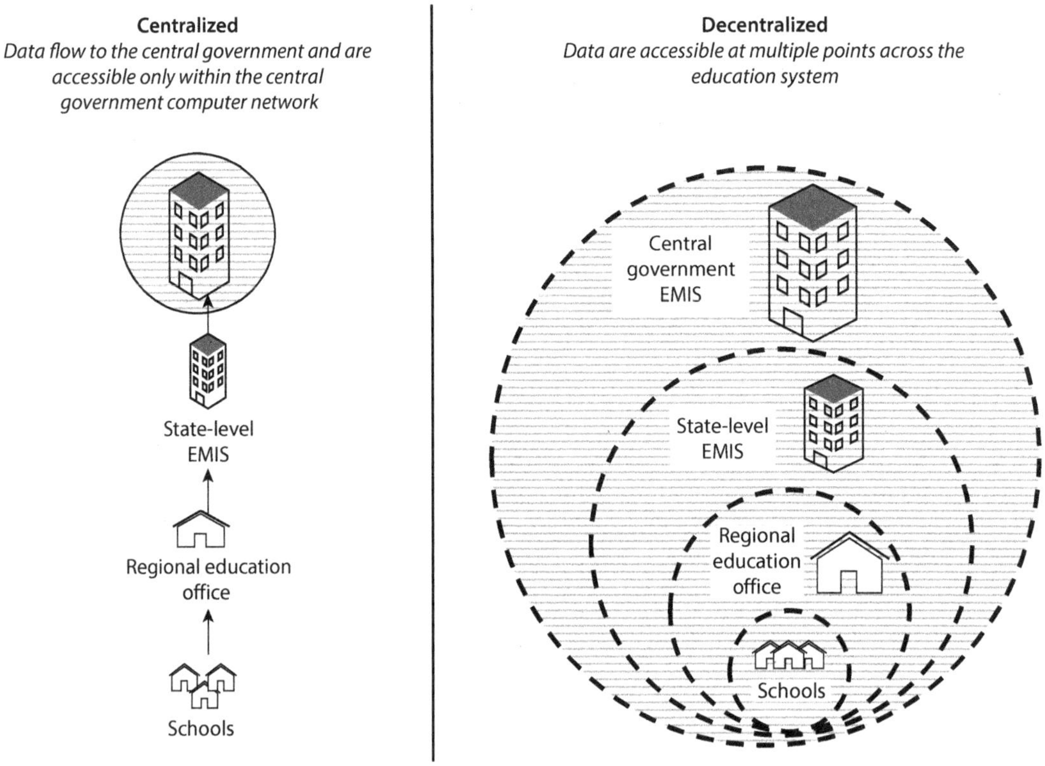

Note: EMIS = Education Management Information System.

Box 3.2 Decentralization in Asia

Decentralization in Asia is currently at different stages. Many populous countries such as China, India, Indonesia, and the Philippines have highly decentralized education systems, whereas countries such as Cambodia, Myanmar, and Vietnam have slowly started decentralization processes. For instance, in Myanmar the government has installed school district offices and decentralized grant mechanisms.

Source: Benete 2014.

Box 3.3 More Community Involvement in Schools

Nepal is undergoing a transition into a more decentralized education system. In fact, Nepal has recently transferred more authority from the state to the community level. Now community schools have more freedom in their management. School committees made up of parents and leaders in the community are entitled to make decisions on teacher recruitment and discretionary fund allocation. The aim is to involve the community in the education process of its own students. At this point it seems as if the project has had a positive impact on school access and equity. It is yet uncertain whether it has also improved learning outcomes.

Source: Bruns, Filmer, and Patrinos 2011.

Table 3.1 Advantages and Disadvantages of Decentralization

Advantages	Disadvantages
Decentralized data systems offer *access* on all levels of the education system. With a decentralized model, users can access data at multiple points. The more authority a stakeholder group has the more access it receives. Nevertheless, even at the school level, some data are already made available to the school staff and parents as well as the community.	The *costs* associated with decentralized systems and enabling access at so many different levels are generally very high. In addition, the architecture of decentralized systems is highly complex and requires more resource input than centralized education data systems. For instance, managing data access and privacy measures for all different levels of authorities is more resource-consuming than sending aggregate data only to the central government.
Decentralized data systems and their multiple data access points encourage *participation*. With appropriate data access, teachers, parents, or students themselves can identify potential weaknesses in individual student learning. At the regional level, data access may contribute to improved learning outcomes by identification of underperforming schools and additional support for those schools. Similarly, at the state level data enable decision makers to make informed decisions about resource allocation. There, the state may provide more funding or additional human resources to school districts that show a history of underperformance.	Ensuring *compatibility* of the different education subsystems within one country may be challenging. Decentralization often includes the establishment of many subsystems across the country. In many cases, the subsystems are divided by state lines and can vary greatly from one another in terms of their EMIS. For instance, they may collect different data sets or use different software or hardware. All of these factors may result in challenges in the data collection, dissemination, and analysis processes. The central government and regional actors should ensure a level of compatibility within the different subsystems so that valuable data can be collected.
A decentralized data system incentivizes *commitment* by stakeholders. The system is built on the participation of stakeholders at all levels and allows for bottom-up initiatives. As such the system is more flexible to adapt to the needs of individual schools and allows for more incentives for human resource development. It is easier to implement a flexible merit-based award and promotion system.	*Efficiency issues* may arise. Depending on the individual country context decentralization may even increase bureaucracy as well as costs and, thus, make the EMIS more inefficient. For instance, small countries may prefer a centralized structure that may be more efficient and easier to supervise. Economies of scale and scope may reverse and become inefficient in small country contexts.

Box 3.4 Examples of a Decentralized Structure

Many countries have successfully implemented decentralized data system structures. In the United States, the State of Maryland has a highly decentralized structure, with information systems at school, county, and state levels. To ensure that data effectively flow from system to system, Maryland has a variety of protocols and processes around information sharing. In the Maryland EMIS assessment (World Bank 2015a), all of the state's counties that were examined had a central data warehouse or database that integrates administrative data and learning outcomes data. This structure is critical for compliance purposes, and schools have access points to the county's information system. With regard to data coverage at the county level, there is minimal integration of administrative and learning outcomes data with financial and human resources data. Some of the county systems incorporate some human resources data, such as teacher evaluations; however, extended human resources data are generally captured in other systems. Likewise, some financial data are captured in these systems, but extended data, especially on salaries or professional development expenses, are captured outside of the EMIS. Of the seven counties examined during the assessment of EMIS in Maryland, none had the same data system structure and all were in different stages of upgrade.

Nigeria also has a decentralized EMIS structure, both practical and necessary for a country that is the most populous in Africa. Sending individual school data to the central government for collection, dissemination, and use would be time-consuming and inefficient. A decentralized structure with subsystems may be costlier, but it ensures that data can be made ready for usage in a timely manner and will be used directly at the local level. On the other hand, some education data may be lost. For instance, funds for Nigeria's education system come from a variety of sources and are distributed through a complex decentralized process. It is extremely difficult to obtain the level of public spending on education, given that 80 percent of education expenses are incurred at state level under constitutional fiscal decentralization arrangements for state and local governments. In addition, a fragmented decentralization process prevents resources from meeting needs. Resources range from schools and school infrastructure to teachers and teaching tools, essentially education inputs and their distribution, utilization, and management. Despite these grievances, a decentralized education structure is the only practical solution in a large country such as Nigeria. In recent years, modern information and communication technologies (ICTs) have enhanced data collection efficiencies and, if employed properly, can also improve communication between the different education subsystems all over the country.

Germany's education data system is highly decentralized. The 16 states in Germany are responsible for the management of their own education systems. This includes the design of curricula, policies, and data management. In fact, the *Abitur* (German high school diploma) is different in each state and difficulty varies. Bavaria is said to have the most difficult one, while other states are more moderate. In general, the federal level does not intervene directly in the local education system but provides guidance on general policies including data collection. The Federal Statistics Agency generally publishes aggregate education data, whereas individual states collect and disseminate in-depth data through the regional ministries of education.

Centralized Systems

In centralized data systems, data flow from schools, to regional education offices, to state-level education offices, and finally arrive at the central government (see figure 3.4). Client–server architecture is common among centralized data systems. Clients are PCs (personal computers) or workstations on which users run applications. Data users rely on servers for resources, such as files, devices, and even processing power (see chapter 6 for further discussion of technology). In such cases, access to data and applications is limited to those who are directly connected to the servers at the central government. Local, regional, and state education offices depend on the central government for information and reporting needs. Even in a centralized system, subsystems based on geography or levels of authority exist that provide feedback to the central system. Frequently, the provision of aggregate data, however, is a stand-alone system. In some countries such as Cameroon dual subsystems exist despite a centralized data structure (box 3.5). Table 3.2 provides an overview of advantages and disadvantages of centralized data systems, and box 3.6 offers a number of examples of countries that have successfully implemented centralized education data structures.

Box 3.5 Subsystems in Cameroon

Centralization may exist despite national education subsystems. For instance, for historical reasons Cameroon has two separate subsystems: Francophone and Anglophone. The two systems are different in their curricula and grading scale but similar in their structure of primary, secondary, and higher education. Thus, data compatibility across the two subsystems is crucial. In recent years, Cameroon has undertaken efforts to decentralize the education data, but at this point the system still remains highly centralized.

Source: UNESCO 2012.

Table 3.2 Advantages and Disadvantages of Centralized Data Systems

Advantages	Disadvantages
Data integrity may be more easily attained in centralized education data systems. The central government is solely in charge of handling, assessing, and utilizing the data collected from the local level. This also means that the sole access point is the central government, which limits potential security threats as opposed to multiple access points in a decentralized system. In addition, the central government can enforce the collection of comparable and usable data at the state level. Given that the central government dictates the use of a unified system, a centralized system is less likely to face the same compatibility challenges as a decentralized EMIS.	There are also some disadvantages of a centralized EMIS, such as *reduced accountability and data access* of a centralized education data system. The availability of few access points limits accountability of the government to other stakeholders because it is more difficult to monitor and ensure that the government takes appropriate steps in its data management. The local actors do not have access to the same data as the central government, so the government is solely responsible for decision making and policy design. In fact, sometimes users need to submit a request to the central government to receive data access.

table continues next page

Table 3.2 Advantages and Disadvantages of Centralized Data Systems *(continued)*

Advantages	*Disadvantages*
Increased efficiency can be achieved by clearly allocating responsibilities assigned by the central government. The responsibility and data access authority are made clear from the very beginning. The central government delegates the data collection to local entities and plainly prescribes the uniform nature of the kind of data, timeline, and method of data collection. Doing so eliminates or severely reduces the possibility of collecting invaluable or useless data. In comparison, in a decentralized system the data collected may not be usable because of the different subsystems.	***Less research and educational dialogue*** may occur if access is not granted to third parties such as NGOs, think tanks, universities, and other research facilities. Education research is crucial in improving education systems and finding innovative strategies to better learning outcomes. If researchers are denied access, this can negatively impact the advance and improvement of an education system. Therefore, it is crucial to ensure access for researchers even in a centralized EMIS. In addition, it is essential that the central government commits to timely reporting. Only by doing so can it ensure that the appropriate steps are taken in time to improve learning outcomes.
Lower learning curves are features of a centralized EMIS. In a centralized system there are fewer, or no, subsystems and fewer access points. This means that the system needs fewer personnel trained in data analytics. At the local level, staff will mostly need to be trained in data entry, but not data analysis, because this occurs at the central government level. This ensures a lower learning curve and eliminates confusion on different subsystems as would be the case in decentralized systems.	***Limited bottom-up initiatives*** exist because of reduced commitment and participation by stakeholders other than the central government. The central government enjoys absolute data access, whereas other stakeholders may be responsible only for data collection without access to the data they collect. This top-down approach hinders grassroots-level innovation and policy input. Moreover, if the staff responsible for data collection do not comprehend the importance and use of the data, it may reduce their commitment to the EMIS. Therefore, appropriate trainings on the importance of data in education systems are particularly important within centralized EMIS structures.

Box 3.6 Examples of Centralized Data System Structures

Fiji implemented a centralized education data system in which data collection occurs at the local level, but analysis, research, and assessment are done at the central level only. At the local level, individual schools can access only school-specific data (for example, attendance, enrollment, and financial data). Thus far, the new system has proven to be highly effective in data collection and data management. However, the government has been restrictive in allowing researchers and assessment teams access to the central data. This potentially limits the spectrum of information that is extracted from the available data.

France's education system traditionally demonstrates a highly centralized structure. The policy decisions and education priorities are defined by the state. This is why the Ministry of Education (MoE) designs, carries out, and analyzes the results of national test scores. The test scores of the *baccalauréat* (high school diploma) are distributed to students through the MoE's website using each student's unique tracking number, and some states offer financial bonuses to high achievers.

Turkey has implemented a highly centralized governance and data management structure since 1973. The Ministry of National Education (MoNE) is responsible for the design and architecture of the system, whereas the 81 Turkish provinces are responsible for the effective execution of the policies and guidelines. The MoNE takes responsibility for planning, structure,

box continues next page

and data management for basic, secondary, and higher education. The Board of Education tracks student achievement and student-focused information such as socioeconomic background. This centralized data assessment enables comparisons across the country and appropriate policy decisions. At the school level the MoNE focuses on data quality with independent provincial inspectors. The Board of Inspections assesses primary schools annually, and ministerial inspectors review secondary schools every three years (OECD 2013).

The Need to Benchmark: Standards and Assessment Methodology

An EMIS comprises three systemic features: data standards, technological standards, and utilization standards. *Data standards* refer to high-quality data that are reliable, accurate, timely, and complete. The data can be of different types: quantitative, qualitative, longitudinal (to measure student performance from K–12 to higher education), and time series (over a period of time). *Technological standards* include data architecture, required capabilities, system compatibility, training and technical support for maintenance of the services, detailed implementation plan, and thorough description of responsibilities. *Utilization standards* include analysis of available information in the form of charts, graphs, and visuals; use of information by stakeholders across the education system from parents and schools to the MoE; accessibility; and dissemination of the information.

Our methodology includes the four actionable areas: (1) enabling environment, (2) system soundness, (3) quality data, and (4) utilization by users. Assessing the state of the EMIS system requires thorough review of these four key EMIS standards. The ultimate objective of EMIS benchmarking is to get a holistic picture of the current system, capabilities, needs, and demand to determine the future implementation course of action. Benchmarking attempts to induce policy change that would enable the policy makers to produce, disseminate, and use high-quality education statistics and is essential for effective education sector planning by the government and enhanced teaching and learning in classrooms. Figure 3.5 describes the set of EMIS standards that are important for a well-functioning EMIS.

The SABER–EMIS Assessment Tool

The SABER–EMIS tool helps build a strategic understanding of the existing data system, provides a foundation for system-wide improvements, and makes recommendations for scaling up and value-added components. It determines relevant examples of best practice and lessons identified by the international community, especially as they relate to the four policy areas. A benchmarking system also allows policy makers to gauge the quality of their EMIS as well as how its data system compares to other systems internationally with similar context (figure 3.5). Appendix A defines each policy lever and highlights assessment scores.

Figure 3.5 Analysis of EMIS Benchmarking Results

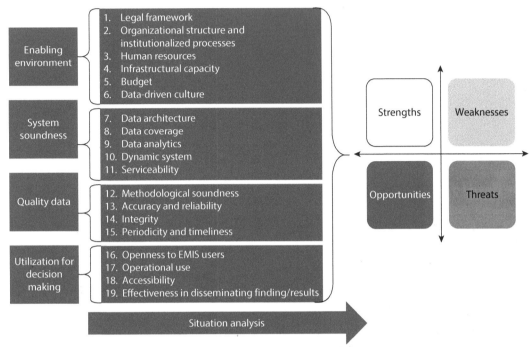

Source: Abdul-Hamid 2014.
Note: EMIS = Education Management Information System.

The aim is to inform the government on policies related to education statistics and indicators, as well as to help countries monitor overall progress related to educational inputs, processes, and outcomes. The assessment in itself is simple enough to be affordable to all governments. In fact, having a solid analysis and guiding principles available is likely to save governments from potential unnecessary expenditure and dead ends. Therefore, governments often use the SABER–EMIS assessment as a first step in the analysis of their current EMIS architecture and use its recommendations for system-wide improvements. Figure 3.6 illustrates an example of the executive summary of a SABER assessment report (Suriname).

The SABER–EMIS tool engages with all levels of governments at every stage of the assessment to seek political support and buy-in. This model can be applied in any country, at any stage of EMIS development. Government participation is crucial not only in the data collection phase but also in the implementation. It is a cooperative process, where the benefits to both the government and the SABER–EMIS assessment team are high. Government participation generally takes place in the form of meetings or conferences, and the provision of key data as well as policy documents. In addition, many education projects by international donor organizations will find the assessment useful in providing them with essential information and a plan toward improvements.

Figure 3.6 Executive Summary of the SABER–EMIS Assessment, Suriname

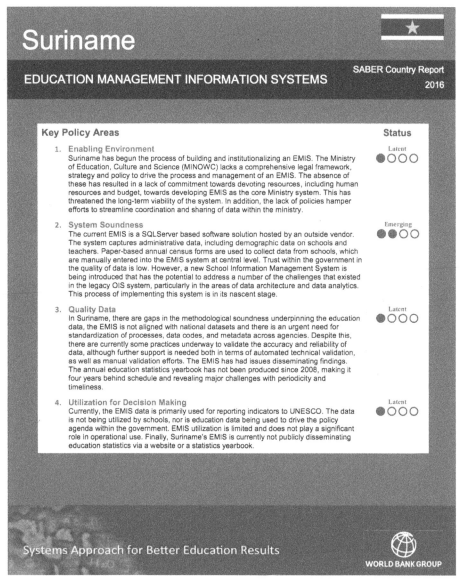

Suriname

EDUCATION MANAGEMENT INFORMATION SYSTEMS

SABER Country Report
2016

Key Policy Areas	Status

1. Enabling Environment — *Latent*
Suriname has begun the process of building and institutionalizing an EMIS. The Ministry of Education, Culture and Science (MINOWC) lacks a comprehensive legal framework, strategy and policy to drive the process and management of an EMIS. The absence of these has resulted in a lack of commitment towards devoting resources, including human resources and budget, towards developing EMIS as the core Ministry system. This has threatened the long-term viability of the system. In addition, the lack of policies hamper efforts to streamline coordination and sharing of data within the ministry.

2. System Soundness — *Emerging*
The current EMIS is a SQLServer based software solution hosted by an outside vendor. The system captures administrative data, including demographic data on schools and teachers. Paper-based annual census forms are used to collect data from schools, which are manually entered into the EMIS system at central level. Trust within the government in the quality of data is low. However, a new School Information Management System is being introduced that has the potential to address a number of the challenges that existed in the legacy OIS system, particularly in the areas of data architecture and data analytics. This process of implementing this system is in its nascent stage.

3. Quality Data — *Latent*
In Suriname, there are gaps in the methodological soundness underpinning the education data, the EMIS is not aligned with national datasets and there is an urgent need for standardization of processes, data codes, and metadata across agencies. Despite this, there are currently some practices underway to validate the accuracy and reliability of data, although further support is needed both in terms of automated technical validation, as well as manual validation efforts. The EMIS has had issues disseminating findings. The annual education statistics yearbook has not been produced since 2008, making it four years behind schedule and revealing major challenges with periodicity and timeliness.

4. Utilization for Decision Making — *Latent*
Currently, the EMIS data is primarily used for reporting indicators to UNESCO. The data is not being utilized by schools, nor is education data being used to drive the policy agenda within the government. EMIS utilization is limited and does not play a significant role in operational use. Finally, Suriname's EMIS is currently not publicly disseminating education statistics via a website or a statistics yearbook.

Systems Approach for Better Education Results

WORLD BANK GROUP

Source: World Bank 2016.

The SABER–EMIS tool produces a high-quality report that is a useful guide to determine the future implementation path for education stakeholders. The process starts with providing the appropriate training to data collectors to ensure that they follow the SABER–EMIS standards. After the training, relevant policy documents are collected and reviewed to evaluate the level of institutionalization of the EMIS in the country. Through meetings with EMIS personnel and users (for example, focus group meetings with teachers, school administration, and parents) data are collected on how and for what the system is used. The government and other education stakeholders are an instrumental part of the assessment and provide valuable information. This enables SABER–EMIS to uncover (potential) discrepancy between policy intent and EMIS utilization. Only then will analysis and benchmark scoring (latent = 1, emerging = 2, established = 3, and advanced = 4) take place. Figure 3.7 illustrates the SABER–EMIS scoring method, including basic explanations. The final step of the SABER–EMIS assessment is data validation, an essential part of the process that ensures all data are accurate, reliable, and complete.

The final score of each of the previously mentioned indicators (enabling environment, system soundness, quality data, and data utilization) is determined by a weighted average of the policy levers. For instance, the benchmarking scores for Romania were determined through the policy lever scores as demonstrated in table 3.3. This detailed analysis allows governments to identify areas of improvement clearly, supported by detailed explanation of the different stages for each

Figure 3.7 SABER Scoring and EMIS Development

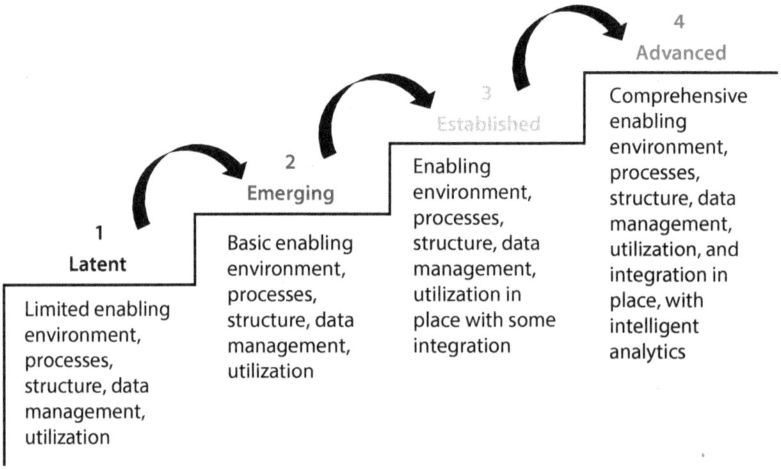

1
Latent
Limited enabling environment, processes, structure, data management, utilization

2
Emerging
Basic enabling environment, processes, structure, data management, utilization

3
Established
Enabling environment, processes, structure, data management, utilization in place with some integration

4
Advanced
Comprehensive enabling environment, processes, structure, data management, utilization, and integration in place, with intelligent analytics

Source: Abdul-Hamid 2014.
Note: EMIS = Education Management Information System; SABER = Systems Approach for Better Education Results.

Table 3.3 SABER–EMIS Policy Lever Scores, Romania

Policy goal	Policy lever	Score[a]	Weight (%)	Benchmark
Enabling environment	Legal framework	2.81	17	Established
	Organizational structure and institutionalized processes	2.67	17	Established
	Human resources	1.71	17	Emerging
	Infrastructural capacity	2.81	17	Established
	Budget	1.90	17	Emerging
	Data-driven culture	2.29	15	Established

table continues next page

Table 3.3 SABER–EMIS Policy Lever Scores, Romania *(continued)*

Policy goal	Policy lever	Score[a]	Weight (%)	Benchmark
System soundness	Data architecture	3.76	20	Advanced
	Data coverage	1.74	30	Emerging
	Data analytics	1.00	15	Emerging
	Dynamic system	2.67	15	Established
	Serviceability	2.97	20	Established
Quality data	Methodological soundness	2.70	25	Established
	Accuracy and reliability	2.56	25	Established
	Integrity	2.96	25	Established
	Periodicity and timeliness	3.70	25	Advanced
Utilization in decision making	Openness	0.74	15	Latent
	Operational use	2.04	50	Established
	Accessibility	2.47	20	Established
	Effectiveness in disseminating findings	1.20	15	Emerging

Source: World Bank 2017.
Note: EMIS = Education Management Information System; SABER = Systems Approach to Better Education Results.
a. 0–0.99 = Latent; 1–1.9 = Emerging; 2–2.9 = Established; 3–4 = Advanced.

policy lever (see appendix A). For instance, in Romania the policy lever scores for data utilization clearly indicate a lack of openness of the EMIS system. The policy lever scores can act as a road map for improvement.

The SABER–EMIS assessment also includes a SWOT (strengths, weaknesses, opportunities, and threats) analysis. This is another level of factoring and/or clustering scores into weaknesses and strengths to provide an assessment summary. The analysis may conclude, for example, that the data clusters in a way that differs from the policy areas. Policy recommendations are then based on the results of the SWOT analysis. By analyzing benchmarked findings, this approach makes SABER–EMIS operational. Table 3.4 illustrates an example of a SABER–EMIS SWOT analysis in the Solomon Islands.

The final results of the assessment (data and report) for each country are published on the SABER portal, which promotes knowledge sharing of lessons learned from different country contexts. In fact, the reports aim to highlight best practices from other countries that are applicable to the context of the assessed country. In addition to producing the report, the SABER–EMIS team often holds workshops with government officials to inform them about their assessment and initiate a dialogue on how to design and implement EMIS improvement and reform plans. The workshops explain the policy goals in depth and emphasize that the goal of any EMIS is to collect useful data that allow for informed decision making and foster student learning.

The SABER-EMIS assessment can be applied to any given country at any stage of EMIS development. From a small and low-income country like Solomon Islands to a large well-established EMIS like that in the United States, the framework for SABER can be used at any stage to (1) determine the progress at different policy areas and (2) help provide a direction for the future stages of implementation.

Table 3.4 SABER–EMIS SWOT Analysis, Solomon Islands

Strengths	*Weaknesses*
• Strong *political buy-in* from high-level officials	• Detailed *policies* supporting EMIS operations do not exist
• The *National Education Action Plan* (NEAP) lays the foundation for EMIS	• Lack of *integration* of different education databases (e.g., assessment/finance) into EMIS
• Linkage of the education statistics with the overall education *strategy*	• *EMIS processes not expanded* to the provincial level
• A *system is already established* at the central level	• Limited *auditing/validation* mechanisms
• *Data analysis tools* already exist	• Flaws in the system that create adverse incentives for schools to *report* inflated education data
	• Poor *Internet* access, especially in remote areas, which inhibits technological activities in the country
	• *Manual processing* of data
	• *No revisions or updates* to school census forms
	• *Limited involvement* of education authorities
	• *Professional development* activities for staff are limited
	• Long delays in *production* of Performance Assessment Reports
Opportunities	*Threats*
• *Involvement of education authorities* beyond collection and distribution of census forms	• Heavy dependence on donors threatens the long-term *sustainability* of the system
• Quality of feedback *reports* provided to schools could be enhanced	• Weak *capacity* of primary data providers and officials at the local level
• Creating awareness, *publicizing*, and regularly updating the content of the existing MEHRD website	• Limited channels for *communication* to inform and update stakeholders
• *Designating MEHRD officials and education authorities closer to schools* (especially in remote areas) to manage/monitor them	• Limited *communication* and *coordination* across different units in the MEHRD
• Existing *donor funding* could be channeled through government systems	

Source: World Bank 2015b.
Note: EMIS = Education Management Information System; MEHRD = Ministry of Education & Human Resources Development; SABER = Systems Approach to Better Education Results.

Other Assessment Tools

Examples of other common international standards/tools are those introduced by the ISO 9000, the Education Data Quality Assessment Framework (Ed-DQAF), Utilization-Focused Evaluation (UFE), and SWOT analysis, which form the construct validity of the tool designed to assess the four policy areas. However, these tools were not designed for benchmarking purposes, which calls for an adaptation process of the standards that will permit international and intertemporal comparisons. In addition, a SWOT analysis is a useful tool for assessing the strength of an EMIS.

The ISO 9000 is typically used for quality management and focuses on the framework for quality management, providing guidance on how to manage for quality and perform internal audits (IOS 2016). These standards have been applied to education and training institutes, including large organizations (Van den Berghe 1998). The ISO 9000 (2005, Principle 7) takes a factual approach to decision making based on analysis of data. This principle corresponds with the demand for data-driven decisions to which an EMIS responds.

The ISO 9000 framework is the backbone of an EMIS. Figure 3.8 adapts ISO 9000 to apply to the soundness (that is, quality) of an EMIS. As outlined in the figure, assessing the management of an EMIS system ensures the continuity of operations. More specifically, the government (or an entity assigned by the government) is the managing authority responsible for the system, which manages its architecture and infrastructure and the realization of such products as statistical reports. Last, the system is analyzed for its continued improvement on the basis of feedback from users and clients. In sum, these features allow for a sustained and effective system.

The Ed-DQAF is an instrument used to benchmark the quality of education data. The International Monetary Fund (IMF) initially developed the generic DQAF to assess the quality of economic data (UNESCO 2010). The framework was then modified and adapted for the education sector in 2004 by the United Nations Education, Scientific, and Cultural Organization Institute for Statistics (UIS) and the World Bank. Since then, it has been referred to as the Ed-DQAF. Ed-DQAF is a diagnostic tool that can assess the quality of education data produced by a government's education statistics agency. It compares education data quality within a country against international standards, allowing a country to identify areas in need of improvement (UIS 2014). Ed-DQAF encompasses the parameters of many other professional standards established to evaluate data quality.

Figure 3.8 Use of ISO 9000 Quality Processes to Assess the Soundness of an EMIS

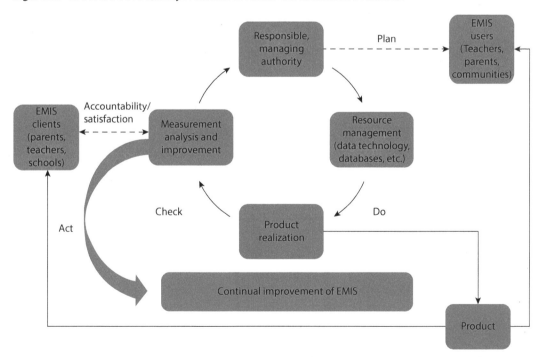

Source: Adapted from IOS, http://www.iso.org/iso/home/standards/management-standards/iso_9000.htm.
Note: EMIS = Education Management Information System.

For example, the professional standards set forth by the American Evaluation Association Program Evaluation Standards (that is, utility, feasibility, propriety, accuracy, and accountability) are analogous to the prerequisites and the five dimensions of data quality of the IMF's DQAF (Yarbrough et al. 2011). Currently, education DQAF has been implemented only in a small number of countries and has not been very effective in examining the quality of the data system.

The UFE evaluates EMIS programs, generating practical results ripe for use. Developed by Michael Patton, it is based on the premise that an evaluation should be judged by its utility and actual use (Yarbrough et al. 2011). Therefore, evaluations should be designed and conducted in a way that ensures their findings are used. Even if an evaluation is technically or methodologically strong, if its findings are not used, it is not considered a good evaluation. The UFE is used to enhance the likely use of evaluation findings and derive lessons learned from an evaluation process (Patton and Horton 2009). In order to enhance use, the UFE framework is based on a comprehensive yet simple checklist of the main steps that should be followed prior to conducting an evaluation, including identifying the main users of an evaluation's findings, the methods that should be used by the evaluation, and the analysis and dissemination of findings.

Although the UFE is theoretically used to assess programs, its original framework has been adapted to assess how an EMIS is used. Instead of focusing on the complete EMIS structure, the UFE assesses the ways different stakeholders use the EMIS. In order to follow this approach, the five key steps highlighted in the UFE checklist have been adapted to assess the utilization of an EMIS (figure 3.9). Using these five steps, an EMIS can identify EMIS users, assess their commitment and use of the EMIS system as a whole, evaluate their access to data and their skills in data analysis, and examine the dissemination strategies in place to distribute information generated by the EMIS. Most important, this approach assesses whether or not the information provided by the EMIS is actually used by education stakeholders.

As previously noted, specific elements of ISO 9000, Ed-DQAF, and UFE are amalgamated in the SABER–EMIS Tool—guided by the three principles of sustainability, accountability, and efficiency—to provide a systematic and practical

Figure 3.9 Key Steps of UFE Adapted to Assess Utilization of an EMIS

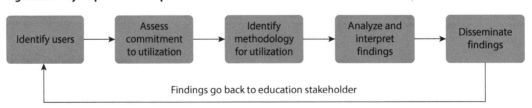

Source: Adapted from Patton 2013.
Note: UFE = Utilization-Focused Evaluation.

way to benchmark an EMIS. Aspects of this tool have already been piloted, validating its use for benchmarking. As such, the construct of the SABER–EMIS Tool aims to be comprehensive and applicable to all contexts.

The SWOT analysis allows evaluators a broad analysis of the EMIS, which could be used to make improvements. SWOT is a situation analysis tool used for the identification and evaluation of strengths, weaknesses, opportunities, and threats. The simplicity of the tool allows it to be applied to complex contexts. The tool is especially appropriate because it can be used in the early stages of strategic decision making; the findings of this tool will thus inform future policy-related decisions (Humphrey 2005). Benchmarking the four policy areas of an EMIS is important, but countries and policy makers are also interested in understanding the strengths and weaknesses of the system.

Lessons Learned from Two Decades of World Bank EMIS Activities

Evidence suggests that an initial and detailed assessment of the existing EMIS structure is key for the success of any EMIS engagement. Since 1998, the World Bank has been involved in over 250 education projects featuring EMIS components, yet some projects fell through in the early stages of development because of lack of alignment between goals and capabilities. Conducting a systematic and specialized "needs assessment" of the EMIS before the start of the project is necessary to fully understand the system needs and guide project preparation and implementation. This plays a critical role in benchmarking an EMIS and provides a valuable foundation for the design of the strategic vision of the EMIS projects. Figure 3.10 illustrates an EMIS value chain and assessment of all factors that should be undertaken by the government to ensure the successful implementation of an effective and fully operational EMIS.

From an extensive review of World Bank EMIS projects from over two decades and all over the world, a number of important dimensions have been derived. As a minimum requirement, governments need to assess the system on

Figure 3.10 EMIS Value Chain

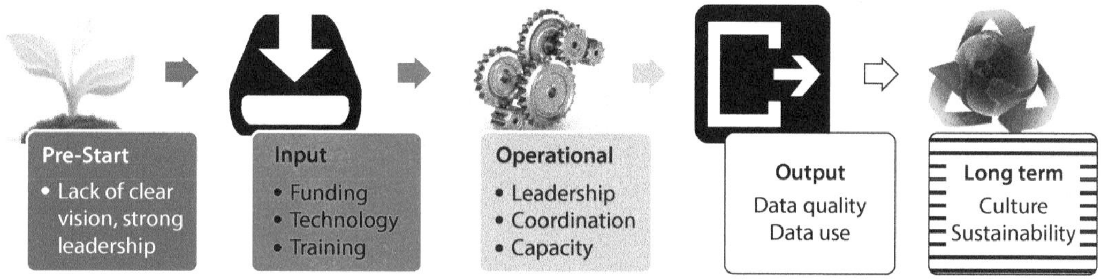

Pre-Start	Input	Operational	Output	Long term
• Lack of clear vision, strong leadership	• Funding • Technology • Training	• Leadership • Coordination • Capacity	Data quality Data use	Culture Sustainability

Note: EMIS = Education Management Information System.

the basis of the following dimensions and questions (Abdul-Hamid, Saraogi, and Mintz 2017):

- **Vision and culture of data**: Is there a clear vision from high-level politicians and other stakeholders regarding EMIS? Is the strategic vision shared by relevant decision makers and education stakeholders? Does a data-driven culture exist? Does the government support the establishment of a data-driven culture? What are the most effective mechanisms to support its implementation?

- **Institutionalization and institutional capacity**: How far has the institutionalization of evidence-based decision making progressed? Is there a clearly defined EMIS organizational structure with a mission statement, structured workflow, and defined roles and responsibilities? What is the existing legal EMIS framework, and will it need to be updated to extend EMIS to all aspects of the education system? Does the statistical agency responsible for EMIS have the appropriate financial, technological, institutional, and human resources to carry out its task? Does a legal policy with a dedicated EMIS budget for its operations exist to avoid funding issues and dependence on donors for EMIS sustainability?

- **Reliable, quality, and timely data**: Are data complete, consistent, and reliable? If not, what are the gaps and the desired data qualities of the new EMIS? Which existing data collection and validation mechanisms need to be improved to attain high-quality data? Is sufficient infrastructure in place to do so, or is there a need to design new data infrastructure? Is data collection comprehensive or does the scope need to be expanded? Is data quality appropriate and timely to allow effective utilization?

- **Dissemination of data**: What are the existing dissemination strategies (for example, reports, online, radio, newspaper, pamphlets, television, and so on)? Do all stakeholders have access to education data? Are the user platforms designed to cater to all types of education stakeholders including those without advanced statistical training? In which format are the data available (for example, only PDF or also Excel)? How often are data available (for example, once a year in the statistical yearbook or more often)? Are data disaggregated sufficiently to be useful to all education stakeholders including parents and the community?

- **Effective data utilization**: Can and do policy makers use data as a basis for informed decision making? If not, which processes need to be improved and institutionalized to ensure that data-based decision making occurs? Are all stakeholders at the central, regional, and local levels empowered to use data for decision-making purposes?

- **System integration and technology**: Is the EMIS system integrated with other databases within the MoE (for example, learning assessment scores) and other government agencies (for example, ministries of finance, health, or labor)? Is the technology able to overcome potential integration challenges (for example, low Internet connectivity, availability of computers, and so on)? Is the structure of the EMIS well defined and supported by database, hardware, and software structures?

Some projects stand out as successful EMIS implementation projects. In Malaysia, an operational EMIS was successfully implemented by clearly stating the overall objectives of mitigating the adverse impact of the regional economic crisis on education and developing students' technical skills. This was achieved through careful assessment of the existing EMIS structure and needs of the education system, high-level political buy-in, and careful operational planning. The system was built on the preexisting EMIS structure, which was improved and made sustainable in the long term with a nationwide reach. Old technology such as databases, software, and hardware were assessed and upgraded or replaced as needed. Institutional capacity was also expanded. The EMIS was integrated into multiple databases and a new information system, Executive Information System (EIS), was developed for planning and policy formulation.

Similarly, the project to establish EMIS as a human resource, teaching, and curriculum planning tool in Nigeria has been successful to some degree. After a comprehensive assessment of the current human resource and information system in primary schools in Nigeria, it was possible to tailor the EMIS to the needs of the country. Consequently, school statistics were made available to the public to be used for evidence-based decision making and to achieve the Education For All objectives. In addition, EMIS equipment and staff capacities were upgraded to manage national data collection, analysis, reporting, and dissemination. The assessment also guided the institutional capacity improvements and institutionalization processes regarding EMIS. This also included procurement of appropriate software and hardware to support the EMIS upgrades.

Using Results-Based Financing as a Structured Approach for Assessment and Development of EMIS

Results-based financing (RBF) is used by the World Bank and international donors to incentivize countries to implement education project components, the financing for which is directly linked with the achievement of pre-agreed outcomes, often referred to as delivery-linked indicators (DLIs) or delivery-linked targets (DLTs). These DLIs act as evaluation indicators of the government's progress toward the overall project's target and are generally based on data obtained through education data management systems. Consequently, almost all projects have one or two subcomponents linked to the strengthening of institutional data management capacities regardless of the target level of education (primary, secondary, tertiary, or vocational training) or target population (teachers, students, or government officials). Since 2012, RBF has been used as an incentivizing tool in over 20 World Bank education projects all over the world.

Box 3.7 provides two success stories where RBF was employed to establish education data management systems.

Using DLIs to monitor a country's education progress automatically provides governments with a clear point of reference for which areas and indicators to focus on. However, such a strong focus on a limited number of indicators may encourage the government to neglect other important areas. Therefore, it is instrumental that the indicators are carefully chosen and broad enough that the underlying education project goals will be achieved and are sustainable in the long term. DLIs should be tangible, transparent, and verifiable and should involve expenditures supported by the program (World Bank 2011). The indicators are critical to achieving the outputs and outcomes efficiently and effectively. If planned well, RBF with DLIs can be a powerful tool to incentivize development in education.

Box 3.7 Success Stories of Results-Based Financing

The Education Reform Project in Moldova clearly stated as one of its objectives the establishment of a consolidated EMIS. Establishing a consolidated EMIS in Moldova was one of the priorities of the project because other DLIs depend on the data provided by the EMIS. The EMIS DLIs included (1) a school-mapping project; (2) data utilization for monitoring, policy making, and planning; (3) semiannual monitoring reports; and (4) establishing an EMIS database with student and school staff records. The DLI of establishing a consolidated EMIS was evaluated in text, but the data provided by EMIS is the basis for many other DLIs that are quantitatively evaluated. These would include, for instance, the percentage of schools attaining the approved quality assurance standards or the number of qualified primary school teachers. The project was successful in establishing an EMIS that was fully functional. In particular, the EMIS was used to closely monitor and mitigate dropout rates, which had not been possible previously. In addition, school report cards based on EMIS data were published by the Ministry of Education and Science and made available to all schools. Although the consolidated EMIS data were not yet fully used for monitoring education reform and policy making, the consolidated EMIS laid the groundwork for data use (Word Bank 2017).

In 2014, the World Bank introduced a Results for Education Achievement and Development project focusing on strengthening the education system, in particular governance and management results, in The Gambia. One of the project development objectives included the establishment of a human resource EMIS system monitoring annual teacher trainings, evaluations, and postings. In addition, the completion of an annual school census (with a minimum 95 percent response rate, including religious schools) is one of the seven DLIs. Another two DLIs focus on average student participation in national assessments for grades 3, 5, and 8 in public schools. A functioning EMIS is the underlying source of this data, and some of the issues faced often come from a lack of technical, institutional, or human resource capacities within the EMIS. In The Gambia, challenges remained with regard to the successful completion of the annual school census, which was directly linked to a lack of statistical skills within the EMIS team.

box continues next page

Box 3.7 Success Stories of Results-Based Financing *(continued)*

Therefore, the government took the following measures: (1) enhance statistical skills and facilitate the use of the statistical software; (2) train end users to conduct data checks, statistical analysis, and results interpretation; (3) develop training plans tailored to attracting young talent; (4) improve EMIS management and cooperation with other teams; (5) set forth a school agenda about data collection, validation, and analysis in the EMIS; (6) establish EMIS documentation processes; (7) integrate national assessment, examination, administrative, and human resource data into the EMIS; and (8) connect regional education offices with the EMIS. Through these measures The Gambia was able to conduct an annual school census with a 95 percent response rate. Analysis and dissemination of the data were also achieved. An early childhood development monitoring and reporting tool was also developed. In addition, training, promotions, and postings of teachers were updated annually in an interfaced EMIS and human resource system (World Bank 2017).

The following represent the structured steps needed for the DLIs to effectively monitor the EMIS development:

- Designing an assessment report with the current EMIS situation, needs, gap analysis, and operational recommendations for the way forward
- Identifying and coordinating with the key stakeholders to discuss the assessment plan and develop a road map to determine timelines, responsibilities, financials, and processes to implement the recommendations. Some of the key things to plan include:
  - Data collection process from schools
  - Education statistics that need to be collected and tracked
  - A data integration framework for linking different types of data sources into one platform
  - A data management system including servers, application types, interfaces, and so on
  - A data analysis and dissemination strategy
  - Short- and long-term financial plans
  - Human resources
  - Data security issues
- Creating a core enabling environment for execution for the outlined road map. This includes development of policies and a data-driven culture.
- Training handbook and EMIS manual for staff professional development
- Long-term plan for longitudinal data collection

Note

1. The IOS develops and publishes voluntary international standards for technology and business. Compliance with IOS standards can be certified by a third party. For more information, see the IOS website at http://www.iso.org/iso/home/standards /management-standards/iso_9000.htm.

References

Abdul-Hamid, Husein. 2014. "What Matters Most for Education Management Information Systems: A Framework Paper." SABER Working Paper Series No. 7, World Bank, Washington, DC.

Abdul-Hamid, Husein, Namrata Saraogi, and Sarah Mintz. 2017. "Lessons Learnt from World Bank EMIS Operations Worldwide: Portfolio Review 1998–2014." World Bank, Washington, DC.

Al Koofi, Ahmed A. Karim. 2007. "A Study of How an Education Management Information System (EMIS) Can Be Effectively Implemented in the Ministry of Education in the Kingdom of Bahrain." Ministry of Education, Kingdom of Bahrain, Al Manamah.

Benete, Lina. 2014. "Decentralization as an Education System Reform." Education UNESCO Bangkok, May 30, http://www.unescobkk.org/education/news/article /decentralization-as-an-education-system-reform/.

Bernbaum, Marcia, and Kurt Moses. 2011. "Education Management Information Systems: A Guide to Education Project Design, Evaluation, and Implementation Based on Experiences from EQUIP2 Projects in Malawi, Uganda, and Zambia." EQUIP2 Lessons Learned in Education, U.S. Agency for International Development, Washington, DC.

Bruns, Barbara, Deon Filmer, and Harry Anthony Patrinos. 2011. *Making Schools Work: New Evidence on Accountability Reforms.* Washington, DC: World Bank.

Humphrey, Albert S. 2005. "SWOT Analysis for Management Consulting." SRI Alumni Newsletter (December). SRI International, California.

OECD (Organisation for Economic Co-operation and Development). 2013. "Chile: Education Policy Outlook 2013." OECD, Paris, November.

Patton, Michael Quinn. 2013. "Utilization-Focused Evaluation (U-FE) Checklist." The Evaluation Center, West Michigan University, Kalamazoo, MI.

Patton, Michael Quinn, and Douglas Horton. 2009. "Utilization-Focused Evaluation for Agricultural Innovation." ILAC Brief 22. ILAC, Bioversity, Rome.

Sampson, Joyce. 2000. "Academy for Educational Development: A Leader in Communications." *Techknowlogia: International Journal of Technology for the Advancement of Knowledge and Learning* 2 (5): 58–59.

UNESCO (United Nations Educational, Scientific, and Cultural Organization). 2010. "Assessing Education Data Quality in the Southern African Development Community (SADC): A Synthesis of Seven Country Assessments." UNESCO, Paris.

———. 2012. "Decentralization in Education: National Policies and Practices." UNESCO, Paris. http://unedsdoc.unesco.org/images/0014/001412/141221e.pdf.

Van den Berghe, Wouter. 1998. "Application of ISO 9000 Standards to Education and Training." *European Journal Vocational Training* (CEDEFOP, European Centre for the Development of Vocational Training), 15 (December): 20–28.

World Bank. 2015a. "SABER–EMIS Maryland State Report." World Bank, Washington, DC.

———. 2015b. "Solomon Islands Education Management Information Systems: SABER Country Report 2015." World Bank, Washington, DC.

———. 2016. "Suriname Education Management Information Systems: SABER Country Report 2016." World Bank, Washington, DC.

———. 2017. "SABER–EMIS Country Report Romania." World Bank, Washington, DC.

Yarbrough, D. B., L. M. Shulha, R. K. Hopson, and F. A. Caruthers. 2011. *The Program Evaluation Standards: A Guide for Evaluators and Evaluation Users*, 3rd ed. Thousand Oaks, CA: Sage Publications.

CHAPTER 4

How to Design and Implement Routine Data Collection from Schools

Key Takeaways

- The school census provides a snapshot of the education system, which is comparable over time and should be integrated into the Education Management Information System (EMIS). It shall include accurate and detailed administrative data on schools, students, human resources, and other resources.
- It is important that questions on the form align with the education goals.
- Ensuring legal backing for data collection and use is crucial for a successful school census.
- Before implementing a school census, the roles and responsibilities and the legal, financial, technological, and administrative capacities need to be assessed. Then, the census processes, system architecture, timelines, budget, and necessary trainings should be planned carefully. Once completed, the school census is generally initiated with proper communication activities at the central level, with local authorities, and in schools. Regional offices collect the school census data (digitally or on paper), which are later verified.
- The school census process needs to be fully institutionalized with defined responsibilities and well coordinated between the central and local levels under the management of a single entity—most commonly the statistical unit within the ministry of education (MoE).
- Digital data collection is becoming affordable and easily achieved. It is also a better way to ensure data accuracy, time saving, and cost reduction.
- Proper internal and external validations are necessary.
- Penalties should be enforced in case of noncompliance with deadlines.
- Timely completion is crucial, and data need to be analyzed and disseminated within no more than four to six months of data collection.

- The process needs to be assessed annually before embarking on a new school census. A comprehensive review of the prior school censuses is helpful for identifying cost-saving measures, achieving better compliance, overcoming challenges, and introducing innovations.
- Schools need to see reports coming out of the census. Schools' ability to see their data and compare themselves with other schools will ensure relevance of the census and will help in school improvement.

A School Census Provides an Aggregate Snapshot of the Education Sector

Data collection via annual school census is one of the key components of an EMIS. Generally, data collection in developing countries takes place by means of annual census forms sent to schools to collect the education information the government needs to monitor the education system. On the basis of the local contexts and capacities, the government decides the appropriate methods (paper-based or technological) and channels (centralized or decentralized) of collecting data from various sources. These census forms are then pilot-tested to ensure that schools understand the instructions, data definitions, and indicators requested before administration at a national scale. Figure 4.1 shows the census's scope of data coverage (data on students, teachers, and schools), which is then processed and managed by the EMIS team at the MoE for analysis and decision making for use by various stakeholders.

The need for collecting and disseminating accurate, timely, and reliable education data has been increasingly emphasized, especially with the onset of the Sustainable Development Goals (SDGs), to ensure that all girls and boys complete free, equitable, and quality primary and secondary education, leading to

Figure 4.1 Data Coverage, Sharing, and Analysis

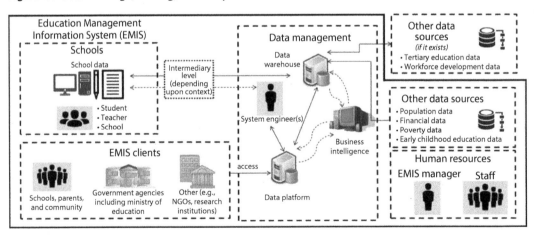

Source: Abdul-Hamid 2014.
Note: NGO = nongovernmental organization.

relevant and effective learning outcomes. This requires a robust school census process, which is able to collect detailed, reliable, and up-to-date school-level data that can strengthen monitoring and improve school administration and student learning. Information collected through a school census can inform key decisions related to planning, budgeting, incentives, accountability, and instruction. It can also facilitate comparison of performance across provinces, local governments, different types of schools, and other countries. Data from a school census can support monitoring and evaluation of projects and programs at schools as well as research and knowledge generation to benefit schools and beyond. This is extremely helpful in developing countries to understand and study relevant statistics for the compression, correlation, and relationship between different education inputs and outputs. Some of the data points that can be collected through a school census include the following:

- Data coordinates to identify school locations within a country
- Material, human, and financial resources at schools
- Breakdown of student administrative information such as family background, attendance rates, enrollment rates, and health records
- Service delivery indicators
- Learning outcomes of students and schools

Figure 4.2 illustrates a common method of deploying a school census process in developing countries. Although some countries have successfully implemented all of the different stages of the data collection process, others are still striving to establish and strengthen their data collection and management processes.

Figure 4.2 School Census Process

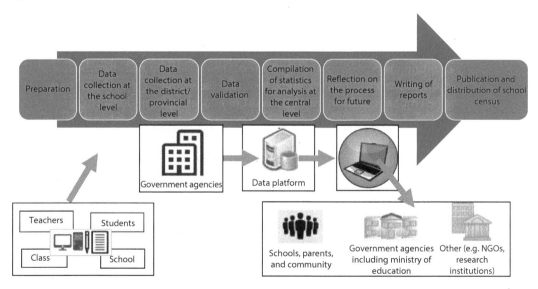

Note: NGO = nongovernmental organization.

Even if a school census is conducted, in many countries the scope and quality of the data collected are still insufficient to inform decision making.

Creating an Effective School Census Process

The life cycle of a school census starts from creating awareness about the process, to developing procedures to set up the process, to execution and continuous review for continuity of operations. The steps involved are outlined as follows:

1. Create awareness campaigns and promote the school census as an important activity toward data-driven culture in education.
2. Ensure enabling conditions and processes are in place.
3. Prepare and execute a realistic project management plan:
   a. Develop standards, policies, and guidelines toward the implementation process.
   b. Develop a sustainable long-term financial plan.
   c. Chalk out a detailed work plan with communication to all relevant stakeholders.
   d. Coordinate between the EMIS team, local authorities, and schools.
   e. Assign roles and responsibilities, given the local context.
   f. Provide continuous training of involved stakeholders.
   g. Prepare all necessary forms and instruction manuals.
   h. Evaluate timelines in accordance with the education cycle.
4. Review the process to ensure continuity of operation. Continuously iterate and adapt the school census to identify emerging data needs or process enhancements.

Creating Awareness of The School Census Process

Creating awareness campaigns and promoting the data-driven culture are crucial for the success of a school census. The buy-in from schools and all involved authorities needs to be established with proper communications. This should be a continuous process around the time of data collection and after the completion of the process and reports. Steps toward a data-driven culture need to continue to be emphasized as an important part of education operations. This can be done through a variety of channels: official government memos, online publication on government and third-party websites, radio coverage, newspaper articles, workshops, and so on.

In many countries, this starts by a ministerial-level decree or letter annually to all local authorities and schools about the school census. The goal is to inform all stakeholders (government officials, school staff, communities, parents, and students) of the need for data in order to make informed choices at each level of decision making. By including everyone affected by data collection in the planning stage, the regional or central government can create a collaborative environment for data collection (box 4.1). Stakeholders will understand all aspects of the data collection and reporting cycle with a full comprehension of what is to be

---

Box 4.1 Creating Demand for Data in Nigeria

In Nigeria, demand for education data has been increased by building a community of stake-holders to improve school quality and accountability. Parents, school staff, local education leaders, and elected community leaders have participated in workshops to help define goals and priorities using comparative school data, resulting in increased demand for and use of school-level information.

Source: EQUIP2 2006.

---

done and why it is important and will help meet the reporting requirements in a timely fashion. Involving the community in the census process has been shown to be effective in some countries because community plays a role in the valida-tion of data.

Education stakeholders need to see data collected using the school census as a flashlight for their use in day-to-day operations, instead of a hammer used for compliance purposes. For example, schools need to understand how timely and accurate reporting of student enrollment allows for allocation of resources such as school fees and textbooks in a timely manner; timely reporting of atten-dance and test scores would allow them to send notifications to parents for reporting absenteeism or performance issues. Having a regular system in which all information is stored and updated would ease many of their administrative processes. For this to happen, training sessions need to be developed for staff and teachers in relation to the collection of data and on the use of data, giving room for attendees to discuss findings and new directions at staff meetings or in written communications; holding discussions that include all staff members so that everyone understands the importance of quality data; and involving all relevant stakeholders from across the education system in every discussion. This process also empowers people who feel motivated to support the ongoing work.

Ensuring that Proper Enabling Conditions and Processes Are in Place

It is important to have standards, policies, and guidelines that determine the implementation of the school census process. The government may need to either develop new policies or update existing ones. The first step is to ensure that all policies are tailored to the needs of the school census and clearly outline the implementation steps, roles and responsibilities, and compliance mechanisms. To ensure sustainability and continuity in school census operations, it is essential to link the collection of education data to national education objec-tives and goals and for schools to fully understand the value of the data. At the policy level, there is a need for a clear strategic direction to guide system-monitoring processes. The strategy needs to spell out what information should to be collected, when, how, and why.

In addition, there needs to be a legal mandate on the type of institutions providing data. In many countries, different types of schools exist, such as independent private, subsidized private, public, religious, missionary, and so on. Not accounting for all schools will give incomplete enrollment rates and a mismatch between administrative and household survey data. Hence the policy on school census needs to be integrated in the school registration legal framework to incentivize all schools to announce their existence as a first step in the legitimization process. Also, sampling and snowballing techniques could be used to identify these schools and complement the numbers. Many governments worldwide struggle with unregistered schools and have taken different approaches. For instance, in Haiti the Inter-American Development Bank (IDB) conducted an extensive school-mapping project in 2014, which included schools with an official and preliminary school license as well as unregistered schools. Box 4.2 highlights three examples of how different governments in Sub-Saharan Africa have tackled unregistered schools.

In addition, the legal framework should define the role of a single entity within the MoE as the sole owner and administrator of the school census process. Having one unit manage the data collection process has many advantages such as avoiding interference with other agencies or institutions within a country that might be involved in some form of data collection process. It is also useful in streamlining processes of planning, collection, verification, and dissemination.

For collection and processing of data, schools need to be bound by state and central policies for compliance that clearly specify what data must be reported,

---

Box 4.2 Examples of Unregistered Schools in Sub-Saharan Africa

Ghana has struggled with unregistered schools. Ever since 2005 when it announced it would close down hundreds of unregistered schools, the government has been trying to monitor and reduce their numbers. In 2014, in the city of Kasoa, 24 percent of schools remained unregistered, 22 percent did not participate in mandatory standardized exams, and only 55 percent submitted the required school improvement plans. Similarly, in Tamale Metropolitan Area, only an estimated 49 out of 300 private preschools, primary schools, and junior high schools are registered (approximately 16 percent). The government aims to close substandard unregistered private schools and elevate well-performing ones to an official status. In general, the Ghanaian Education Service is charged with the responsibility to ensure that all private schools are registered and adhere to the national education standards (Abdul-Hamid, Saraogi, and Mintz 2017; Agyeman and Akweiteh 2014).

Despite high literacy rates, Zimbabwe still struggles with unlicensed schools. Since 2010, "backyard" private schools have appeared all over the country, reducing the quality of education. Often teachers at these schools do not follow national curricula and fail to meet education standards. In addition, the facilities of the schools—ranging from simple homes to churches and backyards—are often not conducive for educational purposes. Generally, unlicensed private schools are for-profit. The private schools charge tuition fees per month,

box continues next page

Box 4.2 Examples of Unregistered Schools in Sub-Saharan Africa *(continued)*

allowing parents to avoid paying large sums up front at the start of the new school year as in public schools. However, this also often means that, if parents are unable to pay for one specific month, children will miss out on the education that month because they are not allowed to attend school unless all fees have been paid. With the support of the Progressive Teachers' Union of Zimbabwe (PTUZ) the government aims to close at least 600 unlicensed schools. The official closure, however, does not guarantee that these schools will not continue to operate: the government would require considerable capacity to monitor all unlicensed schools (Ahimbisibwe and Rumanzi 2017).

In Lagos, Nigeria, only 30 percent of the 15,000 private schools operating in the state have been officially approved and licensed. The Lago State Government is aiming to eradicate unregistered schools by making their operation strictly illegal. A substantial enumeration project including all officially registered private schools will take place to ensure that private schools adhere to the same high-quality standards as public schools (Scott 2016).

how the data must be reported, and the confidentiality of the data. Trainings must be institutionalized into the process of data collection so that schools understand how to complete the school census questionnaire. In addition, they should be responsible and accountable for the information provided by teachers and their staff members, and should have an ethical responsibility to report data accurately. In advanced economies with a culture of data quality, it is easier to meet these policy and regulatory demands.

The data collection process needs to be championed by a central entity responsible for the administration of the school census and institutionalized. The district education authorities can monitor the adherence to the data collection process with existing civil servants as inspectors. Community monitors can be involved in the data validation processes of the school census data and the routine reporting activities. Also community monitors will be relied on in the reporting of incidents at schools.

Evaluation of existing technological and nontechnological resources in the country will help determine what level of automation and technologies already exist and what would be the most efficient use of the existing and potentially new technology. This should include questions such as the following: Are there existing Internet connections and computers/laptops available on a broad scale? Are school staff familiar with computer applications, or will the implementation phase also require basic training in computer skills? Which technology would be the most effective in delivering school census data? For instance, the latest developments in information and communication technology (ICT) such as smartphones and tablets have opened new channels of data collection and maintenance (see chapter 8).

Any investment in technology needs to take cost-effective approaches. In general, technology should be given to individuals already on the education system payroll and *especially to those who could use it for teaching and learning in addition to data collection.* The best suited for this are education inspectors, and additional inspectors might be needed depending on the scope of the work in relation to data collection. This model can be easily adapted to a local, country-specific context. Because paperwork is still the popular means of data collection, careful attention needs to be given to the type of paper: in many countries the use of paper and carbon-backed copies allows for schools to keep a copy, another to go to the local authority, and the original to go to the central collection entity (for example, to the EMIS at the central location). Other countries use a hybrid model combining desktops, laptops, mobile devices, and paper.

An effective school census process requires a long-term financial plan to allocate financial resources. Financial planning is just as important as strategic planning. In line with financial project planning tools, there is a need for a detailed resource allocation structure in addition to contingency plans. From software design, to technology setup, to training and professional development of school staff, all expenses need to be accounted for. The introduction of an effective school census needs to be financially sustainable in the long term. This is particularly true in the case of donor-funded projects, where the donor covers only the initial expenses. The life-cycle costs of the school census project are easily overlooked but need to be accounted for to ensure the sustainability of the census. This is especially true when training government staff and school: these costs are recurring and can be high.

Preparing and Executing a Realistic Project Management Plan

Develop an operations manual. Prepare a technical and operational document detailing steps for data collection, definitions of key education concepts, roles and responsibilities of relevant stakeholders, timelines, and audit and monitoring processes.

Lay out the architecture of the census process. In the planning stage, the MoE should agree on the type of structure (centralized or decentralized) of the school census collection mechanisms, analysis processes, and utilization strategies (refer to chapter 3 for a discussion of centralized and decentralized systems). It also needs to plan the types of data the school census aims to capture and how data collection forms will be constructed. Moreover, the roles and responsibilities as well as timelines during the preparation process need to be assigned. This is necessary to give the project preparation a foreseeable implementation date and ensure its efficiency.

Define roles and responsibilities. Provide clear instructions on the roles and responsibilities in the preparation and implementation phase. The administrators at the government and school levels need to be aware of their responsibilities—for example, data collection, validation, training development, software design, communicating strategy, or coordinating activities. The roles and responsibilities may be communicated through official project memos or by circulating user manuals. User manuals are often distributed to school staff to reinforce their understanding of the importance of data and the guidelines on how data should be collected. The language of the manuals needs to be tailored to the audience and should be concise, simple, and easy to understand.

- **Allocation** of funds. Collection of this data raises accountability and transparency.
- *Learning Data*
  - **Student scores on classroom tests** by subject, class, and gender
  - **Student scores on national examinations** (Grade 4, 6, or 8), as relevant to the countries

The Design of the Form

The design of the school census questionnaire is essential in ensuring that all relevant information will be captured. Generally, the school census is the primary source of education data; therefore, special attention needs to be paid to the types of questions asked. The questions need to be clear and designed to elicit relevant information. The data collected should be representative and useful to obtain important education indicators such as enrollment rates and teacher–pupil ratios.

The design of the questionnaire should be tailored to country-specific requirements in order to fully capture the state of the education sector. Countries conduct school censuses annually by sending out questionnaires to schools for completion. Various types of questionnaires exist, depending on the information the country seeks to collect. Questionnaires may be of different length or format (paper-based/web-based) and may capture different information. For example, some countries may seek information on basic administrative data such as number of schools, students, and teachers, whereas others may collect more comprehensive information such as assessment data, financial data, and information on other education resources. Some standard rules could be followed to design a simple and usable school census form:

- The questionnaires should be designed to be ***reader friendly and simple*** to understand. There is always a risk of asking for unnecessary details that may not be relevant for decision making. This may create a negative interest among the data providers, who may be inclined to provide misleading information. The visual appearance and length of the questionnaire are important criteria that should be taken into account. Excessively long questionnaires should be discouraged, and the font size and space provided to write responses should be adequate. Proper care should be taken that the design of the questionnaire takes into account whether the questionnaire is online or paper-based.
- There should ***be proper guidelines*** on how to complete the questionnaire. Every form should clearly outline the steps that need to be followed to complete the questionnaire. Any technical terms used should be clearly defined so that data providers understand what information they are asked to provide. Figure 4.5 provides a glimpse of the clear, effective instructions in the manual used by Ghana to inform schools on the data collection process. This should be complemented by trainings provided to school headmasters, teachers, and other data providers so that they understand the importance of conducting the exercise and their role as data suppliers.

Figure 4.5 Snapshot of Ghana's School Census Instructional Manual

	INSTRUCTIONAL MANUAL BASIC SCHOOLS
A	All questions MUST BE ANSWERED. District Statistics Officers and Circuit Supervisors to check that the questionnaire is as complete as possible.
B	If requested information is not applicable to your school, please indicate these with N/A or NIL in the spaces provided. Blank means it does not exist or is not needed. If a WHOLE Table is not applicable write in large letters N/A across the whole table. If there is no information for a whole table then write NIL across the whole table. Do NOT WRITE Zeros in every space provided.
C	DO NOT Tick when NUMBERS or HOW MANY is requested. Ticked information in this case is useless. Only tick when a small tick box is provided.
D	All information provided should refer to this academic school year unless otherwise requested in the question. E.g. Enrolment, Textbooks, Teachers, etc in this school year whereas Pupil transfers TO other schools, Staff Leave, etc are requested for the past academic year.
E	Read through questionnaires briefly before completing it. It will minimize the mistakes you may make. Note, where the questionnaires indicates a code, refer to back pages of questionnaires.
Intro	The Annual Census must be signed off by the Head (or Acting) Head of the School. It must be checked and signed by the District Statistic Officer.
1	SCHOOL IDENTIFICATION
1.1	Please put in the full name of the school
1.2	The Year Established refers to the first year the school was opened.
1.4	School Status: Public = State owned, Private= Non-State owned, Registered refers to registration of the school with the Ghana Education Service.
1.5	Registration Number refers to the Number on the School's Registration Certificate. It is only issued to Private schools by the GES
1.6	Levels found in the school: Indicate if the school has more than one level and the School Code or EMIS number assigned to that level in previous Census surveys.
1.7	Location of School: Indicate the names of the region, district, locality, etc in full with the appropriate code (refer to code page). Locality refers to the name given to the surrounding area around the school.
1.8	Type of Locality: Rural is areas with small population(less than 5,000).
1.9	School Address: If your school has no telephone, fax or email leave blank.
1.10	Education Management Unit of School

5	SCHOOL BUILDING
5.1 - 5.2	Condition and Number of Rooms: Indicate the type of wall, roof and floor construction for each level of school according to the categories provided
5.2	No. of Classrooms: Count each room (even if in blocks) as a separate room.
5.3	What is the number and the conditions of the following structures? Don't double count if mentioned above.
	Major Repair refers to a situation demanding complete re-roofing, constructing a wall/cladding a pavilion , or changing the floor of a classroom Minor Repair refers to repair work on windows, fixing door shutters, or replacing one or two roofing sheets
5.4	DON'T COUNT ANY ROOMS IN THIS TABLE THAT HAVE ALREADY BEEN COUNTED IN TABLE 5.1 AND 5.2. Note: Information is being requested on the dormitory block not the hostel block. The hostel block is usually privately owned and not on the school grounds whereas the dormitory block is owned by the school. When reporting on Teacher Quarters, Other Staff Quarters - as a general rule count the bedrooms that are being occupied by a teacher. E.g. If your school has a bungalow and two teachers are staying there then count 2 but if only 1 teacher then count only 1.
6	CHARACTERISTICS OF SCHOOL'S MATERIALS AND EQUIPMENT
6.1	Write the actual number of pieces of furniture available under the specific type on the form separately for each level.
9	ENROLMENT BY GRADE, BY SEX AND BY AGE
9.1	Note that number of classes per grade is the same as the number of streams per grade.
11	TEACHER PROFILES
	Staff number: If no staff number then leave blank. If the teacher has a number do not put Government as a prefix as it will be assumed it is there.
	Year of birth: put last 2 digits of the year in which the person is born.
	Year of First Service: put last 2 digits of the year.
	Rank: refer to codes at back where a letter or number is initialized in bold e.g. S =Subject H = Head Put the appropriate letter or number in the column.

Source: Ghana Statistical Service, http://www.statsghana.gov.gh/nada/index.php/catalog/62.

Box 4.3 Key Questions to Consider While Designing a School Census

While deciding on the data to be collected, it is important to answer these questions:

- What is the purpose of the indicators being tracked?
- Do staff members understand why data are being collected?
- Do staff members see the reports that are created from the entered data?
- Do schools understand how to use the data to enhance teaching and learning?

- The school census has to be constructed so that it *captures all relevant information* necessary to assess the education system. While deciding on the questions to be included in the questionnaire, all education stakeholders (schools, teachers, parents, and governments) should participate in discussions on the key data that would be helpful for planning and monitoring at each stage of decision making (box 4.3). Also, from time to time, revisions must be made to the questionnaire to improve its design and the coverage of data collected. Figure 4.6 provides an example of a school census questionnaire for Ghana.
- Before rolling out the questionnaire, *a pilot test* should be conducted. This is essential to determine whether data providers easily comprehend the language and framing of questions. For example, in the state of Kano, Nigeria, a pilot questionnaire was distributed and the new data collection instrument developed after taking into account feedback from ministry officials, state department officials, school heads, and principals to ensure that data relevant for all education stakeholders was included.

Figure 4.6 Example of the School Census Survey Form in Ghana
a. Basic school profile

ANNUAL SCHOOL CENSUS
2013/2014 ACADEMIC YEAR

BASIC SCHOOLS

REPUBLIC OF GHANA

MINISTRY OF EDUCATION

The Annual School Census is the most important source of information regarding the situation at your school. The information collected will contribute to the Education Management Information System (EMIS) of the region and will be of value to the management, administration, supply of school resources and governing of schools.

Please read the headings and instructions carefully when completing the questionnaire.

I , the Head of ....
fully understand the provision made in the GES Act No 778, 2008 regarding the duty of schools to provide information. This Act requires that every school must provide such information about the school as is reasonably required.

By signing, I certify that the information provided on this form is correct and completed to the best of my knowledge.

Head of School

	Mr/Mrs/Miss	Initials	Surname		Signature	Date
						dd /mm / yyyy

Checked by Circuit Supervisor

*By signing, I certify that the information provided on this form is **accurate and consistent** with my records about the school*

Circuit Supervisor

	Mr/Mrs/Miss	Initials	Surname		Signature	Date
						dd / mm / yyyy

Checked by District Statistics Officer

By signing, I certify that the information provided on this form is thoroughly checked and meets the demand of the Questionnaire

Dist. Stats Officer:

	Mr/Mrs/Miss	Initials	Surname		Signature	Date
						dd / mm / yyyy

I. SCHOOL IDENTIFICATION

1.1 School Name (full name covering all levels offered)   1.2 Year Established

1.3 School Code

1.4 School Status (mark with a tick)   Public ☐   Private registered ☐   Private, not registered ☐

1.5 If private registered, what is your GES registration number?

1.6 Tick which levels are found in the school.

Nursery/Creche ☐   Primary ☐

Kindergarten ☐   Junior High School ☐

1.7 Location of School   (in full)

Region	
District	
Circuit		Circuit Code
Political Constituency	
Locality	

1.8 Type of Locality   Rural (less than 5000 people in community/locality) ☐   Urban (more than 5000 people living in your community) ☐

1.9 School Address for Correspondence

	Telephone:
	Fax:
	Email:

1.10 Education Management Unit of the School   (Refer to Code Page at back of Survey)

1.11 Summary Count

	Nursery/Creche	Kindergarten	Primary	Junior High	
Pupils					*Ensure that the totals for these summary counts correspond with the totals for tables 5.1, 9.5, and 11*
Teachers					
Classrooms					

figure continues next page

Figure 4.6 Example of the School Census Survey Form in Ghana *(continued)*
b. School organization and infrastructure

2 SCHOOL PROFILE AND ORGANISATION

2.1 Indicate **NUMBER** of classes which are Multigrade by level

KG
PRIM
JHS

Multigrade = These are classes where the same teacher teaches pupils in different grades in one classroom, eg. pupils in grade 1 and grade 2 are taught in the same classroom.

2.2 Which of these levels run shift system in your school?

KG
PRIM
JHS

These are schools where there are not enough classrooms to accommodate all pupils. The school day is divided into two sessions where the two groups of pupils are under same head or different heads

2.3 Is your school one of two **DIFFERENT** schools making use of the same building? Yes ☐ No ☐

2.4 If YES, what is the name of the other school you are sharing with?

2.5 Is your school ? Boys only ☐ Girls only ☐ Co-educational/mixed ☐

2.6 Is your school a Special Education School? (*see definition in manual*) Yes ☐ No ☐

2.7 Indicate **NUMBER** of physically challenged pupils by level whether or not your school is a Special School.

	Impairement			Challenges	
	Blind / Visual	Hearing & Speech	Blind & Hearing	Physically Challenged	Intellectually Challenged
KG					
Primary					
JHS					

2.8 Does your school have Ramps for physically challenged pupils? Yes ☐ No ☐

2.9 What type of Support do you need for your physically challenged pupils? *(Tick as applicable)*

Ramps ☐ Hearing Aids ☐ Reading Glasses ☐ Wheel Chairs ☐ Braille ☐ Other ☐

2.10 What Ghanaian language(s) are taught in your school? *(Mark with a tick)*

Asante ☐ Dagbani ☐ Ewe ☐ Ga ☐ Kasem ☐ Wale/Dagaare ☐
Akwapem ☐ Dangme ☐ Fante ☐ Gonja ☐ Nzema ☐ Other ☐

2.11 How far away from the school is ... ?

A. the district education office Less than 5kms ☐ 5 - 10kms ☐ 11 -15kms ☐ More than 15kms ☐

B. the Head's house Less than 1kms ☐ 1 - 5kms ☐ 6 -10kms ☐ More than 11kms ☐

C. the next primary school Less than 5kms ☐ 5 - 10kms ☐ 11 -15kms ☐ More than 15kms ☐

3 SCHOOL INFRASTRUCTURE

3.1 Can a vehicle access your school? Yes ☐ No ☐

3.2 If YES, what is the road made of? *(Tick one box)* Tar ☐ Earth ☐ Gravel ☐

3.3 Does your school own a safe water facility? Yes ☐ No ☐

3.4 What type of safe water facility is available? *(Tick one box)* Pipe borne water ☐ Borehole ☐ Well ☐ Other ☐

3.5 What is the MAIN water storage facility available in the school? *(Tick one)* Tank ☐ Buckets/Pots ☐ None ☐ Other ☐

3.6 Is your school wired for electricity ? Yes ☐ No ☐

3.7 If YES, is it functional? Yes ☐ No ☐ N/A ☐

3.8 Is your community on electricity? Yes ☐ No ☐

3.9 If YES, please specify. National Grid ☐ Local Generator ☐ Other ☐ N/A ☐

3.10 How MANY individual toilet seats are available? Boys ☐ Girls ☐

3.11 How MANY individual toilet seats are functional? Boys ☐ Girls ☐

3.12 Are urinals available and functional? Yes ☐ No ☐

3.13 Which of these problems are experienced in your school?. *(Tick box only if answer is yes)*

Drainage blockages ☐ Soil erosion ☐ Waste water and sewage ☐ Garbage disposal ☐ Other ☐

figure continues next page

Figure 4.6 Example of the School Census Survey Form in Ghana *(continued)*
c. Asset management

7 PUPILS AND TEACHER TEXTBOOKS

7.1 Indicate the NUMBER of Teaching Guides / HandBooks available by grade

	KG 1	KG 2	P1	P2	P3	P4	P5	P6	JH1	JH2	JH3
English											
Mathematics											
Environmental Studies											
Creative Activities/Arts											
Physical Education											
Natural / Integrated Science											
Music & Dance											
ICT											
Psycho social Studies/ RME											
Ghanaian Language/ Language Literacy											
Citizenship Education											
Social Studies											
French											
Basic Design & Tech											
Special Educ Only*											
Audio Therapy*											
Speech Therapy*											

7.2 How MANY Pupil Textbooks for each subject and grade is available ?   (Indicate NIL if none are available)

	KG 1	KG 2	P1	P2	P3	P4	P5	P6	JH1	JH2	JH3
English											
Mathematics											
Environmental Studies											
Creative Activities/Arts											
Physical Education											
Natural / Integrated Science											
Music & Dance											
ICT											
Psycho Social Studies / RME											
Ghanaian Language/ Language Literacy											
Citizenship Education											
Social Studies											
French											
Basic Design & Tech											
Special Educ Only*											
Audio Therapy*											
Speech Therapy*											

figure continues next page

Figure 4.6 Example of the School Census Survey Form in Ghana *(continued)*
d. Teacher qualifications

ACADEMIC Qualifications	CODE
MSLC	01
BECE	02
GCE O'LEVEL	03
SSCE	04
GCE A'LEVEL	05
DIPLOMA	06
DEGREE	07
POST GRADUATE CERTIFICATE	08
POST GRADUATE DIPLOMA	09
MASTERS DEGREE	10
PHD	11
TECHNICIAN	12
HND	13
NO DATA	99

RANKS	CODE
MSLC/BECE	01
GCE 'O' LEVEL	02
SSCE	03
GCE 'A' LEVEL	04
CLASS TEACHER (Unconfirmed)	05
SNR. SUPERVISOR INSTRUCTOR	06
SUPERVISOR INSTRUCTOR	07
PRIN. TECHNICAL INSTRUCTOR	08
SRN. TECHNICAL INSTRUCTOR	09
SENIOR INSTRUCTOR	10
TECHNICAL INSTRUCTOR GD. I	11
TECHNICAL INSTRUCTOR GD. II	12
SUPT. II	13
SUPT. I	14
SNR. SUPT. II	15
SNR. SUPT. I	16
PRINCIPAL SUPT.	17
ASST. DIRECTOR	18
DIRECTOR II	19
DIRECTOR I	20
ASST. DIRECTOR II	22
DEPUTY DIRECTOR	23
CLASS TEACHER CONFIRMED	24
NO DATA	99

PROFESSIONAL Qualifications	CODE
CERT 'A'	01
DIPLOMA	02
DEGREE	03
POST GRADUATE CERTIFICATE	04
POST GRADUATE DIPLOMA	05
MASTERS DEGREE	06
PHD	07
NO DATA	99

MANAGEMENT Unit	CODE
A.M.E. ZION	01
ANGLICAN	02
ROMAN CATHOLIC	03
EVANGELICAL PRESBYTERIAN	04
GARRISON	05
ISLAMIC	06
L.A/D.A/M.A/BODY CORPORATE	07
METHODIST	08
PRESBYTERIAN	09
SALVATION ARMY	10
SEVENTH DAY ADVENTIST	11
T.I. AHMADIYYA	12
BAPTIST	13
PRIVATE	14
D.A/R.C	15
ASSEMBLIES OF GOD	16
L.A/SALVATION ARMY	17
L.A/ANGLICAN	18
L.A/SDA	19
POLICE	20
L.A/PRESBY	21
L.A/METHODIST	22
L.A/E.P	23
PENTECOST	24
OTHER MANAGEMENT TYPE	25
NO DATA	99

Source: Ministry of Education, Ghana 2015.

Establishing Data Validation Mechanisms

The data validation process is one of the most crucial aspects of any effective school census. It ensures that the data are complete, accurate, useful, accessible, timely, clear, and disaggregated to guide all education stakeholders to make informed decisions.

- *Different levels of data validation exist: internal and external.* Data validation and verification can be done in two ways: (1) internal checks in the form of methodologically rigorous techniques and expert views, or (2) external verification in the form of field visits at the schools and local districts. Data validation is essential at each of these different levels.
- *The school registry* should be updated regularly. The system architecture may feature built-in alerts that remind school officials to update. In addition, if the system is online, then access for government or district authorities can be facilitated.
- *The school census forms* need to well designed and up to date. At the government level, even before forms are sent to schools, officials should ensure that all the appropriate and useful data can be captured through the forms. At the school level, school staff should double-check the provided data for their accuracy before submitting the forms. If the submission is conducted online, there might be an additional feature that allows users to correct the entered data before final submission. The school census is the basis for the annually published handbook of education and hence the basis for substantial analysis.
- *Data entry* must be verified. Particularly in the case of manual data entry, human error may cause data distortions (see example in box 4.4). Similar to online school census forms, the data entry software should feature a validation tool before submission is possible.
- *Dissemination processing* should occur only after the data are validated.

Data verification may uncover errors in the data collection process. And what happens if the validation mechanism reveals that the collected school census data are inaccurate? If data collected by independent inspectors vary significantly from the official school census data, this may render the entire school census

---

Box 4.4 Data Validation in North Carolina (United States)

The State of North Carolina has implemented a strict data validation policy for all public schools. In order to ensure high-quality data, the data collected must go through a data auditing and a data profiling process. The Department of Instruction has responsibility for verifying data quality, and each data collection system will undergo an auditing process annually. Most important, data provided by the Data Management Group will not be accepted into the authoritative data process without passing a data validation process.

Source: Public Schools of North Carolina: Data and Statistics, http://www.dpi.state.nc.us/data/management/policies/.

---

outcomes questionable. In severe cases, this may even call for a repeat of the school census on a local, regional, and possibly national level.

Feedback loops are essential to link accountability and school improvements. In addition to a functioning data collection and analysis cycle, there is also a distinct need for feedback mechanisms within the school census construct to ensure a balance between accountability and school improvement. Such a collection cycle needs to be designed so that it effectively collects, maintains, analyzes, disseminates, and uses the data (Abdul-Hamid 2014). This may be achieved with a cyclical feedback loop (figure 4.7), which helps track inputs as well as assess the quality of existing institutions and the education policies in place. The system should be designed so that it provides policy makers and district and school officials with reliable, useful, and accurate data so they can make informed decisions on student learning and policies. To ensure high quality standards, the system will also need to provide feedback not only on collection and analysis processes but also on the feedback loop itself. In some jurisdictions such as Australia, Maryland (United States), and Uganda, the central government has started to provide feedback to individual schools (box 4.5).

Figure 4.7 Information Validation and Feedback Loop

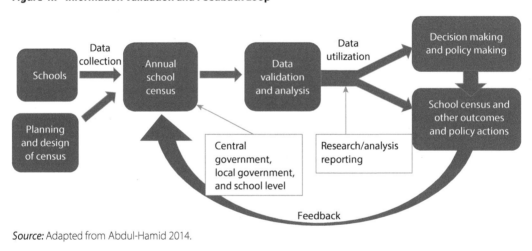

Source: Adapted from Abdul-Hamid 2014.

Box 4.5 Feedback in the Form of Report Cards for Schools

In Uganda, schools are required to provide school-level data annually to the MoE, where the data are processed and analyzed for planning and decision making. In the past, this flow of information has been one way. As part of Uganda's effort to overhaul its EMIS, however, the central ministry now provides feedback to the schools in the form of school profiles generated from data provided by the schools. These reports have been extremely well received over the last several years by headmasters who have used so-called official reports on their schools in communications with parent–teacher associations, elected officials, and visitors.

Source: EQUIP2 2006.

Effective Use of School Census Data

A school census should be able to provide high-quality data that accurately represent the education system in the given country; the information obtained through the data should be useful to decision makers on every level. Active use of the school census should be a priority. Design of the school census should ensure that it provides reliable, accurate, and useful information to support all key stakeholders, including policy makers, school and district leadership, teachers, parents, and researchers, in making data-driven decisions. Evidence-based decision making is the key to success in improving education outcomes.

Within an EMIS, the purpose of the school census is to ensure that all education data are captured and that relevant indicators can be calculated on the basis of the information provided. These indicators are instrumental in the monitoring and evaluating of the education system and of student progress. They are intended to provide information on access, quality, equity, and efficiency of the education system. These indicators range from gross enrollment rates, average class size, and gender ratios to completion, dropout, and transition rates. They can be considered a reference point on what data should be collected.

Access and participation measures include the following:

- *Gross enrollment rate* (GER) and *net enrollment rate* (NER) are relative measures commonly used to calculate the coverage of a group of students, either at a particular level of the education cycle or of student subgroups by age, gender (ratio of boys to girls), race/ethnicity, and other characteristics. They indicate the extent of over-aged and under-aged enrollment.
- *Student intake numbers* provide information on the access of education and capacity of the education system. The capacity of the education system to provide access to students for the appropriate age group is also measured. This, of course, also includes appropriate facilities.
- *Average class size* measures the average number of children being taught together at one time. Average class sizes reflect not only the physical space provided per class but also the burden on teachers. If some areas record higher average class sizes than others, it may demonstrate a lack of teachers.
- *School life expectancy* refers to the total number of years of schooling that a child can expect to receive.

Efficiency indicators include the following:
- *Completion rate* refers to the percentage of a cohort of pupils enrolled in a particular grade who are to complete that level of education. It assesses the likelihood that pupils of the same cohort, including repeaters, complete their education.
- *Dropout rate* offers information on the proportion of pupils from a cohort enrolled in a given grade in a given school year no longer enrolled in the following school year. It illustrates the effect on the internal efficiency of educational systems. By comparing national averages, policy makers may identify and provide additional support to schools with above-average dropout rates.

- *Transition rate* captures the percentage of students that transition from one level of education to the next, for example, from primary to secondary education.
- *Survival rate* measures the retention capacity and internal efficiency of an education system. It is similar to the grade transition rate because it illustrates the retention of pupils (or students) from grade to grade in schools, and conversely the magnitude of dropouts by grade. It uses data on enrollment and repeaters for two consecutive years.
- *Student–teacher ratio* (STR) is often used as an approximation to assess the quality of teaching. The purpose of the STR is to link the level of human resources input in terms of the number of teachers in relation to the size of the pupil population.

Learning indicators include the following:

- *Graduation rate* measures the number of students who graduate a class divided by the population for each single year of age.
- *Student absenteeism rate* is the percentage of days in a given year when the student had unexcused absences from school.

Many developing countries publish a limited number of education indicators, mostly focusing on enrollment. Figure 4.8 illustrates the types of education indicators published on the website of the MoEs in 131 developing countries (Read and Atinc 2017). The results do not necessarily mean that the MoE does not collect data on other indicators; some indicators may be published on different websites, such as the website of the statistics agency.

Along with the data set, many countries publish a statistical guide or a handbook of education that describes the types of education indicators collected and the methods of data collection and analysis. Table 4.1 illustrates an example of

Figure 4.8 Types of Student Data on the Websites of Ministries of Education

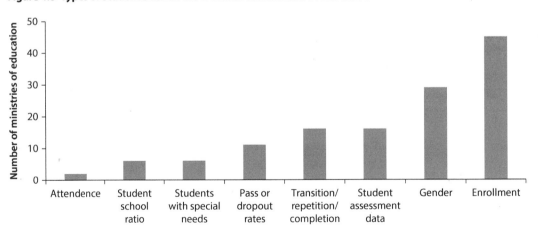

Source: Read and Atinc 2017.

Table 4.1 Table of Contents, Handbook on Education Statistics, Maldives, 2014

table continues next page

Table 4.1 Table of Contents, Handbook on Education Statistics, Maldives, 2014 *(continued)*

Table of contents	Pages
SECTION 5: ENROLMENTS BY SCHOOL	
Male'	56
Haa Alifu Atoll	57
Haa Dhaalu Atoll	58
Shaviyani Atoll	59
Noonu Atoll	60
Raa Atoll	61
Baa Atoll	62
Lhaviyani Atoll & Kaafu Atoll	63
Alifu Alifu Atoll & Alifu Dhaalu Atoll	64
Vaavu Atoll & Meemu Atoll	65
Faafu Atoll & Dhaalu Atoll	66
Thaa Atoll	67
Laamu Atoll	68
Gaafu Alifu Atoll	69
Gaafu Dhaalu Atoll	70
Gnaviyani Atoll	71
Seenu Atoll	72

Source: Ministry of Education, Maldives.

the statistical handbook of education in the Maldives. The table of contents already clearly indicates what data have been captured and which indicators have been calculated. The aim is to cover all necessary data and provide education stakeholders with a comprehensive overview of the state of education in the given country.

Country Examples of School Census Efforts

Somalia—Introducing a School Census

Somalia demonstrates the successful implementation of a school census even in a conflict setting. Its 2012 census was the first since 2006 and had to be designed without a prior system in place. In doing so, the architects had to overcome substantial financial, systematic, and human resource challenges. The MoEs in Puntland and Somaliland worked closely with donor agencies to procure the software, conduct training sessions, and roll out the school census. Within four days of execution, 167 employees at the regional and school levels were trained in the basics of filling out the school census questionnaire. The 167 trained staff members then trained more than 1,400 head teachers in local training sessions. The school census was a milestone in the war-torn country, and finally the MoEs of Puntland and Somaliland were able to plan the education system (Dhayi 2012).

Figure 4.9 EMIS Structure, Somalia

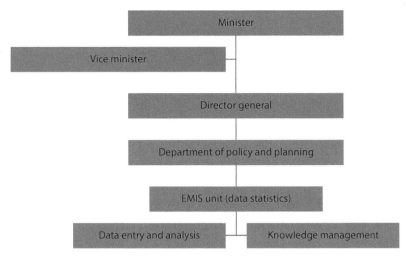

Source: Ministry of Education and Higher Education, Somalia 2015.

Some of the steps taken to execute the system were as follows:

- The MoE set up a dedicated EMIS unit within the ministry to get the institutional support at all levels of the system (figure 4.9).
- The questionnaires were designed in consultation with the donor organizations and needs of the education system.
- The processes were reviewed and piloted in Garowe, the capital of Puntland, and Hargeisa, the capital of Somaliland, and then revised and adapted to the specific regional context. The final version was then translated into Somali and distributed with a detailed instruction manual to head teachers in Puntland.
- Data coverage included basic student administrative information on enrollments, teachers, and schools and was then used for education planning and resource allocation purposes. This was a significant achievement for the MoE because previously all the planning was based on estimates.
- Publication of education statistics became a ritual.
- Efforts have been made to continuously update the type of data collected to include information such as water supply, sanitation facilities, classrooms, transportation, feeding programs, and so on.

Kenya—Adjusting for Age in the Census

To account for the time it takes to complete a school census (as long as one year), Kenya worked to adjust its census language to secure more consistent data. Kenya conducts a national Demographic and Health Survey (DHS) every 10 years. It includes detailed analysis of student data such as attendance and

Figure 4.10 Children out of School by Single Year Group, Kenya

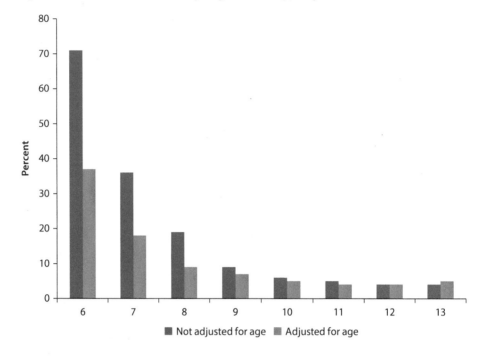

Source: Education Policy and Data Center, http://www.epdc.org/epdc-data-points/how-many-out-school-children-are
-there-kenya.

enrollment figures. The latest census (2009), however, was collected over a period of approximately six months; with two months of data from the old and four months from the new school year. This requires the wording of the census to be very exact: "Has child X attended any kind of school in the school year 2008/09?"

In addition, children's age has to be recorded using a specific reference point. In the case of Kenya, the question specifically asks for the child's age at the beginning of the census data collection and thus corrects for any inconsistencies in age data of students. In total the time lag was as high as 11–15 months, which demonstrates the importance of these precautions. Figure 4.10 shows an extrapolation of the 2009 DHS data for children out of school to demonstrate the difference made by adjustments for age. The example of the Kenyan DHS is applicable to any school census with a time lag.

United States—Detecting Ghost Teachers in Philadelphia, Pennsylvania

Using school census data, the media detected ghost teachers in Philadelphia's school system. A ghost teacher is a teacher who is officially employed and on the payroll but who does not actually teach in the classroom or school. Through the annual school census, the open data project of the school district of Philadelphia revealed that at least 16 ghost teachers earned approximately US$1.7 million in 2014.

These teachers are officially on "release," meaning that they have taken on administrative, informational, or other work serving the teachers' union. Some have not taught in a classroom for over 30 years but are still officially employed as teachers by the district. In 2014, Philadelphia was looking to fill a void of 800 full-time and substitute teachers (Grossman 2015).

Pakistan—Monitoring Schools and Teachers in Punjab

The annual school census of all public schools in Pakistan is the government's primary school facility survey. It captures basic information on school characteristics, enrollment by grade and gender, and teacher-level information. Information for the annual school census forms is expected to come from observation at the school (such as data on the state of school infrastructure and amenities), from interviews in which school staff fill out their own forms (for example, detailed information on teaching staff), or by recording from school registers (for example, student enrollment on the reference date).

The school system in the Pakistani province of Punjab has battled teachers' absentee rates since the 1990s. The government there has tackled this challenge by employing independent monitors, generally retired military, to collect attendance data from schools. The Monitoring and Evaluation Assistants (MEAs) visit up to four schools a day thanks to the existence of specific geographic clusters of schools. At least 90 percent of schools in the district have to be covered in every month. In the past two years, the MEAs have started to use tablets to upload the data directly. The MEAs report to the District Monitoring Office, which also reports to the Government of Punjab. The data provided by MEAs is used for monthly, quarterly, and annual ratings of the schools.

References

Abdul-Hamid, Husein. 2014. "What Matters Most for Education Management Information Systems: A Framework Paper." SABER Working Paper Series No. 7, World Bank, Washington, DC.

Abdul-Hamid, Husein, Namrata Saraogi, and Sarah Mintz. 2017. "Lessons Learnt from World Bank EMIS Operations Worldwide: Portfolio Review 1998–2014." World Bank, Washington DC.

Agyeman, Kojo, and Godwin Allotey Akweiteh. 2014. "Gov't Must Regulate Private Basic Schools—GNECC." *Citifmonline*, October 24. http://citifmonline.com/2014/10/24/govt-must-regulate-private-basic-schools-gnecc/

Ahimbisibwe, Patience, and Perez Rumanzi. 2017. "Uganda: Unregistered Schools Will Not Reopen, Says Government." *The Monitor*, January 25. http://allafrica.com/stories/201701250079.html.

Bruns, Barbara, Deon Filmer, and Harry Anthony Patrinos. 2011. *Making Schools Work: New Evidence on Accountability Reforms*. Washington, DC: World Bank.

Dhayi, Ban. 2012. "A School Census Has Collected Crucial Data to Help Somalia Achieve Quality Education for All." *UNICEF Somalia* (blog), November 27. https://www.unicef.org/somalia/education_12051.html.

EQUIP2. 2006. "PAPERSchool Report Cards: Some Recent Experiences." U.S. Agency for International Development, Washington, DC.

Grossman, Evan. 2015. "Philly Ghost Teachers Made More Than $1.7M Last Year." PennsylvaniaWatchdog.org, April 21. http://watchdog.org/213400/philly-ghost-teachers-made-1-7m-last-year/.

Ministry of Education and Higher Education, Somalia. 2015. *Education Statistics Yearbook 2013/14*. Federal Republic of Somalia.

Read, Lindsay, and Tamar Manelyan Atinc. 2017. "Information for Accountability: Transparency and Citizen Engagement for Improved Service Delivery in Education Systems." Center for Universal Education at Brookings, Washington, DC.

Scott. 2016. "Lagos State Government to Shut Down 10,444 Illegal Private Schools." *The Nigerian Blogger*, September 20.

CHAPTER 5

How to Build and Select an Effective Software Solution

Key Takeaways

- The process of acquiring an Education Management Information System (EMIS) software solution requires the following steps:
  - Assessing the country-specific education needs
  - Deciding on the required education modules (for example attendance, finance, textbook, enrollment, teacher, and staff modules)
  - Designing the system architecture (for example client-server versus cloud-based options)
  - Choosing between self-developed or off-the-shelf software
  - Weighing proprietary ("self-coded") and open-source codes
  - Considering short- and long-term required resources
  - Ensuring data quality
- EMIS software solutions could be procured with a focus on the following functions: data collection/validation, storage/management, and analytics/reporting.
- It is important to think of future sustainability of the system at all levels of procurement and development processes, taking into consideration short- and long-term cost commitments.
- A proper procurement process needs to be carefully designed with a clear process for request for proposals documents and for evaluating tender proposals, ensuring efficient sequencing of functions based on priorities and affordability.
- A software solution needs to fulfill certain minimum requirements. Open-source customizable options are recommended specifically when local talent is available. However, it is important to ensure compatibility, integrability, and security of information. Training is crucial to ensure mastery of relevant staff to customize and update the system. Some open-source applications have hidden costs and need to be selected with care.
- Applications should comply with legal policies in relation to security, protection, privacy, and confidentiality of data.

Technological Solutions Play an Important Role in EMIS Infrastructure

Software solutions are crucial at every stage of the data production chain: collection, validation, analysis, storage, tracking, reporting, and communication activities, to name a few. Whether data are collected physically or through electronic questionnaires, data will eventually be entered, stored, and accessed using modern technology. Appropriate software solutions help to overcome the day-to-day complexities of collecting accurate data and build a data-driven culture and practices where information feeds into policies, planning, decision making, management, and administration. Technology has to be carefully chosen and thoroughly embedded at every step of the data supply and usage chains of each individual country on the basis of need, affordability, capacities, and capabilities.

A software solution needs to fulfill certain minimum requirements. In order to navigate through the vast number of software components, decisions need to be made about the modules needed, the system architecture, and the level of complexity. Figure 5.1 illustrates the main components and processes of EMIS software in the data production and consumption chain. The following are the main components of sound system software:

- *Data collection and entry*: There are data collection applications of different types. For instance, a data collection application is used to feed data, collected from schools and other sources, into a central database. Often, desktop computer, tablet, and smartphone applications are used in the data collection process. This module needs to be compatible with and easily accessible to other modules in the system. Whether data are entered electronically at the local level or manually at the central level, the software needs to have a data entry module with assigned functionalities and a built-in validation process. This is often referred to as "the front end."
- *Data validation functions* ensure the accuracy, reliability, and usefulness of data. Data validation needs to be built into the different modules at all stages of the data production chain: data collection, entry, and dissemination.

Figure 5.1 Components of EMIS Technology

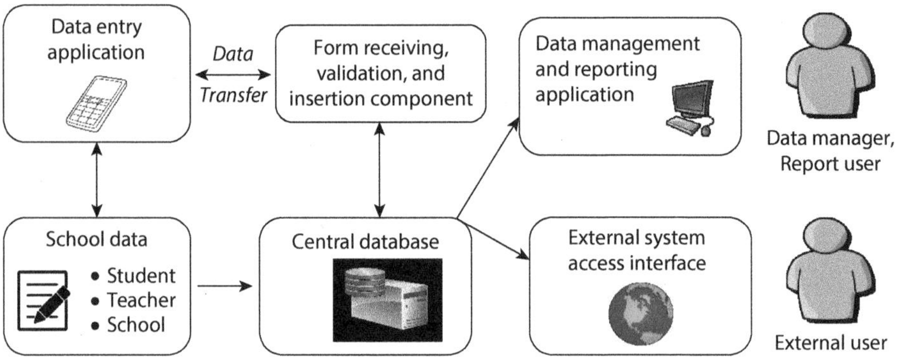

For instance, many software programs allow for a separate screen to reevaluate the data entered before final submission.

- *Database modules* for data storage that are easily accessible are the heart of the EMIS software solution. Databases require secure servers, where the data are stored. A database is organized in a way that its data can be easily accessed, managed, and updated. Often, there is one central database with additional data backup measures at a different location. Generally, the data are stored in specific databases and the software allows for access to this data. This is often referred to as "the back end."
- *Data management and reporting mechanisms* allow EMIS staff and statisticians easy access to conduct data assessments, provide quick reporting, and answer queries. Other mechanisms fetch and manipulate the data, including necessary adjustments, and create indicators for use by government and other stakeholders to inform policy decisions.
- *Data analytics modules* are directly linked to the data. These tools work efficiently when incorporated into the EMIS and when data do not need to be exported for manipulation by external tools such as Microsoft Excel. For dissemination purposes, these modules should be able to visualize data or be effectively linked to data graphic applications such as Tableau or Google Maps.
- *Privacy and security functions* are increasingly important in today's world. Education data can be highly sensitive, and stakeholders must be assured that their data are handled confidentially and in compliance with national privacy laws and policies. The software solution needs to implement the use of passwords and restrict access to data according to a hierarchical structure.

Selecting a Software Solution That Works for You

Implementing an appropriate education software solution can have enormous benefits to the education system as a whole and to student learning, but only when the solution is carefully selected and planned. The right software solution can help secure stakeholder buy-in and establish an effective system. Choosing the wrong software solution can have significant detrimental impacts in the long term, and can result in creating barriers to a data-driven culture and a successful EMIS. The increasing variety of software modules and components can be difficult to navigate and select from. Software packages can substantially differ in complexity and scope, ranging from simple data entry forms linked to central databases to complex early warning systems that support teachers identifying students at risk. The following steps are key for the selection of a software system.

Assessing the Country-Specific Needs and Capacity

Getting a thorough understanding of the needs for a system is the first step when acquiring a new software package for an education information system. The assessment should also review all current systems, including an analysis of whether the current solutions are manual or automated processes.

The assessment should pay particular attention to preexisting smaller sub-systems that have the potential to substantially undermine the EMIS in the long term, for example stand-alone establishment control processes or grant calculation mechanisms that collect and use data identical to that managed by the EMIS. EMIS systems that integrate and/or reconcile well with existing processes tend to have a greater chance of successful adoption—vital in ensuring the longevity of the new system. Integration and reconciliation processes can involve substantial work when deploying a well-functioning EMIS. The assessment should also include any required data migrations and decisions as to whether the existing data are migrated machine to machine through automated means or reentered in the new system manually, poten-tially involving millions of rows of data. In addition, the assessment process should prioritize the needs across all stakeholders, ensuring vital tools are included but allowing room for future expansion without adopting too much at once.

Assessing the needs should be a consultative process involving as many relevant stakeholders and users as possible. A common mistake in imple-menting a new software solution is that the ministry of education (MoE) mandates an information technology (IT) team to identify and roll out a solution, but without wide stakeholder involvement the new system will often fail. Without adequate buy-in or ownership across all stakeholders, data quality will erode over time, eventually rendering the system unusable. Assessments should focus on finding out what kind of information is needed, and for what purpose data will be used, not what information to collect (box 5.1). The information needed will determine what information to col-lect, not the other way around (a common mistake). Getting a thorough understanding of how information will be used and how frequently it needs to be collected will help inform the decisions for an EMIS. In addition, a thor-ough assessment of the skills available within the MoE is needed in order to make decisions on the basis of in-house development or outsourcing. A gap analysis can help here.

Box 5.1 Questions to Ask Prior to Selecting an EMIS Software Solution

To choose the appropriate software option, these questions must be taken into consideration:

- What data need to be tracked, and how frequently?
- What information is needed in order to answer the most pressing policy questions and monitor the performance of the education sector?
- At what level will data be entered, and is the communication infrastructure available to support this choice?
- What level of automated and advanced analysis does the system need to be able to generate?

The analysis should also consider financial, social, and political implications surrounding decommissioning of any preexisting systems or processes. These systems and processes are generally absorbed by the new EMIS, and this calls for the ability of the system to respond to shifting policy requirements, changes in technology, increasing demands from management, and increasing technology awareness in the user base. Additionally, wholesale replacement or upgrade may not be required. Solutions may also exist whereby an existing database requires an enhanced web presence with minimal changes to the existing database(s).

Following the assessment of the existing system and the needs for the new system, it is important to develop a detailed report that highlights the kind of functionality required from the new software solution. Detailed systems requirements should be written up. These should include details on the ability to perform key functions; compatibility, reconciliation, and integration with existing software systems; security; the cost, including capital and running costs like hardware, licenses, training, support, upgrades, customization, and maintenance; user friendliness; and access to technical support. End user training costs can be substantial if training is required at the teacher and/or school level, particularly if geographical and/or Internet availability challenges are present.

Deciding on Education Data Modules and the Sequencing Process

Because the complexity and depth of education information systems vary greatly, decisions need to be made on the scope of data. Information systems commonly track a combination of the following modules:

- School and institution modules (including location, infrastructure, textbooks, and other resources)
- Students and pupil modules (including demographics, enrollment numbers, attendance, graduation rates, and learning assessment data and grade)
- Teachers and staff modules (including human resources and qualifications)
- Finances

Digitization takes place at various stages. Paper-based systems in the form of annual school censuses are still a common method for collecting student-based data, with physical forms being sent from schools to central ministries. In these cases, the MoE at the national level often performs the data entry. This can cause significant delays as the physical forms make their way to the ministry. A government with an existing basic paper and pen–based EMIS system does not have to automate all aspects of the management information system at once because successful systems can include both manual and automated parts. Prioritizing the areas that need to be automated is important to success. Ensuring that flexibility is built into an EMIS will allow continued advancement as the context changes without overwhelming the user base.[1] However, increasingly governments are decentralizing the automation process. In Afghanistan, paper-based forms are sent from the school to regional-level education offices where the data are entered into the national EMIS.

In the most advanced systems, School Information Management Systems (SIMS) are used to manage individual schools. These school-level systems can directly feed data into regional or national systems, providing live data to policy and decision makers. Fiji's Education Management Information System, FEMIS, is an example of this type of comprehensive system, with students, parents, teachers, and regional and national policy makers all able to access data. When implementing a new EMIS, it is crucial to plan for future levels of decentralization and the exponentially increasing availability of Internet connectivity.

Mapping System Functionalities

System functionalities need to be designed before choosing software solutions in order to ensure synchronization and functionality. In simple terms, the system architecture underpins the way in which data are collected, stored, and reported. Every software architecture has distinct components, which change how data are handled. Table 5.1 provides an overview of the most common components of any EMIS software system architecture and their definitions. The initial decision by the government on which software architecture to use is likely to directly influence how the EMIS will develop over time.

There are different types of server modalities: client–server, cloud-based, and hybrid systems. In a *client–server system*, the ministry stores EMIS data on its own hardware (figure 5.2), whereas in cloud-based solutions the data are stored online (figure 5.3). In a hybrid system the ministry's software is installed on client servers, but an external vendor manages the server (figure 5.4). Each has its own advantages and disadvantages. An EMIS can function on client–server models or hybrid systems; data entry and analysis can take place on either type of architecture. It is frequently assumed—erroneously—that accessing a system

Table 5.1 Terminology and Definitions Related to System Architecture

Term	Explanation
System architecture	Software system architecture refers to the blueprint design and structure of a system that meets all the technical and operational requirements. There are a variety of architectural choices available for each software design, and each of these choices can have a substantial impact on the performance, manageability, and overall success of the software solution.
Client server	A client–server system means that the software solution is installed on both the servers and the computers that make up the system. The server connects to the desktop computer, laptop, tablet, or smartphone through a designated network.
RDBMS	A relational database management system (RDBMS) is a database management system (DBMS) that presents the data in views of rows and columns. Since 2009, many RDBMSs use Structured Query Language (SQL) as their main programming language.
Client (desktop and web client)	A client in client–server terminology is a requesting program or user, whereas the server provides the requested information. A *desktop client* installs the program directly on the desktop, and a *web client* requests the information by logging onto the Internet.

table continues next page

Table 5.1 Terminology and Definitions Related to System Architecture (*continued*)

Term	Explanation
Cloud computing	Cloud computing is a technology that allows for the delivery of technological services through the Internet. Clouds are web-based applications and tools that are retrieved from the Internet rather than directly from a server. They generally provide shared computer processing resources, and users can access the data on demand. A private cloud (often referred to as a corporate or internal cloud) delivers services to a single organization. The benefits of a private cloud are the same as public ones: self-service and scalability, multi-tenancy, provision of machines, change of computing resources on demand, and utilization of multiple machines for complex computing jobs (for example, big data).
Front-end layer	The front-end layer refers to the presentation layer of a software solution. These are generally applications designed for direct interaction with the end user, which could be a person or a computer program.
Back-end layer	The back-end layer refers to the data access layer of a software solution. These are generally applications that support the front end in their interaction with the user. This means that the back-end applications do not generally interact with the end user.
First-tier application	The first-tier application is generally the user application ("interface"). It translates tasks and results into something the user can understand.
Second-tier application	The second-tier ("middle") application is often referred to as the logic tier. This tier coordinates the application process commands and makes logic decisions and evaluations. It moves and processes data between the two surrounding tiers.
Third-tier application	The third-tier application stores data in a database or file system. The data are passed back to the second tier for processing and eventually back to the user.
Emulator	Such a feature enables one computer system (hardware or software), the "host," to behave like another computer system, the "guest." Therefore, the host system can use features of the program designed for the guest system. It basically "imitates" another system. Some emulator types, for example Citrix-type emulators, are often difficult to maintain and operate in a developing country, which may pose sustainability issues.
Rendering	Rendering refers to the process in which computer software generates an image from a model. This means that the process is not dependent on graphics software or hardware.

Source: Adapted from TechTarget, http://www.techtarget.com/resources/.

Figure 5.2 Client–Server Model

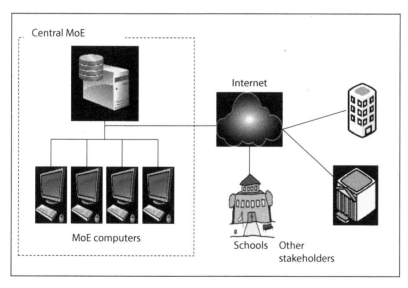

Note: MoE = ministry of education.

Figure 5.3 Cloud-Based System

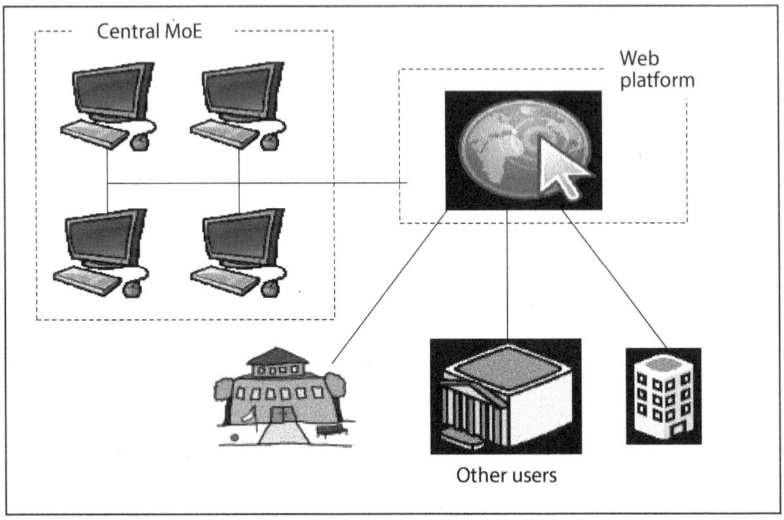

Note: MoE = ministry of education.

Figure 5.4 Hybrid System

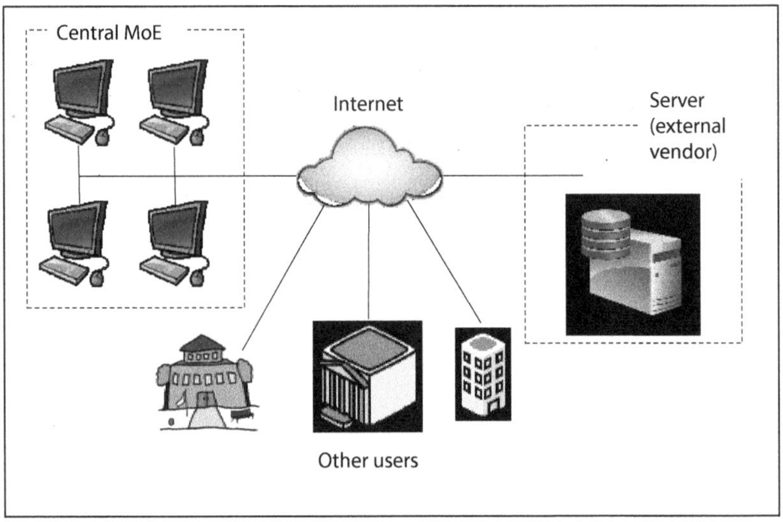

Note: MoE = ministry of education.

from anywhere requires a cloud-based system; however this is not actually the case. Modern-day client–server systems, both cloud-based and hybrid, can allow users to access the system from anywhere using an Internet connection.

In a client–server system, the EMIS software solution is installed on both the servers and the computers that make up the system. Consider the example of Microsoft Outlook: Outlook (the client) is installed on a personal computer, but the mail is sent and received by servers over the network, which in a nutshell describes how client–server systems function. As a result of multiple software installations, the ministry would need to cover the costs of acquiring and maintaining the servers and each computer that needs to access the system (Duan et al. 2012). In a client–server framework, a network connects the server to computers within the ministry. The server can also be connected to the Internet, which allows for remote access to the server by computers that have the software solution installed (figure 5.2).

Most notably, in *cloud-based systems* the software solution is not loaded onto individual computers (figure 5.3). Instead, using a web browser, the server is accessed online. The web server receives the request to access the specified education application from the web browser. It then builds the requested web page and sends data back to the browser, which displays the application. This causes substantial data flow between the browser and server. The data sent back and forth are the same for both a cloud-based and a client–server model. However, the web-based system also passes rendering information back and forth. This model requires more rendering data to be sent to and from the server than a client–server model does while desktop clients typically handle their own rendering.

Cloud servers are hosted by specialized vendors who provide subscription services in exchange for an annual fee. Furthermore, outsourcing such an integral part of a system increases the dependency on a service provider, something many ministries are unwilling to do. If a ministry does opt for a hosted cloud-based solution, issues relating to data security and data ownership need to be addressed because education data can be sensitive and policies may exist that mandate how the data are stored and accessed However, large enterprises—or, in the case of EMIS, governments—may set up their own cloud server, known as a private cloud. These systems achieve the same functionality and the ability to access data through a simple web browser. However, the infrastructure and maintenance of the system often remain in-house. This option is especially attractive to many governments because of the scale of their data needs, as well as the desire to keep data on a privately secured cloud. In many cases a private cloud server is used by a number of different arms of government. If the system does not remain in-house, then the government often hosts a third-party software solution that receives (mandatory and often expensive) updates.

The *hybrid* option is often referred to as a hosted client–server system, where the desktop client and web interface as functionality has gradually migrated away from the desktop to an entirely web-based front end. The web-based EMIS that is accessible from inside and outside the firewall means there are no desktop clients (figure 5.4). However, desktop and web clients can exist side by side, accessing the exact same data. Often, an external vendor provides and maintains the physical servers on its own premises on behalf of the ministry; however, the ministry software solution is loaded on the client's servers. The client is responsible for maintaining the software solution, but the physical servers are maintained by an external vendor, ensuring the system is backed up and remains up to date.[2]

Making the Decision

The success of an EMIS software solution stems from providing an appropriate solution not driven by the wants of donors or the ambition of technology providers. Instead the solution should focus on providing robust, well-functioning, and desirable data services to policy makers at the central, district, and school levels given the specific country context. Today, many education information systems within ministries employ client–server, hybrid, or cloud systems. In fact, many governments have a significant server infrastructure in place servicing multiple ministries. The proposed physical location of the data storage may or may not reside within government-controlled infrastructure. Policy may prohibit or dictate the suitability of "off-site" or "cloud" storage where the ministry has reduced control of the data. The decision of where to store the data should consider that vendors can charge increasing storage fees and/or prohibitive fees to allow for reacquiring data at a later date. Consideration should also be given to whether or not those holding the data are granted permission to view and/or analyze the data.

At the school level, cloud-based private or nonprivate solutions are becoming increasingly popular, with advances in communication technology making increased data transmission possible. In some cases, the ministry hosts cloud-based school information systems, reducing the barriers for uptake in schools. In others, schools contact vendors to provide this specialized service. Here, Internet connectivity and the prevalence of computers at the different levels can have an impact on the decision of which option to choose. For instance, if Internet connectivity is low, then a simultaneous campaign to connect schools to the Internet should be initiated.

Choosing between Off-the-Shelf or Self-Developed Software Solutions

Over recent years, a number of management information software packages have been developed for almost every administrative function and for all sizes of organization, public or private. For some time, the only option available to ministries and governments was to develop EMIS software solutions from scratch, either developed in-house or custom built by a software vendor. However, nowadays a number of management information packages available on the market can fulfill many of the tasks needed within an EMIS and require only minor modifications to the off-the-shelf product. In fact, the market for education software has grown to such an extent that specialized software firms provide individual and integrated software solutions for school, district/region, and national levels at competitive prices. These off-the-shelf software solutions can often be customized for a fraction of the price of developing one from scratch although they can come with conditions such as costly regular mandatory software solution upgrades.

Opting for an off-the-shelf software solution can have a number of significant benefits over developing a new software solution from the ground up. Frequently, vendors will allow a trial period for use prior to purchase, helping to ensure the system functions as expected and according to specifications.

In addition, customizing an existing software solution is a significantly faster process than developing a brand new software package, ensuring a nationwide system can be implemented in a timely and cost-effective manner. Often, software vendors have already ironed out many of the problems a new software package may encounter and aim to achieve industry best practices. Many also offer services attached to the software solution (box 5.2). However, these can be costly in the long term and require intensive external support. In some cases, especially when well procured and negotiated, off-the-shelf solutions that are highly adaptable may provide a cost-saving option, especially when it is hard to

---

Box 5.2 Software as a Service

Software as a Service (SaaS) is a software delivery model that has become increasingly popular with vendors delivering school information management software packages. In this delivery model, software companies host and maintain the servers, database, and applications. These services can be paid for through monthly or yearly subscription fees. This model allows a certain level of flexibility—for example, schools do not have to invest in expensive IT hardware or the personnel to implement it. In addition, it reduces the need for in-house technical expertise because the vendor is in charge of upgrading and maintaining the applications within the system. This model is especially useful for individual schools or small networks of schools because they can realize significant cost savings. However, for district, state, or national levels, self-developed and self-hosted solutions may be more efficient. Shortcomings of an SaaS for stand-alone school systems include the following:

- Data are typically stored at the vendor location, which may or may not comply with national and/or ministry policy on data privacy and or mandatory storage requirements.
- Vendors may sell the data.
- Data aggregation of school-based systems at the district/national level to monitor the performance of the education sector and support policy decisions may not be possible without substantial effort if schools adopt software solutions from numerous different vendors in assorted formats and different technologies.
- Audits of a stand-alone system are complex when that system is not automatically integrated with other government systems, opening the door to inflated student numbers to receive more grant allocation.
- Integration and/or integration with other government systems such as national assessments, human resource management systems, civil registry, and finances are complex, expensive, or not possible, compounded exponentially in difficulty if numerous system types from multiple vendors are in operation.
- Business failure of the vendor can result in complete loss of data.
- Security breaches at the vendor could result in loss of data.

   Once an SaaS is implemented, migrating to another approach later (for example, a ministry-hosted solution) may come at substantial cost. Costs could include purchasing the data back from the vendor and complex data migration processes.

---

sustain an IT cadre as part of the MoE. Opting for an off-the-shelf software solution works best when there are no preexisting computerized systems in place that require integration and/or migration. Stakeholder consultation ensures that all necessary requirements are met.

On the other hand, the key benefits of developing a software solution from scratch involve the flexibility of a completely customized system developed to meet specific contexts and needs. In addition, if a government already has significant levels of internal capacity, developing a software solution from scratch has the potential to provide cost savings. Also, significant levels of internal capacity tend to accompany preexisting systems. It is possible that merging and/or modifying existing systems can produce significant gains in a small amount of time. In Fiji, for instance, FEMIS was initially constructed by simply providing a single website that simultaneously accessed the existing school management information system, the student assessment system, and the ministry human resource system.[3] Another example is Vanuatu, where the government simply added a new web presence to its existing client–server education management system. However, for countries choosing to go down this route, understanding the time, effort, and resources needed to develop a solution from scratch is vital. When making the choice between these options, often the most important aspect is analyzing the internal capacity for developing, implementing, adapting, and maintaining software solutions.

Weighing Proprietary and Open-Source Software

All software solutions, regardless of their architecture, are based on a source code. The source code instructs a computer how to draw pages and screens in reaction to clicked buttons or selected menu options. The pages that are drawn can be as simple as a welcome page with a basic menu or a page that saves the date of birth of a student into a database or as complex as the results of a national resource allocation calculation. When software developers create an EMIS, or any other piece of software solution, they are writing source code files, which include all EMIS functionalities—from the color of the logo to the advanced financial calculations. This is an important concept because it deals with intellectual property rights and the same copyright restrictions apply as to, for example, movies, music, and books.

Broadly speaking, software source codes can be divided into two categories: proprietary and open source. *Proprietary software* is owned by an individual or a company, most frequently the entity that developed it. Because the software solution is owned, there are usually restrictions on its use and clients, here the government, generally do not receive access to the source code. Proprietary software development is frequently driven by specific commercial interests and often involves both licensing and maintenance fees. Examples of proprietary software are the ProgressBook and PowerSchool student information software suites used in schools across the United States and other countries (box 5.3).

Box 5.3 Examples of Proprietary School Information Systems

- Alma
- Class365
- Edsby
- Eduflex
- Edvance School Management Software
- Engage
- Focus School Software
- Gradelink
- LINQ
- MySchool
- PowerSchool
- PraxiSchool
- SAFSMS
- SchoolPRO2

Open-source software solutions are developed as an alternative to proprietary software. The source code for open-source software is available for modification or change by anyone. Open-source EMIS solutions, from school-level to national database systems, are becoming increasingly common, further reducing the barriers to adapting and upgrading existing software solutions. Nevertheless, for the time being most systems are a hybrid. An open-source software solution often demands a greater technical understanding from the user, whereas most proprietary systems require a large commitment—"more funds up front—in exchange for organized training and certain performance guarantees" (Bernbaum and Moses 2011). Most companies that provide fully open-source solutions do so for a basic set of features. These companies will often charge for more advanced features, customization, or support. Examples of open-source software are OpenSIS Community Edition and Project Fedena.[4]

Considering Costs

Developing a thorough understanding of the costs of a proposed system is also vital to ensuring its success. Costs that need to be factored include the initial costs, such as the software solution and any needed licenses, as well as the costs associated with its customization and the hardware needed to run the system. They should also include the long-term costs of running and maintaining the system, ongoing training, maintenance, hardware replacement when warranties expire, Internet bandwidth usage, and staffing. As an example of per student cost, table 5.2 summarizes the different cost components of the data system in the State of Maryland, in the United States (see chapter 7 for more information on Maryland's EMIS).

Table 5.2 Data System Cost per Student in Maryland (United States)

System	Cost per student (US$)
Student information system	9.33
Learning management system	2.68
Data warehouse	7.62

Source: Howard County Public School System 2015.

Box 5.4 Fiji's Affordable EMIS

Fiji has developed an affordable EMIS system. FEMIS utilized Microsoft Structured Query Language (SQL) database software, which is often provided without cost to ministries. Instead there have been some licensing arrangements funded at the federal level. Most resources were employed for the hardware of the databases and training of ministry staff and technical advisors. Fiji's development of an affordable and successful EMIS, despite the country's challenging geography and limited resources, serves as a role model for other countries in the region. Vanuatu, for instance, has already expressed interest in a similar EMIS architecture (please refer to chapter 9 for more detail).

Although donors are often willing to cover the capital expenses related to system development, they usually do not cover the total life cost of a system. In some cases, not budgeting for the long-term costs has resulted in an EMIS that was successful for the duration of a donor project, but was abandoned or scaled down in subsequent years. Some countries have found ways to produce an affordable, sustainable, and operational EMIS. For instance, Fiji has carefully budgeted for a variety of factors and may serve as an example for an affordable EMIS in a small country context (box 5.4).

The decisions made on the system architecture will impact costs in the long term. Cloud computing can potentially reduce the capital expenses of setting up a system, most notably by reducing expenses for hardware, user license fees, and implementation. This is especially the case for individual, or small groups of, schools. For them, cloud-based systems can lower operating costs including energy, maintenance, configuration, upgrading, and general IT staff costs. Finally, because the software solution does not need to be installed on each user's system, cloud-based systems can potentially be implemented rapidly. However, unless the hosted cloud-based system is hosted and maintained by the government, it almost always requires a periodic subscription fee. Such a fee often remains constant and is not depreciated over time—unlike capital investments.

Ensuring Data Quality

Data quality is pivotal to the ongoing viability of an EMIS. The government and school management will not trust or use EMIS data to make decisions if the underlying data are not reliable. Without political and school management support, the EMIS is likely to suffer a slow and painful demise. Therefore, numerous data quality strategies are required.

- *Dedicated data quality staff* must be responsible for (1) ensuring data are collected on time and are accurate and (2) ongoing communication of the need for data quality to those who provide the data.
- Substantial and ongoing *end user training* will ensure data quality.
- *Align data collection and data owners* as closely as possible. Those that use their own data will provide better quality data. For example, schools should maintain school data, whereas engineering staff should maintain facilities data.
- Clearly *state the purpose of data collection*, so that education stakeholders understand the need for data collection. In addition, integrating feedback loops into the data architecture can improve data quality. This is particularly important in paper-based systems (more so than online), where the government needs to demonstrate why the data are collected and return paper reports using the data to the data providers. In online data systems, these features should be integrated to support data quality efforts.
- *Use a single data source* in many places to exert pressure on data quality. For example, use the same student list for assessment, grant calculations, attendance analysis, and infrastructure standards. Doing so ensures that the list is accurate, reliable, and verified at multiples stages.
- *Integrate and compare EMIS data* against other sources, where possible, to ensure data quality. For example, teachers in schools should match teacher pay locations and pay grades in the pay system or national human resource system. In addition, student names and dates of birth should match the civil registry. Through data integration and sharing as well as data comparisons with non-education databases, a higher level of data quality can be achieved.

Designing the System Architecture and Deploying Software Solutions

The components of any software solution include data collection, database management, and data analysis tools. In designing the system architecture, governments can choose to deploy multifunctional software solutions or integrate different solutions, each with a unique purpose. The following section will provide an array of examples and where these software solutions have been implemented.

Purchasing a Multifunctional Software Solution System

Multifunctional software solutions incorporate a variety of functionalities in one single system. The demands on a software solution at the central level differ greatly from those at the local level. Multifunctional systems cater to the needs of individual levels and, consequently, can be used at the central, regional, or local level. These systems are composed of a variety of components, each tailored to the needs of individual stakeholder groups. Many of these multifunctional systems have a proven track record of success and have been implemented in a variety of countries such as Australia, the United Kingdom, the United States, and many more.

At the school level, SIMS are the preferred data entry tool in complex and advanced systems because they can be fully integrated into a national EMIS. SIMS are applications that allow schools to manage various aspects of running a school, frequently including modules to register students, document grades and assessment scores, track student and teacher attendance, and record finances and other aspects of school management. In these advanced systems, teachers and administrators can use a SIMS application to keep track of their day-to-day tasks. These data, used for a school's administration, would automatically be fed into a regional or national EMIS, eliminating the extra step of filling out forms specifically for data reporting purposes. In the most integrated of these systems, data are automatically fed into the central EMIS system as soon as they are entered at the school level. This means that policy makers are able to track changing trends in real time. In most cases, however, these systems provide snapshots, creating flat files or records of the current information in the SIMS that are exported to the central EMIS at planned periods of the year.

Examples of Multifunctional Software Solutions

Capita developed SIMS, which uses a client–server architecture and is based on a Microsoft SQL server system.[5] The system features a student tracking system, enabling teachers to closely monitor academic progress. Furthermore, SIMS offers a built-in financial feature including budgeting, billing, and cash flow modules. SIMS emphasizes school–parent communication through real-time information on the academic progress of each student and, thus, encourages parental engagement in the learning process. SIMS also includes modules for monitoring attendance, punctuality, and behavior of students to encourage improvements. It features staff performance evaluation tools and records staff training and employment details. The personnel feature can be used to track teaching quality, design training programs, and manage appraisals. SIMS offers two separate packages for primary and secondary students, each tailored to their specific needs. In addition, SIMS also has partnered with a variety of vendors to complement the software package.

SIMS—originally developed for use in the United Kingdom, serving over 80,000 primary and secondary students in England and Wales—has expanded to over 22,000 schools in 45 countries all over the world. One of the success factors is its flexibility: SIMS can be tailored to the unique needs of any school. In addition, SIMS has continuously offered training and customer support to help schools in the implementation process.

Sentral Education offers a broad range of school-related tools: (1) administration, (2) finance, (3) assessment, (4) attendance, (5) communication, (6) well-being, (7) learning, (8) scheduling, and (9) staff, student, and parent portal services. It also (1) tracks student profiles and activities, (2) establishes a grade book and continuum tracker, (3) allows for easy report writing, and (4) includes curriculum references, strategic planning tools, and additional resources.[6]

Sentral meets the needs of K–12 schools and is currently used by over 100,000 staff in over 1,800 schools in Australia. The aim of Sentral and similar software companies is to increase efficiencies by eliminating double data entry, manual transfer of data, and wasted time due to corrupted or damaged files. Sentral, in particular, offers a holistic approach, and its package includes maintenance, management, development, and backup of school and student data. It offers single school websites or an enterprise version for groups of schools. Figure 5.5 provides a screenshot of the Sentral applications.

OpenEMIS is an open-source education management system software solution coordinated by the United Nations Educational, Scientific, and Cultural Organization (UNESCO) and developed by Community System Foundation.[7] The software solution can be divided into three distinct categories: data collection, management, and analysis (figure 5.6). The software solution is designed to be flexible and can be adapted to the needs of individual countries. The applications can be run offline or on a desktop computer, on a local network through a client–server infrastructure, or as a cloud-based application hosted on a dedicated OpenEMIS server. The cloud-based system involves an annual fee to cover the maintenance and server costs. The system is designed to work with a MySQL database but is compatible with most database server systems including PostgreSQL and SQL Server. However, it is important to note that OpenEMIS does not mean that the system is open to all users and stakeholders. There are significant costs involved in using the different services, and ownership of information is often held with the vendor.

Figure 5.5 Screenshot of Sentral Applications

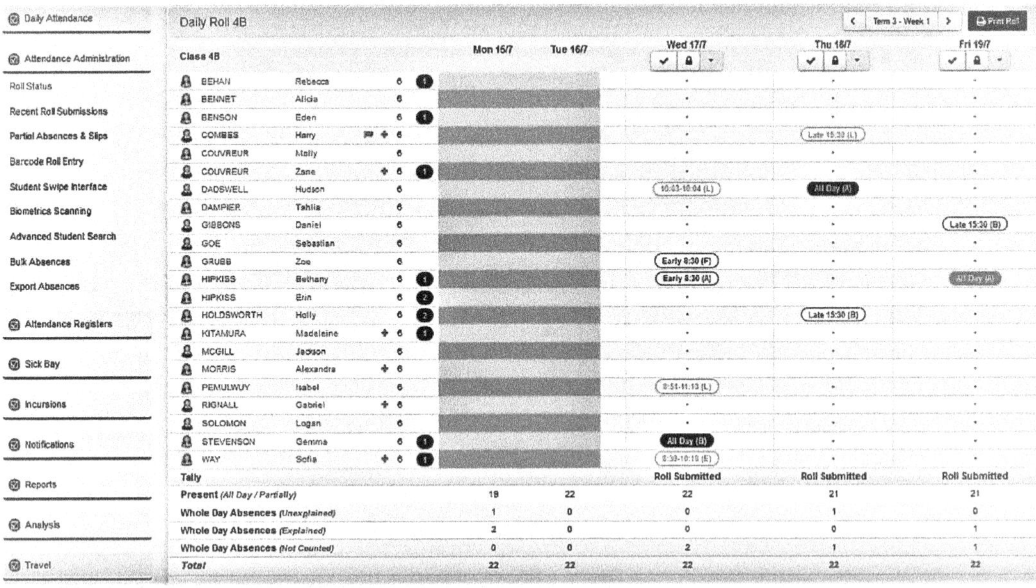

Source: Sentral, https://www.sentral.com.au/.

Data for Learning • http://dx.doi.org/10.1596/978-1-4648-1099-2

Figure 5.6 OpenEMIS Software Suite

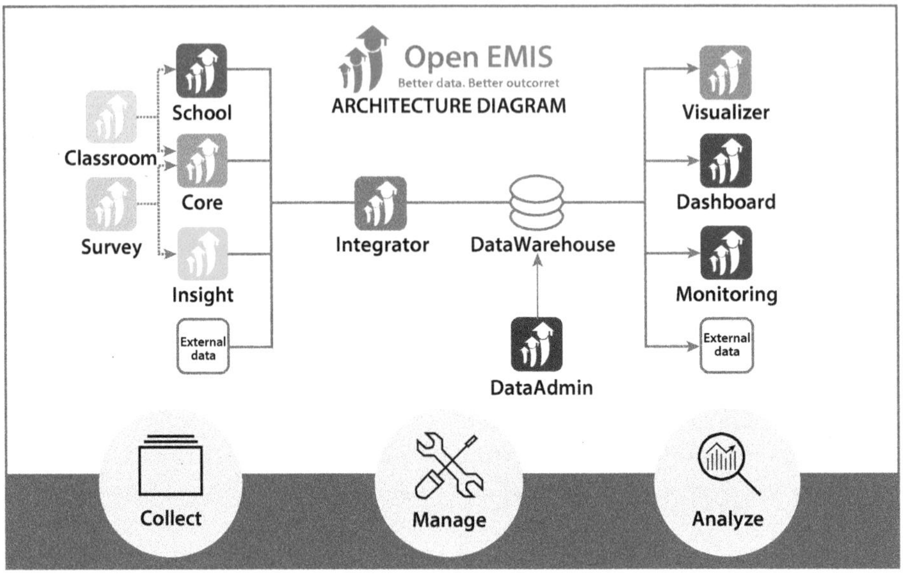

Source: UNESCO 2015.

In schools with strong Internet connectivity, teachers can use the OpenEMIS Classroom software to manage all aspects of their class, including student performance, attendance, and incidents. This information can be fed into the school software, a full information management system. This information then feeds into OpenEMIS Core, the ministry-level EMIS system. When Internet connectivity is low, the survey software can be used to manually import paper-based school census and other educational data at the district, regional, or national level. Alternatively, the survey software can also be used directly by school administrators, bypassing the need for paper-based forms.

The latest version of the OpenEMIS software solution is currently being implemented in Belize, Jordan, Maldives, and St. Vincent and Grenadines (figure 5.7). For example:

- In **Belize**, OpenEMIS School is being implemented across all education levels with the support of the Inter-American Development Bank and UNESCO. It is intended for use at the school level to facilitate the collection, processing, and management of school information.
- In **Jordan**, as of December 2015, the OpenEMIS School was being phased into a number of pilot schools with plans to expand to the rest of the country in the coming years. It is expected to cover more than 2,160,000 students and 140,000 staff in 6,893 schools across the country.
- In **Maldives**, OpenEMIS was initiated in 2015 in response to the changing needs and context of the education system, and to make use of the advancements in technology. As a web-based online analytical processing tool, the

Figure 5.7 OpenEMIS Interface and Snapshot of Training Sessions in Belize and Maldives

Source: OpenEMIS, https://www.openemis.org/.

OpenEMIS Analyzer is designed to support analysis of education data by facilitating user-defined queries to produce customized datasets.

- In ***St. Vincent and Grenadines***, OpenEMIS was adopted in 2013. The OpenEMIS Core system is intended for use at the ministry level to facilitate the collection, processing, and management of aggregate education data. Currently, OpenEMIS has been deployed in 261 schools across the country, and there are plans for further expansion.

Open Solutions for Education (os4ed) has two software packages that provide an integrated EMIS for use at school, district, and national levels: openSIS and openIntel.[8] The basic software package of openSIS is available in 49 languages and is used in more than 16,000 institutions around the world. The community version (a fully open-source software package) includes modules on student demographics, scheduling, report cards, attendance, goals and progress, grade books, transcripts, a parents' portal, advanced reports, medical records, and multi-school support (figure 5.8). Additional modules, including teacher plans and standards-based grading, are available in proprietary versions of the software solution for a fee. Available as a self-hosted cloud-based version, the system is accessed through a web-based interface, allowing users to access it through a simple web browser. Teachers, administrators, and principles can interact with the system directly. Highly customizable, the solution can be set up for use by individual teachers or by a single school administrator. OpenIntel is the second part of os4ed's solution (figure 5.9). Composed of a number of open-source components (for example, Business Intelligence Reporting Tool Runtime and Pentaho Data Integration), the system is designed to use MySQL but can be integrated with most other SQL-based servers.

Initially, openIntel was envisioned as a data warehouse solution for districts in the United States, but soon it was also adapted by other countries. For example:

- In *the United States*, the Oregon Department of Human Services and South Carolina State Department of Education have both used openSIS applications. In Oregon, os4ed worked with the Department of Human Services to fully customize the application to its own needs. The South Carolina Department of Education has recently upgraded to a cloud-based openSIS application, which now also includes integration with other electronic applications outside of os4ed products.

Figure 5.8 Snapshot of the Integrated os4ed Modules

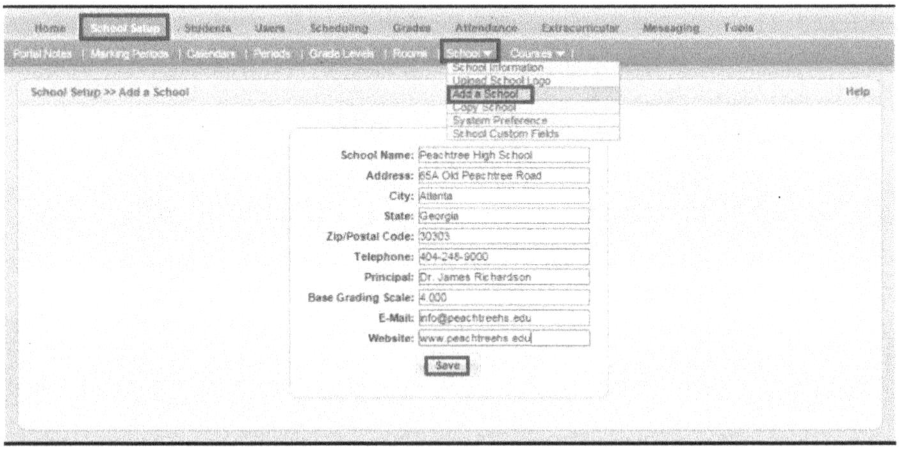

Source: os4ed, http://www.os4ed.com.

Figure 5.9 OpenIntel Sample Screenshots

a. District attendance averages, 2009–10

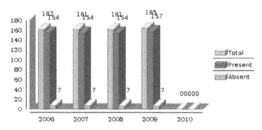

b. Student demographics, 2009–10

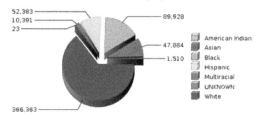

c. District enrollments over time

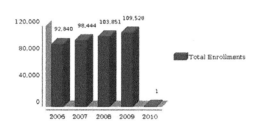

d. District ethnicity over time

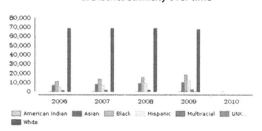

Source: os4ed, http://www.os4ed.com/index.php/openintel.

- In **Dominica**, the MoE incorporated os4ed's solution and has been using it since 2013. All 78 schools in the country have openSIS, covering a student body of 16,500. School principals are trained to use openSIS, and the system is used to support the day-to-day management of each school. In addition, the system is linked to openIntel, housed in the MoE. This allows the MoE to gather real-time data on students' performance and on school finances.
- In **St. Kitts and Nevis**, openSIS has been used to a similar extent as in Dominica. All 46 schools in St. Kitts and Nevis make use of the system. The use of openSIS software in Dominica and St. Kitts and Nevis has also inspired other countries such as Antigua and Barbuda to use the software (UNESCO 2013).

Building the Software Pieces

An alternative approach to developing a multifunctional software solution would be to build the pieces. By doing so, governments have the opportunity to find and develop a software solution tailored to their individual requirements. It allows for more flexibility, but it might also require additional efforts.

Identifying Appropriate Data Collection Applications

Computerized forms, at their simplest, are data entry applications that allow you to enter data into a database, either directly as data are being collected or from paper-based forms. Some database applications, like Microsoft Access, have the capability to create forms that allow data entered to feed directly into a database. In other cases, a separate application is used that interacts with the database. These forms can range in complexity and often include layers of verification, ensuring that data being entered into a field fit certain criteria or fall within certain bounds. In most cases, data entry is done through user-friendly data entry templates prepared and customized by computer programmers.

Because these applications are fairly simple to build and customization is key, in-house programmers are frequently used. However, private consultants or organizations can provide this service if needed. It is vital that programmers work closely with the team designing the survey to ensure data entry is easy and efficient and minimize data entry errors. In many early-phase EMISs, these forms mirror paper-based school census forms. These paper forms are filled out by school administrators, or specially tasked data collection teams, before being sent to a unit within the ministry where data entry operators load them into the database. Figure 5.10 provides an example of a Microsoft Access data entry application that is used in Samoa for collection of education data. Once the paper-based school census forms are collected and sent to the MoE, the EMIS staff enters all the data into the computerized forms. The application has some built-in features that minimize errors in case of manual entry of data.

Increasingly, data entry applications are being developed in a way that allows data entry to take place directly at the school level. Computer-Assisted Personal Interview (CAPI) programs are used for in-person data collection from schools,

Figure 5.10 Microsoft Access Data Entry Application in Samoa

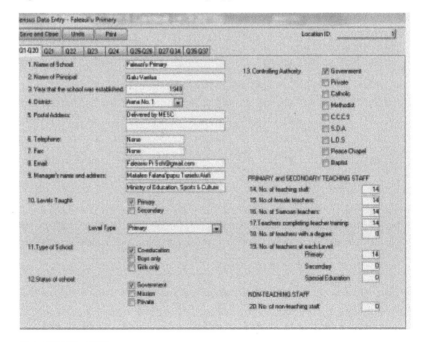

Source: World Bank 2015.

over the phone, or simply self-administered by schools through the program. The answers are then often directly entered into the program using personal computers, smartphones, or tablet computers. A number of models can be used that achieve this, including applications designed for use on mobile devices (both conventional and smartphones) that allow school administrators to submit their data electronically or through cloud-based applications. This allows principals, school administrators, or teachers to enter the data directly, reducing the need for data entry operators and increasing efficiencies. Direct entry can also improve data quality by reducing the number of data processing steps and establishing an increased sense of data ownership.

For example, in Uganda, mobile phones are being used to collect real-time data to improve accountability and evaluation of projects. Taking advantage of the extensive use of smartphones, GPS recordings, photos, and relevant education data are entered into the application. As soon as the reports/data are verified, the data become available on the website and could be used for further analysis and visualization. This technology was mainly adopted to receive feedback from students, teachers, and other beneficiaries on the availability of education resources (Trucano 2014). Figure 5.11 shows the data that are available on the website after entry using the mobile application and that are then used for further analysis for the purpose of decision making.

Examples of Applications for Data Collection

The *Census and Survey Processing System* (CSPro) is an open-source program that allows users to enter, edit, tabulate, and disseminate data.[9] Originated in 2000, CSPro was originally developed for Microsoft Windows. Unlike previous software systems, CSPro offers users a visual approach to data production and manipulation. For those users with advanced programming skills, CSPro offers high levels of flexibility that allow them to make use of many advanced functions and handle complex surveys and censuses (box 5.5). Users without programming skills can rely on the interface to make use of CSPro. CSPro can be used in

Figure 5.11 Example of Data Entry Using Mobile Phones to Transmit Directly to the Ministry of Education Website

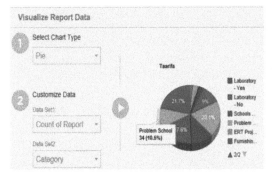
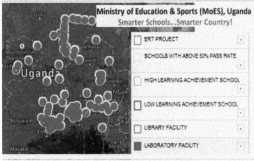

Source: Trucano 2014.
Note: MoE = ministry of education.

Data for Learning • http://dx.doi.org/10.1596/978-1-4648-1099-2

Box 5.5 Examples of CSPro Applications

Funded by the U.S. Agency for International Development (USAID), CSPro has been actively used in over 160 countries. The users range from national statistical agencies, nongovernmental organizations (NGOs), hospitals, and universities to private sector companies. In Indonesia, CSPro has been used for surveys of 235 million citizens and in Djibouti for less than half a million citizens, clearly demonstrating that CSPro can handle any size of survey (CSPro 2017). CSPro surveys are often used for the following:

- Censuses (population and housing, agriculture, and economic)
- Demographic and labor force
- Household income and expenditure
- Large-scale international projects, for example, the Demographic and Health Surveys (DHS), Living Standards Measurement Study (LSMS), and Multiple Indicator Cluster Survey (MICS)

Source: U.S. Census Bureau, https://www.census.gov/population/international/software/cspro/index.html.

---

combination with other statistical programs or as a stand-alone system. If CSPro is used as a stand-alone application, users can enter data directly using tablet technology or manually through the data collection tool. Afterward, the user can manipulate the data and validate them before starting the data analysis process. CSPro has built-in tabulation and data dissemination features. Its simple design, based on visualization, caters to nontechnical staff as well as senior statisticians and programmers (figure 5.12).

Open Data Kit (ODK) is an open-source software system that allows users to (1) design a data collection questionnaire or survey, (2) collect data and send them directly to a database, and (3) manage the collected data on the server and extract them in an appropriate format.[10] ODK is equipped with GPS location and image features, which is particularly helpful in education. It is also used in evidence-based decision making and mapping exercises. ODK is built for touch-screen phones: the program's field interface is oriented to touch and not reliant on programming to answer, change language of the survey instrument, and navigate the questionnaire. Moreover, ODK enables developers to easily capture data as an answer or display data to assist in selecting an answer with ease, something lacking in programming software solutions. The software solution stores data in a portable format and transfers them through a dedicated server application. However, the data storage format often fails to allow for the variable and value labels that are crucial for the management of complex household survey data. Likewise, the server application warehouses the data well but stores the data in a format that makes data export cumbersome; rosters for each survey case are stored in separate files that must be concatenated for use (Shaw et al. 2011). Table 5.3 provides a brief overview of the available ODK tools, and figure 5.13 illustrates examples of data collection with ODK.

Figure 5.12 Sample Screenshot of the CSPro Application

Source: United States Census Bureau. 2017. Census and Survey Processing System (CSPro). https://www.census.gov/population/international/software/cspro/.

Table 5.3 Open Data Kit Tools

ODK tool	Description
Build	To facilitate the design of questionnaire forms, Open Data Kit (ODK) Build uses an HTML5 web-based application and encourages the use of a simple form. Users can design forms simply by dragging and dropping them from a form designer application.
Collect	ODK Collect replaces paper-based data collection with smartphone-based collection. It is built for the Android system and is able to capture data in text, location, photo, video, audio, and barcode features.
Aggregate	ODK Aggregate allows the user to store, view, and collect data. It is flexible and can operate on Android as well as local servers using MySQL and PostgreSQL.
Form Uploader	The Form Uploader allows the upload of a blank form and its media to ODK Aggregate.
Briefcase	The ODK Briefcase allows transfer of data from ODK Collect to ODK Aggregate.
Validate	The OpenRosa is used by ODK Validate to ensure that all data are verified.
XLS2XForm	ODK XLS2XForm ensures that all XForms can be designed with Microsoft Excel.

Source: ODK, https://opendatakit.org.

FHI 360's Mobile Suite is a collection of mobile data collection tools that can be used for collecting and processing surveys on-site, consolidating all data sources into one database using Bluetooth and basic text messaging services. Designed for use by the whole social sector, the suite is not used explicitly for education data. The system is designed for use primarily in remote environments with limited access to communication tools—sometimes being used alongside other existing EMIS tools used in less remote environments. The mobile suite allows on-site and offline data processing, allowing data to be visualized anywhere. Figure 5.14 illustrates two screenshots of the mobile technology for data collection and its GPS application.

Data for Learning • http://dx.doi.org/10.1596/978-1-4648-1099-2

Figure 5.13 Sample Screenshots of Open Data Kit Collect

Figure 5.14 Mobile Technology for Data Collection

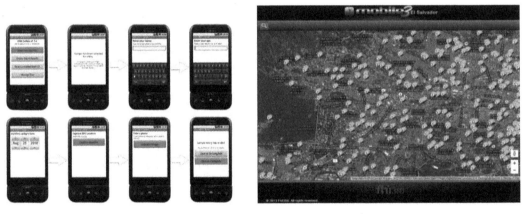

FHI360 has piloted the applications for data collection in El Salvador, Equatorial Guinea, Guatemala, Liberia, and Tanzania. The FHI 360 tools were used for a variety of purposes in these countries, including education in Liberia and Tanzania.

- In **Liberia,** approximately 2,300 government-run schools have been mapped using FHI 360's K-Mobile geographic information system to prevent the spread of Ebola virus in classrooms.[11] One of the main challenges in Liberia's education system was the lack of available data on students, teachers, and schools. After the Ebola crisis hit the country, the government needed information on schools to allocate resources. FHI 360 integrated information from different sources, such as the data on school location, number of students and teachers, ground-level photos of the schools, and infrastructure data (for example availability of roofs, desks, latrines, wells, and blackboards). The MoE was able to compile accurate information on school conditions, students, and teachers, which enabled it to better allocate resources and ensure schools remain free of the virus.
- In **Tanzania**, FHI 360's geographical information system is being used to map approximately 5,500 schools in different regions of the country. Once the system is operational, the EMIS will be used on tablets, smartphones, or laptops to generate reports on a real-time basis on key school performance indicators. Because this information would be available to all government staff at every level of the education system with the help of mobile devices, it is expected to improve the quality of education data.

Blaise is a software package for statistical and scientific research in the form of computer-assisted web, telephone, and face-to-face personal interviews.[12] The software solution can be used for a wide variety of surveys such as education, household, health, labor force, economic, and cross-sectional and longitudinal sample designs. Some of the striking features of the system include the following:

- **Designing easy questionnaires**: Blaise can create questionnaires of different sizes and levels of complexity. The data model can be structured in blocks, tables, groups, and arrays. Data fields can be defined to include question and answer texts, comments, categories such as "do not know," options for multilingual texts, and so forth. In addition, data validation can be conducted at different stages of the survey.
- **Comprehensive documentation and user community**: Strong documentation and an engaging user community enable new developers to gather information on the program's command line programming development environment. The programming language is well designed for most survey design tasks, ranging from issuing "skip" instructions to controlling the graphical interface.
- **Ease of use**: Interviewers find it easy to navigate to various modules of the questionnaire, which is especially useful in case of complex and detailed survey instruments.

Figure 5.15 The Design Process of a Survey Instrument in Blaise

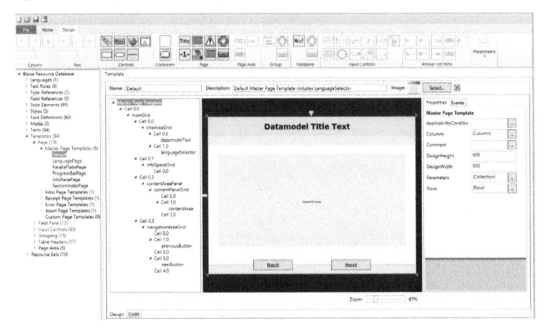

Source: Blaise, http://blaise.com.

The major limitations of Blaise lie with its interface. The development environment offers only command line programming. Although this is helpful for technically advanced users, it might be very difficult for a user with limited experience in programming. Additionally, the interface system relies mainly on the use of keyboard and menus, even though there are some touch-friendly options. Figure 5.15 illustrates a screenshot of Blaise.

Establishing the Database

The core of an EMIS is often a database centralizing school-level data on students, teachers, and resources via an annual school census form and a few other data sources (such as census data, health data, and so on). It is used by education ministries/departments, NGOs, researchers, donors, and other education stakeholders for planning, monitoring, and policy making. Databases are a collection of data points organized in a way that allows information to be accessed, managed, and updated in a highly organized manner. They can be thought of as the back end of an EMIS. These systems can range in complexity, from fairly simple Microsoft Access databases to more complex SQL database systems. SQL databases, some of the most commonly used databases, run on a server, allowing multiple users to access multiple databases simultaneously without compromising data integrity.

A database management system (DBMS) is a software package that allows users to create, retrieve, update, and manage data. The most frequently used systems are called relational database management systems (RDBMSs) (box 5.6).

Box 5.6 Commonly Used Relational Database Management Systems

- Oracle
- MySQL
- Microsoft SQL Server
- DB2
- Microsoft Access

Most databases are relational databases, which organize data using a set of tables with a number of relationships between the different tables. These databases allow users to enter data in any order then reassemble the data in an infinite number of ways without having to physically reorganize the tables themselves. In essence, these programs are the interface that allows users to interact with the database while ensuring that data remain consistently organized and accessible. Oracle Database, Microsoft SQL Server, and MySQL are the most commonly used RDBMSs. Further applications can be layered onto these systems that allow more user-friendly interactions with the database, for example using SQL language to interface with SQL databases.

Examples of Database Applications
In recent years, the number of database software solutions has increased. Some of these solutions include MariaDB, MySQL, PostgreSQL, SQLITE, Firebird, MongoDB, Cassandra, Elasticsearch, and VoltDB. Three examples are highlighted below.

MySQL is simple, easy to use, consumer friendly, and ready for immediate use by governments.[13] It is the most widely used open-source client–server model RDBMS across industries and ensures scalability given the needs of the government. Because of its continuous replication processes, MySQL is able to minimize service disruptions. It is multilayered with advanced security provisions such as network access control, firewalls, authentication requirements, encryption provisions, and audits. MySQL Community, now owned by Oracle, is available for free; however, a number of proprietary versions are available that provide additional functionality. It is fully compatible with other Oracle products and offers cloud services, trainings on software usage, and customer support. The cloud system ensures that the data are continuously backed up and available at any point in time. MySQL comes with an advanced set of different tools that support governments in the management of their education databases. These range from pure database management software solutions to many others such as replication, partitioning, and monitoring software applications. In combination, these software solutions are able to provide all necessary support for effective database management (figure 5.16).

VoltDB is an open-source DBMS with a high-speed in-memory database application. It specializes in fast data and big data (figure 5.17).[14] To visualize

Figure 5.16 Screenshot of MySQL Workbench

Source: MySQL Tutorial, https://www.youtube.com/watch?v=yPu6qV5byu4.

Figure 5.17 Data Process in VoltDB

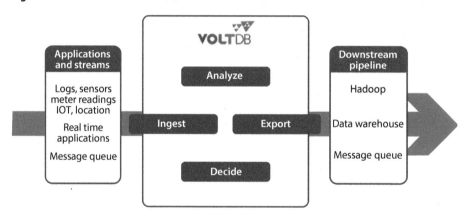

Source: VoltDB, https://www.voltdb.com/.

fast data, it can be thought of in three steps: (1) the software solution applies key function for value production and maps it against existing data, (2) real-time analysis takes place and data-based decisions are made, and (3) data are exported to a warehouse and securely stored. The advantage of VoltDB is that its architecture allows the software solution to be fast enough to stream and process big data in real time, which includes analytics and decision making. VoltDB uses SQL and is compatible with Hadoop to ensure its speed and data monitoring systems such as Ganglia, JMX, Nagios, and New Relic. In addition, the user can also connect applications that are based on C++, C#, Python, Java (Maven), and others. The software application has been designed to avoid loss of data by replicating data through "snapshotting." It is flexible and can easily be expanded to include new modules as required by the government.

PostgreSQL can perform basic math functions, string operations, and cryptography ("data mapping") processes.[15] It is also used for big data and has a large capacity for rows and columns within the database system. For instance, the Generalized Search Tree (GiST) is an indexing tool that combines a wide range of sorting and searching algorithms to produce the desired query results. PostgreSQL is compatible with a wide array of programming languages as well as other open-source software applications (for example Oracle products), which makes PostgreSQL easily customizable to the needs of the education system.

Integrating Applications for Data Analysis

Once data are entered into a database, they need to be manipulated and analyzed in order to provide the indicators and information that can lead to concrete policy action, increase learning, and track compliance issues. Once again, the complexity of the applications used for this varies. In many cases, these are fairly complex, requiring programming language skills: they cannot be used by untrained analysts. SQL-based databases generally require a solid mastery of SQL syntax in order to generate data output and reports.

The complete uses for education data analytics tools to support learning are still being explored; however, a shift from using data for compliance purposes toward using data for increasing learning outcomes and improving education quality is already taking place. A quality learning approach uses information to support and improve a shared accountability model in which all stakeholders—policy makers, principals, teachers, school administrators, parents, and students—are responsible for student learning (Linn 2003). Under the quality learning approach, information is used broadly across the education system with a focus on strengthening education system processes and practices in order to ultimately improve learning outcomes.

As a result, many software packages have been created that facilitate more simplified approaches to analyzing data. They often allow users to create automated queries, generating specific and frequently used indicators, or add levels of advanced analytics. In the private sector, these data analytics packages are often referred to as business intelligence (BI) tools. BI is a set of methodologies and technologies that use data analytics to transform raw data into useful statistics. In addition, advanced BI systems can draw data from a variety of databases, allowing an EMIS to pull from multiple data sources. These systems allow for powerful predictive analysis and help policy makers make predictions and prepare for future trends (box 5.7).

Examples of Data Analytics Applications

There are many analytics tools available from which to choose. Many of these analytics tools also offer advanced predictive modeling. The most common ones include R, Orange, RapidMiner, Dataiku Data Science Studio (DSS), Anaconda,

Box 5.7 Early Warning Systems in Education

Innovative companies like eScholar are designing education-focused BI systems that use data from thousands, or hundreds of thousands, of students with millions of rows of highly granular attendance and assessment data in order to track student progress toward reaching education outcomes. Combining historical datasets with current data, teachers can use these systems to be notified if students are not on track to reach certain education outcomes or need specialized support. The systems aim to analyze and correlate the data in ways that identify at-risk districts, schools, classrooms, teachers, and individual students and to explain why, allowing teachers, administrators, and policy makers to respond directly to the problems identified. Helping teachers identify individualized plans to help student learning outcomes can allow teachers to focus their efforts in ways that will maximize student learning. For example, data on attendance, behavior, and course work in first grade can be used to predict the likelihood of children dropping out of high school later on in their education.

Weka, GraphLab Create, Octave, H_2O, Lavastorm Public Edition, DMWay Basic, Tanagra, PredictionIO, HP Distributed R, KNIME, scikit-learn, Actian Analytics Platform, Apache Spark MLlib, Apache Mahout, LIBLINEAR, Vowpal Wabbit, NumPy, and SciPy. A sampling of these tools appears below.

The open-source software application H_2O is able to manipulate large amounts of data distributed across different systems.[16] The application disseminates data effectively through visualization and provides artificial and visual intelligence focusing on deep learning. It was developed in 2011 and is currently used by approximately 80,000 data scientists and about 9,000 organizations all over the world. H_2O directly connects to application programming interfaces (APIs). In addition, H_2O operates on all standard computer systems: Linux, Windows, and Mac. It can be cloud based or on site, depending on the needs of the government. It can also connect to big data from different databases such as HDFS, S3, SQL, and Hadoop. H_2O is able to compare options and provide the user with a wide array of analysis scenarios. It also offers many additional features such as security and authentication provisions. Figure 5.18 provides an overview of how H_2O operates.

Hewlett Packard (HP) Haven Predictive Analytics is designed to deliver large-scale data analysis from all data points without limits.[17] It is free and compatible with the open-source program statistical software, R. It is powered by HP Vertica and Distributed R and is fully scalable to produce big data analyses and predictions. It can be integrated with Massive Parallel Processing platform, which would allow for even faster data analyses in R.

Actian Vortex Express enables data scientists to conduct massive predictive analytics while inside Hadoop database platform without coding. Actian offers a free graphical community version for predictive analytics platform, which can run data of up to 500 GB on Linux. It is powered by Vortex.[18]

PredictionIO allows governments to download predictive engine templates, which can be tailored and customized at a later point in time.[19] It is a real-time

Figure 5.18 H$_2$O Architecture and Interoperability with Other Programs and Programming Languages

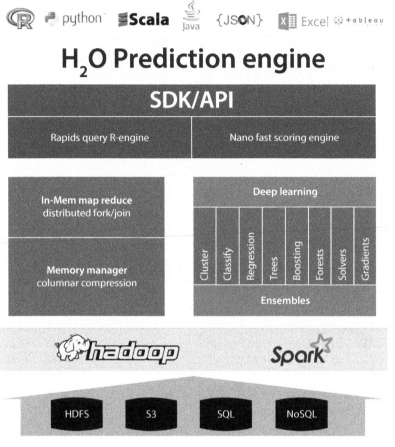

Source: H$_2$O, http://www.h2o.ai/.

application, which is able to unify data from a variety of platforms. It is compatible with data libraries such as Spark MLlib and OpenNLP as well as other programs like HBase and Elasticsearch.

Piwik allows the government to track how education stakeholders make use of their websites.[20] Piwik specializes in four types of services: (1) web, (2) e-commerce, (3) server log, and (4) intranet analytics. Piwik's dashboard can be easily navigated and automatically produces reports customized to the government's needs. In the open-source version, the following models are included: visitor, keyword, browser, referrer information, and many more (figure 5.19). In addition, visitor statistics update every 10 seconds. Graphs and tables can be created online, and data can be easily exported (for example, to Excel, CSV, XLM, and Php). Piwik includes a smartphone application, so statistics can be accessed any time and anywhere. Moreover, EMIS staff can subscribe to daily, weekly, or monthly reports that are directly sent to them via e-mail. There are no data storage limits, and Piwik offers community support and regular privacy and security services.

Data for Learning • http://dx.doi.org/10.1596/978-1-4648-1099-2

Figure 5.19 Piwik Dashboard

Source: Piwik, https://piwik.org/.

Open Web Analytics enables governments to customize their websites according to their specific needs by adding specific modules to the analytics program.[21] Open Web Analytics produces "heat maps" that indicate which links and website functions have been accessed most. These functions are often used for e-commerce tracking, but can easily be adapted for education purposes. In general, Open Analytics has a WordPress and MediaWiki plugin to enable tracking of a website. Alternatively, the government could also add a snippet of Java or Personal Home Page (PHP) code to the existing open-source webpage, which would fulfill the same purpose.

eAnalytics monitors website traffic of up to five million views a month.[22] eAnalytics offers a comprehensive real-time reporting system and allows the government to simultaneously track different Twitter and Google AdWord accounts. eAnalytics follows high standards in privacy measures for the government. The software solution can be seamlessly integrated with other systems such as data warehouse/business intelligence, customer relation management, newsletter, and data-mining systems. In addition, personalized communications regarding content, form, and channel are made possible and affordable. It is distributed under an AGPL 3 license.

Ensuring Compatibility and Interoperability

When selecting and deploying a new software solution, an MoE needs to ensure that the solution is compatible with existing systems because there are likely more than one. The new software system also has to be fully integrated within

---

Box 5.8 Interoperability and Compatibility Programs in Australia

The Australian government introduced interoperability and compatibility programs to ensure that education data reporting systems across the country could be integrated seamlessly. The government realized that the number of information and learning systems applications was growing rapidly across the country. To reduce the risk of data fragmentation, the National Schools Interoperability Program (NSIP) was founded in 2010 and was tasked to develop and promote common approaches to education data. This also included promoting the Systems Interoperability Framework (SIF) Association, which is currently used by 43 education agencies including various local, national, and cross-jurisdictional initiatives. The incorporated tools range from allowing access to online learning resources, online assessment, organization-wide integration applications, and student data transfer to national reporting. The Australian government has published a guiding document on SIF adaptation and implementation to provide stakeholders with information on the process. Three years after inception of SIF, the necessity of having a strong common national approach has amplified further given the growing number of new online products and services. In addition, the Student Information System Baseline Profile (SBP) has also been promoted by the central government and adapted by some states. It aims to reduce complexity and cost for schools, while increasing the ease for vendors in creating interoperability between applications and student (or school) information systems.

Source: NSIP, https://www.mysql.com/.

---

itself, meaning that all parts should function seamlessly with one another. One option would be to provide a system interoperability framework (box 5.8). Such a framework would be particularly helpful to those countries that have granted individual states and schools the freedom to procure software solutions tailored to their specific needs. By doing so, the government acknowledges schools should be granted the option to choose from a vast pool of potential software systems depending on their individual requirements and geographic location.

Another option would be to adopt a central and multifunctional software solution, which covers all necessary software requirements and can be used at the school level. Here, the government should ensure that the multifunctional education software solution is flexible enough to be applied to a variety of different school requirements. Furthermore, it should be easily understandable so that school staff with varying degrees of statistical, software, and computer expertise will be able to make effective use of it.

Implementing Data Security Measures

The database's as well as the application's programming interface should include strict data security, privacy, protection, and confidentiality features. In any software solution a particular focus should be paid to database management security.

Many database software solutions offer their own data privacy measures or can be adapted to the protection measures of the EMIS. Data security can be best achieved through a tiered approach with a variety of data protection layers:

- *Access control and authentication* are often the first steps in data protection. Here, users are issued individual passwords, and a hierarchy of access ensures that the users can access only the data they require to complete their tasks. There may also be a difference of access from within or outside of the network to restrict access.
- *Auditing functionalities* track which data users access and can, thus, ensure that only authorized users access data.
- *A high level of encryption* encodes data so that only authorized users can access it. For unauthorized users, the encrypted data will be made unintelligible. Generally, encryption follows a certain algorithm, and only authorized users are able to decrypt data through the software application. Decryption is generally an automated process in the back end of the software, which does not require coding expertise from the individual authorized user.
- *Firewalls* restrict incoming and outgoing network traffic to exclude unauthorized users. A firewall creates a barrier from the network on which the data are hosted and outside networks such as the Internet.
- *Backups* of data ensure that, even in case of a data breach, all data can be recovered and the data leak removed as soon as possible. Naturally, data backup systems also require protection and security processes.
- *Training* in data security of EMIS staff and all authorized users (for example, statisticians, data collectors, and so on) is necessary so that all stakeholders understand the security and data protection processes.

For example, two data security measures are commonly used: *virtual private networks* (VPNs) and *hypertext transfer protocol secure* (HTTPS). A VPN creates links across private or shared networks, so that you could consider it a "private" Internet. Figure 5.20 illustrates how a VPN establishes a connection between a server and a client (here a laptop computer). VPNs have the advantage that they are generally more secure than hosting data on the open Internet, but they also require additional software and hardware infrastructure to function. HTTPS, however, uses channels of communication such as the Internet but ensures secure communication of data through authentication of the visited websites. It offers strong protection and integrity of the data that are exchanged through HTTPS. Authorized users can generally access websites, but the back-end functions ensure privacy and data protection.

Procurement Procedures

Procurement is the one of the most critical tasks of development of software solutions. Efficient provision of IT infrastructure and services will ease the collection, processing, and management of education data, which in turn will

Figure 5.20 Illustration of a Virtual Private Network (VPN)

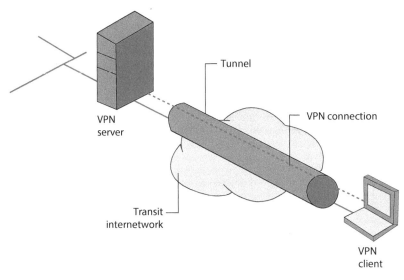

Source: IBM 2005.

contribute to improving the education system. Almost every EMIS has essential software and hardware requirements, whether they are rudimentary or advanced. However, procurement procedures have often been very cumbersome, and governments often find themselves struggling with hiring and contracting vendors.

Meeting with Relevant Stakeholders to Establish the Requirements of the New Software Solution

As discussed in the previous section, the specifications need to be identified in relation to system architecture, wire framing, database, server, hosting, and the other factors mentioned. In any case, narrowing the scope of procurement is key. It has been shown that making sequential steps is better than large procurement of the whole system at once.

Procurement and warranties need solid consideration across the board, in terms of both hardware and software. The operating system and database licenses, short-term costs, and, in particular, long-term costs need to be examined to ensure that the software solution is sustainable. Therefore, the decision about which software solution to procure needs to be carefully planned and prepared. The first step in the procurement process is to assess what is required and expected from the software solution. The following guidelines are laid out to help governments streamline the process of procurement:

- *Establish a clear across-the-board understanding of the education data needs*. While deciding on the product and vendor services, the first important task is to gather information from various school districts on the system needs and lessons learned from the implementation of previous software applications and vendor relations.

- **Bring relevant EMIS stakeholders on board.** Before designing the procurement process, hold consultations with IT and EMIS staff. Insights can be gained from addressing their needs and requirements for the new software solution. They will primarily work with it, so it is important to include them in the decision-making process. In addition, the inclusion of central, regional, and local EMIS and IT staff will help reduce their aversion to change, if it exists.
- **Categorize the main data and IT challenges.** In order to understand what is required from the new software solution, it is necessary to identify and categorize common user errors, training issues, configuration challenges, network hurdles (for example, Internet connectivity challenges), and other potential obstacles to a functioning EMIS software solution. Many of these could be categorized by local IT staff and combined at the central level to paint a clear picture of where the main challenges lie.
- **Inform the public.** Generally, the funding for a new software solution stems from public taxes. Therefore, it is essential to inform the public early on (1) why a new software solution is needed, (2) what the benefits of the new software solution will be, and (3) how the procurement process will take place. The government should design a targeted communication strategy to ensure early buy-in from the public and avoid potential resistance to change from different stakeholder groups.

Designing the Request for Proposals

Once the needs and requirements of the new software solution have been identified, the next stage is to design the requests for proposals (RFPs). Some are open tenders, where all (qualified) companies are allowed to submit proposals for the EMIS solution. Others may be closed tender procedures, where only selected companies are invited to submit their proposals. Regardless of the tender type, both require governments to publish RFP documents.

The RFP documents should be well designed, detailed, and comprehensive. The RFP documents need to clearly state what exactly the government is aiming to procure in order to ensure that only appropriate tender proposals by qualified offerors will be submitted. The aim is to ensure not only that all tender proposals fit the demands and needs as stipulated by the government but also that the selecting committee is able to evaluate tender proposals across the board and compare "apples to apples" (see appendix C). The following sections should be part of any RFP:

- **The general section**: Here the government should describe the (1) scope of the contract, (2) purpose, (3) background, and (4) submittal qualifications. The aim is to provide potential vendors an overview of why the government is calling to tender and what the minimal requirements are.
- **The offer instructions**: The main purpose of this tender section is to (1) inform the offeror of how the process is structured and what is required

to submit a proposal and (2) clearly state the responsibilities of the offeror and the government. Here the government specifies the deadlines for the proposals, how long the offers remain valid, who the tender issuing office is, and the general terms and conditions for the company submitting the tender offer.

- *The program summary*: This section describes in detail what the government is looking for. First, it should start with a description of the current state of the existing EMIS and its architecture, including software, hardware, and communication systems. Second, the government should clearly specify the required implementation schedule, system performance expectation, system components, and access. Third, the government should describe the requirements for hardware installation (for example, databases), training of staff, maintenance, technical support, and the geographic area to be covered by the offeror. Fourth, the government should specify performance-based milestone requirements throughout the lifetime of the project. Fifth, the government should offer an in-depth description of the role and responsibilities of key personnel. These generally include the project manager, senior technical staff, and administrator. By doing so, the government will automatically define their roles and responsibilities throughout the project. Last, the exact timeframe of the project has to be specified.
- *The submission format*: Here the government needs to clearly describe what should be submitted as a proposal as well as how and in which format. After an executive summary, references, description of the offeror's management team, and subcontractor information, it also includes sections on the technical proposal and the price proposal. These are two essential parts of any tender offer and will need to be closely examined. The technical proposal includes how the offeror plans to design the system architecture, its proposed features, and a performance description. In addition, it should include the project approach, implementation schedule, and training structures. Moreover, licensing, maintenance, and technical support offers should be included. The price proposal includes nonrecurring and recurring fees, warranty, maintenance, and alteration pricing.
- *The general evaluation section*: In this section, the government describes the evaluation process, criteria, and basis for tender award. This is an important section that has to be included in any RFP. Not only does it allow offerors to understand how their proposal will be evaluated, but it also ensures for transparency and accountability in the award procedures. Providing this information keeps the tender procedure fair and just.
- *The general provisions*: Here, the government describes a number of important issues for the tender procedures. They range from cancellation of RFP procedures, contract award, and purchase order to tax specifications. They should also include a section on extensions, subcontracting, conflict of interest, price adjustments, liquidated damages, trade discounts, billing, and payment. In addition, there should be some provisions on ethics regulation, assignments, data security, and privacy.

Evaluating the Proposals

Once the RFP has been issued, the government needs to evaluate the proposals. While evaluating proposals, a good practice involves conducting product demonstrations over a period of one week, with the EMIS team inviting key education stakeholders from the central office, schools (teachers, administration), parents, and a few students to express choice and opinion about the systems. This is essential because they are the ultimate users of the system, and involving them in the process would avoid any future issues with implementation. The community, rather than one individual, should choose the final product.

The decision on which software vendor to select can be facilitated by building a matrix with weights and scores of each individual proposal. It ensures a high level of transparency in the software solution procurement process and makes the selection committee accountable to key stakeholders for its decision. The matrix should be based on the requirements stipulated in the RFP and designed accordingly, However, there are also other important questions that need to be taken into consideration when assessing tender proposals. Table 5.4 highlights some of the broad features that are important to keep in mind when choosing a vendor.

Securing the Contract

After all proposals have been evaluated, the government should decide on one vendor and move to secure the contract. It is common that the

Table 5.4 Key Factors to Keep in Mind While Evaluating Proposals

Area to consider	Checklist
System architecture	• Does the technical design of the software and hardware fit the system requirements? • Is the vendor able to support the overall goals of EMIS and deliver appropriate training, administrative support, and upgrades, as and when needed?
Functionality	• Are the functions, features, and benefits of the software/hardware appropriate and tailored to the abilities of the different user groups? • Do these features enable stakeholders to achieve a higher performance level? • Can the system be integrated with the already existing systems?
Adaptability of the system	• Are the new software system and data architecture compatible with the existing structure? • Is the new software solution adaptable and flexible? • Is the system receptive to improvements, upgrades, and expansion, as needed?
Costs	• What is the basic cost per system structure (recurring and one-time payments)? Recurring costs are instrumental and can be the deciding factor between success and failure of a software solution. • Are there any additional costs not covered in the base price (for example, additional training or support services)? • Are the costs in line with the five-year strategic plan for the EMIS?
Licensing	• What are the licensing costs? • What is the licensing arrangement? • What will happen after the end of the project?
Maintenance	• How will the vendor maintain the software solution? • What is included under "basic" maintenance, and what would be additional costs? • What are the stipulated maintenance costs, and what do they include?

table continues next page

Table 5.4 Key Factors to Keep in Mind While Evaluating Proposals *(continued)*

Area to consider	Checklist
Vendor	• What is the track record of the vendor? • How good is the financial strength of the vendor? • Have there been any leadership, corruption, financial, or other challenges in the past?
Management team of the vendor	• How strong is the technical and managerial expertise of the managing team? • Does the team have a proven success record with similar projects?
Customer support	• How strong is the vendor's proposal in the area of customer support for the government, IT, and EMIS units? • Does customer support include questions and additional training sessions, if necessary? • Is ad hoc customer support available in case of system failure or pressing questions by IT staff?
Risks	• What is the likelihood that the new system would fail to work effectively? • What is the likelihood that the new system would fail to meet the education data needs? • How high is the risk of ineffective vendor support?

government shortlists a few offerors and invites them to present their proposals in person. This allows the government to receive a more comprehensive view of each of the shortlisted proposals and aids in its deliberation. The principles of evaluation remain the same, and the evaluation of the tender proposals must remain fair and just. Once the correct vendor has been identified, procurement procedures can progress into the final stage, which finalizes the contract. The vendor will be held by its original tender offer, and the contract should be based on it.

Notes

1. Fiji has a dual data collection system (digital and paper-based). Please refer to chapter 9 for additional information.

2. For an example, see A2C Medical's website at http://a2cmedical.com.

3. FEMIS has since undergone substantial changes and is continuously upgraded, improved, and expanded (refer to chapter 9).

4. Information in this section is from the OpenSIS website, http://www.opensis.com/.

5. Information in this section is from the Capita website, http://www.capita-sims.co.uk /why-sims.

6. Information in this section is from the Sentral website, https://www.sentral.com.au/.

7. For more information about OpenEMIS and its use in different systems, see https:// www.openemis.org/.

8. Information in this section is from the os4ed website, http://www.os4ed.com.

9. For more information about CSPro, see the U.S. Census Bureau website at https:// www.census.gov/population/international/software/cspro/index.html.

10. Information in this section is from the Open Data Kit website, https://opendatakit.org.

11. For more information about FHI 360 in Liberia, see https://www.fhi360.org/projects /liberia-teacher-training-program-ii-lttp-ii.

12. Information in this section is from the Blaise website, http://blaise.com.

13. Information in this section is from the MySQL website, https://www.mysql.com/.

14. Information in this section is from the VoltDB website, https://www.voltdb.com/.

15. Information in this section is from the PostgreSQL website, https://www.postgresql.org/.

16. Information in this section is from the H$_2$O website, http://www.h2o.ai/.

17. Information in this section on Haven is from the HP website, https://www.hpe.com/us/en/home.html.

18. Information in this section is from the Actian website, http://esd.actian.com/.

19. Information in this section is from the PredictionIO website, http://predictionio.incubator.apache.org/.

20. Information in this section is from the Piwik website, https://piwik.org/.

21. Information in this section is from the Open Web Analytics website, http://www.openwebanalytics.com.

22. Information in this section is from the eAnalytics website, http://www.eanalytics.de/.

References

Bernbaum, Marcia, and Kurt Moses. 2011. "Education Management Information Systems: A Guide to Education Project Design, Evaluation, and Implementation Based on Experiences from EQUIP2 Projects in Malawi, Uganda, and Zambia." EQUIP2 Lessons Learned in Education, U.S. Agency for International Development, Washington, DC.

Duan, Jiaqi, Parwiz Faker, Alexander Fesak, and Tim Stuart. 2012. "Benefits and Drawbacks of Cloud-Based versus Traditional ERP Systems." Proceedings of the 2012–13 Course on Advanced Resource Planning, December. http://www.academia.edu/2777755/Benefits_and_Drawbacks_of_Cloud-Based_versus_Traditional_ERP_Systems.

Howard County Public School System. 2015. "Integrated Systems for HCPSS." Presentation delivered to World Bank by Grace Chesney and Justin Benedict, April 2015.

IBM. 2005. "VPN Security and Implementation." IBM Systems and Technology Group.

Linn, Robert. 2003. "Accountability: Responsibility and Reasonable Expectations." *Educational Researcher* 32 (7): 3–13.

Shaw, Arthur, Lena Nguyen, Ulrike Nischan, and Herschel Sy. "Comparative Assessment of Software Programs for the Development of Computer-Assisted Personal Interview (CAPI) Applications." IRIS Center, University of Maryland.

Trucano, Michael. 2014. "Using Mobile Phones to Collect Data in the Education Sector in Uganda." *World Bank EduTech Blog*, April 22. http://blogs.worldbank.org/edutech/using-mobile-phones-collect-data-education-sector-uganda.

UNESCO (United Nations Educational, Scientific, and Cultural Organization). 2013. "Free and Open Source Software, Open Data, and Open Standards in the Caribbean: Situation Review and Recommendations." UNESCO, Paris.

———. 2015. "Using ICT in Policy Planning and Management for Lifelong Learning." *ICT in Education*, October.

World Bank. 2015. "Samoa EMIS Country Report." World Bank, Washington, DC.

CHAPTER 6

Integration of Databases for Decision Making to Improve Learning Outcomes

Key Takeaways

- Data integration requires strategy, standards, collaboration, and systematic data flow to maximize the value of data toward tangible interventions and results in relation to student learning and improvements.
- Learning data need to be added to data on demographics, teachers, schools, and inputs to get the full story.
- Unique identification for schools, teachers, and students should be based on (existing) national identification systems and policies spanning different sectors and ministries. It enables governments to track progress of individuals throughout their academic experience and allows for tracer studies based on longitudinal databases. This may reap substantial integration and benefits and insights into policy making especially in relation to learning outcomes.
- This should be institutionalized through a strong legal framework and policies with (1) data privacy protection provisions and (2) clear allocation of responsibilities and budget to ensure sustainability, efficiency, and accountability.
- Governments should choose between different methodologies/technologies (for example, paper-based, digital, biometric) to find the best fit for their country-specific context.
- Data protection, security, and privacy provisions include a modern cybersecurity architecture, security training for employees, and appropriate data collection and storage rules. The aim is to eliminate the risk of data breaches.

A fully functioning education management information system (EMIS) tracks schools and students and integrates information from different sources (demographics, financials, instructional, personnel, support, resources, and so on) in order to harness the power of data and benefit the system, especially student learning. Good command of data promises big payoffs in student achievement and school success, which are what authentic data-driven decision making implies (Massell 2001; Serim 2003; Streifer 2002). As data use increases, so will the demand to manage different types of data. For that, data on student learning—generated from classroom assessments, standardized tests, and performance and portfolio-type assessments—need to be integrated with other student, teacher, and school data including financing information. The focus could be on patterns of individual student growth over time as well as proportions of student groups meeting standards (Sanders and Horn 1994; Seltzer, Choi, and Thum 2003). Inferences drawn from the data are affected by the scores and variables used and how they are analyzed (Seltzer, Frank, and Bryk 1994; Wainer, Hambleton, and Meara 1999). The answers data provide are also strongly influenced by the questions asked. Countries must develop sophisticated strategies for recording, integrating and analyzing assessment data.

Unique identifications (IDs) for students, teachers, schools, and courses facilitate data collection from different databases and data management. With unique IDs, it is easier to track education users and providers and measure progress over time. It allows the education system to integrate and link data that cover all aspects of the education system and provide important information on the relationships that exist between different actors and services. Even the performance of students who move within the education system (for example, by moving to different schools) or graduate from one education cycle to the next (including courses, behaviors, grades, exams, and so on) can be tracked. This applies to teachers as well as students. For instance, linking teachers' qualifications to students' test results offers insights into learning outcomes for students. Schools need to be included in the system to extrapolate their overall performance. It may also offer information on how a school's performance impacts teacher or student attendance and performance. For instance, there may exist a connection between poor average school performance and the level of teacher qualification or experience schools can attract.

The issue of integration needs to be on the agenda for the education data oversight commissions that in general would coordinate the integration process—regulating and overseeing its implementation—and recommend policy, planning, and investment decisions. These commissions will also work on developing common data standards, data collection guidelines, data flows, and data management practices.

In many developing countries, the foundational challenge to integrating data to the student level is establishing and using unique IDs to track students, teachers, and schools. In order to accomplish proper tracking and integration there is a need for a systematic identification. Many countries have a sort of identification, but many do not use it in education. With nationwide unique identification (UID) systems, as opposed to local identification, schools, students, and teachers can be tracked and supported more efficiently and effectively. In fact, without a tracking system within the EMIS, the opportunity to collect a deeper layer of student learning data will be missed. When UIDs capture relevant information about students, teachers and schools, government, parents, teachers, and students can make informed decisions based on more complete and integrated quality data. Use of such data in the classroom for instructional gains, for example, is expanding. Teachers are able to make use of additional data that might otherwise have been lost in the system. The UID also allows the EMIS to follow students throughout their academic journey and gather important longitudinal information. The more sophisticated the tracking process, the more information can be obtained and used.

Importance and Benefits of Establishing a UID System as Part of the EMIS

UID systems allow for longitudinal research and analysis and can provide important insights on the evolution of academic paths contributing toward the achievement of education goals. In order to achieve education goals, schools and policy makers must trace the links between schools, teachers, and students. Which schools or teachers are in need of more support? Which teachers are achieving good student outcomes? How are students progressing in the different grades and going on to university then to work? Who is dropping out of school, and what are they doing after? Who are the students with special needs, and what's their progress? Are graduates working in their fields of study? Which majors or specialties are not achieving the intended results in the workforce, and how is that related to the curriculum taught at schools? All are crucial questions with serious policy implications. A UID system is key to help answer such questions and establish the links for better targeting and tracking results (figure 6.1).

Different countries have used identification to track students in many ways: (1) simplifying procedures for seeking school admission; (2) establishing mechanisms to verify entitlements such as scholarships and grants; (3) tracking attendance, dropout rates, transitions, and transfer to different schools; (4) tracking the education history of a student over his or her life span; (5) monitoring employment status after school completion; (6) preventing misuse of data by identifying ghost students or teachers; and, most important, (7) monitoring student learning and designing interventions that cater to improving the academic performance of weak students. The aim is to establish a longitudinal tracking system that is able to follow students through all education cycles up to entering the workforce. Similarly, for teachers, identification is used to track data about teacher demographics such as age, gender, academic and professional qualifications, and salaries and payroll transactions. The system also monitors teacher training activities and completion of professional development courses designed for them. The UID system can also be useful to track information about schools, such as (1) management of financial and material resources, (2) asset and financial allocation, (3) civil works, and (4) recruitment of staff.

UID systems have been shown to add financial efficiency. Tracking students makes it easier to plan for resource allocation and financing of schools. Grants and scholarships can be delivered on the basis of the UID system, which can supply information on schools (for example, enrollment rates in real time).

Figure 6.1 Unique IDs Help Integration of Different Data Points to Monitor Quality of Education

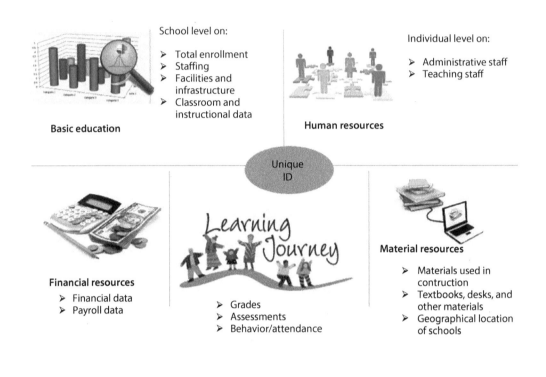

This allows for a higher level of accuracy and also flexibility in the planning process as opposed to relying on a single annual school census that provides only a snapshot of the education system. In addition, UID systems allow for more efficiency in the transferring of transcripts and report cards between schools.

Data quality can also be improved with UID systems. UIDs ensure that all records of the student are correctly identified and related. Students go through a variety of different schools and education cycles until they enter the workforce. Similarly, teachers are likely to move between schools, and without a UID the data on their movements within the education system will be substantially harder to track. A UID system links all of a student's or teacher's records and provides information on his or her academic career. Overall, it improves the accuracy, reliability, and usability of data. It also allows for better tracking and deters corruption (for example, ghost students, teachers, and schools). In Africa, Ghana is often regarded as a model country in terms of UID use (box 6.1).

The expansion of national ID systems could directly benefit education enrollment and completion. Often the key factor of primary and secondary education enrollment is the birth certificate, which is the first proof of identity and is used by school officials for registration purposes. Without a birth certificate children are often barred from receiving school certificates and diplomas because these require valid identification. This deters children from advancing in their academic career. Moreover, if a child wishes to transfer between schools, the lack of a birth certificate or another form of ID can become a true obstacle in the process.

This is why special attention should be paid to birth registration because it is often the first step toward identification. Box 6.2 highlights different examples of how birth and civil registration is conducted and incentivized in Latin America.

The lack of birth registration may jeopardize a child's educational success. An extensive survey conducted by the Inter-American Development Bank (IDB) in Bolivia, Brazil, the Dominican Republic, Guatemala, and Peru reveals that the enrollment rates of children without birth certificates tend to be lower than those of their counterparts with birth certificates (Brito, Corbacho, and Osorio 2013). Table 6.1 illustrates an overview of the results of the study. Children without

---

Box 6.1 Use of UIDs in Ghana

Ghana has built a system in which children are issued UIDs at the age of six. The UIDs are used to track students from primary school to college. The information translates into enrollment numbers, which are then used to allocate resources, infrastructure development, and policy intervention. The system may serve as an example for other countries in West Africa. The Ghanaian authorities explain the importance of the UID on their website:

> The PIN of your child will be captured during enrolment into primary school and this number will be used for admission into every level until the child completes tertiary education. This will help in tracking the progress of your child in the educational sector for necessary policy interventions. It will prevent your being replaced by unqualified ones by some school authorities during admission. Students who qualify for student's loan can use the Ghanacard to establish their identities to eliminate fraud. Data from the NIA [National Identification Authority] database will enable the Ministry of Education [to] plan effectively for the provision of targeted educational infrastructure and other resources for your community.

Source: eServices, Services Portal of the Government of Ghana (accessed November 13, 2016), http://www.eservices.gov.gh /NIA/SitePages/NIA-AreaOfInterest.aspx.

Box 6.2 Examples of Identification and Birth Registration in Latin America

In many Latin American countries, birth registration and identification for newborn children have made tremendous progress in the past decades. Although an estimated 230 million children are still unregistered worldwide, the percentage of unregistered children has dropped from 18 percent in 2006 to 10 percent in 2010 in Latin America and the Caribbean (ECLAC UNICEF 2011).

One of the model countries in terms of registration is Chile, where the UID is needed to access all public services. The UID system is fully institutionalized and integrated into the different databases across all ministries and is protected by data privacy laws and

box continues next page

Box 6.2 Examples of Identification and Birth Registration in Latin America *(continued)*

appropriate data protection software. Similarly, Colombia and Ecuador have established a comprehensive ID system for children and adults. The UID will be used as a tracker across all ministry databases (IDB 2014, 2016).

The IDB has conducted about 62 projects in relation to civil registration in the region over the past two decades. Often services are linked to the registration of children and have been designed to incentivize their identification. For instance, in Uruguay, the government introduced the *Plan Ceibal*, a national "one laptop per child" project in 2009. Because laptops were distributed only to registered students, the project had an interesting side effect of allowing the country to discover several thousand unregistered children. These children were registered and included in the project, and their families received social services and support.

Uruguay also made strides in facilitating the birth registration process. With the support of the IDB, Uruguay implemented a birth registration system, taking advantage of the fact that a large percentage of births take place at hospitals. Once a baby is born, doctors send the certificate of live birth to the National Bureau of Civil Records online and the newborn is assigned a UID number, which is then sent to the hospital and the Civil Registry to be included in the birth certificate. Before infants leave the hospital, they are issued a birth certificate, national ID (valid for the rest of their lives), and a picture ID with biometric credentials. This registration process significantly reduced trafficking of children; because children were fully identifiable, traffickers refrained from abducting them (IDB 2011).

Table 6.1 Relationship between Education and the Lack of a Birth Certificate

	School enrollment	Access to primary education	Finishing primary school	Access to secondary education	Years of completed schooling
Bolivia	−0.25	−0.25	−0.11	−0.1	−0.4
Brazil	−0.17	−0.11	—	−0.15	−0.58
Dominican Republic	−0.08	−0.05	−0.25	−0.18	−0.61
Guatemala	−0.06	−0.1	−0.15	−0.12	−0.42
Peru	−0.1	—	—	—	−0.36

Source: Brito, Corbacho, and Osorio 2013.
Note: These results represent the marginal effects evaluated in the averages of some variables of the econometric analysis presented in Brito, Corbacho, and Osorio 2013. — = not available.

birth registration are often from disadvantaged backgrounds and associated with other basic conditions that affect student outcomes. These factors include access to running water, six or more children in the household, the mother's years of education, the mother's marital status, household wealth, gender, and living in rural areas. Although the study does not establish a causal relationship between the lack of birth registration and educational attainment, a negative correlation persists when controlling for other factors.

National Policies Are the Foundation for the Success of a UID System

Existing national policies and frameworks for a national ID lay the foundation for UID systems in the education sector. Without a national policy on identification it is difficult to implement a strong UID system in education. Studies show that the lack of national IDs, in particular birth registration, can have tremendous consequences for a child's educational development. Over the past decades, countries all over the world have extended their efforts to provide UIDs to their citizens (figure 6.2). A robust identity system involves capturing the unique identity of each individual in a national identity registry. A national registry can then be used across sectors—from education and health care to transportation and urban development—for the delivery of services, both public and private.

A strong legal framework is crucial to ensure sustainability and accountability of a UID system. The legal framework can define the scope of the tracking system and enable the implementation of a UID system, and the government must determine the types of information to be tracked and the uses of the UID system. For instance, the national UID is required for voting, opening bank accounts, or receiving state subsidies in Peru. The information generated from the UID system

Figure 6.2 Civil Registration and Identification Trends, 1960–2014

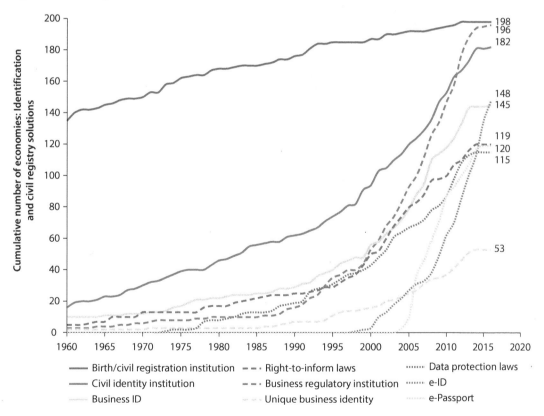

Source: World Bank 2015a.

guides the government in allocating resources, assigning roles and responsibilities within the education system, and beyond. The UID system needs to be fully embedded within the institutions to fulfill its functionality. This includes not only specific laws upholding the legal framework but also a clear assignment of responsibilities. Box 6.3 shows the uses of the national ID in Thailand.

The enabling environment for UID systems starts with an assessment of the existing ID system and its potential for expansion into other sectors such as the education system. It starts with an assessment of the existing norms and practices of national ID systems. Then decision makers have to take the technological and infrastructure capacities into consideration before expanding the existing national ID system toward education. For instance, some countries may find it easier to link education IDs to national birth and marriage registries, whereas others may prefer biometrics-based IDs, which do not require citizens to carry a formal piece of identification. Many national ID programs issue ID cards with a chip containing biometric information to verify a person's identity (box 6.4).

In many countries, UIDs for citizens already exist but are not yet used in the education sector. There is tremendous potential for longitudinal tracking by linking the existing IDs with data collection. For instance, Indian children are enrolled in the Aadhaar program at the age of five, which enables the system to track education enrollment numbers. However, the UIDs are not yet linked to a well-functioning EMIS. Doing so would provide valuable information beyond

---

Box 6.3 A Strong Legal Framework Holds Potential for Expansion into the Education Sector

In Thailand, the national civil registration database is established and maintained by the National Civil Registration Office, Ministry of Interior (MoI). By law, this office is responsible for registering all births, deaths, marriages, divorces, and migrations. A unique 13-digit ID number is generated for each Thai citizen at the time his or her birth and is registered in the national civil registration database. National ID cards are issued to citizens when they reach the age of seven years. This national ID number is already used by health care providers to verify eligibility, track delivered services, settle claims, and build a shared medical record for each patient. The use of the national ID numbers has led to improvements in the efficiency and transparency of the national social health protection system's management, as well as prevented misuse of public resources.

The system should now aim to extend into the education sector. The Thai government has already built a strong data foundation by requiring all Thai citizens to be registered. Schools need to be integrated into an EMIS process, which has the potential to track students' performance and extract data on their learning outcomes. In addition, the Thai government can implement a teacher-specific EMIS that tracks their professional development throughout their careers. By doing so it may be easier to improve students' learning and teachers' performance.

Source: ILO 2015.

---

simple enrollment numbers. Some countries have introduced pilot projects bridging the gap between adult and child identification as well as national UID systems with the education sector (box 6.5).

International organizations such as the World Bank have initiated projects to develop, maintain, or expand ID systems around the globe. Across different global practices such as health, social protection, finance and markets, and so on, World Bank projects have activities related to information systems. Only recently has the Identification for Development (ID4D) initiative materialized as the first step toward harmonizing various cross-practice projects. The ID4D initiative aims to bring different units of the World Bank under one umbrella to achieve the objective of providing a unique legal identity and enable digital ID–based services to all (box 6.6). Providing a legal identity for all (including birth registration) by 2030 is a target shared by the international community as part of the Sustainable Development Goals (SDGs). The examples in table 6.2 illustrate

---

Box 6.4 Example of a UID System in a Strong National Registry Context

Estonia uses a sophisticated civil registration system with a digital system issuing a chip-based ID card with a photograph. This mechanism works well in a developed country with a strong education system, where people are familiar with online services and civil registry is developed. It suffices as a source of data for the education system because it has been well institutionalized and well established. Recently, Estonia has launched a comprehensive website enabling citizens to access personal data and perform many civil rights such as voting, founding a business, or pay taxes.

With regard to education, each student has an individual account that not only records comprehensive academic data, including grades and assessment scores, but also provides an overview of the teaching plan for individual lessons and homework assignments. It also incorporates information on individual teachers and provides detailed attendance records. Parents have access to their child's records and can be notified by text message if their child misses a class. All aspects of academia are captured through the website, and students are tracked throughout their academic career.

Source: e-Estonia, https://e-estonia.com.

Box 6.5 Pilot Studies to Enable Access to Public Services for the Poor

In Guinea, the World Bank introduced a 7,000-household pilot study, which captured data of approximately 42,000 people with unique biometric IDs. These were then used to enable cash transfers that recipients primarily used to pay for food and education. The UIDs were issued in four rural communities struggling with high malnutrition and school dropout rates.

Source: World Bank 2016a.

Box 6.6 Identification for Development

The Identification for Development (ID4D) initiative by the World Bank aims to provide access to services to all citizens in developing countries, in particular the poor. It has been estimated that approximately 1.5 billion people are unable to prove their identity. The majority of them live in Asia or Africa, and a large proportion of citizens without any identification are children and women. Identification is essential in accessing many education, health care, financial, social welfare, economic, and other services. The ability to vote also depends on the ability to identify yourself. It is apparent how crucial identification is to development.

ID4D supports government in adopting new technological means (for example, digital or biometric ID systems) to expand their identification efforts and achieve the Sustainable Development Goal of providing identification to all (including birth registration) by 2030. The ID4D initiative is a collaboration with different international partners, donors, and governments to ensure a broad reach and provide financial technical support to low- and middle-income countries. The World Bank leverages its own expertise and resources to

- Assess a country's ID system and provide recommendations.
- Design an identification model.
- Develop a legal and regulatory framework to support national UID systems.
- Ensure appropriate technological standards and interoperability.
- Promote advocacy and awareness.
- Implement monitoring and evaluation mechanisms.
- Provide finance to establish the identification system infrastructure and streamline the process.

Source: World Bank 2015a.

Table 6.2 Key Facts on Selected Country Examples

Estonia	India
Governing body: Citizen and Migration Board, Ministry of Internal Affairs	**Governing body:** Unique Identification Authority of India (UIDAI), under Planning Commission of India
Registration type: Civil registration	**Registration type:** Biometrics (10 fingerprints and iris)
Credential: Identity card with a photograph and chip for security purposes	**Credential:** a 12-digit unique ID number called Aadhaar (no physical credential)
Target population: 1.3 million people	**Target population:** 1.2 billion people
Use of ID: Personal ID number	**Use of ID based on:** Aadhaar number, along with demographic, biometric, or password
Ghana	Pakistan
Governing body: National Identity Authority, within the Office of the President	**Governing body:** National Database and Registration Authority (autonomous body)
Registration type: Biometrics (fingerprints)	**Registration type:** Biometrics (fingerprints)
Credential: National Identity Card ("Ghana Card") and smart card	**Credential:** National Identity Card with a photograph, smart card, and mobile ID
Target population: 25 million people	**Target population:** 180 million people
Use of ID: National Identity Card and biometrics	**Use of ID:** Smart cards, mobile phones, and biometrics

Source: Atick et al. 2014.

the importance of ID systems in helping the bottom 40 percent of the population to have better access to job opportunities, services, and finance.

Advantages of integrated and multiuse social registries can be significant. Integrated and dynamic gateways for coordinating registration and eligibility processes for multiple social programs can reap benefits in cost reduction and efficiencies. Such efficiencies include, but are not limited to, better coordination of social policies, more effective user programs, and better citizen access. The unified social registries often combine programs across different ministries such as (1) the ministry of welfare or social services for cash transfers, social programs, and pensions; (2) the ministry of energy for tariffs on energy consumption; (3) the ministry of health for health insurance cards; (4) the ministry of education for vouchers for distribution of education materials and training; (5) the ministry of finance for programs to support financial inclusion; (6) the ministry of justice for pro bono legal services; and (7) municipal governments and services for childcare programs. By integrating information from diverse sources—including self-reported information from citizens, administrative information, geospatial information, and integrated data from their beneficiary registries—the unified registries can provide policy makers and the community with information on social benefits. Policy makers are also able to use this information to identify target groups for assistance in education and other public service areas. Figure 6.3 illustrates the number of national programs using a common social registry in select countries.

National ID policies can also help to identify and provide necessary support for marginalized and/or disadvantaged groups because access to identification is

Figure 6.3 Number of Programs Using Common Social Registry, Select Countries

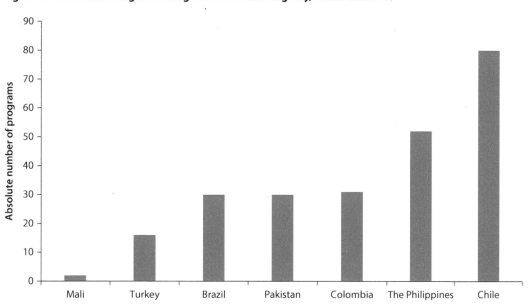

Source: George and Lindert 2016.

generally more challenging for them. UID systems, enabled by modern technological capabilities and infrastructure, can help to identify and provide targeted support to these populations. For instance, for illiterate citizens, there is considerable potential for identification based on biometrics. Many countries have started pilot studies directed at including poor communities (often in rural areas) into national registries and thus allowing them to access public services (box 6.7).

In the field of building information systems, it is important to coordinate among sectors, in particular education. Working in silos brings negative consequences, misalignments, and sustainability issues that have led to failures, missed opportunities, and increased expenditures because funding these systems tends to be expensive. Breaking silos and helping stakeholders to see their contributions to particular goals in an integrated manner is important toward achieving the SDGs. Education often remains outside of national ID programs, which causes substantial loss of important information and lost efficiencies. Often the first step toward student UID systems is the inclusion of children in the national registry, which then offers opportunities and possibilities for expansion (box 6.8).

Table 6.3 provides an overview of which points should be addressed in the process of institutionalizing a UID system. There are several legal questions that need to be addressed to ensure there is no conflict with the existing legal framework. Within the expanded (or new) legal framework, questions as to who,

---

Box 6.7 Examples of National ID Initiatives Targeting the Poor

In Costa Rica, universal health coverage is provided to all poor citizens, who are identified using the national identity card number. When an individual seeks services in a health center, the EBAIS (*Equipos Básicos de Atención Integral en Salud*, or Basic Teams of Global Health Care) can identify individuals according to socioeconomic status through a household survey that the EBAIS team administers and that has 267 variables including health and risk factors. The health center will confirm the information and visit and interview the household before formally enrolling the individual. The identification of the individual is based on the national identity card number and a social security beneficiary card that contains this and other information relevant for administrative purposes (that is, type of beneficiary, employer, work address, and so forth) (Montenegro Torres 2013).

In 2006, the Arab Republic of Egypt implemented a smart card system for its subsidized food program that now covers three-fourths of its population. The Ministry of State for Administrative Development (MSAD) maintains the registry of the individual members of families that have a "family card," which entitles them to receive subsidized food under a program run by another ministry. The same card is used for social assistance payments from a third ministry. The transaction information flows to the MSAD and is then accessible to the other two ministries that use the information to allocate cash and food, respectively, and to track their transactions. Although there are different points of transaction—food shops and post offices for cash—the transaction process and the back-end information system are the same (World Bank 2015a).

Box 6.8 Including Children in the National Registry Is the First Step

In Peru in 2014, more than 96 percent of children were issued a national identification card (DNI) and registered in the National Registry of Identification and Civil Status (RENIEC) system compared to only 2 percent in 2004. In 1995, Peru passed legislation that created RENIEC, a consolidated, single-purpose agency. At that time, it was solely for Peru's adult population and was responsible for both civil registry and national IDs. The ID number is generated for adults, and uniqueness is ensured using biometrics. The ID number is now used for the vast majority of public and private transactions—from voting to opening bank accounts—and is also used for social programs such as cash transfers and social insurance.

In the last decade, efforts to identify children through RENIEC had important implications for the delivery of certain social programs, such as World Bank–supported nutrition programs for young children. Evaluations suggest that issuance of DNIs had a positive impact on identifying beneficiaries, reducing identification costs, and providing targeted support through the Families Targeting System (SISFHO), the National Direct Support to the Poorest (Juntos) Program, and Social Health Insurance (ESSALUD) (RENIEC 2013).

In 2013, the government of Peru received an award from the United Nations Children's Fund (UNICEF) for its efforts to include children from marginalized urban groups and Amazonian and Andean communities into RENIEC. The award was based on the right to identity, but now the ID system should extend to education. RENIEC data has tremendous potential to gear the education system toward a data-driven culture (UNICEF 2013).

Table 6.3 Institutionalization of UID Systems

Subject task	Goal	Questions to ask
Legal authority	Investigate if there are any legal obstacles to establishing a UID system	• Does the government have the necessary authority to implement every task under the UID program proposition? • What are the boundaries of authority in terms of collecting, storing, archiving, accessing, using, disposing of, and modifying identity data? • Is paper identity equal to electronic identity in legal terms? • Which authorities are allowed to collect which data and when? • What are the legal protections for authentication?
Protection of rights	Establish a legal framework to secure the confidence of the population	• Are there laws, regulations and/or guidelines on: – Privacy rights? – Data rights and ownership? – Antidiscrimination? – Antisurveillance? – Recourse for abuse?
Pro-UID policies	Leverage enabling policies to promote UID systems	• Will there be official recognition of the new UID as a new legal category (especially digital IDs)? • Will the new UID allow for the use of signatures (including digital signatures)? • Is the UID established as a trusted platform for interaction between citizens and governments, including in commerce? • Are long-term development polices (for example, ICT inclusion in UIDs) in place?

Source: Adapted from World Bank 2016a.
Note: ICT = information and communication technology; UID = unique identification.

what, when, and how in terms of data collection, storage, security, confidentiality, retrieval, and access should be clearly answered.

The structure of the ID system differs across countries, which impacts the decision on which data source to select. Countries have chosen different paths toward a national registry determining the source for the UID system in education. The data for the national registry usually stem from civil registration (records of births, marriages, and deaths) or a separate identity enrollment scheme. Through the national identity registry, data on education, social protection, and health can be obtained (figure 6.4). There are many variations to how and what data countries track.

UID programs could be fully integrated into a national UID index. A national UID system equips all citizens with a UID and captures their data in a secure database. Some UID systems enroll citizens when they are born (for example, Uruguay) or when they legally become of age. The main aspect is that the national UID index tracks all citizens throughout their (adult) life and grants them access to important public services. Often access to education, health care, and social welfare programs; voting rights; and financial inclusion are dependent on national identification. In some countries such as Chile almost all public services require the individual to present his or her UID number.

Without a UID in these countries, the individual would lose the opportunity to access any public services. To encourage full integration into the national ID system, all public service sectors (including education) may benefit from being included in the national identification index. This means that many programs targeting a subsection of the population should also require registration in the national identification index as a prerequisite. Measures to avoid duplication of entries are also important. Figure 6.5 provides an example of how such a system could be constructed.

Figure 6.4 Potential of Identification Systems to Improve Service Delivery

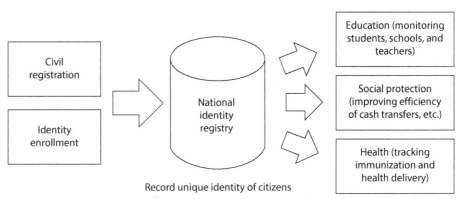

Source: World Bank 2015b.

Figure 6.5 Example of How a Single UID System Can Be Established

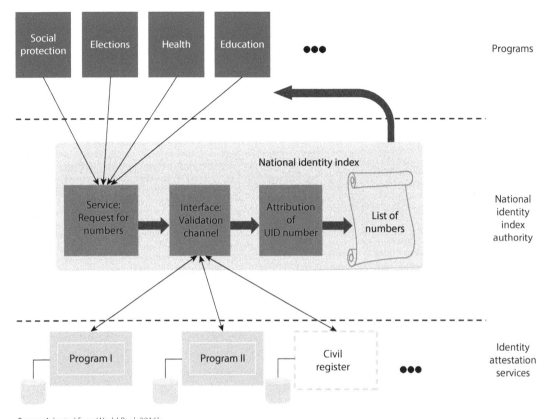

Source: Adapted from World Bank 2016b.
Note: UID = unique identification.

How Is It Done, and What Is the Role of Technology?

Modern technology opens up new possibilities for national UID systems to move beyond traditional paper-based systems (table 6.4). Electronic and digital IDs have become the norm in many countries. Other countries have also expanded into biometric ID systems made possible and even cost-efficient by advanced technologies. For instance, the Indian biometric ID system costs only about US$1 per person and provides immense overall financial benefits (The Hindu 2010).

The success of a UID system is often determined by efficient and sustainable resource allocation, which needs to be taken into consideration before deciding on which technology to employ for UID systems. The decision on which technology to use should be linked to financial capabilities. Some technologies such as biometrics may induce higher up-front costs but reap benefits in the long term. As in any long-term project, financial, administrative, and human resources in the short, medium, and long term are required to ensure the project's success. In the initial phase, resources will be needed for planning and implementation of the UIDs, whereas in the medium to long term the focus should lie on system

Table 6.4 Types of ID Technology

ID technology	Opportunities	Challenges
Paper-based	Paper-based systems are generally easy to establish and require relatively little upfront investment.	It is more challenging to record and track citizens through a paper-based system. Often citizens lose their paper ID or are unable to register in the first place. For instance, often children born in rural areas are not registered at birth because of geographic deterrence.
Electronic/digital	This allows for a general database, where all necessary information is stored. It is often linked to physical IDs, which are equipped with electronic chips storing digital information such as on biometric indicators (for example, fingerprints).	There are general privacy and security concerns. In particular, with online databases, cyber information stealth may occur. Information such as UIDs needs to be protected from third parties and should be handled with care.
Biometric	Biometrics are solely based on physical attributes, which means that citizens do not have to carry any piece of identification. This is particularly important in countries where the poor do not have access to formal IDs.	It requires upfront capital investment into the biometric technology, but economies of scale can be achieved and there is tremendous long-term potential. However, there are often data privacy concerns because the IDs are often centralized in one data warehouse.

improvements and sustainability. Only if the UID system is functional in the long term can longitudinal information on students, teachers, and schools be harnessed.

Modern technology and development efforts have drastically improved and expanded UID systems for low-income countries. This is why modern technology and privacy policies are instrumental components in any UID system. The UID needs to be adapted to the technological capabilities of the specific country context. Countries with highly institutionalized civil registration systems may extend these for UIDs in the education system. Other countries may make use of biometric identification technology to implement UIDs in the education system (box 6.9). Both systems should be connected to a data collection system using an appropriate technology.

To effectively build, store, and use a digital identification system with biometrics, a number of steps need to be taken. Figure 6.6 demonstrates a sample of necessary steps toward establishing a sustainable biometric digital identification solution. Biometrics are often used in countries with weaker institutional structure of civil registry or other ID systems. There are many benefits to biometric UID systems, but they also come with risks. First, the capture of personal data requires strong governance and management provisions by the central government. Second, it often requires a lot of up-front investment to acquire the technology and build the system. Third, there is high demand for technical capacity within the managing agency to cope with the requirements of the system.

Box 6.9 India's Biometric UID System: Aadhaar

India's biometric system, Aadhaar, uses fingerprints and iris scans to issue a unique 12-digit number (Atick et al. 2014). When Aadhaar launched, 70 percent of the population (approximately 910 million people) were not registered and did not possess a valid ID. Most of the unregistered were poor, living in rural areas, and surviving on less than US$2 per day. Today 1.2 billion are registered, and 700,000 are newly enrolled on a daily basis with 200 million people using the service every day. Registering a person costs US$1, and the registration service is offered at public places to make it easily accessible. Today the digital IDs enable targeted cash transfers, which ensure that those who are entitled to subsidies or benefits actually receive them. For example, by implementing cash transfers to Aadhaar-linked bank accounts for the purchase of liquefied petroleum gas cylinders, realizable savings are about 11–14 percent, or US$1 billion per year when applied throughout the country. This is just one of many subsidy programs in India that are being converted to direct transfers using digital ID, impacting over US$11 billion per year (World Bank 2015b).

Figure 6.6 Building a Digital Platform for National IDs

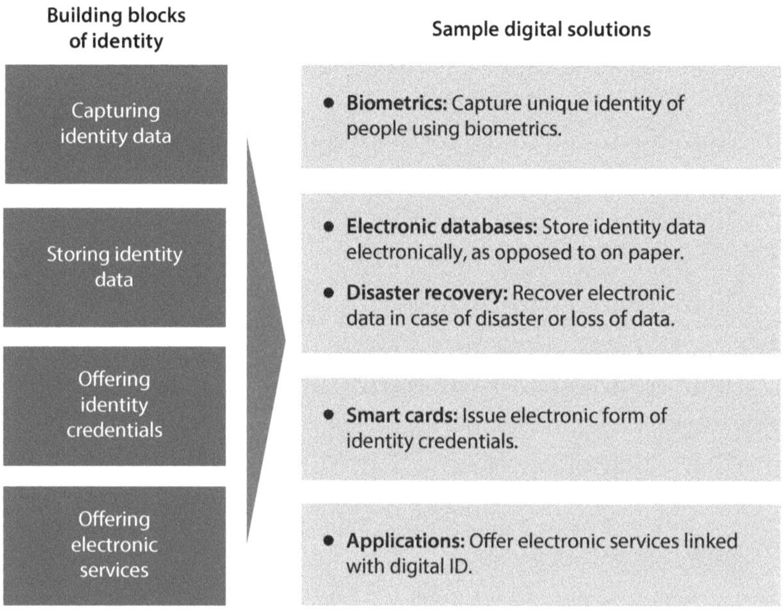

Source: World Bank 2016a.

Last, the government also needs to consider costs and capacity needs for maintenance, updates, and improvements. Countries need to be fully aware of the commitment a biometric UID system requires. If successful, it can reap many benefits and economies of scale over time. Figure 6.7 illustrates the regions in which digital identification platforms with biometrics are used.

Figure 6.7 Number of Biometric ID Systems by Region

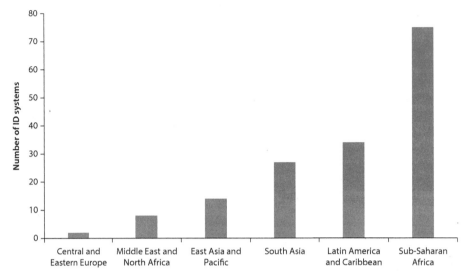

Source: World Bank 2016a.

Box 6.10 Pilot Studies of Teacher and Student IDs Linked to National UIDs in Pakistan

Pakistan's National Database and Registration Authority (NADRA) is one of the earliest agencies in a developing country to use biometrics to ensure unique ID numbers for its citizens. Established in 2000, NADRA now works closely with the Benazir Income Support Program (BISP) to ensure robust identification of the beneficiaries of the country's largest cash transfer program and has helped implement an e-payment system linked to this robust form of identification (World Bank 2015b). In 2013, NADRA conducted a school experiment in the province of Sindh, where 26,000 students and their teachers were issued smart cards. The smart cards track attendance records and have the potential to link to individual student data (Malik 2014). A countrywide application, in collaboration with the existing Child Registration Certificates (CRC) registry, an agency specifically designed for minors under the age of 18, could change the landscape of education data tracking in Pakistan. The NADRA has become a role model for many South Asian countries like Bangladesh and Nepal, and its influence can be strengthened by expanding its role (World Bank 2015b).

Biometric IDs for adults can also be converted into an ID system for children. Similarly, instead of providing UIDs to adults starting at 18 years old, the system could be expanded to children starting at school age. This, of course, requires support and initiative at the local or central government level. Pakistan has introduced a pilot project, which would integrate UID student systems into the existing national ID system (box 6.10).

Privacy and Data Protection Provisions

Privacy and security concerns have become a focal point of discussion. The UID system needs to protect the data collected from its users. Data collection, storage, and analysis have to be secure at every level. The users need to rest assured that only authorized government or school entities can use the UID. To ensure data integrity, third-party users should have access to the data only if permitted by the central or local authority. Many international organizations have started to use modern information and communication technology (ICT) in child registration with tremendous increases in efficiencies, but often there are gaps in the necessary institutional and legal framework (box 6.11).

Unique IDs capture sensitive and highly personal data, which heightens the importance of data protection, security, and privacy provisions. The question of how to successfully protect data privacy and ensure data security needs to be addressed with a holistic approach and a combination of national policies and technical provisions. It starts with understanding what data are to be collected and for what purpose. The next step is to ensure the protection of the collected data through appropriate safeguarding procedures.

National policies lie at the core of privacy and data protection. National guidelines need to follow specific guiding principles that dictate data collection, use, and protection. For this purpose, the Organisation for Economic Co-operation and Development (OECD) has published guidelines governing the protection of privacy and transborder flows of personal data. The guidelines are general and, thus, are highly applicable to education data flows. They range from what data should be collected to the protection and safeguarding of the data.

Box 6.11 Data Privacy and Information and Communication Technology in the Child Registration Process

UNICEF has started pilot projects in some countries where birth registration is done using mobile phones or tablet computers. This allows for significant decreases in the time needed to register a newborn child. For instance, in Ghana mobile phone technology enables parents to register their child within six minutes, which is a substantial increase in efficiencies compared to the average of six months that it used to take. The issue with these new processes and technology is that they are often not supported by the appropriate and necessary legal and institutional framework. There is a strong need for data protection and privacy. This is why some countries have instituted birth notification systems. In such systems, the midwife, parent, or relative can notify the registry of a birth but is not able to actually register the child. This is still done by sworn officials at the national registry level. The notification can, for instance, trigger visits of government officials to remote areas to carry out the proper registration and issue birth certificates. For instance, in Guatemala midwives in remote areas are issued a phone to notify the registration authority of any birth. There are certain codes for gender and other important identifiers. The registration office then sends the registrars to the communities to complete the registration and issue birth certificates as well as identification.

National governments should ensure that the data protection measures include all of the following principles:

- The **data collection limitation principle** specifies the scope of personal data that should be collected. The collection process should follow lawful and fair means and, where appropriate, include the consent of education stakeholders.
- The **data quality principle** ensures that the data collected are relevant to the education purpose. The data should be accurate, complete, and reliable.
- The **purpose specification principle** dictates that the purpose of data collection has to be specified at the time of collection. Clearly stating the purpose of data collection and the data's subsequent use limits data collection and analysis to fulfill exactly that purpose.
- The **use limitation principle** allows dissemination of data according to its specified purpose. The only two possible exceptions to this rule are when given (1) the consent of the data provider and (2) the authority of law.
- The **security safeguards principle** ensures that personal data are protected from risks such as unauthorized access or loss of data, destruction, misuse, or wrongful disclosure.
- The **openness principle** follows the new trend of open data, developments, and new practices. The system should specify which agency is responsible for education data, the purpose of data, and common utilization.
- The **individual participation principle** empowers individuals by (1) providing them with information on what data are collected; (2) allowing direct communication with the relevant data authorities with a reasonable timeframe, an appropriate charge, and in a format understandable to the data provider; (3) granting the right to request data with the legal possibility to challenge a potential denial; and (4) allowing them to modify or delete personal data if necessary.
- The **accountability principle** specifies the need for one data controller that is fully accountable to all previously stated principles and ensures compliance.

Incorporating all principles is necessary to ensure data protection and privacy across borders. One of the main challenges is how to secure data across national boundaries and facilitate safe and protected exchange of data. The European Union (EU) is currently in the process of establishing "a foundation for secure electronic interaction between citizens, businesses and public authorities, thereby increasing the effectiveness of public and private online services, electronic businesses and electronic commerce in the Union" (EU 2014, L 257/74). Among many other aspects, the Electronic Identification and Trust Services (eIDAS) clearly defines minimum obligations for service providers and their liabilities, which raises transparency and accountability in terms of data protection. Thus, it guarantees the trustworthiness of the service providers and their compliance with data protection laws (Rinaldi and Macrelli 2017).

One particular challenge is data breaches. Data breaches can result from careless employees failing to follow proper security procedures, outdated security measures enabling hackers to gain access to the database, or opportunistic thieves. The underlying causes of insufficient employee training, outdated security architecture, inappropriate rules governing access to personal data, data collection beyond the specified purpose, undefined retention periods, or lack of oversight can all contribute to security breaches. The security safeguards principle lies at the core of data protection guidelines, and the previously mentioned causes call for a holistic approach in data safeguarding and protection. Nevertheless, opportunistic thieves and hackers are often perceived to be the main threats to data security.

Technical data privacy and security provisions need to be designed to withstand potential cybercrime and data leaks. Among the most common threats to data privacy and protection are cybercrime attacks and data leaks. Numbers of cybercrime attacks and data breaches have risen dramatically over the past decade, so particular attention should be paid to the protection and security of sensitive, personal, and confidential data. Education data providers, for example, teachers, students, and so on, need to be confident that the data they provide are secure and protected from unauthorized access and data manipulation. Table 6.5 provides an overview of the estimated cost of cybercrime in the past several years. In addition, table 6.6 offers an overview

Table 6.5 Estimated Cost of Cybercrime

Study	Findings
CSIS and McAfee 2014	The global cost of cybercrime is estimated to fall between US$375 billion and US$575 billion, or 0.6 percent of global GDP.
Ponemon Institute 2014	The average per person cost of data breaches increased by over 15 percent in one year. For example, in India it stands at US$51, whereas in the United States it is US$201.
Symantec 2013	The global cost of cybercrime for consumers (excluding businesses) had risen by half in one year and was estimated to be about US$113 billion.
Bauer et al. 2008	The global effects of malware were about 0.5 percent of global GDP.

Source: Adapted from World Bank 2016b.

Table 6.6 Potential Cost of Cybercrime to Infrastructure Providers and Society

Market players	Direct cost	Indirect cost
Software vendors	• Security measures • Patch development and deployment	• Reputation-related revenue loss
Internet service providers, hosting providers, and registrars	• Security measures • Customer support • Abuse management • Cost of infrastructure	• Reputation-related revenue loss • Security countermeasures collateral impact
Computer emergency response team	• Investigation at the organizational level	
Law enforcement	• Law enforcement	
Society at large		• Slower ICT adaptation • Slower ICT innovation

Source: Adapted from World Bank 2016b.
Note: ICT = information and communication technology.

of direct and indirect costs of cybercrime to infrastructure providers, law enforcement agencies, and society at large.

In case of a data breach, certain steps need to be taken.

- *Step I: Uncover how, what, and where* the data breach occurred. A team of specialists (information technology [IT] and other staff) in the ministry of education should clearly identify and list how much and what data have been breached and where the data protection system failure occurred. This may be done through a thorough analysis of the data production chain and data traffic. It may be that the ministry was hacked, but the breach could also have occurred by the actions of a negligent employee. Law may require the ministry to immediately report a data breach to other government agencies.
- *Step II*: Gather a team to respond to the data breach and rectify the issue through an *action plan*. The action plan may include recovering breached data and additional external communications if required (for example, to the public).
- *Step III:* Ensure that no data breach will happen again through *prevention*. Preventive measures may include (1) potentially bringing in external specialists to enhance the data protection architecture, (2) strengthening data protection mechanisms such as the IT infrastructure, (3) training employees, and (4) updating data handling processes to make them more secure.

Modern technology brings new opportunities as well as threats in data protection and security. In the realm of cybercrime, hackers and governments race to include the latest data protection technology in their systems. This is particularly important in countries like Estonia, where almost all aspects of an individual's life are digitized, which includes highly sensitive data on health and education (box 6.12). This calls for additional data privacy and protection provisions.

Box 6.12 Modern Technology Applications to Protect Personal Data

Estonia has adapted new technology to secure personal data available on e-Estonia. The website compiles data ranging from business registry, taxes, voting, parking, academic, and health records. In fact, almost all civil society actions can be conducted through the website (except for marriage and divorce). One of the technologies the website uses is blockchain technology, which is similar to the technology that was originally developed to secure the Internet currency Bitcoin. It is sometimes also referred to as "distributed ledger technology." Once the data have been verified for accuracy, they are coded using complex cryptography. This ensures that the data cannot be changed once added to the blockchain. In fact, the technology uses duplicated ledgers across a variety of servers to ensure that all data are backed up. Therefore, if one ledger is compromised, there are multiple backup versions. This also ensures that data cannot be manipulated once entered. For instance, health records cannot be changed or academic grades manipulated. Moreover, it is a decentralized technology that

box continues next page

allows users to sign on and off from anywhere in the world with a functioning Internet connection. In order to sign on, users insert their personal ID cards into a chip reader that can be connected to any computer through a USB port and then sign on with a personalized password.

Australia also has implemented various technical and legal measures to address public concerns on privacy and to minimize the misuse of data presented through its online data platform My School. Various technical measures, such as preventing data scraping on the site, and legal measures, including copyright restrictions to prevent unauthorized use of content, aim to restrict and provide protection against the misuse of data. More specifically, to reduce the likelihood of computerized mass data gathering (for example, by web robots), My School requires users to enter an alphanumeric code via a Captcha interface and agree to the My School Terms of Use and Privacy Policy to gain access to the information on My School (OECD 2013). Although the Terms of Use and Privacy Policy documents neither prevent nor provide complete protection against the misuse of the data, they do empower the Australian Curriculum, Assessment, and Reporting Authority to litigate if data are used for commercial purposes. For more information on the development of Australia's EMIS, see chapter 8.

Source: e-Estonia, https://e-estonia.com; Williams-Grut 2016.

Examples of Successful UID Implementation in Different Economies

A Comprehensive National Identification System in Morocco

Morocco has established an extensive national ID system, which aims to cover all citizens including school-aged children starting at the age of six years. The foundation of any national ID in Morocco is the civil registry. The civil registry is the responsibility of the Ministry of Interior (MoI), but the process is highly decentralized with about 2,200 offices in different municipalities across the country recording data. The offices send sealed copies of registration documents to the MoI. The system has proven effective and raised birth registration to almost 90 percent, whereas death registration remains at about 60 percent. The robust administrative process makes it difficult to include fraudulent data, and no alterations to the registry are allowed without a court order. The birth registry is often a prerequisite for enrollment in other programs such as the National Electronic Identity (CNIE), which, in turn, is a prerequisite for medical or social security programs. Table 6.7 provides an overview of different national identification programs in Morocco.

The National Registry of Children (MASSAR) is a central database with approximately 10,000 secure access points across the country. It currently covers about 6,512,192 registered and unique students with an annual growth rate in registration of about 10 percent. The coverage of school children is 100 percent; with a primary school enrollment rate of approximately 98 percent, this means that effectively 98 percent of all primary school-aged children are covered under the MASSAR program. There are about 600,000 newly registered children each year, so that by 2024 about 12 million citizens will be covered by the program.

Table 6.7 Overview of National Identification Programs in Morocco

ID program	Registered people	Coverage of segment (%)	Description
National Electronic Identity (CNIE)	17–20 million	75–85	The CNIE has existed since 1977 and is used in every aspect of everyday adult life. It now replaces four documents: birth certificate, certificate of residence, proof of life, and certification of nationality. Citizens are registered ensuring uniqueness and issued a smart ID card, which uses state-of-the-art Automated Fingerprint Identification System (AFIS) technology. There are about 100 enrollment centers in Morocco, and the cost to citizen per enrollment is 75 dirhams.
National Registry of Children (MASSAR)	6.5 million	98	It covers all children between the ages of 6 and 18 years, who are not included in other databases. No identity card is issued, but each child receives a unique identification number for the duration of the child's schooling.
Non-contributive Medical Assistance Program (RAMED)	7.1 million	80	RAMED targets the poor and is designed to enable disadvantaged groups to benefit from health services. The RAMED database contains information on the socioeconomic condition of households, which (if eligible) are issued a RAMED identity card valid for three years. The maximum contribution for households is DH 600. The enrollment in CNIE is a prerequisite for RAMED, encouraging registration of the poor. The card itself lacks security mechanisms and may be counterfeited.
Social Security (CNSS)	3 million	85	The employer submits the application on behalf of the employee. The enrollment process is extensive and requires the CNIE, which makes the system robust. However, because spouses and children are often included in the registration of one employee, duplications often occur if a spouse or child joins the rank of an employee.

Source: World Bank 2016b.

The database infrastructure is ready for integration with other national databases, but this has not yet happened.

MASSAR issues UID numbers to children between 6 and 18 years of age who are not covered by any other national identification program in Morocco. MASSAR is an initiative undertaken by the Ministry of Education and Vocational Training (MENFP) and is institutionalized under the general overarching privacy protection law 09-08 from 2009, which covers all identification programs in Morocco. MASSAR was officially launched in 2013 with the aim of providing identification for all school-age children. The children are issued a UID number, but no identity card. The ID number will remain the same for entire duration of a child's scholastic life. Therefore, even if children transfer to a different school anywhere in the country, they can be easily tracked.

With the launch of MASSAR, the government has the opportunity to track students throughout their academic experience. It directly links individuals to their attendance, assessment, and academic performance indicators. By analyzing such data, the government can derive important policy conclusions to achieve education goals and improve student learning. The next step would be to integrate it across the MENFP and also with other government databases.

MASSAR offers many benefits to parents and students. Students and parents are able to access personal data such as transcripts and assessment scores. The system allows parents to access the timetable of their child, including attendance and examinations, and directly communicate with school staff. For instance, parents can submit appointment or certificate requests through the system. Teachers and school administrators also benefit from the communication and individual student tracking possibilities (World Bank 2016a).

Longitudinal Tracking in Florida (United States)

The State of Florida serves as an example of how to build a successful UID for students with a focus on longitudinal student tracking (see chapter 7 for further discussion). Every student is issued a unique tracking number, which is applied through the entire academic career, including tertiary education, within the state. Florida is one of the country's pioneers in collecting and tracking student-level data with the oldest longitudinal data system in the country dating back to 1995. In 2014, the Florida Department of Education (FDOE) served nearly 2.7 million students, 4,200 public schools, 28 colleges, 192,000 teachers, 47,000 college professors and administrators, and 321,000 full-time staff throughout the state. Figure 6.8 provides an overview of the structure of the longitudinal tracking system.

The UID system in Florida provides an example of a fully operational and utilized longitudinal data system. In fact, Florida's statewide longitudinal data

Figure 6.8 Example of Longitudinal Tracking

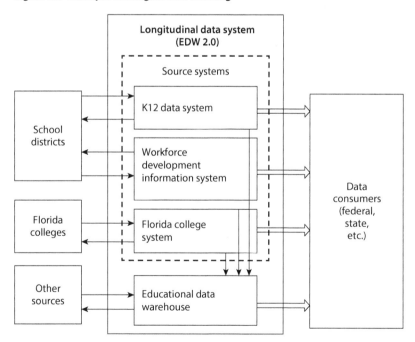

Source: FDOE, http://www.fldoe.org/accountability/data-sys/statewide-longitudinal-data-sys/.

system helped to institutionalize the EMIS in the education system, while culti-vating a data-driven culture. State educational accountability policies date back nearly 50 years, positioning Florida at the forefront of efforts to track and learn from education data (DQC 2015).

The statewide longitudinal data system tracks 2.7 million students across different education agencies and stores data in a centralized database. The cen-tralized database architecture was set up in 2003 and, more than ten years later, was ready for upgrades and enhancements. One of the most important improve-ments was the introduction of a more efficient UID system that uses a common, statewide UID as opposed to a local UID that has a cumbersome and inefficient process for tracking student movement. Many countries wishing to establish a sustainable UID system should follow Florida's model, which has established funding mechanisms that will maintain the system after the initial federal grants expire. This was supported by a strong commitment from politicians who cre-ated the appropriate state legislation to make sustainability possible. Matching of grants and ongoing funding ensure the long-term viability of the system (McQuiggan and Sapp 2014).

Student UIDs in Primary Schools in Kenya

In rural Kenya the first phase of the iMlango program has equipped 195 primary schools with UID systems for their pupils and modern technology serving approximately 150,000 children. In a country where regular teacher and student attendance is often a challenge, it is important to introduce and maintain effec-tive monitoring mechanisms. The iMlango program is designed to provide schools with an attendance monitoring system as well as Internet access via satellite to introduce students and the community to digital learning and a new digital economy.[1]

Every school is issued two Android tablets, which are used for attendance monitoring. Every day students swipe their noncontact ID cards to monitor attendance, and the data are immediately uploaded to the Android app. The app has been specifically developed for this purpose by the Kenyan company sQuid (figure 6.9). In addition, the system allows students to create an individual learn-ing platform, where they can choose between different subjects such as English, math, and life skills. After each successful completion of a new module, the student receives a medal to monitor his or her own progress. Teachers, schools, and program sponsors all use the information provided by the attendance and learning monitoring system to track their students' progress.

Generally, iMlango students come from poor and deprived communities, where many children fail to attend school regularly. Often class sizes are too big for teachers to provide sufficient support and track students' attendance and learning outcomes. Existing evidence suggests that iMlango was well received by the school community, with particularly high levels of interest and enthusiasm among stu-dents and teachers. Some teachers reported that the time needed to take roll was reduced, enabling them to focus more on instruction, and that the use of projec-tors engaged students (Ndiku and Mwai 2015). The African storybooks were

Figure 6.9 Screenshot of the sQuid Android App and Learning Center

Source: iMlango, http://www.imlango.com/index.html.

Box 6.13 Mary's iMlango Success Story

There are many success stories of the iMlango program such as the one of Mary, a student in Kenya. Mary, like many of her classmates, comes from a poor family in a single parent household. Initially, her academic performance ranged in the bottom 30–40 percent. The new technological possibilities sparked her interest so that she would come to school even over the weekends to practice and learn. iMlango tracked her academic progress through her UID and tailored exercises to her needs. Within one term, Mary was able to receive targeted support and monitor her own learning progress so that her math scores alone increased by 19 percent. Mary's teacher stated, "At first she was scared of even touching a computer, but now she can do everything on her own. She has developed an interest in eLearning and she even comes to school on the weekends to learn." Mary understands how much she has benefitted from iMlango and hopes that it will continue to help many students like her in the future. In fact, she says, "Thanks iMlango and continue to help us." Mary serves as an example of how UID can help not only in monitoring attendance but also in designing student-specific learning modules and, thus, improve learning. This demonstrates that monitoring can directly improve student progress.

Source: iMlango, http://www.imlango.com/index.html.

also popular, with students reading all 70 stories in a single month (Welch and Glennie 2016). Furthermore, with the help of iMlango, students have been able to take charge of their own attendance and learning and have made substantial progress such as the success story of Mary (box 6.13). In addition, the U.K. Department for International Development (DfID) and the Ministry of Education in Kenya have introduced financial support programs for families of children with a strong attendance record.

Pilot Studies of Student Tracking Using Aadhaar UIDs in India

The Indian state of Kerala piloted a project where students were issued Aadhaar UIDs. In 2011, in the first phase of its initiative, the Government of Kerala issued Aadhaar UIDs to 60 students. The aim was to expand the project to all 12,000 schools in the state. The initiative was then able to collect and track student data throughout their academic careers. The strength of the scheme is that it is linked to a nationwide ID system and can benefit immensely from economies of scale. The Aadhaar enrollment costs only US$1 per participant and can be done quickly almost anywhere in the country. The Aadhaar UID will remain active throughout the entire lifetime of the student.

In its first phase, the initiative collected only the data prescribed by Aadhaar (date of birth, gender, and address) as well as minimal education details such as class name, admission details, and name of the local school. It issued photo IDs in addition to the student's Aadhaar number. However, this initiative is only a first step toward a student tracking mechanism and there is great potential for expansion (The Hindu 2010).

The UID initiative is a first step toward expanding Aadhaar to students and schools. The system could be improved by tracking learning outcomes longitudinally. Longitudinal tracking of students allows for important policy conclusions, which can be used directly to improve student learning outcomes. Longitudinal tracking in combination with predictive analytical tools reaps high benefits for long-term planning and education policy decisions. The tracking systems need to be directly incorporated into the EMIS structure and cover students throughout their entire academic career. This also includes linking the system to the tertiary education sector by sharing student data with universities.

Teacher Tracking in Bihar, India

In the Indian state of Bihar, all 320,000 teachers are issued unique personal IDs including a photograph, which serves as an attendance monitoring tool. In fact, teachers' attendance rates are accessible online in real time. The system is accessible on a subdistrict, district, and state level. In addition to attendance monitoring, the system now also enables teachers to set personalized goals, which, once achieved, their supervisor has to approve in the system. The system that started out as a monitoring tool of teachers' attendance is in the process of being converted into what will eventually become a teacher-focused human resource management information system. It will serve as a master data record platform and improve data collection on teachers and their professional development.

Bihar has integrated teachers' attendance monitoring into professional and human resource development. It developed a sophisticated intervention tool to reduce ghost teachers and teacher absenteeism in general. The Teacher Education Management Information System (TEMIS) is a special tool established to address ghost teachers and teachers' absence within the broader Enhancing Teacher Effectiveness in Bihar (ETEB) operation. It includes data on the teachers' educational level, professional qualifications, and personal history in addition to the current school posting, commencement date of teaching service, and training status.

The TEMIS with UIDs has the potential to make accurate projections on staffing needs, human resource expenses, and foreseeable retirement dates of teachers (World Bank 2015b).

Unique Learner References in The Philippines

The Philippines issues a unique learner reference number to each student enrolled in public schools and the Alternative Learning System (ALS), which tackles illiteracy within the adult population. The 12-digit number enables the government to track student progress throughout the entire education system. It is entered into the Learner Information System (LIS), which is managed by the Department of Education. The Philippine government successfully established a Learner Registry on the basis of the unique learner reference numbers collected with the LIS. The aim is to track students longitudinally and create a basis for decision making. The LIS is able to generate automatic report templates for the individual students, enabling teachers to focus their attention and time on teaching rather than administrative matters. The system increases efficiencies through all levels from the individual school to the central government. Even though the system is an excellent example of how to track students throughout their academic career, it is still in need of certain improvements and upgrades to be able to capture all necessary student learning data (Department of Education, Philippines 2015).

Longitudinal Tracking in Vocational Training in Australia

In 2014, Australia launched a system of UIDs for vocational trainings (see chapter 8 for a detailed case study of Australia's EMIS). The Unique Student Identifier (USI) system, launched in January 2015, allows students and providers of vocational education training (VET) to find, collate, and authenticate students' VET achievements into a single transcript. It assigns a unique tracking number for each student enrolled in the VET course, tracks individual progress, and ensures that students' VET records are not lost. Any vocational training the student undergoes will be uploaded to his or her training transcript, which is accessible online to the student using the USI. The system provides accurate and timely information on the training courses completed, courses currently enrolled in, and progress on the course for students as well as the training providers. The training providers are responsible for data collection and reporting of enrollment details. Online access to an authenticated record of student attainment can help training providers not only streamline the assessment of course prerequisites, credit transfer, and eligibility for funding assistance but also provide tailored training, where needed.

The USI system is integrated into the Australian Vocational Education and Training Management Information Statistical Standard (AVETMISS 7.0), which is a national standard to ensure that all data are consistent and accurate. The USI system does not actually increase the frequency of reports, but it ensures higher-quality data. Overall, USI improves the efficiency of the education system, allows for more accurate vocational planning, and provides data on an individual student's progress through his or her vocational training from which important information may be extrapolated (Australian Government 2016).

Note

1. Information in this section is from iMlango's website, http://www.imlango.com/index .html.

References

Atick, Joseph, Alan Gelb, Seda Pahlavooni, Elena Gasol Ramos, and Zaid Safdar. 2014. "Digital Identity Toolkit: A Guide for Stakeholders in Africa." World Bank, Washington, DC. http://documents.worldbank.org/curated/en/2014/06/20272197/digital-identity -toolkit-guide-stakeholders-africa.

Australian Government. 2016. USI RTO Webinar: "New Functions and Expert Tips." USI Office, Australian Government, August. https://www.usi.gov.au/system/files /documents/usi_webinar_presentation_-_new_functions_and_expert_tips_-_10 _august_2016_0.pdf.

Bauer, Johannes, Michel van Eeten, Tithi Chattopadhyay, and Yuehua Wu. 2008. "ITU Study on the Financial Aspects of Network Security: Malware and Spam." http:// www.itu.int/ITU-D/cyb/cybersecurity/docs/itu-study-financial-aspects-of-malware -and-spam.pdf.

Brito, Steve, Ana Corbacho, and René Osorio. 2013. "Birth Registration: The Key to Social Inclusion in Latin America and the Caribbean." Inter-American Development Bank, Washington DC.

CSIS (Center for Strategic and International Studies) and McAfee. 2014. "Net Losses: Estimating the Global Cost of Cybercrime." http://www.mcafee.com/us/resources /reports/rp-economic-impact-cybercrime2.pdf.

Department of Education, Philippines. 2015. "Education for All 2015 National Review Report: Philippines."

DQC (Data Quality Campaign). 2015. "EMIS in Different Country Contexts." Presented by Paige Kowalski at the World Bank Education Staff Development Program, Washington, DC.

George, Tina, and Kathy Lindert. 2016. "Social, Protection and Labor Delivery Systems: Solving the Challenges of Fragmentation and Static Systems." Presentation, World Bank, Washington DC.

IDB (Inter-American Development Bank). 2011. "Newborn Citizens on BIDtv." IDB, Washington, DC. https://vimeo.com/29405202.

———. 2014. "Factsheet: Civil Registration and Identity Management in Latin America and the Caribbean." IDB, Washington, DC.

———. 2016. "Civil Registry and Identification." IDB, Washington, DC. http://iadb .libguides.com/registros.

ILO (International Labour Organization). 2015. "Social Protection in Action: Building Social Protection Floors." ILO, Geneva.

Malik, Tariq. 2014. "Technology in the Service of Development: The NADRA Story." Center for Global Development, London. http://www.cgdev.org/publication/ft /technology-service-development-nadra-story.

Massell, D. 2001. "The Data-Driven Theory of Change: Effects and Implications." Paper presented at the annual meeting of the American Educational Research Association, Seattle, WA.

McQuiggan, Jaime, and Armistead Sapp. 2014. *Implement, Improve and Expand Your Statewide Longitudinal Data System: Creating a Culture of Data in Education.* Hoboken, NJ: John Wiley & Sons.

Montenegro Torres, Fernando. 2013. "Costa Rica Case Study: Primary Health Care Achievements and Challenges within the Framework of the Social Health Insurance." Universal Health Coverage (UNICO) Studies Series 14, World Bank, Washington, DC.

Ndiku, Mbenge T., and Naomi W. Mwai. 2015. "Equalizing Utilization of Information among Rural Schools in Kenya through Satellite Technology." Department of Information and Knowledge Management, Technical University of Kenya.

OECD (Organisation for Economic Co-operation and Development). 2013. "Chile: Education Policy Outlook 2013." OECD, Paris.

Ponemon Institute. 2014. "Cost of Data Breach Study: Global Analysis." Study for IBM. http://public.dhe.ibm.com/common/ssi/ecm/se/en/sel03027usen/SEL27USEN.pdf.

Rinaldi, Gian Marco, and Viola Macrelli. 2017. "The EU eIDAS Regulation and the SPID Scheme." *Bird & Bird News Centre*, March 21.

Sanders, W., and S. Horn. 1994. "The Tennessee Value-Added Assessment System (TVAAS): Mixed-Model Methodology in Educational Assessment." *Journal of Personnel Evaluation in Education* 8 (3): 299–311.

Seltzer, M. H., K. Choi, and Y. M. Thum. 2003. "Examining Relationships between Where Students Start and How Rapidly They Progress: Using New Developments in Growth Modeling to Gain Insights into the Distribution of Achievement within Schools." *Educational Evaluation and Policy Analysis* 25 (3): 263–86.

Seltzer, M. H., K. A. Frank, and A. S. Bryk. 1994. "The Metric Matters: The Sensitivity of Conclusions about Growth in Student Achievement to Choice of Metric. *Educational Evaluation and Policy Analysis* 16 (1): 41–49.

Serim, F. 2003. *No More Flying Blind: Using Data-Driven Decision Making to Guide Student Learning.* Washington, DC: Consortium for School Networking.

Streifer, P. 2002. *Using Data to Make Better Education Decisions.* Lanham, MD: Scarecrow Education and American Association of School Administrators.

Symantec. 2013. "The Norton Report 2013." https://msisac.cisecurity.org/resources/reports /documents/b-norton-report-2013.pdf.

The Hindu. 2010. "Students to Get UID Number." *The Hindu*, Kerala, September 17. http://www.thehindu.com/todays-paper/tp-national/tp-kerala/students-to-get-uid -number/article673940.ece.

UNESCO (United Nations Education, Scientific, and Cultural Organization). 2014. "Regional Report about Education for All in Latin America and the Caribbean." Report for the Global Education for All Meeting, Muscat, Oman, May 12 and 14. UNESCO, Santiago, Chile.

UNICEF (United Nations Children's Fund). 2013. "UNICEF Annual Report: Peru." UNICEF, New York.

UNICEF and ECLAC (Economic Commission for Latin America and the Caribbean). 2011. "The Right to an Identity: Birth Registration in Latin America and the Caribbean." *Challenges: Newsletter on Progress toward the Millennium Development Goals from a Child Rights Perspective*, No. 13. http://repositorio.cepal.org/handle/11362/35984.

Wainer, H., R. Hambleton, and K. Meara. 1999. "Alternative Displays for Communicating NAEP Results: A Redesign and Validity Study. *Journal of Educational Measurement* 36 (4): 301–35.

Welch, Tessa, and Jennifer Glennie. 2016. "OER Contributing to Early Literacy in Africa: Evidence from Saide's African Storybook." Saide, Johannesburg.

Williams-Grut, Oscar. 2016. "One Picture Shows Just How Hot Fintech Is Right Now— But People Are Talking about 'Froth.'" *Business Insider Australia*, February 10.

World Bank. 2015a. "Identification for Development (ID4D)." World Bank, Washington, DC, (accessed on March 13, 2017), http://www.worldbank.org/en/programs/id4d.

———. 2015b. "The Role of Identification in the Post-2015 Development Agenda." World Bank, Washington, DC.

———. 2016a. "Identification for Development: Strategic Framework." World Bank, Washington, DC, January 25.

———. 2016b. *World Development Report 2016: Digital Dividends*. Washington, DC: World Bank.

CHAPTER 7

Innovation in Advanced and Decentralized Systems: The Case of the United States

Student data isn't the whole story, but it is a critical part of the story. Data underpins key aspects of our work. When that data is effectively collected, managed, and utilized, opportunities emerge that make the entire education system stronger.

—Dr. Jack Smith, Superintendent, Montgomery County Public Schools

Key Takeaways

- Success in data systems in education in the United States is due to proper policy, financing, and collaboration across levels of government and civil society.
- In a decentralized model structure such as the United States, management of data is central. Data culture is derived from a strong and comprehensive legal framework at the federal and state levels to ensure collection and use of crucial information around common goals.
- The State of Maryland, a best-practice example, has focused on data for learning, especially bringing data to benefit schools and classroom teaching and learning. Data are accessible and transparent, so schools can monitor progress toward their improvement goals.
- Maryland incorporated learning-focused data tools such as academic indexing to identify students at risk and improve stakeholder communication, efficient teacher evaluation, and teaching resource–sharing modules to support school leadership and teachers in fostering learning outcomes.
- Policy makers in Maryland and all stakeholders are involved in the design of the data systems. School districts are encouraged to improve education quality through supportive dissemination of data.
- Maryland has been successful in achieving advanced Education Management Information Systems (EMISs) at reasonable cost using competitive

procurement processes and selecting optimal solutions by taking advantage of public-private partnerships.

• The federal and local governments provide grants to support longitudinal tracking of schools, teachers, and students to inform decision makers. In Maryland, individual student data are integrated with higher education and workforce data to align education with market needs and productivity. In the State of Florida, the longitudinal data system covers all aspects of an individual's schooling experience, including tertiary education.

• Decentralized data systems should be conducive to continuous improvements and adaptable to changes in technology, education needs, and innovative ideas to foster learning.

The Data-Centered Education System in the United States

The United States has an advanced data-centered education system that spans a decentralized system. Much can be learned from advanced systems around the world, such as the United States, where the use of data to inform, enhance, and complement learning in education is undergoing significant growth. With 150 years of experience collecting and analyzing education data, the United States has a plethora of successes and challenges from which others can learn. The United States is unique in that it is at the forefront of innovation in education data systems. The data have been continuously helpful in tackling issues related to dropouts, graduation, targeting, transforming learning outcomes, and supporting all education stakeholders in making evidence-based decisions—ultimately driving continuous improvement of the entire education system.

This chapter has three distinct parts. First, the decentralized structure of the U.S. education system and varying actors influencing data are outlined, with emphasis on the legal framework, financing, and data collection, management, and utilization. Second, it provides a spotlight on the State of Maryland, examining its data system from the lens of state and counties. Third, the chapter reviews longitudinal data systems across the United States as examples of innovation in taking education data to the next level of excellence.

Policy Drivers for Data in a Decentralized System

The United States has a decentralized education system. From the time of the country's inception, the U.S. Constitution designated the majority of power over the education system to state and local authorities. States have direct oversight over most aspects of the public education system, performing political, administrative, and fiscal functions that are often the work of ministries of education in countries with centralized education systems (U.S. Department of Education 2008).

Table 7.1 U.S. Federal Legislation Influencing EMIS

Federal legislation	Summary descriptions
ESEA/NCLB *(Elementary and Secondary Education Act/No Child Left Behind)*	Provides funding, promotes equal access to education, established standards and accountability. Also provides an opportunity to move from data for compliance to data utilization for student learning outcomes.
FERPA *(Family Educational Rights and Privacy Act)*	Protects the privacy of student educational records and applies to all schools that receive funding from the U.S. Department of Education.
COPPA *(Children's Online Privacy Protection Act)*	Governs the collection of information that is gathered online from children under the age of 13, and applies to the operators of websites and online services directed at children. Enforced by the Federal Trade Commission.

Source: U.S. Department of Education; Federal Trade Commission.

EMISs in the United States have been especially influenced by three policies: (1) the Elementary and Secondary Education Act (ESEA) of 1965, reauthorized in 2001 as the No Child Left Behind (NCLB) Act; (2) the Family Educational Rights and Privacy Act (FERPA) of 1974; and (3) the Children's Online Privacy Protection Act (COPPA) of 1998 (table 7.1).

At the federal level, ESEA/NCLB outlines accountability steps that have critical implications for EMISs. Key legislation is included in Improving Basic Programs Operated by Local Education Agencies (ESEA/NCLB Part A, Section 1111), which specifically mandates:

- Each state shall have *a statewide accountability system* that ensures all local educational agencies, public elementary schools, and public secondary schools make adequate yearly progress (AYP) toward the state's student academic achievement standards.
- Each state shall define the *adequately yearly progress* in a manner that is statistically valid and reliable.
- Each state shall establish statewide *annual measurable objectives* and intermediate goals to meet objectives.
- Each state shall develop a uniform averaging procedure to *track the progress of schools* toward reaching AYP.
- Each state shall establish *a set of high-quality, yearly student academic assessments* that include, at a minimum, academic assessments in mathematics, reading or language arts, and science that will be used as the primary means of determining the yearly performance of the state toward meeting its student academic achievement standards.
- Each state educational agency may *incorporate the data from the assessments* under this paragraph into a state-developed longitudinal data system that links student test scores, length of enrollment, and graduation records over time.

- Each state that *receives assistance* under this part shall prepare and disseminate an annual state report card in a concise, understandable, and uniform format.
- Each state shall collect and disseminate information in a manner that *protects the privacy of individuals*.

Financing Functions

Several other key federal policies and grant initiatives have supported states in building data systems. For example, as part of the American Recovery and Reinvestment Act (ARRA) of 2009, Race to the Top (RTTT) is a US$4.35 billion initiative built on the framework of comprehensive reform in four core areas: (1) adopting rigorous standards and assessments that prepare students for success in college and the workplace; (2) recruiting, developing, retaining, and rewarding effective teachers and principals; (3) *building data systems* that measure student success and inform teachers and principals how they can improve their practices; and (4) turning around the lowest-performing schools.

Not only is there greater decision-making authority at state and local levels, but the bulk of financing also comes from state and local governments. According to Cornman and Zhou (2016), during fiscal year 2014, the United States reported spending US$623.2 billion for public elementary and secondary education. Of that amount, state and local governments provided US$568.7 billion (91.3 percent) and the federal government contributed US$54.5 billion (8.7 percent of all revenues). Total allocations per pupil averaged US$12,460. Current expenditures per pupil averaged US$11,066 at the national level but varied significantly across the country, from US$6,546 in Utah to US$20,577 in the District of Columbia (map 7.1).

Other funding (as highlighted in the next section) comes from nongovernmental agencies in support of data collection and sharing because there is much public interest in quality education data.

Roles in the Data Chain

At the federal level, the National Center for Education Statistics (NCES) was established by Congress in 1867 with a mandate to collect and share education statistics. NCES continues today as the primary federal entity for collecting and analyzing U.S. education data. It is housed within the U.S. Department of Education's Institute of Education Sciences. NCES fulfills a Congressional mandate to collect, collate, analyze, and report complete statistics on the condition of U.S. education; conduct and publish reports; and review and report on education activities internationally (for example, in its annual report, "The Condition of Education").[1] All state systems report data to the federal government on predetermined schedules.

State policies define the education system within each state, including critical factors such as curriculum, assessments, teacher qualifications, resource distribution, and what data are collected and when they need to be reported. Local education agencies (LEAs) at the county (or district) level implement and enforce these requirements. In operating local school systems,

Map 7.1 Current Expenditures per Pupil for Public Elementary and Secondary Education, by State, 2014

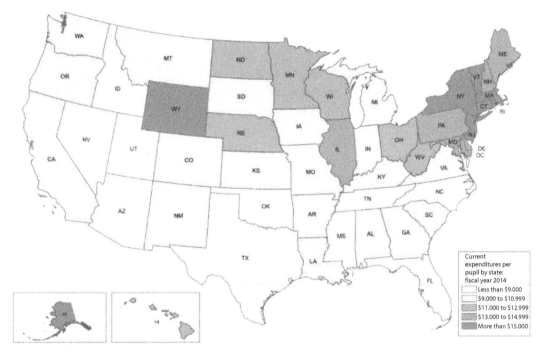

Source: Cornman and Zhou 2016.

they also develop and implement their own policies, hire and supervise teaching staff, and raise money. LEA structures vary by state and region but are generally managed by a governing body referred to as the education board. Education data are often a central part of the board and the school system's decision making. Given this decentralized education system, EMISs vary significantly from state to state, and in some states they vary from county (local government) to county.

The private and social sectors are also essential parts of this ecosystem. The Data Quality Campaign (DQC), a nonprofit organization, is a strong example of the social sector playing a key role in promoting effective use of education data. *EdSurge*, an independent information resource and community for education technology stakeholders, reported that education technology start-ups in the United States raised a total of US$1.85 billion through December 16, 2015 (Winters 2015). Of that figure, companies whose tools target K–12 accounted for US$537 million, whereas those serving higher education raised US$711 million. Across the ecosystem, additional organizations, solutions, and communities help to unleash the potential of data to drive learning.

In 2009, the DQC released "10 State Actions to Ensure Effective Data Use." The goal, according to the DQC, was for states to move from collecting data only for compliance and accountability purposes to using data to answer critical policy questions, inform continuous improvement, and ultimately support student paths to success. In 2014, the final year DQC surveyed state progress toward the 10 State Actions, three states had implemented all of them: Arkansas, Delaware, and Kentucky. The 10 State Actions (DQC 2009) include the following:

1. *Link state K–12 data systems* with early learning, postsecondary, workforce, and other critical state agency data systems.
2. Create stable, sustained support for *longitudinal data systems*.
3. Develop *governance structures* to guide data collection and use.
4. Build state *data repositories*.
5. Provide *timely, role-based access* to data.
6. Create *progress reports* with student-level data for educators, students, and parents.
7. Create reports with *longitudinal statistics* to guide system-level change.
8. Develop a *purposeful research agenda*.
9. Implement policies and promote practices to *build educators' capacity* to use data.
10. Promote strategies to *raise awareness* of available data.

Important to note with this campaign is the momentum and progress demonstrated by the states over the three-year period from 2011 to 2014 (figure 7.1).

Figure 7.1 Number of States with Each Action

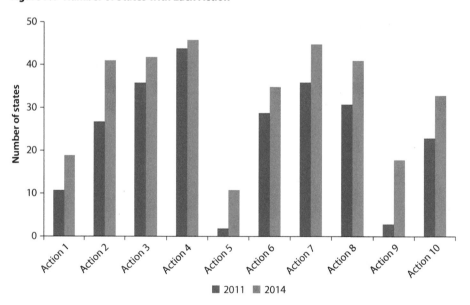

Source: DQC, dataqualitycampaign.org/why-education-data/state-progress 2016.

Spotlight on the State of Maryland

Maryland's public school system is among the highest performers nationwide. Maryland is also at the forefront of a national trend toward using data in innovative, learning-centric practices. At both state and county levels, a variety of good practices and key insights emerge that are relevant to education stakeholders around the world who are rethinking their education data systems. Maryland is located in the Mid-Atlantic region of the United States, bordered by Delaware, Pennsylvania, Virginia, Washington, DC, and West Virginia.

Education System and Data Responsibility

Maryland comprises 24 school districts (or counties) that serve more than 866,000 students (MD Report Card 2014). The State Board of Education governs the state's education system, and the State Superintendent leads the Maryland State Department of Education (MSDE). The MSDE has three key offices: the Office of the Deputy for School Effectiveness, the Office of the Deputy for Teaching and Learning, and the Office of the Deputy for Finance and Administration. The state-level EMIS is managed by the Office of Teaching and Learning in the Division of Curriculum, Assessment, and Accountability (DCAA). Maryland's decentralized education system creates a significant amount of variation in the management of education data across the state. MSDE is the central collector of education data and is responsible for sharing county data with the federal government for compliance purposes.

Education policy in Maryland has been consistently ahead of the curve, with legislation that pushes the limits of education data and strives toward improving accountability and learning outcomes. In the early 1970s, Maryland passed an educational accountability law that mandated statewide goal setting and testing and was among the first pieces of legislation to mandate school-level report cards. Although common today, such report cards were innovative, even revolutionary, at that time (Michaels and Ferrara 1999). Between 1976 and 1982, Maryland adopted and implemented Project Basic to account for gaps in the Maryland Accountability Testing Program report, such as the lack of attendance information and disaggregated performance data. The driving concept behind Project Basic was that school is an incubator for skills that lead to an effective and fulfilling adulthood. Hornbeck (1977) notes that Project Basic prepared students with a fundamental ability to cope with self and others in a variety of settings, from family to the workplace, to the community, and to the nation. In the early 1990s, the Maryland School Performance Assessment Program (MSPAP) was first administered and used to evaluate schools and to provide information to guide school improvement efforts. More recently, the Maryland General Assembly passed the Education Reform Act and the State Board of Education adopted the Common Core State Standards, a more rigorous and thinking-based set of content standards. These and other policies and programs illustrate Maryland's focus on using data to drive school improvement and learning outcomes.

Data use is enhanced through a common culture that recognizes the value of data. With this foundation, data are used in decision making by different stakeholders at all levels of the education system (for example, policy makers, principals, teachers, administrators, parents, students, and so on). Parents and students have real-time access to student learning data. Teachers use data to track progress toward Student Learning Objectives (SLOs). Principals and school administrators actively use data to evaluate teachers, monitor school progress, and manage school plans. Policy makers use data to monitor education quality and equity, improve accountability, and gauge effectiveness of policies and programs.

Bringing Data to Life in Schools and Classrooms—Examples of Data Models in Crucial Functions

In Maryland, schools depend on data to track progress toward SLOs and to better understand student needs in general. In Maryland, SLOs are designed to evaluate instruction. SLOs are measurable instructional goals established for a specific group of students over a set period of time. Additionally, they serve as one of the measures of student growth for the State Teacher Evaluation model and may represent 20–35 percent of a teacher's evaluation. An effective education data system is a critical tool for teachers throughout the SLO process. An SLO begins with planning and documenting intended objectives and moves on to capturing a baseline of student knowledge; the next step is design and delivery of curriculum, followed by another assessment, and finally analysis and use of student learning outcomes data. Box 7.1 illustrates how an EMIS can support teachers in answering many questions related to the progress of students.

Cecil County, Maryland (United States)

The county uses a sophisticated information system that combines demographic student data with instructional data to track student learning by various disaggregated demographics (for example, gender, ethnicity, and so on). The system also employs an Academic Index, which pulls data from academic factors that may impact success in school such as absence, discipline, and assessment scores. In addition to tracking general class performance, this report is a predictive tool

---

Box 7.1 An EMIS Supports Teachers in Answering Many Questions

- What do students know and not know before and after the curriculum is delivered?
- Are there gaps in the curriculum that prevent students from learning?
- Do certain students have special needs and require further intervention?
- Are such interventions working?
- Is a student's poor performance due to absence or inability to understand the content?

---

that identifies students at risk of dropping out of school. The Academic Index is calculated on the basis of cut-off points, with 4 or more points displayed in blue (indicating need for intervention), 2–3 points displayed in orange; and 0–1 point displayed in green (figure 7.2 and table 7.2).

Teachers gain greater insight into the classroom, and supervisors benefit from aggregate data. Reflecting on the Academic Index, Regina Roberts, a school principal in Cecil County commented, "This is a system that builds off of what

Figure 7.2 Cecil County, Maryland (United States) Academic Index—Marking Period 1

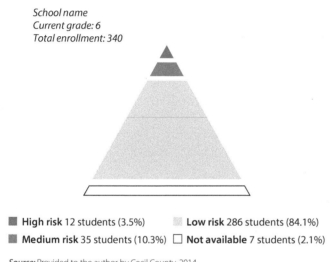

School name
Current grade: 6
Total enrollment: 340

■ **High risk** 12 students (3.5%)   ▨ **Low risk** 286 students (84.1%)
■ **Medium risk** 35 students (10.3%)   □ **Not available** 7 students (2.1%)

Source: Provided to the author by Cecil County, 2014.

Table 7.2 Cecil County, Maryland (United States) Academic Index

Assessments		
Grades (*no. of Ds or Fs*)	0	0
Grades	1	1
Grades	2	2
Grades	3+	3
Discipline (suspensions per school year)		
Suspensions	0	0
Suspensions	1	1
Suspensions	2–3	2
Suspensions	4+	3
Attendance (excused & unexcused)		
Absences	91–100%	0
Absences	85–90%	1
Absences	80–84%	2
Absences	0–79%	3

Source: Provided to the author by Cecil County, 2014.

teachers already know individually and creates incredible value by aggregating that knowledge in an efficient, easy-to-use format. We can interact with information in a more dynamic way to address student needs. Teachers—and principals as well—have access to information that significantly shifts the way we do business, making it more efficient, reliable, and fast."[2]

Use of data in the classroom for instructional gains is expanding; however, the programs used are often not linked to the local-level EMIS, meaning stakeholders miss an opportunity to collect a deeper layer of student learning data. Learning programs such as DIBELS, Fountas & Pinnell, Scholastic Reading & Math Inventory, and many others are commonly used in the classroom; but data are still not fed into the county EMIS. This is more of a technical integration gap that vendors should work to improve. That said, the MSDE could monitor for, identify, and suggest to counties any instructional programs that have good integration capabilities.

Kent County

An EMIS can also help cultivate a culture of data use among teachers. In Kent County, the school system uses *SchoolNet*, a product under the Pearson-owned PowerSchool student information system. SchoolNet combines student information with instructional data and allows teachers to create, store, and share their own mini-assessments (also referred to as formative or short-cycle assessments). While launching SchoolNet, the school system was also rolling out the professional learning community (PLC) model, a workplace strategy to foster collaborative learning among colleagues.

The SchoolNet EMIS, combined with the collaborative PLC framework, was catalytic for teachers, who immediately started working together around assessment data. Karen Couch, the Superintendent of Kent County schools, described the benefit of the combined tools: "We have become more sophisticated in understanding the value of a benchmark test and the resulting data." Dr. Couch continued, explaining the collective benefits,

> Independently, it changed how teachers view assessments and how they use data in planning their SLOs. Collaboratively, it transformed the dialogue and collaboration between teachers to be more data-driven and more energetic. They are required to meet twice a month, but many now meet once a week to collaborate and discuss data. Working together as a collaborative culture ensures the effective use of data is a true partnership.

Charles County and a Data System for Evaluation and Professional Growth

Across Maryland, principals use EMISs to manage staff and plan more effectively. They rely on data to understand and make decisions about their schools. Principals use data to answer many questions, such as those listed in box 7.2. Charles County worked with the vendor Insystech to customize The Evaluation & Assets Management System (TEAMS). Although TEAMS works best on the cloud in an environment with Internet, it can also be customized for regions without Internet or with limited Internet access. Because Charles County has

---

Box 7.2 An EMIS Supports Principals in Answering Many Questions

- Are the teachers in my school effective, and are students learning?
- Is my school on track to meet district and state student–teacher ratio goals?
- Is learning at my school equitable? Is it fair across demographic groups such as gender and ethnicity?
- Is professional development effective, and what is the return on investment in professional development?
- What is my school budget, and is it managed efficiently?

---

consistent Internet access, the full capabilities of the system are available and include Staff Evaluation, Admin Management, Student Assessment and Student Information Systems, Asset Management, and Search.

Principals were brought in to help design the evaluation system, and they now use it throughout the evaluation process. This user-driven design process helped to create a product that truly responds to the needs of principals. Specific user requests included spell-check, automatic saving every 30 seconds, and color codes to differentiate automatic and manual correlations.

The Asset Hub allows teachers to share, vet, and collaborate around instructional assets. Teachers also have the opportunity to rate assets. Assets with higher ratings float to the top of the system, making them more visible to users, while weaker assets drop to the bottom of the list. Asset management makes teaching more efficient and collaborative.

In addition, an automated, intuitive evaluation system improves the rate and quality of teacher evaluations. Prior to the system, a single teacher evaluation took a principal between four and five hours. That process included scheduling the class observation, conducting the observation, writing up notes, analyzing notes, scheduling the follow-up, and finally meeting with the teacher to discuss results. Maryland state law requires two evaluations per teacher per year. The inefficient process led principals to put off evaluations until they stacked up at the end of each semester, forcing principals to rush through the built-up evaluations to meet deadlines. The purpose of the evaluation, as an instrument to monitor and strengthen the skills of teachers, was largely lost.

The new approach to evaluation supports principals in scheduling an observation, sending calendar invites, collecting and managing notes, and sharing documents. When conducting an observation, principals use the tools to schedule the initial observation with the teacher. During the observation they take notes directly in the system, on a tablet or laptop. Following the observation, the principals review notes and then click "Correlate," which automatically selects phrases from the notes that are relevant to the state evaluation methodology (box 7.3) and correlates the notes with the relevant domain, saving principals the extra time of rewriting notes into the evaluation framework (figure 7.3).

Data for Learning • http://dx.doi.org/10.1596/978-1-4648-1099-2

Box 7.3 Teacher Evaluation Model—An EMIS Opportunity

The state evaluation model examines a 50/50 split between qualitative professional practice measures (inputs) and quantitative student growth measures (outcomes). On the basis of the Charlotte Danielson Framework, four practice domains are evaluated that make up qualitative professional practice: (1) planning and preparation, (2) instructional delivery, (3) classroom management and environment, and (4) professional responsibilities. Performance in each domain is worth 12.5 percentage points. The TEAMS teacher evaluation product includes both qualitative and quantitative measures, effectively comparing teacher inputs with student outcomes. Integrating this model with an EMIS provides an opportunity to effectively track teacher inputs and student learning outcomes over time.

Source: MSDE 2015.

Figure 7.3 Innovation in Data Collection for Teacher Evaluation

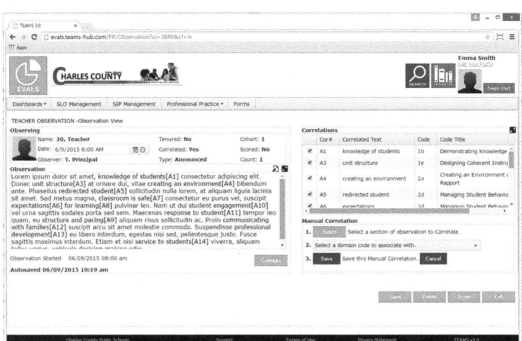

Source: Provided to the World Bank by Insystech, 2015.

After the automated transfer, principals have the opportunity to edit domains in case anything was missed in the automated correlation process. During training to use the system, principals are taught the terminology to use for maximizing correlations, and the correlation taxonomy in the system can also be added to and revised. Next, the correlated domains are transferred into the framework for scoring. The principal scores the teacher's performance on a scale of 1–4, with an option to add notes next to each score. Scores and notes are aggregated over time to show changes in professional development. Perhaps the most critical aspect of the tool is that it cultivates conversation and transparency. After each observation, the teacher has access to the scores and write-ups before meeting with the principal to discuss results, reducing surprises and adding to a dialogue that is truly focused on teacher professional development.

Kim Hill, Superintendent of Charles County schools, emphasized the importance of the dialogue between principal and teacher: "Throughout development and design of this product, principals were at the table. They were demanding, as they should have been, because they were taking away obstacles and barriers. Their insights focused on what is important, which is the conversation." Amy Hollstein, Assistant Superintendent of Instruction, supported this point, stating, "The best part of the whole process is the dialogue between the principal and the teacher. We call it the courageous conversation."

With the school management system in place and integrating with student assessment data, shifts in the work culture are taking place. A focus on true professional development—genuinely improving teaching and management expertise—has taken hold. All parties are happy with the system, which is quick, easy to use, and accurate. "It sounds so simple, but it is so incredibly profound," stated Dr. Smith, as he reflected on Charles County's success, "To help your staff develop as professionals from the day they walk in the door is a huge step in the profession, a fundamental shift that raises the level of professionalism for teachers and principals."

The State Central Data System

Policy makers use data to monitor education quality and equity, and for planning. Using data to monitor quality is not easy, especially when it comes to communicating results in a way that effectively brings about results and does not alienate or antagonize stakeholders. For example, transparently disseminating aggregate examination results or graduation rates across a state or country informs all education stakeholders about the health of the education system, but challenges may arise for low-performing states or districts.

Administrators and decision makers in regions with lower results may dispute the data, divert responsibility, or use other methods to defend their position. Such defensive tactics fail to improve the situation and often run the risk of making the conditions worse by spreading negative attitudes. The responsibility falls on policy makers to share data in such a way that negative responses are minimized and instead encourages stakeholders to collaborate and improve.

Maryland developed an effective and collaborative strategy for sharing cohort graduation rates with county decision makers. Instead of sharing the actual graduation rate of each county, policy makers calculated the state average and shared data in relation to that average (map 7.2). Green counties included those that were within five percentage points above or below the state

Map 7.2 Collaborative Approach to Sharing Cohort Graduation Rates

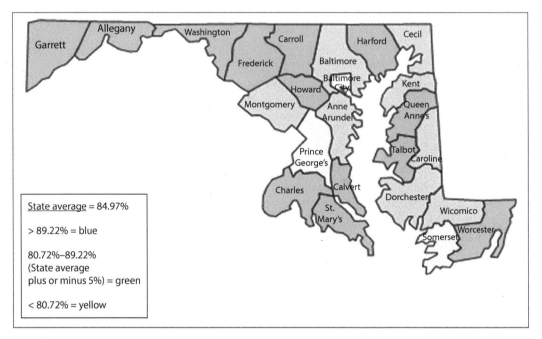

State average = 84.97%

> 89.22% = blue

80.72%–89.22%
(State average
plus or minus 5%) = green

< 80.72% = yellow

Source: MSDE 2015.

average. Blue counties were those that scored above that bracket, and yellow were those below that bracket. Policy makers carefully selected coloring as well. Instead of using traditional colors—for example, coloring low-performing counties in red—policy makers used neutral pastel colors, so as not to invoke an immediate defensive response. The result was a meeting that was characterized by productive dialogue and action, as opposed to one with defensive and divisive conduct.

A key tool that policy makers in Maryland use to hold schools accountable is the School Progress Index (SPI), which reports EMIS data and analysis through a transparent platform. The SPI came about as a result of federal reforms to NCLB, which initially tracked accountability through AYP. In 2011, the U.S. Department of Education gave states the opportunity to develop a new system for measuring and reporting school performance. Maryland redesigned its accountability system focusing on the progress schools are making toward improving student achievement, closing achievement gaps, and enabling students to move toward readiness for college and career by mastering grade-level and course-level curriculum goals each year (MSDE 2012).

The SPI is based on high multiple measures that include student achievement data in English/language arts, mathematics, and science. It includes growth data in English/language arts and mathematics; gaps, based on the gap score between the highest-achieving and lowest-achieving subgroup in mathematics, reading, and science; and cohort graduation and cohort dropout rates. The SPI guides interventions from policy makers by categorizing schools into one of five strands that determine the district and state support schools receive. The state affords top-performing schools with greater flexibility whereas lower-performing schools receive progressively more prescriptive technical assistance, expectations, and monitoring.

The change is further evidence of Maryland's transition from a compliance-focused system to one that targets student growth and learning. The SPI provides more in-depth, student-level information than AYP, which simply tracked how a school's scores would change from year to year (figure 7.4). The SPI evaluates schools on a continuous scale on variables of Achievement, Growth, Gap Reduction, and College- and Career-Readiness, and makes results of each school available publically via the annual Maryland

Figure 7.4 Maryland School Progress Index

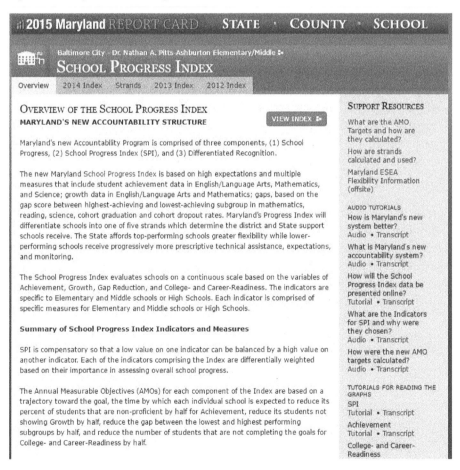

Source: MSDE, reportcard.msde.maryland.gov.

Data for Learning • http://dx.doi.org/10.1596/978-1-4648-1099-2

Report Card. The index identifies schools for intervention, support, and recognition depending on their progress.

During the transition from AYP to the SPI, MSDE was careful to provide ongoing communication about the reform and what it meant for schools, staff, students, and parents. The *Maryland Classroom* newsletter is a good example of this communication effort, with the December 2012 issue providing frequently asked questions as well as detailed information on methodology and use of the index (MSDE 2012).

Various tools are built into the webpage to educate the user on understanding and using the index. The SPI is reported through the Maryland Report Card, which also contains demographic data, enrollment and attendance rates, absentee rates, student mobility, teacher qualifications, and data about students receiving special services. A similar use of EMIS was tremendously successful in Australia and is detailed in chapter 8.

For a strategy like the SPI to be successful, schools must be armed with the tools to effectively design and achieve improvement plans. To effectively position schools for success, national, state, and local governments provide schools with data that they use to benchmark their student performance against student performance metrics at local and national levels, as well as tools to organize and analyze those data.

Maryland's Howard County provided school management with an Excel table to track improvement plan performance data. Table 7.3 shares a portion of that table, tracking national performance measures over a five-year period, including results from the national, state, and local levels. The county provided a separate table for each school to track student-level progress on state and local exams. Providing templates to schools not only makes recording easier at the school level but also improves data sharing by limiting multiple versions and formats.

Constructing an Advanced System at the Local Level: The Case of Howard County in Expanding the Data System

Between 2012 and 2015, Maryland's Howard County implemented a cutting-edge EMIS. The success of the new system stemmed from the county's ability to develop key enabling conditions for its EMIS, most notably, vision, strategy, and human resources. The process started in 2012, when the county hired a new superintendent. With the support of the new superintendent, Howard County created the Office of Accountability and hired a chief accountability officer to steer the process of identifying and implementing an effective EMIS and a strong accountability strategy.

Meetings with stakeholders were crucial in the EMIS design process. Following an extensive assessment, including internal dialogue and focus groups, as well as several external audits conducted by the Center for Education Policy Research at Harvard University, IMPAQ International, and Pearson, the chief accountability officer and her team determined that existing data systems did not provide adequate data to support the

Table 7.3 School Improvement Plan Based on Data and Results

National Performance Measures	Trend data										Targets				Benchmarks				
	2011		2012		2013		2014		2015		2015	2016	2017	2018	College and career readiness				
PSAT G10	N	%	N	%	N	%	N	%	N	%	Percent				College and career	National (2009)	MD (2014)	S (2014)	S (2015)
PSAT Composite	1709	41.4	1630	41.8	1557	40.5	1569	39.9	1583	41.7	n.a.	n.a.	n.a.	n.a.	145	27	—	39.9	41.7
PSAT Math	2168	52.5	2011	51.6	1914	49.8	1861	47.3	1982	52.2	n.a.	n.a.	n.a.	n.a.	47	35	—	47.3	52.2
PSAT Critical Reading	1680	40.7	1613	41.4	1497	38.9	1634	41.5	1570	41.4	n.a.	n.a.	n.a.	n.a.	49	27	—	41.5	41.4
PSAT Writing	1563	37.8	1429	36.7	1486	38.6	1487	37.8	1487	39.2	n.a.	n.a.	n.a.	n.a.	48	26	—	37.8	39.2
PSAT Participation Rate	4131	90.3	3899	91.6	3847	95.0	3936	94.1	3796	95.6	n.a.	n.a.	n.a.	n.a.	—	—	—	94.1	95.6
PSAT G11	N	%	N	%	N	%	N	%	N	%	Percent				College Board	National (2009)	MD (2014)	S (2014)	S (2015)
PSAT Composite	1639	46.3	1815	47.0	1717	47.0	1742	47.7	1759	47.6	n.a.	n.a.	n.a.	n.a.	152	36	—	47.7	47.6
PSAT Math	1901	53.7	2115	54.8	2037	55.7	1887	51.7	1982	53.6	n.a.	n.a.	n.a.	n.a.	50	44	—	51.7	53.6
PSAT Critical Reading	1756	49.6	1905	49.4	1749	47.8	1894	51.9	1929	52.1	n.a.	n.a.	n.a.	n.a.	50	40	—	51.9	52.1
PSAT Writing	1659	46.9	1707	44.2	1749	47.8	1882	51.6	1847	49.9	n.a.	n.a.	n.a.	n.a.	49	38	—	51.6	49.9
PSAT Participation Rate	3539	87.0	3859	90.2	3656	91.1	3649	92.5	3699	92.5	n.a.	n.a.	n.a.	n.a.	—	—	—	92.5	92.5

table continues next page

Table 7.3 School Improvement Plan Based on Data and Results (continued)

AP (Graduates)	N	%	N	%	N	%	N	%	N	%	N	%	N	%	Percent			College Board	National (2013)	MD (2013)	S (2013)	S (2014)
Enrolled in 1+ AP Course	2224	57.1	2076	54.2	2456	60.0	2319	60.7	—	—	—	—	—	n.a.	n.a.	—	—	—	—	60.0	60.7
Graduates Taking 1+ AP Exams	1816	47.8	1768	46.1	2037	49.7	2025	53.0	—	—	—	—	—	n.a.	n.a.	—	—	33.2	47.4	49.7	53.0
Earned a 3+ on 1+ AP Exams	1602	41.1	1518	39.6	1715	41.9	1712	44.8	—	—	—	—	—	n.a.	n.a.	—	—	20.1	29.6	41.9	44.8

SAT (Graduates)	N	%	N	%	N	%	N	%	N	%	N	%	N	%	Percent			College Board	National (2013)	MD (2013)	S (2013)	S (2014)
SAT Composite	944	45.1	1563	50.3	1755	53.2	1737	54.4	—	—	—	—	—	n.a.	n.a.	—	—	1650	—	—	53.2	54.4
SAT Math	1064	50.8	1743	56.1	1883	57.1	1856	58.1	—	—	—	—	—	n.a.	n.a.	—	—	550	—	—	57.1	58.1
SAT Verbal	305	43.2	1497	48.2	1675	50.8	1701	53.3	—	—	—	—	—	n.a.	n.a.	—	—	550	—	—	50.8	53.3
SAT Writing	898	42.9	1527	49.1	1716	52.1	1654	51.8	—	—	—	—	—	n.a.	n.a.	—	—	550	—	—	52.1	51.8
SAT Participation Rate	2095	53.8	3109	81.2	3296	80.5	3193	83.6	—	—	—	—	—	n.a.	n.a.	—	—	—	—	—	80.5	83.6

Source: Howard County 2015.

Note: n.a. = not applicable; — = data not available.

county's strategic plan. The team needed multiple data points to effectively inform decision making, and they needed data to actively monitor progress toward goals. Constructing a system that could integrate these data and make them readily available and easy to analyze was key. Guided by a strategic timeline (figure 7.5), the decision was made to build a comprehensive, integrated system including a student information system, a learning management system, and a data warehouse.

Project Cost

The cost structures for each system were negotiated and ultimately fell within budget requirements (table 7.4). According to Howard County, the budget for the integrated system totaled US$5.8 million (spent over five years), which is just under 1 percent of the fiscal year 2015 operating budget of US$758.8 million.

Integration of Components

There were a few crucial aspects to the new EMIS:

- **The student information system** is a comprehensive, web-based system that includes student demographics, enrollment, registration, scheduling, attendance, grading, discipline, transcript, and master schedule builder. It equips teachers, administrators, and parents with the power to obtain up-to-the-minute access to student information.
- The **learning management system** is a cloud-based learning platform that teachers, students, and parents can access on any device at any time. It integrates with the student information system to seamlessly populate class information and pass on critical student data.
- **The data warehouse** is a centralized repository of data that empowers administrators, principals, and school staff with timely and accurate longitudinal data to inform instructional practices and student performance, and provides an opportunity to increase student achievement. Reflecting on the implementation of the integrated EMIS, Howard County identified key advantages that the new system introduced and challenges for its implementation (table 7.5).

A key outcome in addition to the advantages below is that the new system provides a meaningful foundation for data-driven target setting. Before the integrated system was established, performance management targets were not aligned to the overarching strategy, nor were they consistently tracking and facilitating growth (Hitch and Fullerton 2013). Howard County also provided a list of what it identified as key success factors. Box 7.4 lists the essential elements that made implementation possible and helped overcome obstacles. Any EMIS requires some or even all of these aspects to be successful in the long term and to provide valuable information to education stakeholders at all levels for data-driven decision making.

Figure 7.5 A Thoughtful Strategic Plan Is the Road Map for an Effective EMIS

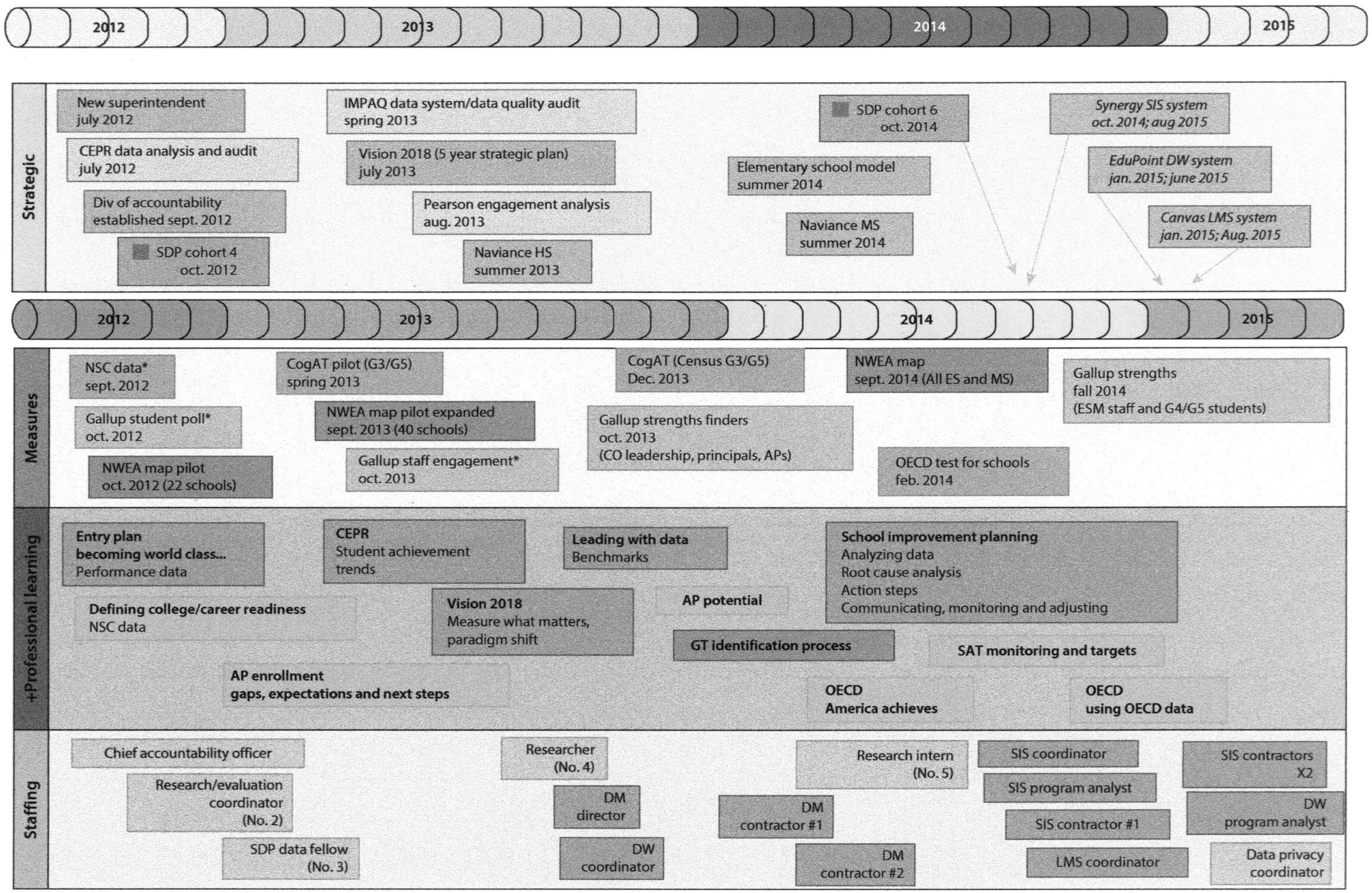

2012 | 2013 | 2014 | 2015

Strategic
- New superintendent july 2012
- CEPR data analysis and audit july 2012
- Div of accountability established sept. 2012
- SDP cohort 4 oct. 2012
- IMPAQ data system/data quality audit spring 2013
- Vision 2018 (5 year strategic plan) july 2013
- Pearson engagement analysis aug. 2013
- Naviance HS summer 2013
- SDP cohort 6 oct. 2014
- Elementary school model summer 2014
- Naviance MS summer 2014
- Synergy SIS system oct. 2014; aug 2015
- EduPoint DW system jan. 2015; june 2015
- Canvas LMS system jan. 2015; Aug. 2015

Measures
- NSC data* sept. 2012
- Gallup student poll* oct. 2012
- NWEA map pilot oct. 2012 (22 schools)
- CogAT pilot (G3/G5) spring 2013
- NWEA map pilot expanded sept. 2013 (40 schools)
- Gallup staff engagement* oct. 2013
- CogAT (Census G3/G5) Dec. 2013
- Gallup strengths finders oct. 2013 (CO leadership, principals, APs)
- NWEA map sept. 2014 (All ES and MS)
- OECD test for schools feb. 2014
- Gallup strengths fall 2014 (ESM staff and G4/G5 students)

+Professional learning
- Entry plan becoming world class... Performance data
- Defining college/career readiness NSC data
- AP enrollment gaps, expectations and next steps
- CEPR Student achievement trends
- Leading with data Benchmarks
- Vision 2018 Measure what matters, paradigm shift
- AP potential
- GT identification process
- School improvement planning / Analyzing data / Root cause analysis / Action steps / Communicating, monitoring and adjusting
- SAT monitoring and targets
- OECD America achieves
- OECD using OECD data

Staffing
- Chief accountability officer
- Research/evaluation coordinator (No. 2)
- SDP data fellow (No. 3)
- Researcher (No. 4)
- DM director
- DW coordinator
- Research intern (No. 5)
- DM contractor #1
- DM contractor #2
- SIS coordinator
- SIS program analyst
- SIS contractor #1
- LMS coordinator
- SIS contractors X2
- DW program analyst
- Data privacy coordinator

Source: Howard County 2015.

Note: EMIS = Education Management Information System.

Table 7.4 System Cost per Student

System	Cost per student (US$)
Student information system	9.33
Learning management system	2.68
Data warehouse	7.62

Source: Howard County 2015.

Table 7.5 Howard County, Maryland (United States) Reflections on Implementation of Integrated EMIS

Advantages	Challenges
• Ability to obtain accurate, real-time data • Single point of entry • Longitudinal analysis • Predictive analysis • Promotes equity	• Communication outside division • Aggressive timeline for implementation • Training of 8,000+ staff on three products • End-user buy-in

Source: Howard County 2015.
Note: EMIS = Education Management Information System.

Box 7.4 Key Factors of Success

• Leadership support and vision
• Funding
• Parallel approach to project implementation
• Skilled technical staff
• Project timeline and milestones
• Monitoring (daily, weekly)
• Communication within division and with vendor
• Collaboration, internally and externally
• Detailed training plan
• Managing and understanding the functional details (specifications) of systems
• Ability to influence change in culture
• Staff equipped with the right tools and technology
• Flexibility

Designing Longitudinal Data Systems

Data collection over the past century had a heavy emphasis on how to collect and organize student data, generally with a focus on demographic, academic, and financial information as it comes in on a yearly basis. These efforts have helped to build the enabling environments and digital architectures that we find today. Over the last two decades, advanced systems have started pursuing longitudinal data systems. Longitudinal data systems track student data over time and across institutions. Some platforms are making it possible to track students from preschool through primary, secondary, and tertiary education, and into the workforce. These platforms are referred to as P–20W. This section examines the evolution of longitudinal data systems in Maryland and another U.S. state, Florida.

The U.S. government encourages longitudinal data systems through the State Longitudinal Data Systems Grant Program (SLDS). The Education Sciences Reform Act (ESRA) of 2002 initiated the SLDS Grant Program to support the development and implementation of states' longitudinal data systems, as well as the expansion of K–12 systems and P–20W. Additionally, the SLDS program seeks to help states, districts, schools, and educators make data-informed decisions to improve student learning. As of 2012, SLDS had awarded grants totaling US$514 million.

Examples of Longitudinal Data Systems
The Maryland System

The Maryland Longitudinal Data System (MLDS) is a statewide data system that aims to integrate individual-level student data and workforce data in order to inform decision making and ultimately improve the state's education system. Maryland received three SLDS grants: US$5,690,718 (2006), US$5,990,186 (2009), and US$3,963,473 (2012). To drive state-level implementation of the longitudinal data system, Maryland enacted the Maryland Longitudinal Data System Act (Chapter 190, Senate Bill 275) in 2010 to establish the MLDS as a statewide data system containing certain student data from all levels of education and into the state's workforce. The MLDS is complex, consisting of multiple data owners, interagency data stewards, robust data architecture, and a myriad of data security, quality, and analytical tools and processes (figure 7.6).

The Maryland Longitudinal Data System Center is a state agency responsible for overseeing and maintaining the MLDS, mandated to effectively organize, manage, disaggregate, and analyze individual student data and to examine student progress and outcomes over time, including preparation for postsecondary education and the workforce. The MLDS Center (2015) has a clearly defined set of responsibilities, which include the following:

- Serving as a *central repository* of student and workforce data
- *Ensuring compliance* with the federal FERPA and other relevant privacy laws and policies
- Designing, implementing, and maintaining strict system *security procedures*
- Conducting research pursuant to the Governing Board's *research agenda*
- Maintaining a *public-facing website* and data portals
- Fulfilling *public information requests*

To fulfill these responsibilities, the Center works in partnership with the Maryland Higher Education Commission (MHEC), the MSDE, the Maryland Department of Labor, Licensing, and Regulation (DLLR), and

Figure 7.6 Maryland Longitudinal Data System Center, Data Process Flow

Maryland Longitudinal Data System Center data process flow
Person, organization, and transactional files provided by interagency data stewards, custodians, and owners

Last update: 05/13/2014

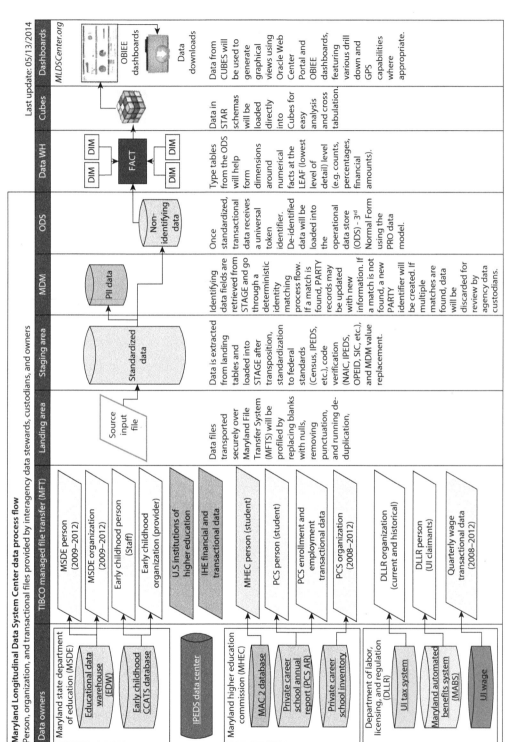

Source: MLDS Center 2014.

181

Figure 7.7 Maryland Longitudinal Data System

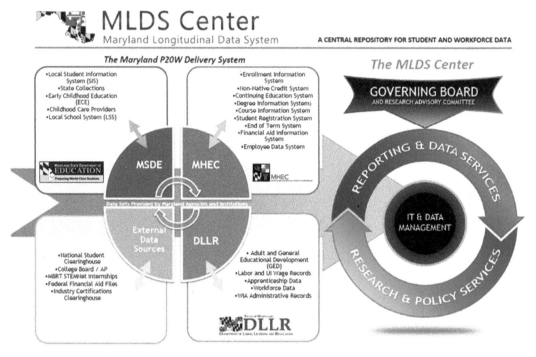

Source: MLDS Center 2014.

the University of Maryland School of Social Work and College of Education (figure 7.7).

The longitudinal system is used to answer key questions about students and the education system. In 2010, former Governor Martin O'Malley passed Senate Bill 275, Chapter 190, which established the MLDS. The bill authorized the MLDS Governing Board to oversee the project and mandated that the Governing Board comprise high-level officials from across the participating agencies. This leadership support and collaboration was an essential element to the success of the project.

As part of the design phase, the Governing Board identified 15 key policy questions that each participating agency needed answered; and, from there, it worked backward to build a system capable of answering these key guiding questions in three areas:

1. **Postsecondary Readiness and Access**
   a. Are students academically prepared to enter postsecondary institutions and complete programs in a timely manner?
   b. What percentage of high school exiters go on to enroll in postsecondary education?
   c. What percentage of high school exiters entering college are assessed to need to take developmental courses, and in what content areas?

    d. Which financial aid programs are most effective in improving access and success for students?

2. **Postsecondary Completion**

    a. How likely are students placed in developmental courses to persist in postsecondary education and transfer and/or graduate?

    b. Are community college students able to transfer within the state to four-year institutions successfully and without loss of credit?

    c. What are the differences in performance, retention, and graduation, including time to degree, of students across various postsecondary programs?

    d. What are the characteristics of two-year institutions that are most effective in allowing students to persist and either graduate or transfer?

    e. Which four-year institutions are most effective and timely in graduating students?

3. **Workforce Outcomes**

    a. What happens to students who start at community colleges and do not go on to four-year institutions?

    b. What are the educational and labor market outcomes for individuals who use federal and state resources to obtain training at community colleges or other postsecondary institutions?

    c. What economic value do noncredit community college credentials have in the workplace?

    d. Are college graduates successful in the workforce?

    e. What are the workforce outcomes for students who earn a high school diploma but do not transition to postsecondary education?

    f. What are the workforce outcomes of Maryland high school noncompleters?

The Governing Board also has oversight of the MLDS Center research agenda, which is guided by the 15 policy questions. The research agenda also has basic guidelines, for example, that all research analyses and reports intended to inform policy and programming will use data from at least two of the three partner agencies (MSDE, MHEC, and DLLR).

The foundation of the MLDS is established, including consensus across stakeholders, governance structures, management, and infrastructure. However, the system is not yet fully operational or populated with data. The last data inventory shows that most data from participating entities have been approved, although data are in various stages of preparation and loading into the system (MLDS Center 2014). Having data fully loaded in the MLDS and ready to use will mark a major milestone for Maryland's education system as a whole.

Maryland's process of establishing the foundation and infrastructure for the MLDS can guide other institutions. In general, longitudinal data systems do not need to be extremely robust, they simple need

- An identifier system,
- Common code sets that track information over time, and
- Systems and processes to keep data secure.

In addition to these technical elements, key ingredients are ongoing participation and support from high-level decision makers and thorough consensus building and communication efforts across stakeholder groups.

MLDS is part of a national movement for states to implement longitudinal data systems. In 2005, as part of the Educational Technical Assistance Act of 2002, the SLDS Grant Program started awarding grants and technical assistance to states in order to catalyze the successful design, development, implementation, and expansion of K–12 and P–20W (data from early learning to workforce) longitudinal data systems. Additional national efforts supported this movement, such as the Common Education Data Standards (CEDS) project, a national collaborative effort to develop voluntary, common data standards for a key set of education data elements to streamline the exchange, comparison, and understanding of data within and across P–20W institutions and sectors.

The DQC also supports this effort by tracking the progress of states toward achieving the 10 Essential Elements of statewide longitudinal data systems and the 10 State Actions to Ensure Effective Data Use. In 2014, Maryland scored 10 out of 10 on the Essential Elements of statewide longitudinal data systems, and 8 out of 10 on the 10 State Actions to Ensure Effective Data Use.[3] The two-point loss was a result of the lack of a fully operational and utilized LDS. DQC's State Actions assessment consists of 24 questions. Maryland answered "Yes" to all but the three following questions:

- Do parents, teachers, and appropriate stakeholders have access to student-level longitudinal data?
- Does state policy ensure that teachers and parents have access to their students' longitudinal data?
- Are teachers and principals trained to use longitudinal data to tailor instruction and inform school-wide policies and practices?

The Florida System

The state of Florida provides an example of a fully operational and utilized longitudinal data system (figure 7.8). In spite of a turbulent start due to political restructuring, Florida's statewide longitudinal data system helped to institutionalize the state's EMIS while cultivating a data-driven culture. State educational accountability policies date back nearly 50 years, positioning Florida at the forefront of efforts to track and learn from education data.

In 2014, the Florida Department of Education (FDOE) served nearly 2.7 million students, 4,200 public schools, 28 colleges, 192,000 teachers, 47,000 college professors and administrators, and 321,000 full-time staff throughout the state. It is one of the country's pioneers in collecting and tracking student-level data with the oldest longitudinal data system in the country dating back to 1995. Florida's statewide longitudinal data system tracks 2.7 million students across multiple agencies via a centralized data

Figure 7.8 Florida Longitudinal Data System

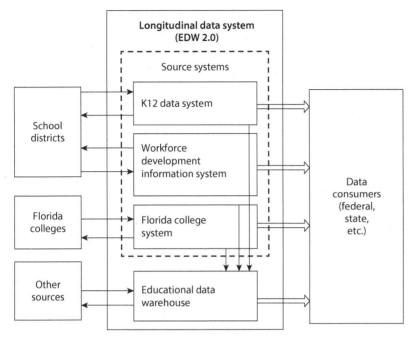

Source: Adapted from FDOE, http://www.fldoe.org/accountability/data-sys/statewide-longitudinal-data-sys/.

warehouse. According to the DQC (2006), Florida's use of data includes the following:

- *Accountability and reporting* across the education system
- Reporting almost immediately *after the two-to-three-week submission* period
- *Districts provided with files containing data* on their own students who are included in calculations for accountability purposes by the state
- *High use of data* by teachers and administrators
- *FDOE staff working with legislative staff* to ensure or strengthen understanding of the data used by legislators
- Florida Office of Program Policy Analysis and Government Accountability use of student level data to *examine performance in various areas in the context of costs of education*

Although Florida was certainly a pioneer in longitudinal data systems, the centralized data warehouse architecture was set up in 2003, and, more than ten years later, is ready for upgrades and enhancements. Florida pursued the same federal grant funds for upgrades that Maryland pursued (ARRA/RTTT, ESRA/SLDS).

MicQuiggan and Sapp (2014) note that Florida's key upgrades include the following:

- Improving data quality through *a feedback loop* that reports data quality issues back to the agency where the quality issue originated
- A *more efficient unique identification (UID) system* that uses a common, statewide UID as opposed to a local UID that has a cumbersome and inefficient process for tracking student movement
- A *better process for researcher access to data* with greater automation and use of data marts and cubes, as well as business intelligence—improved from Florida's initial process that was highly manual and time consuming
- Organization of a *data governance board*, which, surprisingly, was not established with the initial SLDS and which, in retrospect, would have benefitted the state, especially in the management of metadata

These upgrades also reveal lessons learned. A key lesson from Florida is the importance of establishing funding mechanisms that will maintain the system after the initial federal grants expire. Commitments from the state legislature, either in the form of matching grants or ongoing funding, ensure the long-term viability of the system (McQuiggan and Sapp 2014).

Central to this discussion of longitudinal data systems is the notion of when and how data are collected, their ability to integrate with other data sets, and the platforms that will catalyze data use in the future. Examples of innovation in advanced systems that will become increasingly prevalent in the coming years include the following:

- *Greater interoperability and integration capabilities* across data systems and types of data—for example, the ability to integrate classroom learning technologies with student information systems—will provide greater insight into student learning outcomes.
- Increasingly advanced systems will look to *gather and use real-time data, and integrate data* with other data systems. Collected data are often not used until after grades for a term or year have been completed, meaning that educators are not acting on data in real time.
- *Cloud computing* leverages a network of remote servers hosted on the Internet to make a variety of services from applications to database storage available at users' fingertips. Cloud platforms will continue to make education delivery more affordable, accessible, and collaborative in the years to come.

Notes

1. For more information about NCES and to access its annual report, see the NCES website at https://nces.ed.gov.
2. Comments in this chapter from Maryland educators and education officials come from personal and telephone interviews.
3. Scores at the time of writing, but these may have changed.

References

Cornman, Stephen and Lei Zhou. 2016. "Revenues and Expenditures for Public Elementary and Secondary Education: School Year 2013–14 (Fiscal Year 2014)." U.S. Department of Education: National Center for Education Statistics, Washington, DC. http://nces.ed.gov/pubsearch.

DQC (Data Quality Campaign). 2009. "10 State Actions to Ensure Effective Data Use." DQC. https://www.uschamberfoundation.org/sites/default/files/publication/edu/DQC_10%20State%20Actions%20To%20Ensure%20Effective%20Data%20Use.pdf.

Hitch, R., and J. Fullerton. 2013. "SDP Strategic Use of Data: Howard County Public School System." Harvard University Strategic Data Project, Harvard University, Cambridge, MA.

Hornbeck, David W. 1977. "Maryland's 'Project Basic.'" *Educational Leadership*, Association for Supervision and Curriculum Development.

Howard County. 2015. "Integrated Systems for HCPSS." Presentation delivered to World Bank by Grace Chesney and Justin Benedict, Washington, DC, April.

McQuiggan, Jaime, and Armistead Sapp. 2014. *Implement, Improve and Expand Your Statewide Longitudinal Data System: Creating a Culture of Data in Education*. Hoboken, NJ: John Wiley & Sons.

Michaels, H., and S. Ferrara. 1999. "Evolution of Educational Reform in Maryland: Using Data to Drive State Policy and Local Reform." In *Handbook of Educational Policy*, edited by G. J. Cizek. San Diego: Academic Press.

MLDS (Maryland Longitudinal Data System) Center. 2014. "Building a System to Protect Identities." Paper presented by Chandra Haislet to the MIS Conference, Washington, DC, August 1.

MSDE (Maryland State Department of Education). 2012. "School Progress Index." *Maryland Classroom* 18 (3), December.

———. 2015. "Maryland Student Records System Manual." MSDE, Baltimore, MD.

NCES (National Center on Education Statistics). 2016. "The Condition of Education 2016." U.S. Department of Education, Washington, DC.

U.S. Department of Education. 2008. "Organization of U.S. Education: State Role I - Primary and Secondary Education." International Affairs Office, U.S. Department of Education, Washington, DC.

Winters, Michael. 2015. "Christmas Bonus! US Edtech Sets Record with $1.85 Billion Raised in 2015." *EdSurge*, December 21. https://www.edsurge.com/news/2015-12-21-christmas-bonus-us-edtech -sets-record-with-1-85-billion-raised-in-2015.

CHAPTER 8

How to Build Progressive Centralized and Hybrid Data Systems: The Cases of Chile and Australia

My School is an important step in the Government's Education Revolution—providing unprecedented transparency and helping drive vital improvements in school education.
—Julia Gillard, then Deputy Prime Minister and
Minister of Education in Australia

Key Takeaways

- Both the Chilean and Australian governments demonstrated strong leadership and ensured buy-in from all stakeholders by clearly articulating the rationale for harnessing education data and actively communicating the need for an advanced Education Management Information System (EMIS).
- Cementing a strong legal framework with clearly defined guidelines, reporting mechanisms, and the ability to withstand changes in leadership was pivotal in building and ensuring continued development of the EMIS in both countries.
- Incentivizing data collection and reporting effectively ensured the viability of the EMIS. Both Chile and Australia incentivize the reporting of school-level information by linking it to school funding.
- Establishing a central, independent authority responsible for collecting, processing, and disseminating data ensures effective coordination across different stakeholders and well-functioning information management.
- Data are widely disseminated and communicated to foster transparency and accountability on the path of establishing a data-driven culture.
- Feedback loops ensure constant updates and monitoring of improvements in the education system. Both Chile and Australia continuously seek to expand, innovate, and upgrade their EMISs in order to adapt to changing needs.

Toward a Sound EMIS

The use of data to inform, enhance, and complement learning in education is undergoing significant growth across the world. Advanced EMISs have the potential to increase transparency, strengthen accountability, and support all education stakeholders in making evidence-based decisions that can ultimately drive continuous improvement of the entire education system and considerably improve student learning.

This chapter follows Chile and Australia on their journeys in the development and enhancement of their EMISs. Chile and Australia have both established well-functioning education data management systems in very different country contexts. Chile has striven to establish a comprehensive and reliable central EMIS over the past decades, under the strong leadership of the Ministry of Education (MoE). The Australian experience illustrates how the government galvanized efforts to develop a national system in a highly decentralized education model, making it a hybrid of centralized and decentralized structures. Launching education data platforms made education data more accessible and transparent for all education stakeholders at all levels. Despite the large differences in educational and social context, the cases of both countries underscore key factors and lessons crucial for the development and improvement of education data systems.

Driving Informed Decisions through EMIS—The Centralized Case of Chile

Chile has one of Latin America's oldest and most sophisticated EMISs, in which data are crucial at every step of the decision-making process. In a country in which a large majority of students attend private schools (tables 8.1 and 8.2), the education data system has played a fundamental role in not only informing parental school choice but also propelling a series of key reforms that aimed to improve quality and equity in education. Chile's longstanding EMIS provides a comprehensive set of educational data to the public and has been increasingly used as a key tool to improve school management and planning. Although Chile is yet to cultivate a data-driven culture among all stakeholders as in the case of Maryland, the Chilean EMIS can shed light on the process of developing and refining the system to facilitate informed decision making and to promote transparency and accountability in education (figure 8.1).

A reliable education data system has long been recognized as critical to improve quality at the national and school levels. Chile's education data system was developed along with the market-oriented reforms in the 1980s that gave birth to the current school voucher system, under which the government pays a flat subsidy to the public or private school of individual choice. Because the decision on where parents send their children to school has a direct effect on the funding for schools, the availability of accurate and timely data on student enrollment was fundamental to the voucher system. The government recognized that a prerequisite for such market-based approach to education is a reliable data

Table 8.1 Education Indicators at a Glance, Chile

	Male	Female	Total
Gross enrollment rates (2015)			
Primary	103.3	100.0	101.6
Lower secondary	103.7	101.8	102.8
Upper secondary	98.2	101.1	99.6
Gross graduation rates (2014)			
Primary	94.8	94.9	94.8
Lower secondary	96.3	97.1	96.7
Upper secondary	84.5	91.7	88.0
Pupil–teacher ratio (headcount basis, 2013)			
Primary	19.5		
Secondary	21.0		
Public expenditure on education (2014)			
As % of total government expenditure	19.9		
As % of GDP	4.8		

Source: UIS 2017.

Table 8.2 The Percentage of Students Enrolled by Sector and Level

	Primary (%)	Secondary (%)
Government	39.1	35.9
Private, subsidized	53.3	50.8
Private, nonsubsidized	7.6	8.3
Delegated administration	0.01	5.0

Source: MINEDUC 2015.

Figure 8.1 Evolution of EMIS in Chile

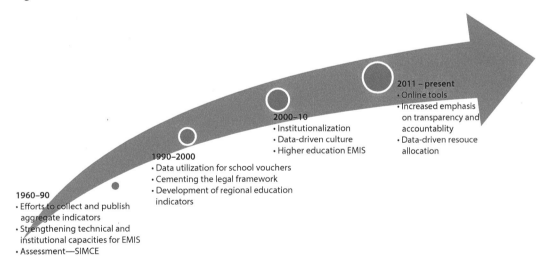

Note: EMIS = Education Management Information System; SIMCE = National System for Measuring the Quality of Education (*Sistema de Medición de la Calidad de la Educación*).

system that provides information on not just enrollment but also performance (Delannoy 2000; Himmel 1996), and developed a comprehensive education data system over the years.

EMIS development in Chile started as early as the 1960s and continues to expand and improve. Over the years, Chile has ensured that all decisions are rooted in information and data derived from the centralized education data management system. Five distinct stages in the EMIS development process emerge: (1) strengthening technical and institutional capacities, (2) cementing the legal framework to support data-guided policy decisions, (3) improving the quality and management of the information system, (4) institutionalization of a data-driven culture, and (5) expanding feedback loops and incentivizing data collection. Figure 8.1 illustrates the evolution of an EMIS in Chile. This chapter will detail the development stages and processes to establish a well-functioning EMIS that facilitates informed decision making.

Strengthening Technical and Institutional Capacities

As a first step toward developing an operational EMIS, Chile aimed to build the necessary technical and institutional capacities to collect and disseminate education data. Chile has been a forerunner in collecting and disseminating comprehensive education data. Since the late 1960s, the MoE has been collecting and publishing aggregate indicators on the education system (for example, coverage, education level, and literacy rate) and school types (public/subsidized and non-subsidized private) (UIS 2017). Through the early use of a school recordkeeping system, Chile also aimed to strengthen school-level data management and improve administrative efficiency by expediting tedious administrative tasks such as keeping student registers and scheduling. Cassidy (2006) documents that many schools, especially those located in remote areas, were encouraged to use and did use a packaged application for school-based data collection.

In the initial stage of developing education indicators and compiling educational statistics, Chile also cooperated with international agencies to strengthen its technical capacity. In the mid-to-late 1990s, Chile began participating in developing and producing education indicators through international initiatives such as the World Education Indicators Program and Mercosur (*Mercado Común del Sur*, a subregional bloc in South America) Education Indicators Project (Cassidy 2006). In 1998, in cooperation with OREALC (the regional education bureau, or *Oficina Regional de Educación para América Latina y el Caribe*) of the United Nations Educational, Scientific, and Cutural Organization (UNESCO), Chile led the development and implementation of the Regional Education Indicators Project (PRIE). The objectives of PRIE were to (1) develop a basic set of comparable education indicators for the Americas, (2) strengthen the capacity of national education statistics systems and analyze comparable indicators for the region, and (3) publish and promote the use of education indicators to inform the design of education policies (UNESCO 2011). Chile's MoE—along with a number of international organizations including the U.S. Agency for International

Development (USAID), UNESCO Institute for Statistics (UIS), and World Bank (through UIS)—provided funding support (US$856,205) as well as technical assistance on data collection and indicator development (PRIE 2003). Through this project, a range of education indicators on access, participation, coverage, progress, education finance, and resources were developed and relevant data were collected.

Through collaboration with various internal actors, Chile cultivated its technical and institutional capacities to design, maintain, and improve its EMIS. In developing its current system to evaluate student performance and disseminate information on educational quality, the MoE closely cooperated with the Catholic University of Chile. A multidisciplinary team of experts including engineers, psychologists, educators, and sociologists at the university was entrusted to design the first national census-based student assessment, the Performance Evaluation Program (PER) from 1981 to 1984. To ensure homogeneity in testing procedures, a total of 12,000 examiners were trained under the network of 640 supervisors (Himmel 1996). Technical pamphlets describing the program and manuals for interpreting test results and audiovisual aids were distributed to national and local officials, school principals, and teachers.

Despite these efforts, the program was short-lived, partially because of the lack of strong leadership, political commitment, and limited managerial and institutional capacity, in addition to the high cost of provision that amounted to roughly US$2 million—or US$5 per student (Himmel 1996). Having encountered such challenges, the MoE strategically planned to reinstate the system. The MoE continued to collaborate with the Catholic University to pool expertise and strengthen institutional capacity while clearly defining managerial responsibilities. It assigned an independent team within the MoE to be held responsible for administration, data management, and hiring and development of professionals. The tasks of information dissemination and system logistics and computations were delegated to the university. Through these efforts, the National System for Measuring the Quality of Education (*Sistema de Medición de la Calidad de la Educación*, SIMCE) was created and has been operating since 1988.

Cementing the Legal Framework to Support Data-Guided Policy Decisions

A strong legal framework was key to enabling continued development of Chile's EMIS. Since the passage of the Constitutional Law on Education (*Ley Orgánica Constitucional de Enseñanza*, LOCE) in 1990, data collection and use have evolved in scale and scope and from a compliance-driven approach to a learning-driven approach. Figure 8.2 outlines a series of policies that laid a strong foundation for improved transparency and accountability and ultimately the institutionalization of a data-driven culture.

LOCE, decreed in 1990 and governing the Chilean education system until 2008, secured the viability and sustainability of SIMCE. As Meckes and Carrasco

Figure 8.2 Timeline of Influential Policies

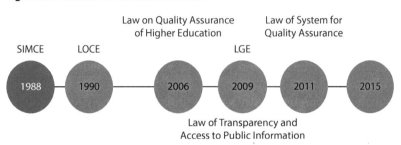

Note: LGE = Law of General Education (*Ley General de Educación*); LOCE = Constitutional Law on Education (*Ley Orgánica Constitucional de Enseñanza*); SIMCE = National System for Measuring the Quality of Education (*Sistema de Medición de la Calidad de la Educación*).

(2010) note, LOCE institutionalized SIMCE within the framework of the MoE and assigned the following responsibilities:

- *Evaluate the achievement of national curriculum objectives* on a regular basis at the end of primary and secondary education, at the minimum.
- *Design and conduct assessments* and analyze data at the regional and school levels.
- *Publish assessment data* (except data on individual student performance) in a newspaper.
- *Submit the assessment system* for the approval of the Higher Education Council.

In accordance with LOCE, SIMCE was administered to fourth and eighth graders in alternate years between 1988 and 1994. SIMCE included tenth graders and has been operating on a yearly basis since 1994.

The legal mandate to publish school-level SIMCE results paved the way toward greater transparency and accountability. Until 1995, school-level SIMCE scores were shared confidentially only with school principals and teachers. As the public increasingly voiced its demand for transparency and educational quality, in 1995 SIMCE began publishing school-level results and rankings of schools in newspapers with national and regional coverage. The newspaper supplement included mean scores and changes in scores from the previous assessment, from the national mean, and from that of schools with similar socioeconomic student population—allowing parents to compare school performance in context and holding schools accountable. Since 1998, school reports were distributed to all schools usually at the beginning of the next school year as a means to provide pedagogical support. In addition to student performance data, the report included examples of test questions with an analysis of the contents and skills required to correctly answer them and workshop guidelines for the schools to establish improvement plans.

Chile has undertaken its first steps toward effective data use at different levels. Under the school voucher system, high-quality data on student performance and school characteristics were imperative to effectively allocate resources and generate appropriate incentives for schools. Since the early 1990s, the Chilean government used SIMCE scores to inform key policy decisions. For instance, the P-900 program, introduced in 1990, used average fourth grade SIMCE scores to allocate additional resources to about 900 underperforming schools (Mizala, Romaguera, and Urquiola 2007). The program was institutionalized and scaled in 2008 with the Law on Preferential Subsidies (*Ley de Subvención Escolar Preferencial*, SEP).

Improving the Quality and Management of the Information System

A single entity is responsible for the management of a particular set of information. The Department of Evaluation, Measurement and Educational Registry (*Departamento de Evaluación, Medición y Registro Educacional*, DEMRE) at the University of Chile is responsible for the management of information on the standardized university admissions examination (*Prueba de Selección Universitaria*, PSU). The Higher Education Division within the MoE has developed and is responsible for the National Higher Education Information System (SIES). Other entities include the National Board of Student Aid and Scholarships (*Junta Nacional de Auxilio Escolar y Becas*, JUNAEB), responsible for managing information related to student vulnerability (EVI-SINAE). ENLACES, or the Center for Education and Technology in the MoE, is responsible for data related to use of information and communication technology (ICT) in education based on data collected from the Digital Census, SIMCE, and administrative data. The National Accreditation Commission (*Comisión Nacional de Acreditación*, CNA) is responsible for issuing accreditation of educational institutions and managing relevant information.

The Center for Research in the MoE coordinates the information gathered from various agencies to disseminate timely and quality education information. It supports the process of collection, validation, processing, and integration of databases; conducts impact evaluations; and publishes reports on official statistics. The links to the abovementioned datasets are published on the Center's website and are accompanied by the e-mail addresses of staff who can be contacted for inquiries. In addition to these data sources, the official database incorporates information from the National Demographic Census and the National Household Surveys that collect information on the average years of schooling of the adult population. The Center for Research comprises an interdisciplinary team of professionals, organized in seven units by function and level of education: Statistics, Evaluation, Early Childhood Education, School Education (primary and secondary), Higher Education, Research Promotion, and Cabinet Support units. There are currently 35 professionals including multiple trained statisticians and statistical engineers at the Center.

Technology has facilitated data collection, processing, and dissemination. The National Statistics Institute (*Instituto Nacional de Estadísticas*, INE) creates a computer database by scanning paper-based questionnaires and applying optical mark recognition (OMR) and intelligent character recognition (ICR) software.[1]

These processes of data capture and computer-assisted coding are outsourced to experienced external vendor(s) selected through a tender process. Box 8.1 describes an example of one of the private companies that undertook this task.

As in the case of the census, the government uses OCR/ICR and data capture technologies to process SIMCE data and to create a digitized database (*Agencia de Calidad de la Educación* 2014). It divides the tasks of digitizing and processing SIMCE data into several parts and distributes them among the external document management companies selected through a tender process. For instance, Dimacofi, a software company specializing in copying, printing, and document management tasks, participated in SIMCE processing for three years. Dimacofi provided *Soluciones Web Y Portales* (SWYP) *Ltda* using the ABBYY FormReader software bundled with scanners to replace manual data entry with automatic capture of information from the paper-based questionnaires. Figure 8.3 depicts a typical workflow of the data capture process. Upon receipt of the sealed SIMCE

Box 8.1 Example of Chilean Data Collection Software

Developed by a Chilean system engineering company Serpro, *CSProX* is software that simplifies designing complex questionnaires through its intuitive interface and a relatively simple programming language and development environment. The Computer-Assisted Personal Interview supports the use of the software by adding user-friendly features such as pop-up menus, assisted-coding algorithms, and interactive error correction to the data entry core operations. It can also be used on different devices with the Windows Operating System and can adapt the way it displays a questionnaire (for example, multiple questions per screen or one per screen) to the device on which it is operating, all using the same data collection application.

Source: Serpro, http://www.serpro.com.

Figure 8.3 A Typical Process of Data Capture

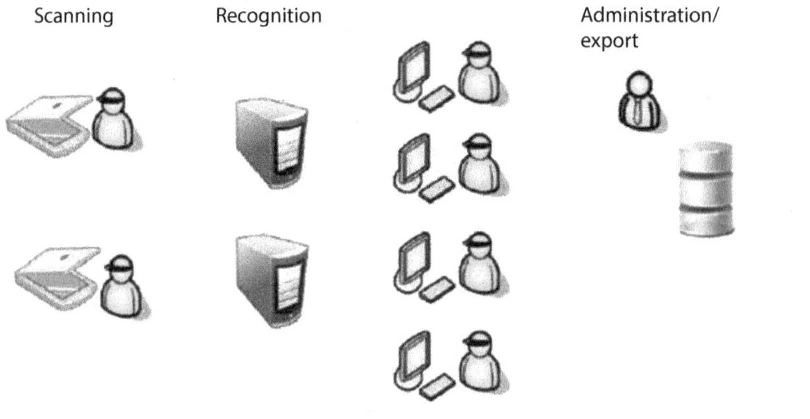

Source: ABBYY 2016.

questionnaires, the documents are scanned by five to six workers. Then data are processed sequentially from scanning and recognition to verification and correction, and automatically exported to a central repository. This automated process enables high-quality text recognition and data extraction, and reduces common errors associated with manual data entry.

Improving the Quality and Management of the Information System

In recent years, greater emphasis has been placed on transparency and quality assurance. Chile has focused extensively on establishing and institutionalizing a data-driven culture. With the ratification of a series of legislations outlined in table 8.3, Chile aimed to improve the quality of its education system through improved performance measurement, monitoring, and dissemination of information. The following centralized, independent agencies have been established to monitor adherence to educational standards, conduct quality inspections, and manage relevant information systems:

- The **National Education Council** (*Consejo Nacional de Educación*, CNED) is an autonomous education advisory body that reviews and approves ministerial proposals, including quality standards and curricula. It also manages the ÍNDICES system through which it collects, processes, and validates a large set of data on higher education (that is, matriculation, tuition, institution infrastructure, library resources, and retention).
- The **Agency for Education Quality** (*Agencia de Calidad de la Educación*) shoulders the prime responsibility of managing SIMCE. The agency is also responsible for guiding schools in their institutional and pedagogical improvement, providing additional technical assistance to low-performing schools, and informing the school community of these processes through school

Table 8.3 Policy Measures to Improve Transparency and Quality of Education

Year	Legislation	Description
2009	Law of General Education (*Ley General de Educación*, LGE)	The LGE aims to improve quality of education by setting learning standards, measuring and monitoring the overall quality of education, and outlining consequences for schools that fail to meet the standards.
2009	Law on Transparency and Access to Public Information (*Ley de Transparencia de la Función Pública y Acceso a la Información*)	The Law on Transparency and Access to Public Information requires all branches of government to publish up-to-date information, including expenditures, salaries, and subsidies.
2011	Law of System for Quality Assurance (*Ley del Sistema de Aseguramiento de la Calidad*)	The Law of System for Quality Assurance aims to strengthen monitoring of national educational progress and to improve educational quality and equity. It established the National System for Quality Assurance of School Education (*Sistema Nacional de Aseguramiento de la Calidad de la Educación Escolar*, SAC).

inspection reports. It coordinates, analyzes, and disseminates information on international assessments.

- The **Superintendent of School Education** (*Superintendencia de Educación Escolar*) is responsible for monitoring the use of resources and schools' compliance with educational standards, laws, and regulations to ensure that schools meet minimum requirements to provide quality education to their students.

The push for transparency and quality has translated into publishing more and better information. The scope of the information system has now expanded to cover schools, teachers, and higher education. More information has led to wider use of data to support evidence-based decision making by all key stakeholders.

The Chilean EMIS has expanded to include higher education. The rapid expansion of higher education and an exponential growth in the number and diversity of institutions signaled a need for robust and reliable data. The Law on Quality Assurance of Higher Education (2006) entrusted the Higher Education Division within the MoE to develop a data system. The National Higher Education Information System (*Sistema Nacional de Información de la Educación Superior*, SIES) was created in the subsequent year. Prior to the establishment of SIES, the data on tertiary education were not centralized but were with different institutions providing often inconsistent data, leading to misinterpretations and lack of confidence in data (Zanderigo, Dowd, and Turner 2012). Currently, the SIES collects, systematizes, analyzes, and disseminates information on higher education and supports students to make informed decisions about their future career trajectories.

Along with school inspection and evaluation data, Chile has been collecting, publishing, and monitoring information on education finance at the aggregate and school levels. The MoE collects and provides data on national and school-level budget and resources received via the per-pupil voucher, preferential voucher (weighted voucher), and shared financing (tuition). It also collects information on resource use within each school, for example, how much is invested in the school improvement plan, teacher salaries, and school facilities (UIS 2017). Such information is then shared with the Superintendent of School Education that monitors the use of public resources and publishes detailed school budget and investment information on its website. With the 2015 passage of the Law of Inclusion (*Ley de Inclusión*), the Superintendent of School Education is required to keep a register of schools' bank records as evidence that funding is being used for educational purposes.

In addition, Chile has established a comprehensive teacher evaluation and information management system. The MoE has been collecting and publishing individual-level information (with specific codes for confidentiality) on teacher education (type of institution), specialization (type of program), initial training and professional development, years of experience, type of contract, and work schedule of teachers and teacher assistants. This teacher data system also consolidates information from the national, standards-based, mandatory teacher evaluation system (commonly referred to as *Docentemás*) including evaluation results and resulting rewards. The evaluation uses a composite measure of teacher quality from information collected, including portfolios, self-evaluations, and value-added measures of student achievement; and the results are distributed to teachers and directors to identify training needs and provide pertinent support to ultimately improve instructional practice. This evaluation system is complemented by a range of reward programs that provide individual and group rewards for teachers and by the recently introduced teacher career system. Teachers who receive a Basic or Unsatisfactory rating are required to participate in Professional Development Plans (*Planes de Superación Profesional*, PSPs), and those who receive a second consecutive Unsatisfactory rating in the evaluation are to be dismissed.

Institutionalization of a Data-Driven Culture, Expanding Feedback Loops, and Incentivizing Data Collection

Policy makers and researchers have long used school management, finance, and student achievement data to design, improve, and monitor policies. The focus has been expanded to empower all education stakeholders—including parents and the entire school community—and to further promote evidence-based decision making in the education system.

The system of school performance evaluation generated a feedback cycle, allowing school administrators and teachers to monitor their schools' performance and improve practice. As stipulated in LOCE, the Agency for Education Quality conducts regular school performance evaluations with the objective of strengthening self-evaluation and institutional capacities of schools and promoting continuous improvement of educational quality. The Agency uses multiple indicators to evaluate school performance, including school climate, school reputation, school motivation, civic education, school attendance, retention, gender equity, and technical and professional qualifications. It engages in direct data collection through three-day school visits, during which the inspectors collect information using various tools, such as surveys and interviews with administrators, teachers, teacher aides, parents, and students.

On the basis of the information collected, the evaluators deliver an external qualitative diagnosis of schools and identify schools that are failing or are in need of active intervention. High-performing schools are given the autonomy to design their own school improvement plan and engage in internal capacity building. Others are to receive technical support from either the MoE or certified institutions to draft their improvement plans.[2] Low-performing schools that fail to improve after receiving assistance face the risk of losing their operating license or eligibility for government subsidy. Existing evidence suggests that low-performing schools under high accountability pressures modified internal policies and practices in meaningful ways and improved student achievement (Elacqua 2015; Mizala and Torshe 2013).

Chile is steadily moving toward establishing a data-driven culture through actively communicating school-level data to the public and generating feedback loops. With the slogan "More information, better education," the MoE's web page of the same title provides information on schools, including school-level SIMCE and PSU results, teacher evaluation results, and the selection process, to guide parental school choice. The website also has an interactive tool that allows anyone to search for school results by name, unique school ID number, type of school, municipality, and urban/rural location. It provides rich information on student academic indicators as well as social and personal indicators (figure 8.4). Based on SIMCE data, the academic evaluation result page displays trends in student achievement (for example, comparison of current and past SIMCE score), comparison of results with schools with similar characteristics, and information on how the community should and should not use the data. Social and personal indicators include sanitary standards, learning environment, community engagement, and school motivation level, among others. Raw datasets containing information on average scores for each subject disaggregated by various student and school characteristics since 1998 can be downloaded from the website.

Chile has also increased efforts to actively engage families and provide them with digestible and actionable information so they can make informed school choice decisions and improve student learning. With the implementation of the

Figure 8.4 Sample School Performance Report Available to the Public on the SIMCE Website

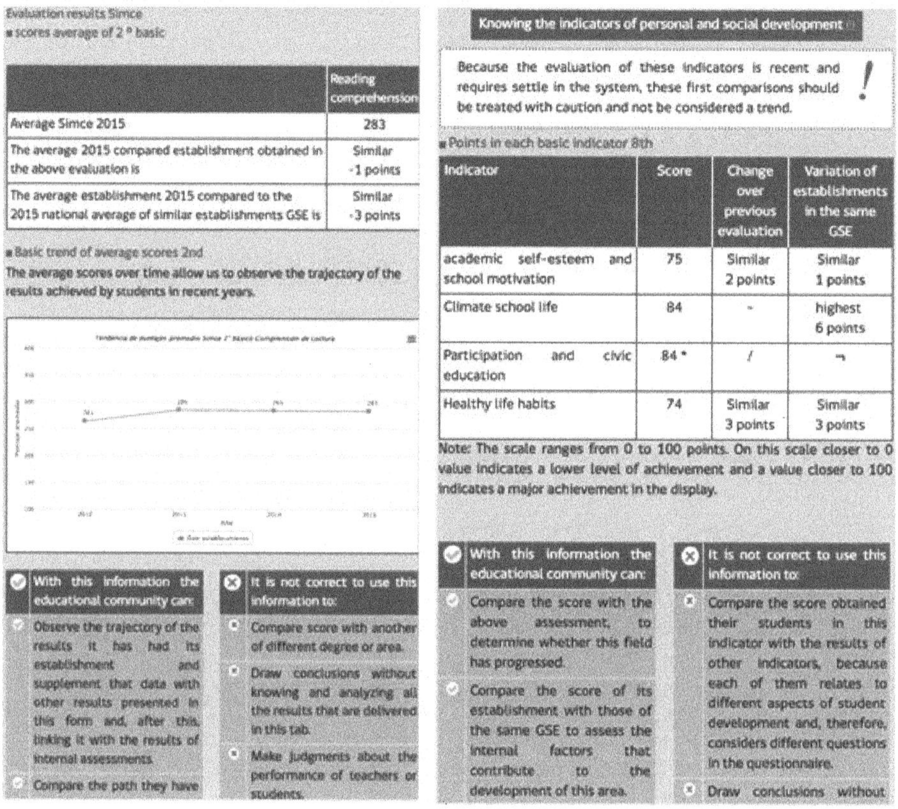

Source: Agencia de Calidad de la Educación, http://www.agenciaeducacion.cl.

school voucher system that determined the amount of school subsidies largely based on the number of students enrolled, school principals were incentivized to enroll more students and thereby engaged in multiple efforts, including informing families of each school's good academic results or unique features. The Agency for Education Quality prepares and publishes the Information Card, an annual report specifically for parents and guardians that includes detailed explanation of SIMCE test results using nontechnical terms as well as recommendations on how parents can support their children's learning at home (figure 8.5).

As simply demonstrated by the change in the design and number of booklets distributed—from a few black-and-white flyers per school in 2010 to color-print booklets and digital copies available to all parents in 2014—the MoE has increased efforts to improve dissemination of information to parents and enhance parental engagement. If the initial dissemination efforts were focused on cost efficiency, the MoE now places greater emphasis on user friendliness and accessibility, mandating that these reports are sent to each school and holding the school directors responsible for distribution. Another effective means of informing parental school choice is a geo-referential system available online through the SIMCE website (map 8.1). It displays a user-friendly, interactive map with each balloon corresponding to a school and displaying the average SIMCE score of the school in the last three tests.

Although existing evidence suggests that families' school choice decisions tend to be influenced more by school proximity, infrastructure, socioeconomic characteristics, and other factors (Elacqua and Fabrega 2004; Barrera-Osorio, Linden, and Urquiola 2008), the wide dissemination of school-based results became a driving force in promoting a standards-based reform and signal a step toward improving accountability and transparency.

SIES supports students in making informed decisions about their future. Under the SIES, the My Future (*Mi Futuro*) website provides information from multiple databases focusing on the four main areas: (1) *Futuro Laboral* on expected returns by program and institution (table 8.4); (2) *Ficha Financiera* on indicators on the financial situation of institutions; (3) *Ficha Académica* on academic attributes, including enrollment rates and number of professors; and (4) SIES *Técnico* on information on vocationally oriented institutions. Since its creation, the number of visits has nearly doubled, jumping from 856,000

Figure 8.5 Examples of Reports Specifically for Parents and Guardians

| 2nd basic | basic 4.° | basic 6.° | basic 8.° | II medium | III means |

Source: Agencia de Calidad de la Educación, http://www.agenciaeducacion.cl.

Map 8.1 A Display of Schools in Santiago, Chile

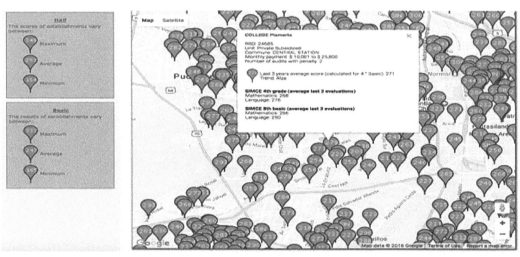

Source: SIMCE, http://www.agenciaeducacion.cl/evaluaciones/que-es-el-simce/.

Table 8.4 Information on Employability and Income Prospects Available through *Mi Futuro* Website

Institution	Accreditation of the Institution	Career	% Students of subsidized establishments	Retention of 1st year	Actual Duration (semesters)	Employability 1st year	Average income at the 4th year	Annual Tariff 2016
Pontifical Catholic University of Chile	7 years	Nursing	57.0%	92.1%	10.8	99.5%	From $ 1 million 300 thousand to $ 1 million 400 thousand	$ 3,818,000
Pontifical Catholic University of Chile	7 years	Chemistry and Pharmacy	78.4%	93.3%	14.2	97.6%	From $ 1 million 400 thousand to $ 1 million 500 thousand	$ 3,672,000
Pontifical Catholic University of Chile	7 years	Law	22.2%	94.1%	14.4	96.6%	From $ 1 million 900 thousand to $ 2 million	$ 4,739,000
Pontifical Catholic University of Chile	7 years	Commercial engineering	12.0%	95.1%	12.8	96.5%	From $ 2 million 100 thousand to $ 2 million 200 thousand	$ 5,398,000

Search criteria above table: Type: Universities · Institution: Pontificia Universidad Catolica de Chile · Career: All · Change search criteria · Search results:

Source: Mi Futuro, http://www.mifuturo.cl/.

in 2010 to 1,600,000 in 2012 (Zanderigo, Dowd, and Turner 2012). In addition to the My Future website, the *Elige Carrera* website managed by CNED provides information on different career trajectories to inform student educational choice.

The MoE publishes various education statistics to facilitate research and support informed decision making. Some of the education indicators available through the MoE include enrollment, dropout, retention, and graduation rates; spending as a percentage of GDP; per-pupil spending; class and school size;

Table 8.5 Indicators Presented in the Annual Report on Education Statis of Education, Chile, 2015

Areas presented	Data presented in the report
Educational institutions	• Number of schools (preprimary, primary, and second geographical area, religious orientation, monthly co: • Number of higher education institutions by region • Number of schools that provide each level of educat unit, region, geographical area, etc.
Student participation	• Student enrollment (preprimary, primary, secondary, ... region, level of education, type of program (technical/general), gender, etc.
Teachers and assistants	• Total number of teachers • Number of teachers by institution, region, geographical area, age, gender, etc. • Total number of assistants • Number of assistants by type, region, geographical area, age, gender, etc.
Supporters	• Number of supporters, establishments, students, teaching positions, and assistant positions by type of supporter and region

Source: Translated from *Centro de Estudios* 2016.

literacy rates; school achievement; school and teacher evaluation results; school mission; and student demographics. Table 8.5 shows some of the indicators included in the MoE's Annual Report on Education Statistics. Datasets can be downloaded in Comma-Separated Values (CSV) or Microsoft Excel format to facilitate data sharing and statistical analysis.

In fact, studies suggest that data-driven policies have been effective in improving educational quality and equity. Since 2008, SEP has provided additional financial and technical support to public and public-subsidized private primary schools for enrollment of socioeconomically disadvantaged students. On the basis of data from the centralized enrollment system, the weighted per-pupil funding formulas compensate for the higher costs of educating disadvantaged students and aim to ensure equitable access to quality education (Elacqua 2015; OECD 2013). The recently ratified Law of Inclusion aims to further promote equity by increasing preferential subsidy by 20 percent and launching a common school application platform, in which an objective, transparent, and nondiscriminatory algorithm will be used to allocate students when demand for seats exceeds supply.

A number of studies have found positive effects of SEP on improving student achievement, as measured by scores on SIMCE, and on reducing income-based achievement gaps (*Centro de Estudios* 2012; Murnane, Page, and Vegas 2010). An impact evaluation of Chile's scholarship for academically strong teacher candidates (*Beca Vocación de Profesor*, BVP) demonstrates that BVP has been successful in attracting those with higher academic performance, as measured by scores on the PSU, than the average for teacher training candidates (Alvarado 2009). Analysis by Wales et al. (2014) shows that the effectiveness of Chile's education policy benefitted from the availability of significant amounts of data that induced external research on policies, which then enabled the government to phase out or suspend ineffective policies or modify them to ensure successful implementation. Such a feedback loop would not have been possible without the culture of monitoring and evaluation within the MoE that welcomed external expertise to inform policy design and implementation.

Looking Ahead

Although Chile has made strides in expanding access to education and reducing gaps in school learning, several challenges remain in improving educational quality and equity. One of the gravest challenges is the narrowing yet persistent income-based achievement gap. Although a large majority of students attend private schools, there is no obligatory system of supervision for nonsubsidized private education providers. There is also an overlap in the functions of supervisory agencies, and the various providers operate according to different rules. There is no obligatory system of supervision for private providers, allowing them to control the population they were serving in a way that municipal schools could not, leading to further stratification between students of different socioeconomic backgrounds. For instance, studies suggest that private voucher schools, with higher salaries and more flexible wage structures, are able to hire higher-quality teachers, which explains a large portion of the achievement gap between public and private voucher schools (Behrman et al. 2016; Correra, Parro, and Reyes 2014).

The unregulated nature of the nonsubsidized private institutions and non-mandatory submission of institutional data naturally limit access to and reliability of data. The empirical evidence on the performance of private schools, particularly small-scale independent schools, is limited because of thin data. This poses a concern given the high proportion of students attending a private institution and the large heterogeneity in the quality of these institutions. The government has increased efforts to collect and disseminate information on these schools by requiring all institutions to participate in SIMCE and incentivizing all schools to disclose information through its open portal. For instance, although filling out the section on information on school characteristics on the SIMCE website is not required, most schools, including nonsubsidized private schools, provide information. However, the website notes that the accuracy of the data is solely the school's responsibility. Similarly, higher education institutions voluntarily submit data to SIES, with the exception of those regarding licensing and accreditation. Despite the voluntary nature, participation rates have remained high and ÍNDICES covers more than 90 percent of all higher education institutions since 2008 (Zanderigo, Dowd, and Turner 2012). Nevertheless, participation varies across the different institutional types, with universities systematically providing more information than vocationally oriented higher education institutions.

Although Chile has established a strong foundation for a successful operation of the data system, more can be done to strengthen the feedback loop to propel continuous improvement in education. The Chilean experience of developing and effectively using education data also illustrates the critical importance of sustained commitment and engagement of key stakeholders and long-term planning and consensus building. Yet there is not much available evidence of use of data to inform instructional practice. Improved integration of the educational data system ensures a functioning EMIS in a coordinated manner. In addition, it increases support for all key stakeholders and enables them to use data for making informed decisions. This would ensure active stakeholder participation and strengthen school accountability, and ultimately enable transitioning from a compliance-based to learning-focused system.

Overall, Chile has made substantial progress toward a data-driven culture and a strong compliance system. Chile has been at the forefront of collecting and disseminating information to inform parental choice and policy decisions to improve educational quality and equity. In particular, Chile's longstanding EMIS has evolved according to the changing needs and objectives throughout its life cycle over the past three decades and has been used to transmit incentives to teachers and schools. Through the use of online tools and dissemination efforts, along with passage of laws mandating public disclosure of information, Chile has been striving to promote transparency and accountability and has moved a step closer to securing a data-driven culture. Although the Chilean system still faces challenges in involving and incorporating data from the private sector, it can serve as a role model for countries wishing to uphold national learning standards in an environment where private schools dominate the education system.

Strengthening National Accountability and Transparency through Data while Maintaining a Decentralized Model—The Hybrid Case of Australia

The Australian Commonwealth Government established a hybrid education management system. Even though states collect data and disseminate reports, the government has focused on national accountability, reporting, and transparency standards to enable all stakeholder groups nationwide access to education data (table 8.6). The government allocates funds to all schools, sets national education standards, drives education reform, and ensures national performance measurement and reporting. Nevertheless, as defined by the federal system of government, the state and territory governments remain responsible for the provision of education to all children of school age. Therefore, the national government in Australia had to carefully design measures to establish national education standards, improve nationwide transparency, and strengthen accountability. One of these efforts is the online platform My School that allows the public to access and compare education data nationally. Figure 8.6 provides an overview of Australia's EMIS evolution.

Establishing the Legal Framework for Education Goals, Performance Monitoring, and Reporting

In an advanced system such as in Australia, policy goals are aligned so that they contribute to institutionalizing and promoting a fully operational EMIS (figure 8.7). Education stakeholders are informed about the national goals and objectives as well as the specific plans and actions to achieve them.

Table 8.6 Education Indicators at a Glance, Australia

Level	Number of schools	Enrollment (full-time students)	Student enrollment in govt. schools (%)
Schools and Enrollment (2015)[a]			
Primary	6,224	2,135,076	69.5
Secondary	1,409	1,595,618	59.0
Combined	1,323	—	—

Gross enrollment rates (2014)[b]			
	Male	*Female*	*Total*
Primary	106.4	105.8	106.1
Lower secondary	114.0	109.9	112.0
Upper secondary	193.0	179.3	186.4

Gross graduation rates (2014)[b]			
	Male	*Female*	*Total*
Primary	106.4	105.8	106.1
Lower secondary	114.0	109.9	112.0
Upper secondary	151.9	159.5	155.6

Pupil (full-time equivalent)–teacher ratio (2015)[a]			
Primary			15.4
Secondary			12.0

Public expenditure on education (2013)[b]			
As % of total government expenditure			14.0
As % of GDP			1.3

Note: GDP = gross domestic product; — = not available.
a. Information from ABS 2016.
b. Information from UIS 2017.

Figure 8.6 Evolution of the EMIS in Australia

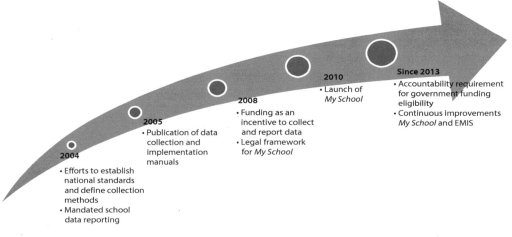

Note: EMIS = Education Management Information System.

Figure 8.7 Institutionalization of the Australian Education Data System

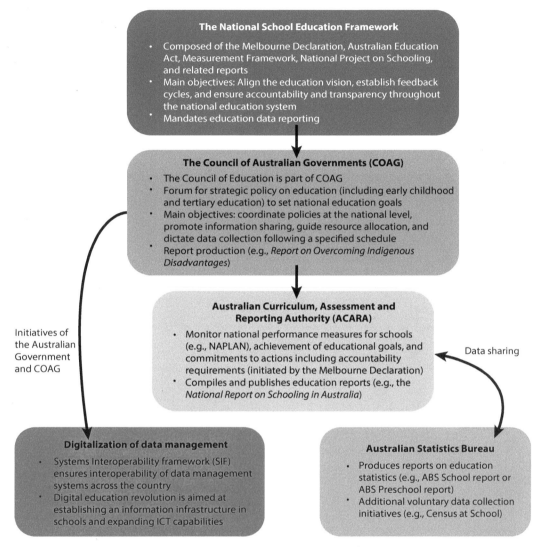

Note: ICT = information and communication technology.

Improving transparency and accountability through structural dissemination of education statistics has been a long-term priority in Australia.

Given the decentralized nature of the education system, it was imperative to establish common definitions of variables and data collection methods; this ensures comparability across the nation in order to accurately assess the state of its education system and track improvement in schools and student learning. Table 8.7 provides an overview of the policy milestones that contributed to the evolution of the data system.

Table 8.7 Evolution of Policies toward a Data System

Influential policy measures	Description
Australian National School Education Policy Framework	The Policy *Framework* connects national priorities/commitments and policies across the system so that they reinforce each other. The framework consists of five key policy documents and reports: • The Melbourne Declaration on Educational Goals for Young Australians sets national educational goals and commitments to action for schooling. • The Australian Education Act, the National Education Agreement, and the National Education Reform Agreement lay the foundation for performance measurement and reporting. • The focus of the Measurement Framework for Schooling in Australia lies on student (1) participation: enrollment, attendance, and participation in assessments and vocational training; (2) achievement: literacy, numeracy, ICT, science, and citizenship; (3) attainment: school completion and post-learning pathways; and (4) equity. • The *National Report on Schooling in Australia* presents the nationally agreed key performance measures defined in the Measurement Framework. • Related documents include the annual Report on Government Services and the biennial COAG *Report on Overcoming Indigenous Disadvantages.*
Schools Assistance (Learning Together–Achievement Through Choice and Opportunity) Act 2004	The Act outlines the *principles* for reporting to which all education authorities must commit their funding agreements. All schools are required to report information on their students and staff, progress on the school plan, and school performance in four domains—(1) learning and teaching, (2) student environment, (3) leadership and management, and (4) community involvement—through the *Annual School Board Report.* The Act allows the government to set national educational standards and collect quantitative information on schools. The amended version is currently in force.
Schools Assistance Act 2008 and Australian Education Act 2013	The Acts serve as the principal *legislation* for the provision of school funding and create financial incentives for schools to collect and report information. The scope of funding and financial assistance has been expanded to nongovernment primary and secondary education. The Australian Education Act supersedes the Schools Assistance Act 2008.
Schools Assistance Regulations	The Regulations outline the *school performance* and transparency requirements to receive government funding under the Act. The funding requirements specified in the regulations include (1) national school assessments, (2) national reports on the outcomes of schooling, (3) individual school information, (4) reporting to parents, (5) publication by schools of information relating to schools, and (6) national curriculum.
National Data Standards Manual	The manual aims to *assist schools* in data collection and storage processes. First introduced in 2005, the original edition, titled *Data Implementation Manual for Enrolments,* provided guidelines on designing enrollment forms and collecting and managing data. The manual includes (1) standard definitions for the following student background characteristics: sex, indigenous status, language and socioeconomic background, and geographic location; and (2) technical specifications for collecting data. The manual was updated and published in 2007, 2008, 2009, 2010, and 2012.

Source: Adapted from ACARA 2014; Australian Government 2006: PNQ Systems, http://www.pnqsys.com/contact.aspx.
Note: COAG = Council of Australian Governments; ICT = information and communication technology.

The National School Education Policy Framework ensures that measurement and reporting are aligned with educational goals and creates positive feedback cycles. The framework governs the collection and publication of student and school data with the objectives of (1) promoting accountability to students, parents, and the community; (2) tracking the achievement of educational goals; and (3) providing evidence to support future policy reforms and system improvements including smart resource allocation. The national priorities and commitments along with the key policy

Figure 8.8 The National School Education Policy Framework

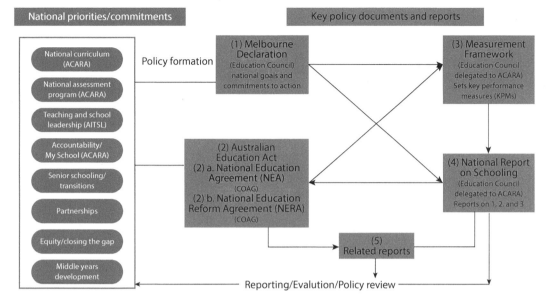

Source: ACARA 2015.

documents and reports identified in the framework are organically connected and reinforce each other in policy formation, reporting, and evaluation (figure 8.8).

The legal framework assigns data responsibility. The key governing bodies are the Education Council and the Australian Curriculum, Assessment and Reporting Authority (ACARA). The Education Council, established in 2013 as part of the Council of Australian Governments (COAG), acts as a forum for strategic policy on school education, early childhood education, and higher education.[3] It coordinates policies at the national level, promotes collaboration on information sharing, and guides resource allocation. Under the supervision of the Education Council, the ACARA monitors and reviews the national performance measures for schools, achievement of educational goals, and commitments to action stated in the Melbourne Declaration, and the accountability requirements established by intergovernmental agreements (ACARA 2015).

Mandating and Setting Standards for Reporting to Ensure Comparability and Quality of Data

The COAG sets education targets, defines education indicators, and collects data following a specified schedule. These objectives are directly drawn from the performance reporting frameworks (figure 8.8) and have been strategically designed to ensure data comparability across Australia. The government has employed the Systems Interoperability Framework (SIF) to ensure that all education data monitoring and reporting systems are compatible with each other. This is particularly important in hybrid systems, where different schools, states, and territories may use individual school management applications. Compatibility and integration of the different systems ensure the smooth transfer of education data to the central level. To this end, SIF has been endorsed by the National Schools Interoperability Program (NSIP) Steering Group, representing Australia's State and Territory Education Departments and the nongovernment school sectors.[4]

The focus of data collection lies on student (1) *participation*: enrollment, attendance, and participation in assessments and vocational training; (2) *achievement*: literacy, numeracy, ICT, science, and citizenship; (3) *attainment*: school completion and post-learning pathways; and (4) *equity*: indigenous status, sex, disability, geographic location, language, and socioeconomic background. The key performance measures and data sources are specified in the Measurement Framework for Schooling in Australia. Table 8.8 provides an example of how the reporting schedule of one of the focus areas may look like.

Table 8.8 Extract of Key Performance Measures, 2014–18

Measures	Target population	Data source(s)	Frequency	2014	2015	2016	2017	2018
1. Student participation								
(a) Enrollment Proportion of children aged 6–15 years who are enrolled in school	6–15-year-olds (disaggregation by jurisdiction only)	National Schools Statistics Collection; ABS Estimated Resident Population	Annual	✓	✓	✓	✓	✓
		Census of Population and Housing	Quinquennial			✓		
(b) Attendance rate The number of actual full-time equivalent student-days attended by full-time students in Years 1–10 in Semester 1 as a percentage of the total number of possible student-days attended in Semester 1	Years 1–10	National Student Attendance Data Collection (ACARA) (administrative data)	Annual	✓	✓	✓	✓	✓
(c) Attendance level The proportion of full-time students in Years 1–10 whose attendance rate in Semester 1 is equal to or greater than 90 percent	Years 1–10	National Student Attendance Data Collection (ACARA) (administrative data)	Annual		✓	✓	✓	✓

Source: ACARA 2015.

Data collection for national reports starts at the school level. Schools are required to report data to the Department of Education and Training, which then analyzes and disseminates the data in the form of education reports. There is a wide array of different reports at the national level, and some states also produce their own reports. Each report covers a different area of focus in the education system, ranging from performance indicators to enrollment figures. Table 8.9 illustrates an overview of different national reports in Australia. In addition, some reports published by the national government focus on a particular target population, for example, the biennial COAG report on "Overcoming Indigenous Disadvantage: Key Indicators."

One of the main education reports is the National Report on Schooling in Australia. It is published annually[5] and reports on progress toward the achievement of national educational initiatives including the educational goals and commitment to action of the Melbourne Declaration. It covers all aspects of the education system from new national policies to student performance in the National Assessment Programme—Literacy and Numeracy (NAPLAN) and school finances (table 8.10). The reports on years 2009–13 are publicly available on ACARA's website, and editions prior to 2009 can be accessed on the SCSEEC website (ACARA 2016).

The National Government Provides Principals and Teachers with Tools to Foster Student Learning

The government has gone to great efforts to ensure that schools receive the appropriate and useful tools to support them in school management and teaching. The Digital Education Revolution (DER) initiative pledged more than

Table 8.9 Overview of National Reporting in Australia

Report	*Description*
Report of Government Services	The focus lies on the performance assessment of public education delivery. It evaluates the performance of schools and students at the national level.
ABS Schools Australia	The Australian Bureau of Statistics (ABS) compiles an annual report of private and public school enrollment figures.
ABS Preschool	Similarly, the ABS compiles a report on all children attending preschool across the country.
NAPLAN	The National Assessment Programme—Literacy and Numeracy (NAPLAN) analyzes national assessment scores. It summarizes the performance of the students undertaking the Year 3, 5, 7, and 9 examinations.
National Report on Schooling in Australia	This is the report describing educational outcome statistics (see below) and is published by the Australian Curriculum, Assessment and Reporting Authority (ACARA).
My School	ACARA enables user to access individual school data on the My School website (refer to section: "Enabling Access and Data Use for All Education Stakeholders through the My School Platform").

Source: Department for Education and Child Development South Australia, https://www.decd.sa.gov.au/department/research-and-data/statistics-reports-and-publications/state-and-national-school-and-preschool-data-publications.

Table 8.10 Indicators Presented in the National Report on Schooling in Australia, 2013

Areas presented	Indicators
Schools and Schooling	• Number of schools (primary, secondary) • Number and proportion of schools and students by sector (government, Catholic, independent) • School enrollment (primary, secondary) • School staff by sector (primary, secondary)
Student Participation	• Student enrollment (absolute numbers, in percentage of population aged 6–15) • Progression rates (years 9–10, 10–11, and 11–12) • Retention rates for different years by sector (government, Catholic, independent) • Attendance rates (sector, year level, sex, state, and territory)
Student Achievement	• Reading, persuasive writing, and numeracy (year 3, 5, 7, and 9) • Proportion participating in the National Assessment Programme (NAP) (year 3, 5, 7, and 9) • Proportion of students achieving below, at or above proficiency level in civics and citizenship
Senior Schooling and Transitions	• Australians in Vocational Educational Training (VET) completing at least one unit under the Australian Qualification Framework (absolute number, percentage, by sector and highest academic qualification) • Students in VET (in school-based apprenticeships and other school programs) • Percentage of Australians in full-time training, employment, or education (percentage of 15- to 19- and 20- to 24-year olds) • Proportion of Australians having attained at least year 12 or higher level of qualification
School Funding	• Recurrent funding for government and nongovernment schools (national and state funding) • Total funding (by state and territories) • Average funding cost per student (government and nongovernment) • Specific purpose payments for government and nongovernment schools (recurrent expenditure, capital expenditure, and national partnership payments, including trade training centers, additional teachers, digital education revolution, and focus on specific territories) • Operating expenditure (in-school and out-of-school expenditure) • Per capita cost and income of nongovernment schools • Recurrent income by student by government, Catholic, and independent schools (primary, secondary, and special education)

Source: Adapted from ACARA 2016.

$A2 billion to the integration of ICT to support teaching and learning in Australian schools. The funds were used to purchase computers and software solutions, establish an ICT and data infrastructure in schools, develop leadership, foster professional development, and expand resource availability. The main objectives of the initiative are to facilitate four factors of change: (1) infrastructure, (2) leadership, (3) teaching capability, and (4) learning resources. This includes the provision of access to appropriate technology to promote contemporary learning and deliver a nationally consistent online curriculum that incorporates stimulating and challenging learning opportunities for children (DERN 2013).

Complementary to DER, the Australian Institute for Teaching and School Leadership (AITSL) is funded by the government and provides information and support to all schools and their staff across the country. The website is one of the first points of reference for principals and teachers to help them navigate the demanding school environment and focus on student learning. The tools on the website have been designed to support principals and teachers in the impact evaluation of their leadership and teaching efforts. Nationally available tools are often complemented by state-specific ones to cater to the context of individual states.

Supporting Principals

The AITSL supports principals in their leadership task by catering to their individual needs. AITSL developed a 360-Degree Reflection Tool for principals. This tool is open to all principals in Australia for a fee. The registered principal selects his or her raters (line manager, leadership team, staff, peers, and others), who then complete the questionnaire. The principal later receives a data-driven feedback report and is guided in developing key practices to improve his or her leadership skillset. The 360-Degree Reflection Tool supports principals in (1) identifying themes and key messages, (2) developing an action plan, (3) scheduling time to debrief with the principal's raters, (4) developing key leadership attributes, and (5) monitoring progress. AITSL suggests retaking the 360-Degree Reflection Tool within 12–18 months to carefully track leadership progress.

AITSL developed the Interactive Leadership Profile tool, which is free of charge and highlights three leadership lenses, which have been divided into 12 areas of focus (table 8.11). Principals are able to select each area of focus and one additional area to create an individual profile. This profile is then compiled into a report and ready to be downloaded. In addition, the profile can also be saved in the principal's own folder on the website, if he or she chooses to register. AITSL offers a school leadership eCollection, where many best-practice reports are available to principals. This ensures that the national government has a channel to disseminate new insights into school leadership and support principals in their role.

Supporting Teachers

AITSL has also designed tools that support teachers in their teaching tasks and improve student learning outcomes. A particular focus lies on the software application "My Standards," available for Google and Apple phones as well as tablets (figure 8.9). The software application allows teachers to create individual profiles by storing and uploading artifacts about students, curricula, and classroom activities.

Table 8.11 Leadership Lenses and Areas of Focus to Support Principals in Their Task

Professional practices lens	Leadership requirements lens	Leadership emphasis lens
Leading teaching and learning	Vision and values	Operational
Developing self and others	Knowledge and understanding	Relational
Leading improvement, innovation and change	Personal qualities and social and interpersonal skills	Strategic
		Systemic
Leading the management of the school		
Engaging and working with the community		

Source: AITSL, http://www.aitsl.edu.au/.

Figure 8.9 Example of Screenshots of the My Standards Application Designed to Support Teachers through Data

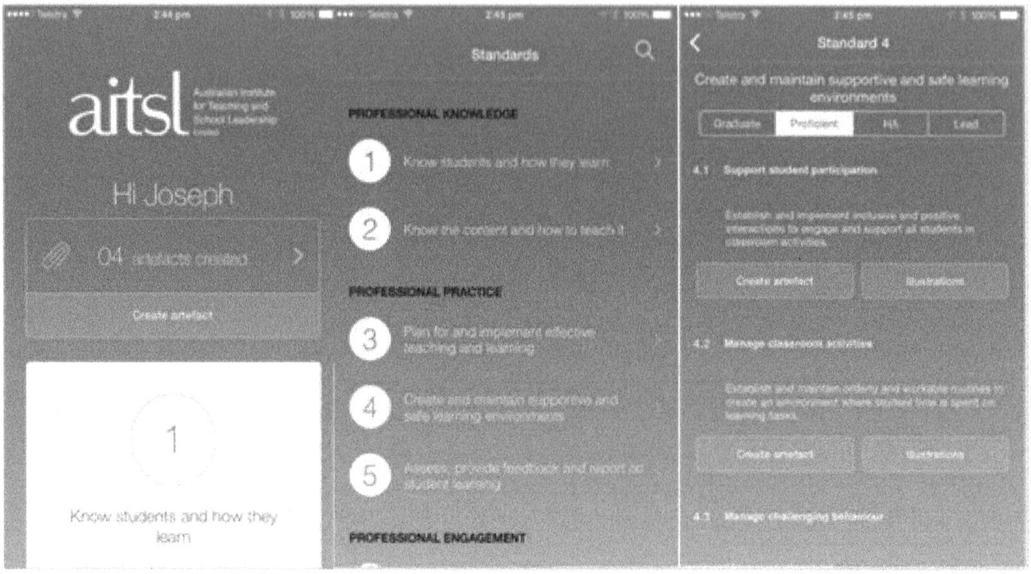

Source: iTunes 2017.

In addition, the software application provides teachers with evidence-based professional knowledge to support them in their teaching task.

Enabling Access and Data Use for All Education Stakeholders through the My School Platform

The Australian government developed My School, an online platform to provide rich, comparable information about school performance and characteristics to education stakeholders and, thus, foster transparency and accountability.[6] It was developed to address a lack of clear and consistent public information on Australian schools. After years of strategic planning and discussions among education leaders in all states and territories, the government officially launched the My School website in 2010. As the first national data repository of rich and detailed information on all schools in the country, My School offers profiles of all Australian schools, specifically "government and non-government school sectors that receive funding from governments through either the National Education Agreement or the Schools Assistance Act 2008" (ACARA 2014, 2). It aims to "give parents and the wider community more information than they have ever had before about their local school and how it is performing." Overall, My School provides a wide range of nationally comparable information on school performance and characteristics to support evidence-based decision making, empower parents to use education data, enable knowledge sharing, and ultimately improve student learning. The information sheet explaining My School and the indicators it presents are available in 21 languages on the

Figure 8.10 A Snapshot of Australia's My School Website

Source: My School, myschool.edu.au.

My School website. Figure 8.10 portrays the user interface of the My School online platform.

Information Coverage of My School

My School provides key education indicators and a detailed analysis of schools. The School Profile page provides key indicators about the school, including the type of school, enrollment and attendance rates, and various data about the school population (figure 8.11 and box 8.2). It also includes data on school resources and finances, such as gross and net recurrent income received by a school over a calendar year in lump sum and per student amount. My School also provides information about student performance on the NAPLAN by each test domain and student and school cohort (that is, schools serving students of similar socioeconomic backgrounds) to measure student progress over time ("student gain") and allow for statistical comparisons (figure 8.12).

My School uses the available information to produce the Index of Community Socio-Educational Advantage (ICSEA). The index is based on a range of descriptive statistics on schools including total number of enrolled, information on staff, and student background characteristics. The data are collected directly from the

Figure 8.11 Example of Gordon East Public School Profile, Gordon, New South Wales

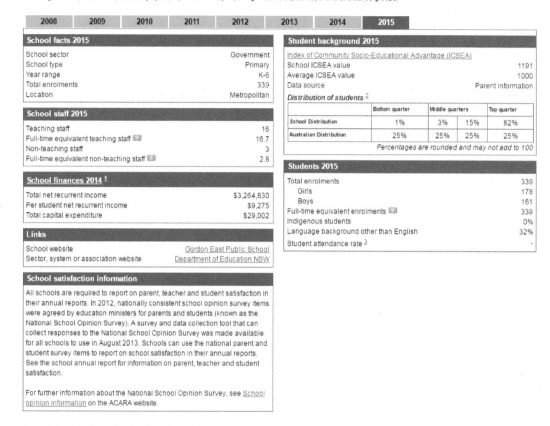

Gordon East Public School, Gordon, NSW

School comments

Gordon East Public School is a high performing school situated on spacious, picturesque grounds in Gordon. An outstanding feature of our school is the sense of shared purpose by the school community and the supportive relationships that underpin this. We value high expectations for student learning, enabling all students to strive for and experience success. Highly professional and dedicated teachers implement quality learning programs across all key learning areas. Gordon East provides innovative and well-resourced programs that engage, motivate and inspire students to achieve excellence. Students participate in a variety of opportunities including robotics, chess club, Maths Olympiad, representative sport, string ensembles, bands, choirs and dance groups.

| 2008 | 2009 | 2010 | 2011 | 2012 | 2013 | 2014 | 2015 |

School facts 2015

School sector	Government
School type	Primary
Year range	K-6
Total enrolments	339
Location	Metropolitan

Student background 2015

Index of Community Socio-Educational Advantage (ICSEA)

School ICSEA value	1191
Average ICSEA value	1000
Data source	Parent information

Distribution of students [2]

	Bottom quarter	Middle quarters		Top quarter
School Distribution	1%	3%	15%	82%
Australian Distribution	25%	25%	25%	25%

Percentages are rounded and may not add to 100

School staff 2015

Teaching staff	16
Full-time equivalent teaching staff [?]	16.7
Non-teaching staff	3
Full-time equivalent non-teaching staff [?]	2.8

Students 2015

Total enrolments	339
Girls	178
Boys	161
Full-time equivalent enrolments [?]	339
Indigenous students	0%
Language background other than English	32%
Student attendance rate [3]	-

School finances 2014 [1]

Total net recurrent income	$3,264,830
Per student net recurrent income	$9,275
Total capital expenditure	$29,002

Links

School website	Gordon East Public School
Sector, system or association website	Department of Education NSW

School satisfaction information

All schools are required to report on parent, teacher and student satisfaction in their annual reports. In 2012, nationally consistent school opinion survey items were agreed by education ministers for parents and students (known as the National School Opinion Survey). A survey and data collection tool that can collect responses to the National School Opinion Survey was made available for all schools to use in August 2013. Schools can use the national parent and student survey items to report on school satisfaction in their annual reports. See the school annual report for information on parent, teacher and student satisfaction.

For further information about the National School Opinion Survey, see School opinion information on the ACARA website.

Source: School Profile: Gordon East Public School, Gordon, NSW (My School website), ACARA, Sydney, Australia (accessed September 13, 2016), https://www.myschool.edu.au/SchoolProfile/Index/94042/GordonEastPublicSchool/41270/2015.

Box 8.2 Information Coverage of My School

The information available on the My School website centers on three main factors:

1. Student performance
   a. School-level NAPLAN scores
   b. Students' score gains
   c. Vocational education enrollments
2. School resources and finances
   a. Gross and net recurrent income

box continues next page

Box 8.2 Information Coverage of My School *(continued)*

    b. Capital expenditure

    c. School staff

3. Operational context

    a. School profile

    b. ICSEA

    c. Student enrollment

Source: ACARA 2016.

Figure 8.12 A My School Snapshot of a Similar School's Page: The King's College, Wellard, Western Australia

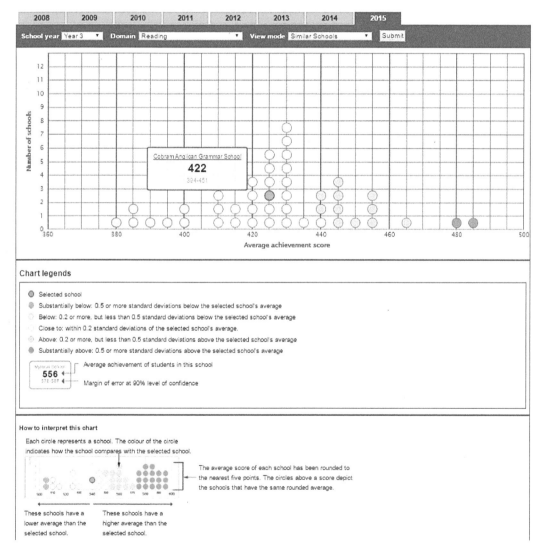

Source: My School 2016.

Box 8.3 Index of Community Socio-Educational Advantage

The Index of Community Socio-Educational Advantage (ICSEA) score is based on four factors:

1. Parents' occupation
2. Parents' education
3. Geographical location
4. Proportion of indigenous students

Source: ACARA 2016.

schools to ensure accuracy and reliability of data. ICSEA scores enable parents to compare schools across Australia. ACARA calculates the ICSEA score for each school on the basis of the factors highlighted in box 8.3.

The Path toward a Successful My School Website

The education information system played a fundamental role throughout the reforms and the creation of My School. Before these reforms took place, the Australian government struggled with unreliable data. Communities, especially parents, did not have access to data and therefore had little ability to understand how their schools fit into the larger picture and had few ways to exert any influence over instruction. Further, Australia had no nationally comparable, single source of data (ACARA 2016). A number of key reforms have been guided by My School data, including a review of government education funding, and the Making Every School a Great School program. Australia's example offers several policy lessons that may be especially relevant for countries with a federal–state and hybrid data system. Figure 8.13 outlines the timeline and key milestones that helped My School establish the delivery capabilities for national school reporting.

The success of My School was facilitated by the following key factors:

- *Policy window*: My School was linked to the broad education agenda as set forth by the government to strengthen its role as an education data platform for all stakeholder groups. This was achieved through a strong top-down buy-in from high-level politicians and commonwealth relations. Australia's path was a reflection of the general push for a higher level of transparency and accountability in the commonwealth countries. These factors were aided by parental support for the project. The project anticipated potential obstacles—such as stakeholder resistance (for example, unions, school administration, teachers, and parents), coordination challenges between states and territories, and limited school choice—and was able to overcome these.

- *Structural advantages*: Intergovernmental coordination mechanisms ensured that all agencies related to education could focus on the integration of My School with the national education strategy, which strengthened the

Figure 8.13 My School—Establishing Delivery Capabilities for National School Reporting

Budget Funding for Independent Data Collection and Reporting
- Funding received in 2008–09 federal budget for new independent collection agency for school data.
- The Council of Australian Governments (COAG) commissioned report, the "New National Architecture for School Curriculum, Assessment, and Reporting," recommended that a single new national statutory body be established to implement curriculum, assessment, and reporting policy (Sept 2008). Budget funding directed toward this.
- Adopting this recommendation and linking the three elements of national school system governance-- curriculum, assessment, and reporting—provided the basis for establishing ACARA.

Australian Curriculum, Assessment and Reporting Authority (ACARA)
- Established under the ACARA Act 2008 and became fully operational by May 2009.
- Independent authority responsible for development of a national curriculum, a national assessment program, and collection and reporting of national school performance data.
- Legislated to perform its functions and exercise its powers in accordance with the Charter and under direction of MCEECDYA.
- Developed My School to present publicly, for the first time, nationally comparable school performance information on all Australian schools.

My School (launched 1/28/2010)

Source: OECD 2013.

My School project. The COAG in cooperation with ACARA was the main agency involved in the negotiations and development of the project.

- ***Government funding***: A centralized funding mechanism was important to clearly track and monitor resource allocation. This also facilitated the incorporation of school financials into the system. The Australian government was able to leverage the financial agreements by directly linking the provision of data for My School to the continued allocation of education funding. The previously described Schools Assistance Act of 2008, the Intergovernmental Agreement on Federal Financial Relations of 2008, and the National Education Agreement of 2009 required that government and nongovernment schools report on school characteristics and performance. Moreover, they also mandated a stable source of funding for My School.

- ***Availability of existing data***: My School could tap into preexisting data collection structures, which already produced reliable data. The most important existing data sources were the school census, schools (states and territories had already been collecting a lot of education data relevant for My School), and NAPLAN assessment scores. The ability to disaggregate data and access to growth data were strong supporting factors. In addition, support from main COAG players was highly beneficial to ensure buy-in from the government and provide leadership throughout the project. This helped pull other territories and states on board and averted the potential challenges associated with a decentralized education system structure.

- **Access to technology**: Given that My School is an online platform, high Internet connectivity for all education stakeholders was key to reap its benefits. This also includes access to computers or other ICT. In addition, data providers and users already demonstrated an existing level of digital literacy. Acknowledging that My School's success depends on Internet access and digital literacy skills, the government was instrumental to ensure stakeholder buy-in by launching a national initiative to expand Internet access. This was particularly important in rural and/or disadvantaged communities.

Decrease in Costs over Time

The costs of the My School project decreased over time. In total, the My School website development and maintenance cost, security testing, legal services, focus groups, and staffing costs amounted to approximately $A2.1 million in 2010. Table 8.12 illustrates how the operational costs have decreased since the project's initial release. These costs include the main site and disaster recovery site hosting, financial insurance, web development, maintenance, and testing provided by external suppliers.

Staff expenses make up the majority of the total budget for the administration of My School. In 2012–13, almost 64 percent of the total budget was allocated to reporting and information technology (IT) staff, including web developers and data analysts. The remaining 37 percent consisted of project expenses, including web hosting costs, travel and meeting costs, financial data insurance, website testing, and salaries of help desk staff to provide user support (table 8.13). The staffing needs are divided into three roles: (1) policy, data collection, analysis, and management (excluding NAPLAN work) requires on average 5.4 full-time

Table 8.12 Operational Cost of My School Website

	Total operating costs (in $A)
2013–14	726,000
2012–13	705,000
2011–12	747,000
2010–11	1,577,907

Source: Gerbase et al. 2016.

Table 8.13 My School Website Budget, 2012–13

	In $A
Total MySchool expenses	2,363,000
Staff expenses	1,498,000
Project expenses	864,000

Source: Gerbase et al. 2016.

employees; (2) IT design, developing, and testing requires 1.9 employees; and (3) communications requires 0.6 full-time employees. In total, My School is expected to need approximately eight full-time employees to operate (Gerbase et al. 2016).

Communicating the Advantages of My School

To inform and encourage active use of the new public information service, ACARA launched a comprehensive communications campaign prior to the launch of My School. The key elements of the communication strategy included (1) identifying target audiences and key education stakeholders, (2) selecting effective communication channels, (3) identifying key spokespersons and key messages as well as tailoring them to the audience, and (4) aligning timelines and key activities until the launch and final release dates. With this communication strategy, ACARA introduced the system through a variety of means including television commercials, media interviews with key spokespeople, presentations by the deputy prime minister at the principal's forum, newspaper articles, brochures, and a series of online fact sheets and frequently asked questions. Prior to the official website opening, principals gained early access to their school's web page on My School. It also disseminated information packs and supporting materials in plain language to describe the development of the ICSEA measure and its intended purpose.

Using My School

The My School website is frequently visited by policy makers, teachers, parents, and education researchers. On the launch day, the number of page views for My School hit an unanticipated high level—30 million views, comparable to that of large news websites over the course of a month (OECD 2013). A study found that initially the states and territories with performance levels below the national average were the main users, but over time the variations across states disappeared. In 2013, the My School website had approximately 1.45 million visitors (Gerbase et al. 2016).

- *Policy makers*: Policy makers use My School at varying degrees. My School has proven to be particularly effective in informing decisions on resource and funding allocations. The information collected and presented on My School led to redistributions of funding to provide additional funding for underfunded schools, often in disadvantaged communities, to effect school improvements. However, Australia still adheres to its original school funding formula, which reduces policy makers' flexibility to reallocate school funds.
- *Teachers*: Although My School data hold the potential to support teachers in improving their classroom practices, teachers do not yet use the site to its full potential. Qualitative findings suggest that teachers generally do not discuss or use My School because many face difficulties in interpreting the data (Gerbase et al. 2016).

- *Parents*: Findings from focus groups suggested that many parents consider My School a good starting point when choosing schools for their children. However, some raised concerns regarding the accuracy of information in depicting true school conditions (Colmar Brunton 2014). Surveys show that over 80 percent of parents are aware of the website, but less than half of parents actually make use of the data to guide their decisions. This limited use of the website may stem from differences in digital literacy skills among parents. A study confirmed that My School seems inaccessible to parents who do not possess the necessary skills to navigate through the website and interpret its data (Gerbase et al. 2016).
- *Education Researchers:* My School offers numerous benefits to education researchers and is widely used by the education research community. It encourages a dialogue surrounding education in Australia and has raised demand for data.

Eliminating Data Misuse to Ensure Sustained Success

My School is constantly undergoing restructuring and has increased efforts to address data misuse and privacy. In the initial stages of My School implementation, educators feared that data may be used to unfairly compare schools without contextualizing the differences in student body and available resources. To address these concerns and minimize the misuse of data presented, ACARA implemented tight controls through various means. These include technical measures (for example, preventing data scraping on the site), legal measures (for example, copyright restrictions to prevent unauthorized use of content), and regulations prohibiting the use of data for creating league tables (Gerbase et al. 2016).

More specifically, in order to reduce the likelihood of computerized mass data gathering (for example, by web robots), users are required to enter an alphanumeric code via a Captcha interface and agree to the My School Terms of Use and Privacy Policy to gain access to the information on My School (OECD 2013). Although the Terms of Use and Privacy Policy documents neither prevent nor provide complete protection against the misuse of the data, they do empower ACARA to litigate if data are used for commercial purposes. ACARA also reviews applications for data requests. The ACARA Data Request Panel is responsible for reviewing and authorizing access to general data and the ACARA Research and Data Committee for unpublished data. The review process generally takes four to eight weeks, and upon receipt of approval the applicant must sign a legal agreement with ACARA (Gerbase et al. 2016).

My School as an International Role Model

The success of My School serves as a role model for other countries striving to empower local stakeholders to access and use education data. It is not always easy for policy makers to find ways to empower all education stakeholders to effectively use national education data. The Australian My School model has received international attention, and some countries like the Philippines have

---

Box 8.4 Example of a Website Similar to My School

The aim of the web platform Check My School in the Philippines is to enable stakeholder access to education data and, thus, enable stakeholders to improve public service delivery and the overall quality of education. Check My School is a participatory monitoring initiative designed to collect, validate, and disseminate education data online and in schools by engaging parents and the community. It operates in three distinct stages:[a]

1. It guarantees **data access** through continuous data updates as data on individual schools are collected (for example, enrollment, classrooms, seats, textbooks, budget, and test results data).
2. **Feedback mechanisms** consist of meetings with key stakeholders including community volunteers to discuss and raise education issues.
3. **Issue resolution** is facilitated by mapping key stakeholders and assigning responsibilities.

Even though the platform has not yet reached its full potential (Shkabatur 2012), it has been successful in encouraging citizen engagement, in particular committed and trained volunteers; establishing partnerships with different organizations and, thus, tapping into local networks of civil organizations, youth groups, and active individuals; and making use of official and social media tools (for example, Twitter and Facebook) to facilitate access and strengthen monitoring efforts.

The next phase of Check My School aims to strengthen the issue resolution process. One of the main objectives is to design a clear avenue for complaints and discussions beyond the Department of Education, expanding the process to utility companies and other government agencies. The initiative has placed the focus on answering the following questions: How will communities and citizens tap into existing resources? How can the process for requests become more efficient and less difficult? Who has the authority to effect certain decisions and resource allocation? (Read and Atinc 2017)

a. Information in this section is from the Check My School website, http://www.checkmyschool.org/.

---

adapted similar platforms specific to their own education system needs and country context. Box 8.4 describes the Check My School website in the Philippines.

Additional Data Collection and Dissemination Efforts
Data Reporting in Higher Education
Australia has established an online Higher Education Information Management System (HEIMS) to facilitate data collection, verification, and reporting. Under the Higher Education Support Act 2003 (HESA), all higher education providers are required to report data to the Higher Education Student Data Collection. The required data for reporting include information on courses, students (enrollment, study load, student debt, HELP loan), and units of study completion. To manage and monitor data on students' Higher Education Loan Program (HELP) entitlements, the government issues each student a Commonwealth Higher Education Student Support Number (CHESSN). The CHESSN is a

unique identifier for students receiving HELP assistance or Research Training Program support from the Commonwealth government. The following three applications are provided by the government to facilitate data entry, verification, and submission.

- **HEIMS Administration** manages CHESSN allocation through the CHESSN Toolkit and supports reporting on Commonwealth Scholarship data through the Commonwealth Scholarship toolkit.
- **HEIMS Online** allows providers to check and verify the reported data and provides access to the secure Program Funding System for entering and submitting estimated student data where advance payments are made.
- **Higher Education Provider Client Assistance Tool (HEPCAT)** is an application for approved higher education and vocational education and training (VET) providers to prepare, validate, and submit data to HEIMS. Most data are reported using the HEPCAT. The HEIMS Help website provides detailed guidelines on installing and using HEPCAT as well as training resources, including online training videos, webinars, and information on in-person training, to help providers fulfill reporting and verification requirements. The latest version, HEPCAT 23.0.0.0010, was released in December 2016.

All data submissions are validated through HEPCAT and HEIMS. Data collected through HEPCAT and HEIMS Online can be accessed and downloaded from the Higher Education Datamart. Access to these systems is by application, and all registered users must acknowledge the conditions associated with the application's use. The Department of Education and Training of the Australian Government is responsible for the management of the Higher Education Datamart, HEIMS Administration, HEIMS Online, and HEPCAT systems as well as other user accounts associated with these systems. Both HEPCAT and HEIMS systems produce error reports each time the user runs the validation process (figure 8.14). All validation error messages must be resolved before submission.

Vocational Education and Training Data Collection

The Australian Government has expanded its data collection efforts to VET. In fact, HESA also requires all VET providers to report data to the VET FEE-HELP[7] Data Collection. In addition, a Unique Student Identifier (USI) system for VET, similar to the CHESSN, was launched in 2014.[8] It creates a secure online record of accredited training and qualifications. The USI is a reference number made up of 10 numbers and letters and allows individuals to easily access their training records and transcripts of training and qualifications gained in Australia, anytime and anywhere. As the name suggests, USI is unique to an individual and stays with that individual throughout his or her lifetime. Students enrolled in VET cannot receive their qualification or statement of attainment without a USI.

Figure 8.14 An Example of a HEIMS Data Validation

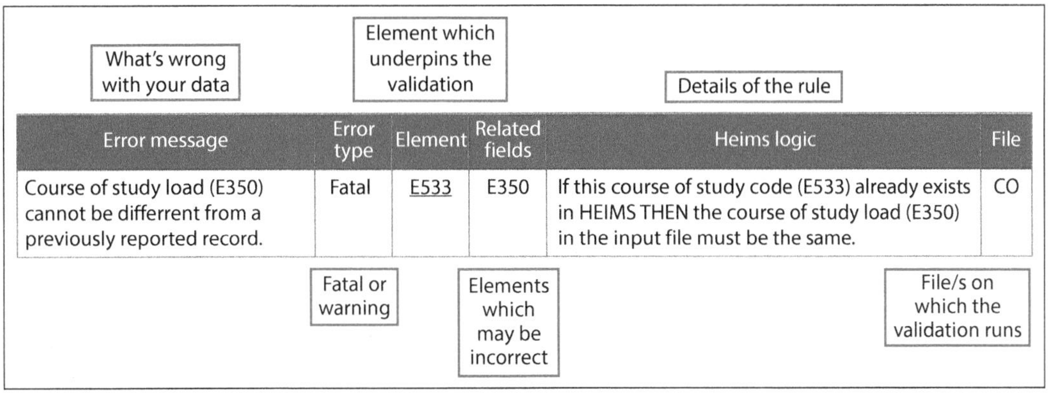

What's wrong with your data		Element which underpins the validation		Details of the rule	

Error message	Error type	Element	Related fields	Heims logic	File
Course of study load (E350) cannot be differrent from a previously reported record.	Fatal	E533	E350	If this course of study code (E533) already exists in HEIMS THEN the course of study load (E350) in the input file must be the same.	CO

	Fatal or warning		Elements which may be incorrect		File/s on which the validation runs

Source: HEIMS 2017.
Note: HEIMS = Higher Education Information Management System

The USI system enables training providers to immediately assess students' skills and progress and thereby support them to provide targeted training. The VET providers are responsible for data collection and reporting of their students. The system itself is fully integrated into the Australian Vocational Education and Training Management Information Statistical Standard (AVETMISS) 7.0, which is a national standard to ensure that all data are consistent and accurate. So far the Australian government has not recorded an increase in the frequency of reports, but it established high quality standards. Overall, USI improves the efficiency of the education system and allows for more accurate vocational planning and tracking of an individual student's progress through data on his or her vocational training.

Voluntary Data Collection at the School Level

In addition to mandatory reporting through My School and the annual school census, the Australian Bureau of Statistics (ABS) has also launched a number of voluntary initiatives to collect data. Advanced systems aim to capture any relevant information that may impact a child's learning and schooling experience. Because learning takes place everywhere—inside and outside the classroom—it is particularly important to understand students' home and school learning envrionments as well as their habits and preferences to provide individualized education and create an environment conducive to learning. Australia's CensusAtSchool (C@S) was a flagship project of the ABS that collected various data on students from 2006 to 2014.[9]

During its development stage, ABS actively consulted experts and key stakeholders. For example, education departments and teachers helped to develop the educational strategy and teaching materials, while students and teachers identified areas of interest and refined the wording of the questions.

The questionnaires and data entered were managed confidentially under strict privacy and security measures. Although the project—along with Education Services as a whole—concluded in 2014, all data collected from the project are publicly available on the C@S website (ABS 2014).

Even though participation in the C@S was voluntary, almost 24,000 student responses were recorded in 2013. The questionnaire asked students 31 noninvasive questions about their everyday lives, ranging from favorite takeaway food, daily breakfast, favorite music, transportation to school, height, and hobbies to recycling habits in their homes. Furthermore, online games were intended to be fun as well as educational. For instance, one of these games is an online version of "memory" that tests not only students' short-term memory but also their ability to use ICT effectively. This enabled policy makers to gain important insights into Australian society and revealed interesting facts about Internet use and social, environmental, and child development issues (figure 8.15).

National Efforts to Ensure Data Privacy and Avoid Data Misuse

The Australian government has introduced protective measures to ensure data privacy and, thus, eliminate data misuse. ACARA's security protocols around data collection, storage, access, and use comply with best practices and support

Figure 8.15 A Sample Infographic Created Using Data Collected in the 2013 CensusAtSchool Questionnaire

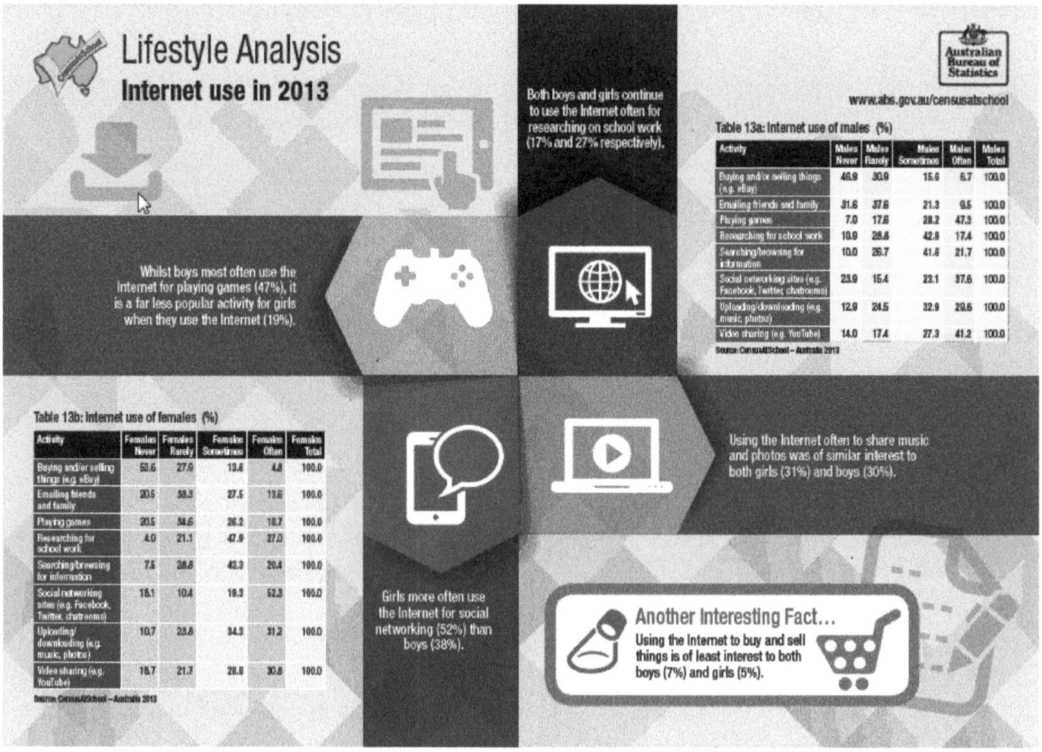

responsible use of information. Education ministers agreed upon and ACARA adopted rules that support meaningful and comparable reporting of school data and responsible use of this information. These rules include (1) protection of individual student privacy, (2) not publishing comparative data without contextual information, and (3) publication of confidence intervals, caveats, and explanatory notes to ensure accurate interpretation. The rules are intended to suppress the publication of information in situations where it could result in the identification of individual students. These rules also apply to My School data as discussed earlier.

ACARA also reviews applications for data requests. The ACARA Data Request Panel is responsible for reviewing and authorizing access to the data underlying published indicators, and the ACARA Research and Data Committee manages requests to access unpublished data. The review process generally takes four to eight weeks, and upon receipt of approval the applicant signs a legal agreement with ACARA (Gerbase et al. 2016). For the HEIMS, the Department of the Higher Education Datamart Protocols set out arrangements to ensure that disclosure of higher education data through the Datamart complies with all legal and policy requirements. The principal aim is to protect the privacy of individuals and maintain the confidentiality of the data.

In addition to these national efforts, a number of data protection initiatives exist outside of the government. For instance, the Independent School Council of Australia (ISCA) and the National Catholic Education Commission (NCEC) jointly produced a Privacy Compliance Manual to support nongovernment schools in complying with privacy standards. The Manual was initiated in 2001 and updated in 2004, 2007, 2010, 2013, 2014, and 2016 to address changing privacy issues for nongovernmental schools along with the introduction of new policies and initiatives. For instance, the introduction of NAPLAN Online raised concerns related to the storing (cloud computing) and movement of electronic student background data and test data from schools to outside agencies such as ACARA.[10]

Looking Ahead

Overall, Australia has successfully implemented a nationwide compliance system with a focus on feedback mechanisms, data access, and learning in the context of a hybrid education data system. Australia's experience offers several policy lessons that may be especially relevant for countries with a federal–state system. The strong legal framework in Australia ensures regular and mandatory reporting by all schools despite the decentralized structure of the education system. Funding allocation is dependent upon data reporting, which incentivizes data collection and school buy-in. In addition, these factors directly contribute to a data-driven culture with open data access for education stakeholders and a focus on learning of disadvantaged groups.

As the first national data repository of rich and detailed information on all schools in the country, the My School platform serves as a key tool to disseminate information. It allows all stakeholders to assess the current state of education and fairly compare schools across the country. Australia is also exploring additional EMIS applications such as unique student IDs in higher education and vocational and technical training. Moreover, voluntary data collection initiatives (for example, C@S) were launched to expand data collection. Overall, the additional EMIS applications can be used to foster increased education efficiencies and could be expanded in the future. The rich, comparable data readily accessible to the public present enormous potential in guiding policy decisions, supporting teachers to improve their classroom practices, empowering parents and informing school choice, and ultimately improving student learning outcomes as originally intended.

Although Australia has made substantial progress in improving transparency and accountability through the introduction of the My School platform, challenges in moving toward a true learning focus persist. The national focus remains on compliance with national education targets and does not yet focus on learning at all levels of the education system (for example, the classroom level). However, there have been many initiatives by the Australian government, such as the DER, to enable school staff to effectively manage school, student, and teaching data to improve learning outcomes. In addition, the government-funded AITSL offers principals and teachers a pool of resources to improve school leadership and teaching quality to attain improved educational outcomes. Nevertheless, existing evidence suggests that not all key educational stakeholders are ready to take full advantage of tools such as My School, mainly because of limited digital literacy and numeracy skills. With improved communication efforts and tailored training, all key stakeholders (that is, district and school leadership, teachers, school administrators, parents, and students) would be able to actively use the online tool, moving a step closer to creating a positive feedback cycle and fostering a data-driven culture.

Notes

1. For more information, see the INE website at http://www.ine.es.

2. For more information, see the *Agencia de Calidad de la Educación* website at http://www.agenciaeducacion.cl.

3. Information on the Education Council is from its website (accessed September 30, 2016), http://scseec.edu.au/.

4. Please refer to Chapter 5 for more information on successful software solution procurement in Australia.

5. At the time of writing, the latest available report was the *National Report on Schooling in Australia 2013*.

6. Information in this section is from the My School website (accessed September 7, 2016), http://www.myschool.edu.au/.

7. VET FEE-HELP is the Australian program to grant education loans to students enrolled in VET programs.

8. Information in this section is from the USI: Unique Student Identifier web page of the Australian Government (accessed August 19, 2016), https://www.usi .gov.au/.

9. CensusAtSchool was based on a project developed by the Royal Statistical Society Centre for Statistical Education and the Office for National Statistics in the United Kingdom. In addition, the ABS also drew on best-practice experiences from other countries in creating CensusAtSchool (ABS 2015).

10. Information in this section is from the ISCA website, http://isca.edu.au.

References

ABBYY. 2016. "ABBYY FormReader 6.5 Is Used for National Educational Tests Processing in Chile." ABBYY, Moscow. https://www.abbyy.com/media/1121/4286e_ss_govern ment.pdf.

ABS (Australian Bureau of Statistics). 2015. "School Census 2014." ABS, Melbourne, February 2. http://www.abs.gov.au/AUSSTATS/abs@.nsf/Lookup/4221.0Main+Featu res12014?OpenDocument.

———. 2016. "Summary of Findings." ABS, Melbourne, February 2. http://www.abs.gov .au/ausstats/abs@.nsf/mf/4221.0.

ACARA (Australian Curriculum, Assessment and Reporting Authority). 2014. "Factsheet: Frequently Asked Questions about the My School Website." ACARA, Melbourne http://www.acara.edu.au/verve/_resources/FAQs_2014.pdf.

———. 2015. "Measurement Framework for Schooling in Australia." ACARA, Sydney.

———. 2016. "National Report on Schooling in Australia 2013." ACARA, Sydney.

Alvarado, Felix. 2009. "Complementary Uses of Information Systems in Decision Making, Planning and Democracy: An Example in the Education Sector." *Journal of Education for International Development* 4 (2): 1–12.

Australian Government. 2006. "Fiji Access to Quality Education Program—Framework for Delivery." Canberra, http://dfat.gov.au/about-us/publications/Pages/fiji-access-to -quality-education-program-framework-for-delivery.aspx.

Barrera-Osorio, Felipe, Leigh L. Linden, and Miguel Urquiola. 2008. "The Effects of User -Fee Reductions on Enrollment: Evidence from a Quasi-Experiment." Columbia University Working Paper, New York.

Behrman, Jere R. Michela M. Tincani, Petra E. Todd, and Kenneth I. Wolpin. 2016. "Teacher Quality in Public and Private Schools under a Voucher System: The Case of Chile." *Journal of Labor Economics* 34 (2): 319–62, Part 1.

Cassidy, Thomas. 2006. "Education Management Information System (EMIS) Development in Latin America and the Caribbean: Lessons and Challenges." Working Paper, Inter-American Development Bank, Washington, DC, August.

Centro de Estudios. 2012. "Impacto de la Ley SEP en SIMCE: una mirada a 4." Ministerio de Educación, Chile.

———. 2016. "Anuario Estadísticas de Educación." Ministerio de Educación, Chile.

Colmar Brunton. 2014. "ACARA: Perspectives on the My School Website." Colmar Brunton, Sydney, Australia, November 3.

Correra, J. A., F. Parro, and L. Reyes. 2014. "The Effects of Vouchers on School Results: Evidence from Chile's Targeted Voucher Program." *Journal of Human Capital* 8 (4): 351–98.

Delannoy, F. 2000. *Education Reforms in Chile, 1980–98: A Lesson in Pragmatism*. Country Studies, Education Reform and Management Series. Washington, DC: World Bank.

DERN (Digital Education Research Network). 2013. "DER Mid-Program Review: Assessing Progress of the DER and Potential Future Directions." DERN, Australian Council for Education Research (ACER), Canberra (accessed March 21, 2017), https://dern.acer.edu.au/dern/ict-research/page/der-mid-program-review-assessing -progress-of-the-der-and-potential-future-d.

Elacqua, G. 2015. "School Choice, Private Schooling, and School Reform in Chile." Lecture presented at Princeton University, Princeton, NJ, October 22.

Elacqua, G., and R. Fabrega. 2004. "El consumidor de la educación: El actor olvidado en la libre elección de colegios en Chile." Mimeo, Universidad Adolfo Ibañez, Santiago, Chile.

Gerbase, Diana Engel, Chiara Lawry, Sarah Lux-Lee, Surya Kiran Palukuri, Hannah Poquette, and Vincent Lee Quan. 2016. "My School Australia Case Study." Capstone Project, School of International and Public Affairs, Columbia University, New York.

Himmel, Erika. 1996. "National Assessment in Chile." In *Measuring Student Outcomes*, edited by Vincent Greaney and T. Kellaghan. Washington, DC: World Bank.

MINEDUC (Ministro de Educacion Chile). 2015. "Estadisticas de la Educaion 2015." MINEDUC, Santiago, Chile.

Mizala, Alejandra, Pilar Romaguera, and Miguel Urquiola. 2007. "Socioeconomic Status or Noise? Tradeoffs in the Generation of School Quality Information." *Journal of Development Economics* 84 (1): 61–75.

Mizala, A., and F. Torshe. 2013. "Does a Means-Tested Educational Voucher System Equalize Educational Achievement? Evidence from Chile." In *ICERI2013 Proceedings*, 3341–42. Valencia, Spain: International Academy of Technology, Education, and Development.

Murnane, Robert, Lindsay Page, and Emiliana Vegas. 2010. *Distribution of Student Achievement in Chile: Baseline Analysis for the Evaluation of the Subvention Escolar Preferencial, SEP (Preferential School Subsidy)*. Washington, DC: World Bank.

OECD (Organisation for Economic Co-operation and Development). 2013. "Chile: Education Policy Outlook 2013." OECD, Paris.

PRIE (Regional Education Indicators Project). 2003. "The Experience of the Regional Education Indicators Project 2000–2003." UNESCO, Santiago, Chile. http://www .prie.oas.org/english/documentos/The%20experience%20of%20the%20Project%20 2000-2003%20en.pdf.

Read, Lindsay, and Tamar Manelyan Atinc. 2017. "Information for Accountability: Transparency and Citizen Engagement for Improved Service Delivery in Education Systems." Center for Universal Education, Brookings Institution, Washington, DC.

Shkabatur, Jennifer. 2012. "Check My School: A Case Study on Citizens' Monitoring of the Education Sector in the Philippines." World Bank, Washington, DC.

UIS (UNESCO Institute of Statistics). 2017. *Estimation of the Numbers and Rates of Out-of-School Children and Adolescents Using Administrative and Household Survey Data.* Information Paper No. 35. Montreal: UIS.

UNESCO (United Nations Educational, Scientific, and Cultural Organization). 2011. "Regional Education Indicators Project (PRIE)." UNESCO, Paris.

Wales, Joseph, Ahmed Ali, Susan Nicolai, Francisca Morales, and Daniel Contreras. 2014. "Improvements in the Quality of Basic Education: Chile's Experience." Case Study Summary: Education, Overseas Development Institute, London.

Zanderigo, Tony, Elizabeth Dowd, and Sarah Turner. 2012. "Delivering School Transparency in Australia: National Reporting through My School." OECD Publishing. http://www.oecd-ilibrary.org/docserver/download/9812071e.pdf.

CHAPTER 9

Developing an Affordable and School-Centered EMIS: The Case of Fiji

We want our planning section to use our data frequently. We want our policy section to use that data and show us graphs of the exact status of the education system....
[F]rom there we can make recommendations to the honorable Minister and Permanent Secretary to make those decisions that can improve the system.

—Ms. Releshni Karan, Director Corporate Services, Ministry of Education Fiji

Key Takeaways

- The success of the Fiji Education Management Information System (FEMIS) stems from developing an affordable EMIS solution focused on providing well-functioning and desirable data services to policy makers at the central, regional, and local levels.
- Policies were designed that mandate timely, efficient, effective, and reliable data collection from districts and schools at specific deadlines to ensure a high response rate.
- Publicly available concept notes and direct trainings were pivotal in promoting awareness and buy-in from the Ministry of Education, Heritage and Arts (MoEHA) and other key education stakeholders to communicate the opportunity of FEMIS in providing value to schools and governments for decision making.
- The successful development of EMIS in Fiji was due to political support from the government as well as the buy-in and involvement of staff at each level of the education system.
- The MoEHA allocated dedicated, quality staff to train school officials. During the training sessions, actual school data were entered into the system to save time and financial resources.

- The new individual student records at the school level encourage schools to consume their own data, driving up the quality of student data. Individual records are shared throughout the education system, leading to the creation of a longitudinal dataset for assessment purposes.
- Data are entered at the school level, which provides for stronger ownership for schools.
- Clear responsibilities and data ownership roles were defined following the premise that an entity maintaining data must use consistent methods to ensure quality of data and cost efficiencies.
- FEMIS demonstrates a clear security clearance hierarchy, with the MoEHA as the highest level down to individual student records.
- New modules such as financial, material assessment data were added to the FEMIS to provide an integrated and comprehensive dataset used to assess education sector performance.
- Fiji's experience could be replicated in countries with similar context.

Introduction and Country Overview

FEMIS has successfully established an affordable EMIS tailored to its country-specific context, resources, and education requirements.[1] FEMIS is a success story despite a challenging environment that is dependent on donor funding. In this chapter, we present how Fiji developed its data system, elaborating on the guidelines used, cost-effective measures, risk mitigation measures taken, and anecdotal experiences that may prove helpful to other countries involved with developing a data system in similar context.

Fiji is an upper-middle-income country located in the South Pacific and consists of more than 300 islands. The estimated population of Fiji in 2015 was 871,986, and the estimated number of children from the age of 5 to 18 years old was 223,192 for the same year. Of this number, 17,245 children were 5 years old (of preschool age), 129,901 children were of primary school age (between 6 and 13 years of age), and 76,046 were in the secondary school age group (between 14 and 18 years of age) (MoEHA 2016). There are several ethnic groups, with indigenous Fijians and Indo-Fijians the most prominent. The geographical distribution contributes to the scattered distribution of schools and students, which poses some challenges to the education system.

The country is divided into nine education districts and four divisions. Approximately 90 percent of schools have access to the Internet. Although only 90 percent of schools have Internet connections, the estimated remaining 10 percent of schools without Internet are typically small primary schools located in rural or remote areas.

The school system is governed by the Education Act and the policies of the MoEHA. The system is characterized by a public-private partnership, where approximately 98 percent of the schools are faith based or community owned but are funded by the government. The remaining 2 percent are government schools.

The government initiated a Tuition Free Grant in 2014 to ensure that parents do not have to bear the burden of paying tuition for their children attending primary and secondary schools (MoEHA 2016).

The overall budget for Fiji's MoEHA in 2015 was F$401,649,600 (US$193 million) equating to 11.8 percent of the total government budget.[2] The MoEHA supports over 210,000 students, including early childhood education (ECE) and employs 5,815 primary, 4,690 secondary, and 100 special education staff.

The gross domestic product (GDP) of the country is approximately US$4.5 billion, and Fiji is one of the most developed countries in the Pacific region. It is richly endowed with forests, minerals, and fish. Agriculture is the main contributor to GDP and employs more than 70 percent of the workforce. Remittances, particularly for military staff, are increasing steadily, eclipsing traditional sectors such as sugar and garment manufacturing. Sugarcane contributed significantly to the industrial growth, and sugar exports and tourism add to the foreign exchange reserves. However, cyclones and coups have had an adverse impact on investments and pose a significant economic challenge.

The education system is structured so that primary education runs for six years, lower secondary for four years, and upper secondary for three years (table 9.1). Although education is not compulsory, it is free for the first eight years.

Table 9.1 Education Indicators at a Glance, Fiji

Number of schools[a] 2016	
ECE	942
Primary	734
Secondary	181
Number of students	
ECE	15,577
Primary	145,867
Secondary	66,827
Net enrollment rate (%)	
Primary	100
Secondary	83.6
Student–teacher ratio	
ECE	14
Primary	25
Secondary	13
Public expenditure on education	
% of total government expenditure	13.7
% of GDP	3.8

Source: Provided by MoEHA on request.
Note: ECE = early childhood education; EMIS = Education Management Information System; GDP = gross domestic product.
a. Using 2016 end-of-year EMIS data post-Cyclone Winston.

Fiji's schools are operated mostly by the government, by religious communities, or by the districts.

How Did Fiji Develop an EMIS?

Building on What Already Existed

Early assessment of the data system determined a need to integrate the three existing main education databases of the MoEHA into a unified, web-based platform. These three main databases held partially overlapping data but did not communicate with each other. Development of the FEMIS started in 2012 and was tailored to its surrounding environment, taking into account the national availability of Internet, culture, per capita income, and existing MoEHA information technology (IT) resources.

Development Stage I: Before FEMIS

The goal of system development was to produce an EMIS with one single data source over a period of four years. This demonstrated a substantial change from the initial system, where three databases made up the data storage: SIMS (School Information System), FESA (Education Staffing Information System), and LANA (Literacy and Numeracy Assessment System) (box 9.1). Before FEMIS, access to all databases was via computers on the MoEHA network. Access to these databases via the Internet was blocked.

Development Stage II: After FEMIS

At the time of writing, FEMIS consists of two physical databases, LANA and FESA, which are, respectively, the assessment and staffing databases (figure 9.1). Each database has a corresponding web application. The FESA application maintains staffing data in the FESA database. The LANA application maintains assessment data in the LANA database, but schools administer the class lists in the LANA database using FEMIS. The hardware design consists of a web server to serve web pages and reports over the open Internet,

---

Box 9.1 Three Main Databases Prior to FEMIS

- **FESA**—Fiji Education Staffing Appointments: Used to manage all aspects of teacher placements. FESA is web based but accessible only on the government network.
- **SIMS**—School Information Management System: Used to collect aggregated paper-based school survey data on teachers, students, finances, and assets. SIMS was a Windows-based system installed on personal computers (PCs) at district offices and the Statistics Unit.
- **LANA**—Literacy and Numeracy Assessments: Used to issue, mark, and report on national literacy and numeracy assessments for years 4, 6, and 8. FILNA is web based and accessible only on the government network and only within the Examination and Assessment Unit (EAU).

Figure 9.1 Components of FEMIS

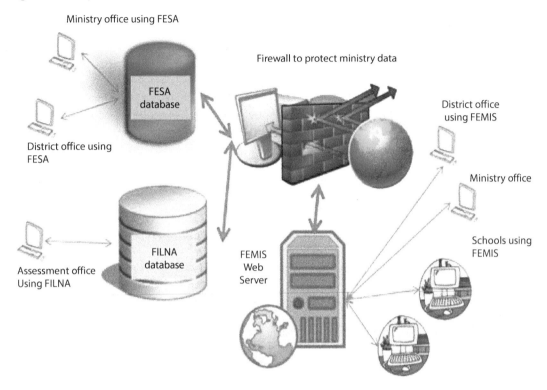

Note: FEMIS = Fiji Education Management Information System; FESA = Fiji Education Staffing Appointments; LANA = Literacy and Numeracy Assessment; SIMS = School Information Management System.

connected to a single (large) database server housing the FESA and LANA databases. Each primary server has a matching redundant twin used for backup in the event of catastrophic hardware failure of a primary server. The redundant pair also function as the quality assurance (QA) testing area where new features are tried out and refined before installation on the primary live servers. In addition to the above, a copy of the two main live databases is taken each night and stored on the redundant server. This nightly copy is used exclusively for ad hoc querying by statistics officers. This allows statistics officers to build and execute queries that are not in standard reports in the EMIS. Typically, day-old data suffice for most data queries received by the statistics officers. This copy does not function as a data warehouse; instead it contains an exact replica of the live data.

Senior staff approved the prototype for general use in 2012. Crucially, security was established to allow as much *visibility* of data as practical while restricting edit/update. For example, schools can see their staffing records but cannot alter their pay. However, schools can comment that their staffing data are incorrect, allowing the FEMIS team at the ministry level to follow up and make adjustments as required. The school-centric approach brought rapid and substantial buy-in from schools. The first year of FEMIS focused on rolling the system out to schools. An attendance module was quickly introduced along with rudimentary modules for tracking school fees, acquittals against the grant, recording of parent information, student health, an online library for teachers, and other features designed to engage schools in maintaining the core, ministry-required student data of gender, date of birth, and class.

The success and affordability of FEMIS is why it now serves as a potential model for other countries in the region. A similar model is now being developed in Vanuatu. It is an excellent example of low-cost system development, implementation, and use. Much of the web technology was successfully attached to the existing EMIS, saving countless hours of software development time. In Vanuatu, ministry buy-in to the same concept is strong, and the system is already substantially improving the quality of data on staff and students. The parallel paper-based system in FEMIS is crucial as a model for countries such as Vanuatu, where Internet connectivity is considerably behind that of Fiji and paper remains the main data collection instrument.

Establishing a Policy Framework to Institutionalize FEMIS

MoEHA introduced a FEMIS policy in 2014 to support the functioning of FEMIS operations. The purpose of the policy is to provide a framework that will enhance and facilitate effective, efficient, and timely data collection from schools and reporting to the MoEHA and all stakeholders throughout Fiji. This policy is also designed to ensure that the collection and entry of data are undertaken with care and concern to continually raise the quality of data held in FEMIS (MoEHA 2016, 2). The policy document builds on a number of relevant policies and legislations (box 9.2). It is the first step toward institutionalizing FEMIS in the country.

The policy document clearly articulates the processes and mandates for successful implementation of the system. The 10-page document includes

---

Box 9.2 List of Supporting Policies for FEMIS

The supporting and relevant policy documents are the following:

- The Constitution of the Republic of Fiji—2013
- ICT Development Policy
- Information Technology Centre Government Policy
- National Strategic Development Plan (2015–20)
- Education Sector Strategic Development Plan (2015–18)
- Education Act (1978)
- Examination Act
- Public Service Act 1999

Source: MoEHA 2016.

---

aspects such as FEMIS processes, validation mechanisms, timelines, allocation of responsibilities, privacy assurances, some indicator coverage, government utilization and disciplinary action in case of wrongdoings. It also sets forth reporting requirements for the MoEHA. The MoEHA has to follow clearly outlined performance reporting requirements. By institutionalizing reporting requirements, the MoEHA ensures that the education data are integrated with other ministerial and international donor reports (box 9.3).

The ownership and responsibility of data collection and management rest with MoEHA. Clear data ownership and responsibility are essential to ensure reliability and accuracy of the data. This is why, where practical, FEMIS has a single entity responsible for each data area with numerous entities using that data. At the same time, however, the entity responsible for maintaining an area of data must have significant interest in the accuracy of that data. This is based on the premise that having an entity maintain data it does not use consistently results in poor quality data.

Political Support

The successful development of an EMIS in Fiji was due to the political support from the government as well as the buy-in and involvement of staff at each level of the education system. The MoEHA was keen on developing the EMIS as a tool to better manage the performance of education system business processes. To this end, creating awareness among all the different levels of stakeholders was key. As a result, during the early days, a concept note was developed and shared across staff at different levels to get their support. In addition, substantial effort was undertaken to train staff on the concept and benefits of

---

Box 9.3 Reporting Requirements by the MoEHA

The MoEHA is required to share education data with the following entities:

- Fiji Bureau of Statistics Report
- MoEHA Annual Report
- MoEHA Strategic Development Plan (2015–18)
- Ministry of Finance Quarterly Report
- Ministry of Strategic Planning, National Development and Statistics Report
- Peoples Charter for Change Peace and Progress (2008)
- Roadmap for Democracy and Sustainable Socio-economic Development (2009–14)
- Implementation Coordinating Office (ICO) Report
- United Nations Education, Scientific, and Cultural Organization (UNESCO) Statistical Data on Educational Attainment
- UNESCO's Sustainable Development Goals and Education for All achievements
- UNESCO Institute of Statistics

Source: MoEHA 2016.

---

developing the EMIS, and how the system could be a useful tool to help improve and expedite their current work. At the ministry level, most senior staff members demonstrate significant awareness of FEMIS. However, detailed knowledge and an understanding of the system as well as its potential will not be fully leveraged until the potential of data is fully understood and exploited by different stakeholders. As FEMIS develops, the focus should move from the use of data for monitoring business processes to assessing the performance of the education system. Government should play a leading role in making the data available to other education stakeholders so they can analyze and use the data to improve the quality of education.

The MoEHA has a dedicated staff overlooking the functioning of FEMIS. MoEHA supports an IT Unit manager, an officer dedicated to training and support, a data cleaner who phones schools to ensure accurate data, and a senior programmer. The Australian Access to Quality Education Program (AQEP)[3] supports an additional programmer and a data quality analyst. The data quality analyst is responsible for data quality strategies and education. The assessment unit maintains two full-time IT staff dedicated to maintaining the assessment component in the EMIS to reduce dependence on third-party software by increasing EMIS assessment functionality such as online marking and distribution of exams. Additionally, AQEP is funding temporary positions of an online training materials producer and a procedure writer. As the project nears completion, the MoEHA will perform training remotely or online at substantially reduced cost.

Training

Continuous training for EMIS and IT staff at the MoEHA was another component that promoted the growth of the system. This achieved three simultaneous objectives: (1) the ministry became capable of providing ongoing support of the EMIS, which is a positive step toward the system's long-term sustainability; (2) the use of ministry staff avoids the involvement of IT support companies with profit-driven agendas that typically are contrary, and often destructive, to ministry needs; (3) international organizations and donors are freed from the software development issues and can focus on technical assistance. FEMIS was rolled out without the assistance of dedicated Technical Advisors (TAs) in other areas of the MoEHA. Despite the advantages of a ministry-focused approach, the delivery of the EMIS could have benefitted substantially from dedicated TAs supporting other areas of the MoEHA. For instance, TA support in the human resource, finance, and assessment areas typically places high demands on an EMIS.

A key factor that led to the buy-in and support of FEMIS was the provision of training in schools to demonstrate the use and importance of student data. Schools that had access to the Internet received training on the use of data. This training faced substantial logistical hurdles because of the number of remote islands involved. "Training of trainers" model was piloted but was not successful.

Direct sessions required schools to complete the registration of all student records at the time of the training, sometimes taking up to two full days. The training was repeated at the start of the school year and again at the end of the school year. Training at the start of the school year focused on rolling over and setting up new classes. Training at the end of the year focused on ensuring high accuracy of student data. This not only solved the buy-in dilemma in obtaining student data but also allowed working examples of classes and students. Tools were developed specifically to engage and coerce schools into maintaining their own data.

Although training was designated as EMIS training, much of it consisted of learning basic computer skills. Numerous approaches were used to identify those who were not equipped to work on computers and to provide additional training where possible. Over time, training was refined to target those more in need than others. Data quality reports were developed to determine which schools needed training and which did not, reducing training costs and acknowledging compliant schools. The training generally covered the basic skills that staff would need during the school year, such as how to produce certain reports and how to enter requirements related to staff into the system.

The training sessions at the central, district, and school levels resulted in acceptance of FEMIS as a handy tool for monitoring outcomes. Each school has a FEMIS administrator responsible for maintaining and updating records in the EMIS. Regular training sessions for the administrators and school principals helped them to understand the tool better and work more efficiently. The IT helpdesk at the MoEHA was a huge success in solving real-time questions and concerns the schools had with regard to information being entered in the system. At any point, administrators or teachers could e-mail the helpdesk and get an immediate response that helped smooth the process. Moreover, the training provided to the staff at the MoEHA helped them use the system more effectively. Figure 9.2 provides a snapshot of the available training modules for teachers on using the FEMIS website.

FEMIS had built-in mechanisms that allowed its staff to identify schools in need of additional training. Figure 9.3 depicts the school data summary report, which shows missing early childhood school data. The point rating system is used to identify schools requiring training; schools scoring less than 5 are identified as being in need of training.

Selecting Between Different System Options and Balancing Finances

During the development stage of FEMIS, government officials and AQEP—the implementing agency funded by Australia's Department of Foreign Affairs and Trade (DFAT)—balanced the needs of the education system with the available financial resources. In cost planning, both initial (development, training, and acquisition) and long-term (maintenance, upgrades, and improvements) costs were taken in consideration. The key factor was that FEMIS was not driven by the wants of donors but designed to accommodate

Figure 9.2 Training Sessions Provided for Teachers on Using FEMIS

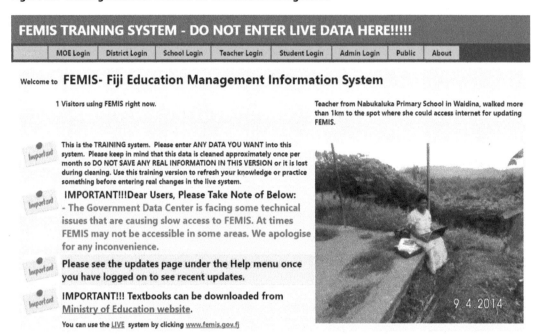

Source: FEMIS, http://www.femis.gov.fj/femis/.

Figure 9.3 School Data Summary Report

FEMIS School Data Summary Report - District Report

For: 2016 Ra

	Sch Type	Code	Teachers	Classes	Students	Attendance Data Up To Date	Students 5 Days Absent	School Details	Points
Ra									
y School	Primary		7	8	164	100%	13%	Yes	7
al School	Primary		1	8	42	0%	0%	Yes	2
rgarten	ECE		1	0	0	0%	0%	0	0
ary School	Primary		5	8	111	88%	11%	Yes	4
strict School	Primary		4	8	92	75%	11%	Yes	4
ndergarten	ECE		1	0	0	0%	0%	0	0
ct School	Primary		4	8	145	100%	15%	No	3
A Kindergarten	ECE		1	0	0	0%	0%	0	0
lim Primary School	Primary		4	8	109	100%	16%	Yes	6
c School	Primary		9	8	195	100%	20%	Yes	7
			0	2	32	0%	0%	No	0
ary School	Primary		9	8	172	44%	9%	No	4
School	Primary		4	9	83	90%	0%	Yes	5
nary School	Primary		6	8	157	0%	0%	No	0
mary School	Primary		1	8	53	0%	0%	Yes	4
School	Primary		5	8	112	38%	6%	No	4
y School	Primary		7	8	153	100%	2%	Yes	7
indergarten	ECE		1	0	0	0%	0%	0	0

◄ ► ►│ Report 05 02 Student Data Summa

Source: FEMIS, http://www.femis.gov.fj/femis/.

the requirements of the Fiji education sector. The FEMIS team constantly weighed different options and assessed each regarding its costs, needs, and utility to the overall system. The following are some of the choices the FEMIS team made:

- Should the MoEHA acquire a new database software or use an existing one?
  - In Fiji, the Structured Query Language (SQL) database software was provided without cost to the MoEHA through licensing arrangements already in place with the federal IT body that covered its costs.
- Who provides necessary hardware equipment for software development?
  - AQEP funded the system.
- Who provides and pays for training of FEMIS and other staff?
  - Initially, the costs of training were borne by AQEP, but as the project evolved most of the training costs were borne by the MoEHA. All FEMIS staff (besides the IT technical support) are funded by the MoEHA as well.
- Will hardware equipment (for example, laptops) be provided to the end user (that is, schools)?
  - The MoEHA did not provide additional laptops to end users for the purpose of FEMIS training and use. During FEMIS training sessions, all schools were required to bring their own or borrowed laptops. In addition, schools were also responsible for ensuring Internet connectivity for all training without exception and without additional resources.

System Cost

One of the main positive features of FEMIS is its affordability. Some cost features were particularly important contributors to the system's affordability: (1) SQL database software was provided without cost to the MoEHA through licensing arrangements already in place with the federal IT body; (2) the cost of Internet bandwidth is also paid by the federal IT body; (3) software development costs such as labor, desks, and personal computers (PCs) are provided by the MoEHA; (4) at the time of writing, the MoEHA is in the process of recruiting a national resource specifically to develop online training materials. This will allow the MoEHA to cease costly donor-funded direct training and independently sustain a more cost-effective online training program in the longer term; and (5) no laptops were provided to end users. All schools brought laptops and their own Internet connectivity to all training without exception.

Regarding system development costs, the FEMIS team needed to select the appropriate software solution that could be tailored to the country-specific needs and requirements of the education system. These cost features were particularly important contributors to the system's affordability. The initial development of FEMIS entailed a cost of about $A800,000, which included software procurement, training, and staffing (especially IT support). Table 9.2 provides a brief overview of the software choices and costs for a variety of required FEMIS components.

Table 9.2 Cost of System Development

Component	Tool	Approx. cost ($A)
Software development tools used to build web pages and reports	Microsoft Visual Studio	600 to 1,500 per developer
Database technology used to store data	Microsoft SQL Server	Approximately 3,000 for each of two servers
Server software	Windows Server 201X	Usually less than 1,000 for each of the four servers.
Physical server hardware	2x web servers plus 2x database servers	60,000 for all four servers
End user training	Ministry staff and technical advisor(s)	Approximately 100,000 per annum exclusive of TA costs.

Note: SQL = Structured Query Language; TA = Technical Advisor.

System Functionalities

FEMIS features a school-centric approach that brought rapid and substantial buy-in from schools. Every school was assigned a FEMIS administrator whose primary role is to input education data on a real-time basis into FEMIS. Every morning, the administrators enter attendance data provided by teachers, which makes it easy to track student absenteeism on a daily basis. In addition, administrators continually update records and data as and when they become available. Previously, teachers had done this work but found that it took time away from teaching. On the downside, this reduces the interaction of teachers with FEMIS and their potential use of its data because they are no longer entering the information. Figure 9.4 demonstrates the number of successful school and ministry-level logons since the inception of FEMIS, clearly illustrating how FEMIS has become a regular component of school life.

FEMIS has ensured that all schools (government and community-based) are integrated into its system. FEMIS is fully digitalized and generally uploads data directly or extracts data from other systems. However, because approximately 10 percent of schools in Fiji remain without Internet connectivity, most school-level data input pages have paper equivalents allowing nonconnected schools to complete and submit data to district offices for entry into the EMIS.

FEMIS includes individual-level data on assessments, enrollment, attendance, and infrastructure for basic (primary and secondary) education. Currently, FEMIS collects data from primary and secondary schools, but there are plans to integrate data from ECE and technical colleges. This would allow information on student progression and performance from ECE to technical and higher education, and would have important implications for designing interventions to monitor and improve outcomes.

Staffing and personnel data are also integrated into FEMIS. Data from the staffing system FESA are displayed as read-only data in FEMIS along with selected payroll/pay slip data from the national pay system, leave balances, professional development history, qualifications, and teacher registration data. Teachers may not alter any of these data but can provide feedback to district offices in the form of a comment on the staffing details page in FEMIS. Districts can list the feedback

Figure 9.4 Successful FEMIS Logons by Schools and Ministry

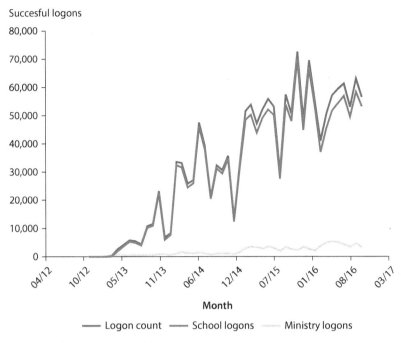

as the "Staffing Problems" report and follow up as required (figure 9.5). Once an issue is resolved, the district can clear it from the problem report. A tally of problems per district is visible on all ministry and district pages. Currently, however, there is less use of this feature at the district level, and mostly the IT unit within the MoEHA resolves the issue of errors in reporting.

Registration for external exams is derived directly from FEMIS. One of the many achievements of FEMIS is that student registration for external exams and national literacy and numeracy assessments is fully integrated into the system. The Exams and Assessment Unit uses the student registry in FEMIS to automatically enroll students for the appropriate external exams and LANA (years 5 and 7 since 2016; previously years 4, 6, and 8). This ensures additional buy-in from schools because it makes registration of all students in FEMIS a necessity while eliminating a previously separate cumbersome registration process and allowing for the entry of marks for some exams by schools and the printing of student assessment reports. This also facilitates the printing of some national exam papers at schools, saving on vast resources previously required to securely ship exam papers.

The introduction of individual student and teacher records at the school level improved communication between staff members and made real-time monitoring of education data possible. This enabled school staff to quickly

Figure 9.5 Staffing Problems Report

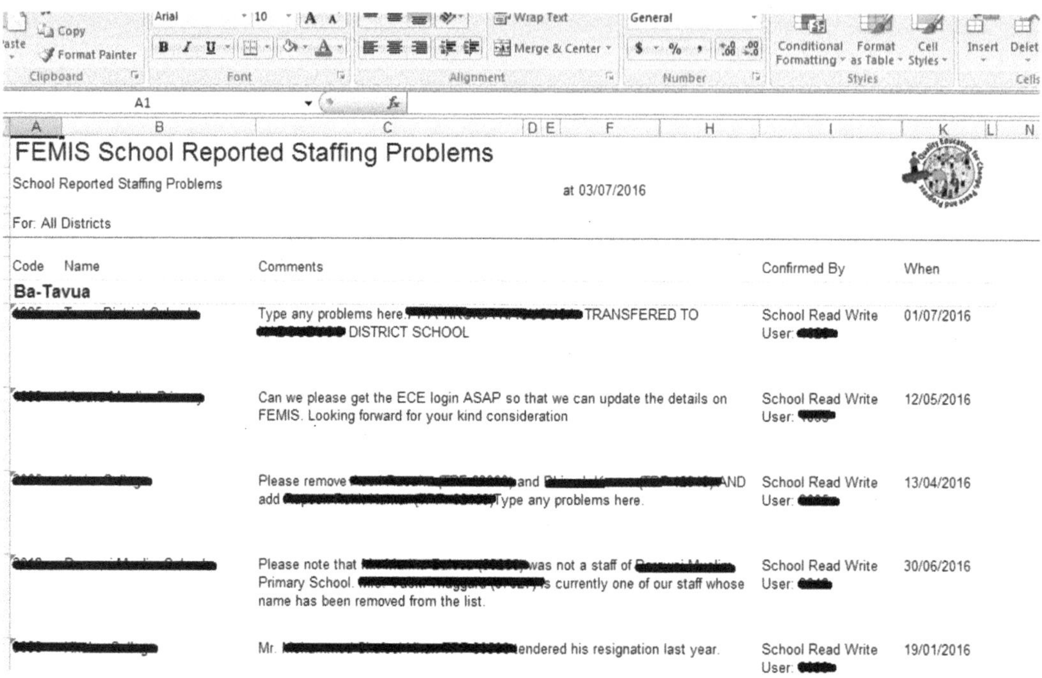

FEMIS School Reported Staffing Problems

School Reported Staffing Problems at 03/07/2016

For: All Districts

Code Name	Comments	Confirmed By	When
Ba-Tavua			
[redacted]	Type any problems here.[redacted] TRANSFERED TO [redacted] DISTRICT SCHOOL	School Read Write User: [redacted]	01/07/2016
[redacted]	Can we please get the ECE login ASAP so that we can update the details on FEMIS. Looking forward for your kind consideration	School Read Write User: [redacted]	12/05/2016
[redacted]	Please remove [redacted] and [redacted] AND add [redacted] Type any problems here.	School Read Write User: [redacted]	13/04/2016
[redacted]	Please note that [redacted] was not a staff of [redacted] Primary School. [redacted] s currently one of our staff whose name has been removed from the list.	School Read Write User: [redacted]	30/06/2016
[redacted]	Mr. [redacted] endered his resignation last year.	School Read Write User: [redacted]	19/01/2016

Source: FEMIS, http://www.femis.gov.fj/femis/.

respond to the needs of individual students and teachers. Individual data records also enable government staff in allocation of grants and resources and developing policies that cater to individual student characteristics. In addition, it enabled school administrators to integrate student transfers from other schools more easily. Figure 9.6 provides an example of individual student records in FEMIS.

Most countries collect pre-aggregated school data instead of individual records. Two arguments can be made: one for and one against individual student records (table 9.3).

FEMIS facilitates Internet discussions, in which school administrators can request and share information on students. If students transfer from one school to another, schools have to ensure that there are no duplications of the student records through sharing of data to track individual students over time. Figure 9.7 illustrates such a discussion board with request for information or action. Each school has a unique identifier number (blacked out on the left for privacy reasons), which allows all users to know the basic characteristics of the school (school level, geographic location, and so on).

FEMIS allows for tracking and monitoring business processes for the government. At first, many modules may not seem relevant to the MoEHA but in fact provide valuable information and encourage school buy-in.

Figure 9.6 Snapshot of Individual Data Records in FEMIS

Source: FEMIS, http://www.femis.gov.fj/femis/.

Table 9.3 The Debate on Maintaining Individual Student Records

The case for individual student records	The case against individual student records
• Individual student records are required for detailed attendance recording and analysis. Attendance reporting is required to get school buy-in, which is required to improve data quality. Individual student records offer a higher level of detail orientation toward reliable and useful individual student data with improved accuracy across the board as well as significantly reduced effort.	• The EMIS is perceived as more work during the initial population of the individual student records. Although a one-off exercise, this is typically done during the first month of school, which is an already busy time of year. Schools associate the additional workload with the new system, discouraging school buy-in.
• A well-functioning EMIS should identify ghost teachers and ghost students, not aggregate them efficiently into widely distributed reports.	• Dedicated employees are required on an ongoing basis to monitor discrepancies with individual student data and engage with schools to correct issues as they arise.
• Comparing individual student records against civil registry data will improve the accuracy of the grant calculation and improve student registration accuracy, simplifying assessment processing.	• The first year of individual student records renders lower (more accurate) gross student counts than the previously aggregated data submitted that was used to calculate the grant the previous year. This affects national statistical reports and can affect gross grant amounts.
• If each individual student record in the EMIS has a birth certificate, this implies that school age records in the civil registry that are not in the EMIS are children out of school. This allows generating a report from the civil registry that lists specific details of children out of school.	• The second year of collecting individual student records tends to continue to produce appropriate (more accurate) gross student counts; however, schools tend to struggle with the concept of carrying students over, in particular early childhood education to primary and primary to secondary, where schools must locate the student in the previous, different, school.
• Schools are no longer required to fill out exam registration forms, the existing class list *is* the exams registration list, again saving time and improving data quality, also allowing convenient longitudinal recording of exam results over years including students who move between schools. The time required is significantly less than the time to submit a series of aggregated tables on assorted student data.	• By year 3, with substantial effort from dedicated staff in the MoEHA IT Unit, the rate of students appearing in two schools at the same time has dropped to 0.4 percent.

Note: EMIS = Education Management Information System; IT = information technology; MoEHA = Ministry of Education, Heritage and Art.

Figure 9.7 Screenshot of the FEMIS Forum Showing Schools Communicating to Clean Student Data

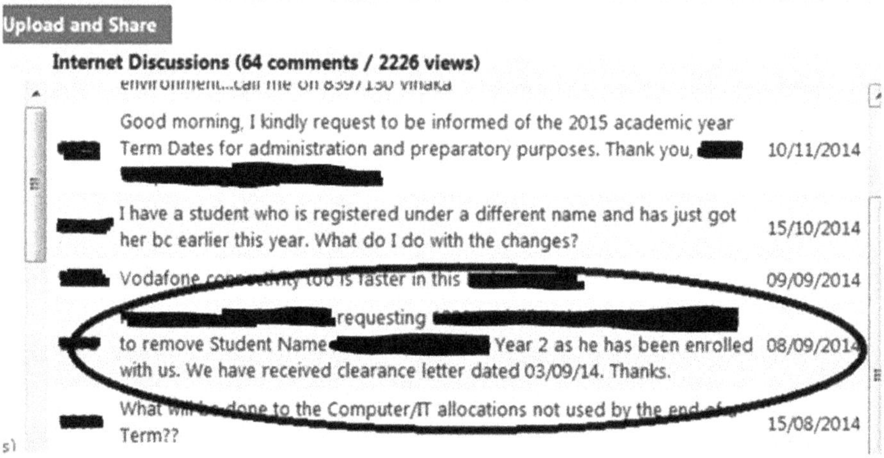

For example, a school uniform fees module forces a school to maintain accurate student records in order to record fees. Although the MoEHA may have no interest in uniform fees, it has substantial interest in the underlying core student data. Another approach to help solve the buy-in dilemma was to populate perhaps one-quarter to one-third of the student data from the existing assessment system as part of the initial rollout. This saved schools the effort of populating 50,000 of the 210,000 initial student records from scratch and offered an operational working example. The MoEHA allocated dedicated quality staff to this monumental task.

All students are equipped with unique identifiers (IDs). For Fiji students, the birth certificate ID and student ID are recorded; for foreign students, their passport number is recorded. This technically allows for students to be tracked throughout their academic career. It also is easier to track student movements at the beginning of, during, and at the end of the school year. This prevents two schools from claiming the same student simultaneously. Students with disabilities are also integrated into the regular schools under the Special and Inclusive Policy, and their special needs are included in the FEMIS. Teachers are uniquely identified through their staffing system ID and also their provident fund ID. Schools are uniquely identified by school registration numbers issued by the Assets Management Unit. ECE centers are gradually receiving their own unique ID numbers as separate entities from their attached primary schools. This latter process is ongoing. Numerous attempts to link the EMIS to the civil registry have not been successful. The EMIS records height and weight of students for use by the Ministry of Health although data sharing has not progressed past initial meetings.

Data Quality and Accuracy

Clear data ownership and responsibility are essential to ensure reliability and accuracy of the data. This is why, where practical, FEMIS has a single entity responsible for each data area with numerous other entities using that data. At the same time, the MoEHA is responsible for maintaining overall accuracy of the data, relying on the premise that an entity using its own data will provide higher-quality data for its own use. Other areas of the MoEHA benefit from sharing the higher-quality data, which puts additional pressure on data accuracy.

School heads are responsible for the accuracy of student, finance, and other school data. Head teachers and principals have to follow the guidelines presented by the MoEHA to ensure that the data are current, correct, and complete. If school heads fail to do so or even deliberately falsify data, they will be subject to disciplinary penalties. Disciplinary actions include, but are not limited to, salary suspension, disciplinary proceedings, and criminal charges.

The FEMIS administrator is responsible for data validation mechanisms such as updating and uploading accurate student, finance, and other school data into FEMIS at the school level. In addition, the FEMIS administrator is responsible for noting incorrect staff movements that exist in FESA, such as teachers whose leave is not reflected. Moreover, the FEMIS administrator reports to key stakeholders (for example, head teachers and principals). School heads and principals then carry out mandatory class edits at specified times. During those class edits, the head teachers or principals have to verify and confirm the student enrollment data for each year level. They check and compare all student data in the following parameters: age, citizenship, ethnicity, new students, repeaters, start or end of term, and boarders. All of this is done electronically in the FEMIS database by simply ticking a box associated with the class for the given term. Audited financial data are submitted by the school management within four weeks of the school Annual General meeting, and the school management is expected to submit all audited financial reports. Figure 9.8 shows the types of data quality reports generated by FEMIS for QA purposes.

Increased demands for analysis of the FEMIS data drive up the quality of data. The FEMIS team was pivotal in encouraging and spreading this perspective to schools and the MoEHA. Naturally, the discussions in the early rollout questioned data availability and data quality. As FEMIS data quality improved and availability increased, these discussions gave way to solid analysis of education performance using FEMIS data. Questions now focus on the analysis of data, not quality or availability. Conversely, non-ministry-related donor projects that do not buy into the EMIS will administer potentially vast and redundant data sources that can conflict with EMIS data. This draws the reliability of both ministry- and non-ministry-related data sources into question, thoroughly undermining the EMIS.

Figure 9.8 Options for the Data Quality Report

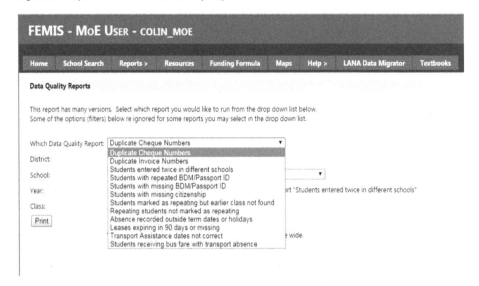

Source: FEMIS, http://www.femis.gov.fj/femis/.

Security and Data Privacy Provisions

A security system was to be established to allow as much visibility of data while restricting edits and updates to ensure accuracy and reliability. FEMIS uses a self-sustaining approach to security. It is not realistic to expect a small under-staffed IT Unit to manage passwords for more than 10,000 teachers, 1,000 schools, and several hundred MoEHA employees. FEMIS has four broad account types with different levels of data access: MoEHA, district, school, and teacher (figure 9.9). The IT Unit manages only the MoEHA and district accounts.

1. **Ministry-level access** is generally fewer than 600 users. MoEHA account types include general ministry staff, emergency relief workers, engineers, finance, highly restricted Examination and Assessment Unit (EAU) access, and so on. MoEHA account types can see all schools in all districts with restrictions on what is visible within the school according to the actual account type. For example, engineers do not have access to individual student records, and emergency relief workers have restricted views of school data but can run disaster management reports on all schools. Ministry-level accounts have extremely limited *write* access but tend to have broad visibility of data.
2. **District-level access** consists of two different types:
   a. District *read-only* users are the same as MoEHA users in that they can see all data and change nothing, but this access type is restricted to viewing schools in only one district.
   b. District *read-write* users are also restricted to schools in one district, but this user type can change school data sufficiently to act as a proxy for schools

Figure 9.9 Hierarchy of Data Access

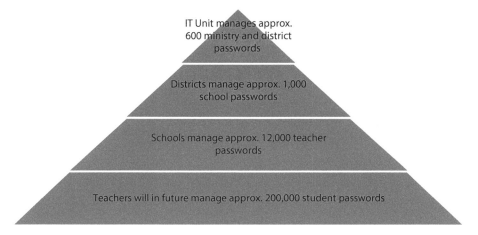

that do not have an Internet connection. Policy mandates these users to maintain data for schools without Internet.

   c. Districts are responsible for managing passwords for all schools in their district.

3. *School-level access* allows a school to log on and manage all students in all grades in the school. School-level access can also see all finance, facilities, and teacher data for teachers currently in the school. Schools are responsible for managing passwords for all teachers attending the school. The staffing system FESA determines the school a teacher is in at any given time. If FEMIS determines any inconsistencies in the FESA staffing information, teacher access is denied until the issue is resolved. Schools log on with a school code.

4. *Teacher-level access* allows teachers to see their own professional development, leave, and other staffing information. If the school-level logon has assigned a teacher a class, that teacher can manage all students in that class, including student attendance, student fees, student health, and so on. Teachers can also view assessment results for students in their assigned class(es). Teachers log on using their teacher ID.

5. *Student-level access and community-level access* are under development at the time of writing.

6. *Public-level access* is not permitted by the MoEHA, although preliminary work is underway to allow public access to generic maps and basic graphs generated by the EMIS.

Data Use

FEMIS is used for a variety of basic reporting, tracking, and resource allocation functions. Currently, FEMIS data are used for national assessment registration and dissemination; grant allocation; attendance tracking; determination of textbook requirements; calculation of transport subsidies; school finances including detailed expenditure against allocation with budget tracking at the school level;

staff professional development; teacher qualifications; teacher leave; teacher sala-ries, positions, and history; school type; school infrastructure; teacher subject loading; school mapping; disaster resource tracking; drug usage; an online library and forum; school library data; school lease, property, and legal data; substantial individual student data such as fees, health, assessments, family, and subjects; and determination of staffing requirements.

The introduction of individual student and teacher records at the school level encouraged schools to consume their own data, driving up the quality of student data. This also improves communication in schools between staff members because they can monitor real-time education data and respond to the needs of individual students and teachers. Individual data records also enable government staff in allocation of grants and resources and in developing policies that cater to individual student characteristics.

As an integrated system, FEMIS can leverage attendance reporting, national assessment report, financial data, and so on to compare and draw inferences. For example, the outcome data on student's assessment can be linked to the attendance data and allocation of material resources. This is especially useful when analyzing the impact of inputs on outputs. Schools can draw up their own attendance records (students and teachers), data on facilities, and financial data. Figure 9.10 illustrates some examples of reports that are available through FEMIS for individual schools.

FEMIS data are not yet used effectively to support senior-level decision making or monitor the implementation and effectiveness of policy, beyond the Sustainable Development Goals and parliament reporting. However, FEMIS has the potential to inform a broader variety of operational uses. For example, releasing 50,000 exam results is fairly effortless, but a closer look at the data could reveal problems like skewed grades by gender that have been effectively ignored.

There is a strong culture of data retention for internal consumption instead of making the data available to external stakeholders. The MoEHA is very protective of education data: although data quality may be moderate to high, it often retains data rather than sharing data transparently with stakeholders. At present data are used more to drive and manage internal ministry processes than to support decisions and monitor policy. The use of data in the ministry has seen improved management of finances and vast improvements in assess-ment and other processes.

Looking Ahead

Despite the success of FEMIS to date, substantial work remains for future FEMIS development. This includes:

- Further work with senior MoEHA staff in the use of FEMIS as a decision sup-port tool
- Analysis of FEMIS data to monitor teaching and learning

Figure 9.10 Material Resources and Attendance Module in FEMIS

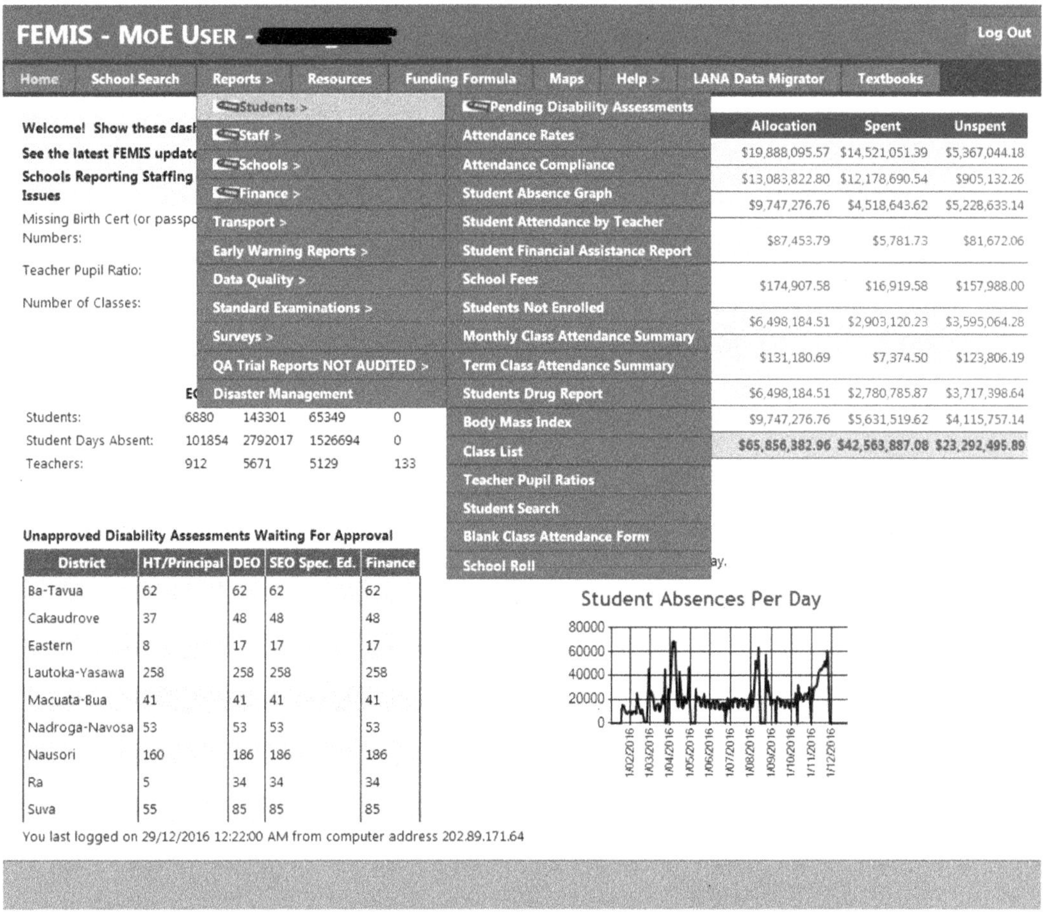

Source: FEMIS training video, https://www.youtube.com/watch?v=AwmzWXakeU8&feature=youtu.be.

- Enabling access by students and the wider community to FEMIS
- Integration of ECE, Technical Education, and Higher Education to track longitudinal outcomes
- Encouraging use of the eLearning, Online Library, and Educators Forum areas
- Integration of the EMIS with other ministries, primarily the Ministry of Health
- Integration with the Births Deaths Marriages database

Given FEMIS's successful implementation and buy-in from all education stakeholders at the local and central levels, the next step requires transition from a compliance-focused to a learning-focused approach. That journey is complicated, but it is also a game changer. At the core of this transition is a behavior change in the way that data are valued. The shift moves from seeing data as a tool to monitor progress to understanding that data, as well as the larger EMIS, can be used to promote teaching and learning as well as management and planning.

When designing a new system, start with the policy questions that key stakeholders want the system to answer. By answering these questions early in the process, the risk of ending up with a fragmented and limited system is reduced. This requires multiple efforts to build consensus across a variety of departments and stakeholders (Abdul Hamid et al 2017).

Notes

1. Information on FEMIS comes from its website, http://www.femis.gov.fj/femis/.
2. This information was provided to the World Bank by the MoEHA Finance Unit on June 21, 2016.
3. AQEP is the agency working with the MoEHA and DFAT to implement FEMIS in the country. The budget for the project is from the Australian government.

Reference

MoEHA (Ministry of Education, Heritage and Arts). 2016. "Policy on Fiji Education Management Information System." MoEHA, Suva, Fiji, December 10. http://www .education.gov.fj/images/2016/FEMIS_Policy_-Reviewed_2016.pdf.

CHAPTER 10

Building an Education Management Information System in a Fragile Environment: The Case of Afghanistan

The availability and use of valid and timely information, evidence based decision making, results based management, timely provision of services, consistent monitoring of the operations and evaluation of the results constitute the backbone of our endeavors.

—Dr. Assadullah Hanif, Minister of Education, Afghanistan

Key Takeaways

- By prioritizing education data, the Government of Afghanistan has successfully established a functioning Education Management Information System (EMIS) and demonstrates how an EMIS can be designed, implemented, and sustained even in highly fragile environments. EMIS data is now used for policy making.
- The EMIS has proved to be instrumental at tracking teacher payroll and student attendance, especially for girls.
- Decentralization of the data collection process and improved information and communication technology (ICT) capacities have increased efficiencies and response rates and alleviated safety concerns, with data now sent to school district offices.
- Constant review, feedback, and improvements—along with staff training ranging from data collection, entry, and verification to ICT skills—ensured that Afghanistan's EMIS developed its full functionality.

- Data validation mechanisms through the support of outside consultants and a newly decentralized structure helped Afghanistan reduce doubts about data quality and secure funding from international donors.
- Data are widely disseminated through the Ministry of Education (MoE) website not only to foster transparency and accountability but also to pave the way toward establishing a data-driven culture.

Introduction and Country Overview

Education systems suffer immensely in fragile and conflict-affected areas. The ability to access accurate student data, as well as data on teachers, schools, and other education inputs and outputs, is an essential component of the postconflict rebuilding process. As such, an EMIS plays a critical role in supporting a country's education sector as it evolves from a fragile context. This chapter details the experience of Afghanistan and its journey to develop, reform, and decentralize its EMIS following three decades of conflict and war. The Afghan experience provides insights that are valuable to education stakeholders—in both fragile and nonfragile environments—seeking to reform their education data systems.

This chapter follows the development of an operational EMIS in Afghanistan. It provides a country overview to frame the context followed by a detailed description of the different development stages. Afghanistan started the journey toward a comprehensive EMIS in 2005 and is still progressing. During the process many lessons have been learned that may be applicable to countries facing similar challenges.

Afghanistan has been under a protracted state of conflict and instability for over three decades, severely impacting the country's economy, infrastructure, and education system. The protracted conflict has had wide-ranging effect, with more than half the population living below the poverty line and one-third of the population struggling to reach food security. Out of a population of 30.5 million, just under a million Afghans are classified as internally displaced, with an additional 2.6 million Afghan refugees having fled the country. The ongoing insecurity, especially in the south and east of the country, continues to limit effective education delivery and data collection.

Afghanistan's education sector has been particularly hard hit by insecurity, with girls' education the worst affected. In 2001, just after the fall of the Taliban, the net enrollment rate was estimated at 43 percent for boys and less than 3 percent for girls (World Bank 2009). In addition, there were only 21,000, mostly undereducated, teachers in the country. Since 2002, however, the education sector in Afghanistan has undergone a national rebuilding process. In 2014, net enrollment of all children had risen to 8.8 million, 38 percent of which were girls (table 10.1). Of these children, 5.8 million were enrolled in primary education. Over the same period, the number of teachers had grown from 21,000 to 187,000 (figures 10.1 and 10.2).

Table 10.1 Education Indicators at a Glance, Afghanistan

Schools and enrollment (2016)[a]

Institution	Schools	Enrollment	% Female
Primary	6,216	6,037,663	41
Lower secondary	3,990	1,599,485	36
Upper secondary	4,875	946,558	36

Gross enrollment rates (2014)[b]

	Male	Female	Total
Primary	130.7	91.8	111.7
Lower secondary	82.7	48.6	66.2
Upper secondary	57.3	29.6	43.9

Pupil-teacher ratio (headcount basis)[b]

Primary (2013)	45.7
Lower secondary (2013)	45.0
Upper secondary (2007)	30.7

Literacy rates[b]

Age	Male	Female
Youth (15–24 years) (2015)	69.6	46.3
Adult (15+) (2015)	52.0	24.2
Elderly (65+) (2011)	20.7	19.7

Public expenditure on education (2014)

As a percentage of government expenditure	18.4

a. Ministry of Education n.d.
b. World Bank data.

Figure 10.1 Number of Teachers, Afghanistan, 2001 and 2014

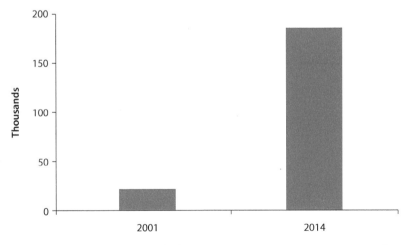

Source: Ministry of Education, http://emis.af/index.aspx.

Figure 10.2 Student Enrollment, Afghanistan, 2001 and 2014

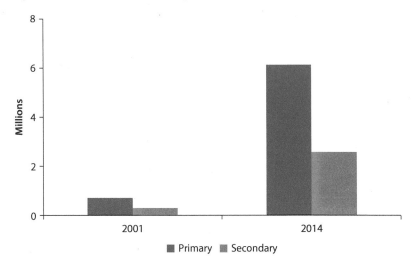

Source: Ministry of Education, http://emis.af/index.aspx.

The difficult terrain combined with a lack of public and private infrastructure has led to geographic isolation for a number of provinces. Landlocked, the country lies to the northwest of Pakistan, east of the Islamic Republic of Iran, and south of Tajikistan, Turkmenistan, and Uzbekistan. The Hindu Kush Mountains, an 800-kilometer-long mountain range, divide the country into three distinct geographic regions: the Himalayas, the Southern Plateau, and the Northern Plains. Politically, the country is divided into 34 provinces, each with a provincial governor appointed by the President of Afghanistan.

In 2003, the country adopted a new constitution, under which rebuilding the education sector became one of the first priorities supported by the new government and the international community. However, with no accurate or reliable data, planning and financing of the sector proved difficult. Data collection, collation, and analysis except in the most rudimentary forms were virtually nonexistent. Most of the reports were based on extrapolation of historic data available through provincial education staff.

Increasing use of ICT in the education sector and strengthening the EMIS have been a priority under donor projects. With the support of the World Bank and the Afghanistan Reconstruction Trust Fund, the Education Quality Improvement Project (EQUIP) was launched in 2004. With a budget of US$460 million, EQUIP is the largest education sector program in the country today.

Building an EMIS amid Fragility

Developing a comprehensive data management information system poses significant and unique challenges. Afghanistan's unique context of fragility added additional complications. However, building and strengthening an EMIS in the country has been a long-term priority for the MoE. The concerted effort first

Figure 10.3 Evolution of the EMIS in Afghanistan

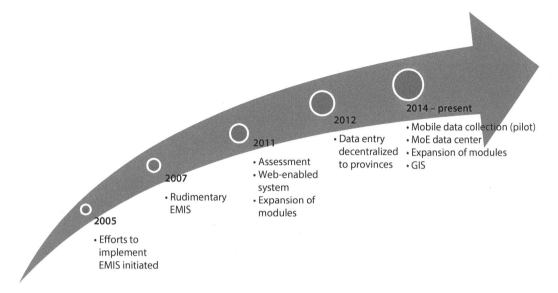

Note: EMIS = Education Management Information System; GIS = Geographic Information System; MoE = Ministry of Education.

began in 2005, with improvements and developments ongoing through today. Figure 10.3 illustrates the evolution of Afghanistan's EMIS, divided into five distinct phases.

Creating a Rudimentary EMIS

The Central EMIS Directorate was created in 2005 and began to develop a software application, relying on in-house expertise. With the support of the international community, the government began the process of systematizing data collection with the creation of a basic EMIS based on a client–server environment. This initial software package included modules for school management, infrastructure management, student registration, informal education reporting, and *Shura*, or parent–teacher association reporting. The development process for these modules, however, was somewhat ad hoc, meaning that a well-defined system development approach was not followed.

The data collection depended on paper forms centrally printed at the EMIS department and circulated to schools through the Provincial and District Education Offices (DEOs). Schools filled out the forms and physically sent them to the MoE in Kabul. The Central EMIS Directorate received full ownership of the data, meaning that it was responsible for the full cycle of data production from collection, entry, and analysis to reporting and dissemination.

Conducting a First Education Data Survey

Afghanistan began the process of institutionalizing an EMIS in 2007. In the middle of that year, the Central EMIS Directorate conducted its first school survey (box 10.1), with 196 survey teams visiting nearly 9,000 of the country's

Box 10.1 Data Collection in Insecure Environments

Although an important first step, the 2007 school survey was not entirely complete. Because of insecurity in 8 of Afghanistan's 34 provinces, an estimated 600 of the 9,500 schools could not be reached. In most cases, when survey teams were unable to visit schools, the head teachers were asked to travel to the regional capital with documentation to fill out the survey. However, for 200 schools even this was not possible because the principals did not feel safe enough to travel. For these schools, estimates were derived from data at the provincial education department.

Source: Adapted from Ministry of Education 2009.

9,500 schools over a seventy-day period. The survey report was made available in January 2008 and its results constituted the first data entered into Afghanistan's nascent EMIS. Since 2007, the MoE has successfully positioned EMIS as the point of reference system that collects, processes, and disseminates education data on a regular basis.

Since that initial survey, paper forms were sent annually to schools across the country. Once filled out, the forms physically travelled from the schools to DEOs. From the district level they were transported to Provincial Education Departments (PEDs) and finally to the Central EMIS Directorate. The EMIS team would then process and enter the data into the electronic EMIS system. Because the paper forms passed through multiple levels of administration and were entered into the system without an effective validation procedure, the reliability of the data was low.

Challenges Emerged

This highly centralized structure resulted in a number of challenges, primarily in the areas of data collection, quality, access, and integration. Data collection was especially challenging in insecure provinces where individuals collecting and transporting education data were putting themselves at great risk. Cases of education data forms being "smuggled" into Kabul in milk containers or other innocuous devices were not uncommon. In addition to security-related challenges, data collection was also hampered by distance and mountainous terrain. Transporting data from remote provinces was time-consuming. In addition, the lack of systematic data entry validation procedures and training led to inaccurate data, reducing quality and reliability.

The architectural challenges led to problems with access and integration. Access to data and applications was limited to those who were directly connected to the local servers within the EMIS department in Kabul. As a result, all stakeholders depended on the EMIS department for their data and reporting needs. In addition, the lack of integration across systems amplified data quality problems and inefficiency stemming from duplication and inconsistency in data collection and reporting.

Most of the staff in the EMIS team had an ICT background with limited technical knowledge of the education sector. As a result, the relevance and importance of various data points, and their impact on education indicators, were not completely understood. This meant that the EMIS team did not have the capacity to spot anomalies or flag data discrepancies during the data entry phase. Furthermore, insecurity and geographic barriers made physical data validation efforts both costly and dangerous. The need for data to be owned and managed by respective government units—while being supported by the EMIS team—became clear. In addition, the length of time involved in physically transporting the forms to the MoE meant that data were out of date when entered into the system, reducing their value for planning purposes.

Evaluating and Strategizing

In an effort to address some of the issues, the Government of Afghanistan decided to implement a thorough assessment of the system. The review undertook a detailed study of the MoE's data and information needs in order to propose an integrated information technology (IT) solution that could meet the long-term needs of the MoE. Decentralizing the system, allowing data entry to take place at the regional level, became a priority. As part of this assessment, the following eight areas were prioritized:

1. Developing an ICT Vision and Education ICT strategy for the MoE
2. Analyzing each of the MoE's processes with the aim of reengineering them in order to allow automation
3. Creating an architecture solution complete with hardware, soft applications, and networking
4. Creating a detailed project plan for the implementation of the developed solution
5. Providing budget estimates for the project
6. Creating a training and change management plan for the project
7. Developing and articulating the rollout plan for the project
8. Detailing sustainability issues

Increasing Ownership

Decentralizing Afghanistan's education data system involved two steps: (1) decentralizing responsibility within the MoE and (2) decentralizing data entry down to the provincial level. The EMIS team, headed by a chief information officer, would continue to be responsible for the development, implementation, and testing of EMIS applications and processes. Individual line departments would become responsible for the data relating to their units. A new organizational structure for the flow of data (figure 10.4) was proposed, leading to the handover of data entry responsibilities to line departments. This change of management resulted in increased ownership over the data by individual units, with the aim of improving scrutiny on data quality.

Figure 10.4 Suggested Organization for Data Management at the Ministry of Education

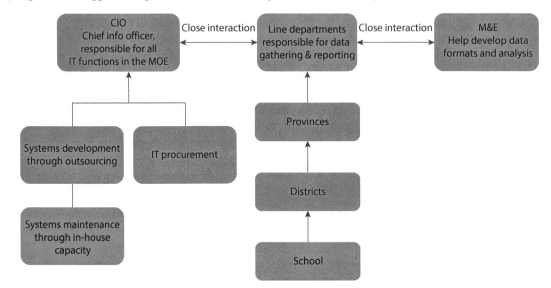

Note: IT = information technology; M&E = monitoring and evaluation; MOE = Ministry of Education.

Decentralizing Data Entry

Decentralizing data entry down to the provincial level had a number of advantages. The significant geographic barriers and lack of infrastructure meant that data reaching Kabul often took months. Insecurity meant that data could get lost en route and those transporting forms were at risk. Decentralizing data entry to the provincial level meant that forms still had to travel from schools to the provinces but that the travel period would reduce significantly. Future plans to decentralize data entry even further to the district level were considered, but connectivity and capacity issues meant that this next step did not happen immediately.

Increasing ICT Capacities

The review process also found a strong need to enhance the existing ICT capacities within the MoE in general and at the provincial level specifically. The availability of computing resources, power, and Internet connectivity within the provincial MoE offices would allow the data entry to be decentralized down to the provincial offices, increasing the efficiency and effectiveness of the EMIS.

Upgrading to a New Web-Enabled System

Following the assessment period, the MoE developed a detailed plan to upgrade its data system. Short-, medium-, and long-term goals were identified (box 10.2). Modernizing the ICT system, adding or redeveloping modules,

---

Box 10.2 Short-, Medium-, and Long-Term EMIS Goals

Short-term goals

- Transfer the existing student management information system to a web-enabled environment, allowing data entry to be decentralized.
- Create synergies with other departments including the Ministry of Communication and Information Technology (MoCIT), Central Statistical Organization (CSO), in order to capitalize on existing expertise and avoid duplication of work.
- Build capacity both at PEDs and within the wider MoE through an extensive training program.
- Develop and deliver change management workshops in order foster a data-driven culture within the MoE.
- Undertake a comprehensive review of the data needs within the MoE including
  - Monitoring and evaluation (M&E) and compliance requirements, and
  - The requirements of an ICT infrastructure and architecture that could support the development and implementation of a data-driven MoE.

Medium-term goals

- Foster institution buy-in of the implementation plan developed under Phase I through a process of dialogue and consensus building.
- Develop additional modules through outsourcing or a hybrid strategy.
- Continue capacity building and training.

Long-term goals

- Maintain, sustain, and scale up.
- Add more modules and capabilities to existing EMIS applications.
- Develop and pilot a mobile data collection system.

---

providing extensive training for staff, increasing data verification efforts, and introducing core policies were prioritized in the short term.

Modernizing the ICT System

Modernizing the ICT systems that underpinned Afghanistan's EMIS became a priority. The desire to decentralize data entry to the provincial level meant that the existing system architecture needed to be changed. Running through a rudimentary client–server environment, access to the legacy system was limited to computers that were directly connected to the local area network within the EMIS department. In addition, all stakeholders depended on the EMIS department for their data and reporting needs. The existing system could not be decentralized, limiting its functionality. In 2011 the system was brought online and dramatically modernized, paving the way for data entry to be decentralized to the provincial level. The decentralization process—shifting data entry from the central ministerial level to the district level—involved a number of steps. These steps and the time frames associated with them were as follows:

- Migration of applications to .NET Microsoft framework: 3 months
- Hosting of the migrated applications and databases at the central data center: 6 months (in parallel with the application migration)
- Establishment of local area networks and ensuring Internet availability at each of the PEDs: 12 months for the 34 provinces
- Training of PED staff in using the web-enabled applications and entering data: 12 months from the date of migration and systems going live from the national data center in Kabul
- Change management program: Ongoing support of district and provincial staff in the shift from using physical processes to automated systems.

Selecting an EMIS Platform

Because the original applications had been developed using Microsoft technologies, the EMIS team decided to use Microsoft's .NET platform in the switch to a web-enabled system. The in-house EMIS team had significant levels of expertise using Microsoft systems, making it a logical choice. All the existing applications were migrated to a single .NET platform, supported by a common Structure Query Language (SQL) server relational database. As the existing database already ran on an SQL server platform, making the transition to a web-enabled relational database platform was straightforward.

The shift to a self-hosted web-enabled system meant that the applications making up Afghanistan's system could now be accessed through a web portal. Figure 10.5 illustrates the structure of the web-enabled system. Data entry applications are accessible through a cloud-based system, and data entry operators with the right credentials can upload data on any computer connected to the Internet. As a result, the PEDs can now input the data directly. Shifting to the provincial level has significantly reduced the distance paper forms need to travel before being entered into the system, an important step in modernizing Afghanistan's EMIS and significantly reducing the time it takes for data to be available within the EMIS.

The MoE also began developing a state of the art data center that hosts all EMIS data. Initially, from 2011 to 2014, the National Data Center of the Ministry of Communication and Information Technology (MoCIT) in Kabul hosted all EMIS data because it was the only data center available to government departments. However, in 2014 the MoE opened its own center, using Cisco ASR 1002 routers with a three-tiered security architecture.

Developing New EMIS Applications

As part of the process of modernizing Afghanistan's EMIS, a number of applications used today were developed or redeveloped during this phase. Central to the system were a School Management System, a Student Management System, and a Teacher Training Management System. In addition, a number of

Figure 10.5 Structure of a Web-Enabled System

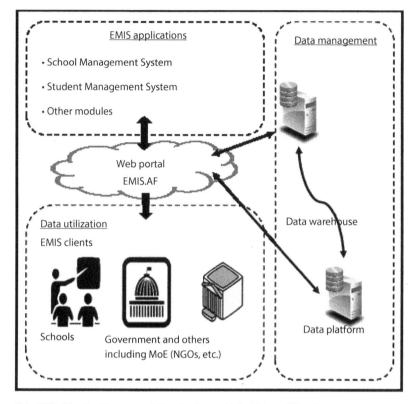

Note: EMIS = Education Management Information System; MoE = Ministry of Education;
NGO = nongovernmental organization.

smaller applications were developed and incorporated into the EMIS. Each of
these modules is described in brief below.

- *The Student Management System* provides a platform for managing student
  data, including their demographics, class status, and examination results. Each
  student is mapped to a school and each school is identified by a unique code.
  As a result, the system allows details of all students in any given school to be
  viewed by eligible staff. Some of the data in this application are collected in the
  annual school census.
- *The School Management System* collects and stores details of all schools,
  including information on school location, type of school, number of classrooms, infrastructure, toilets, library, science labs, and so on. It provides stakeholders with important information on the number, types, and quality of
  school infrastructure in Afghanistan. Data for this system are also collected as
  part of the annual school census.
- *The Teacher Training Management System* tracks the education, training, and
  professional development status of hundreds of thousands of teachers, for the

Teacher Education Department (TED) within the MoE. In addition, the system has the potential to fine-tune training plans.

- **The Certificate Distribution System** provides students with a graduation certificate. The System allows the MoE to rapidly verify that a student has been registered within the education system and has fulfilled his or her graduation requirements. A database of verified students is maintained in the General Education Department. The system collects data from this database, prints the certificates, and distributes them to the relevant parties. This automated process has immensely reduced the time needed to distribute certificates to graduating students.

- **Human Resource Management System for the Technical Assistants** was developed to manage the entire life cycle of technical assistants in the MoE. This application streamlines the management of thousands of technical assistants, including their selection, induction, performance assessment, payment, and promotion. Using this system as a model, an initiative has begun to roll out a comprehensive Human Resource Management Information System (HRMIS) for all *Tashkil* (civil servants) of the MoE. This system will eventually cover over 250,000 employees, including all public school teachers.

In 2012, education data were entered into the electronic applications at the provincial level for the first time (figure 10.6). Blank paper-based forms are sent from the central EMIS directorate to each PED. The PEDs distribute these forms to DEOs, who then distribute them to the schools. School principals fill out the forms, after which they return them to the DEOs. These district offices consolidate the forms and send them to the PED. At the provincial level, the data from these forms are entered into the School and Student Management Systems. After data entry, the physical forms are sent from the PEDs to the EMIS directorate in Kabul.

Training Staff and Building Capacity

Training and capacity building—viewed as the most effective strategies to institutionalize a data-driven culture within the MoE—were recognized as priorities for the MoE at an early stage of EMIS development. Various training programs were provided to all levels of MoE staff. These included specific data collection, data entry, and verification modules. In addition, ICT training programs were developed and delivered to EMIS staff, focusing on developing, implementing, and maintaining a modern EMIS system (box 10.3).

Figure 10.6 Afghanistan EMIS Data Flow

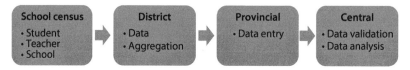

School census	District	Provincial	Central
• Student • Teacher • School	• Data • Aggregation	• Data entry	• Data validation • Data analysis

Note: EMIS = Education Management Information System.

Box 10.3 Types of Training

- Installing operating systems (OS) on desktop and laptop machines
- Loading OS on local servers
- Loading applications on servers and clients
- Generic ICT training including training on application development using .NET Framework
- Training the trainers on data entry processes
- Training in using the EMIS programs for entering the data
- Data verification and correction

Training was also vital in allowing data collection to be decentralized to provincial levels. A significant portion of the training effort focused on training new data entry operators in the PEDs, ensuring that data entry would take place effectively and efficiently. These training programs involved ICT-specific trainings such as installing operating systems and accessing the applications from client servers, as well as data entry and verification training programs. The Central EMIS Directorate developed all the training programs and delivered these at the PEDs. Training in the EMIS directorate happens on a regular basis, with refresher programs provided throughout the year. In addition, EMIS employees have been trained in mobile application development.

Training programs and workshops were also used as part of a change management process. Individual MoE departments were introduced to data concepts and how data use could streamline their work programs. This helped create an environment where "data ownership" could shift from the central EMIS team to the departments themselves. The Central EMIS Directorate developed all the training programs and delivered these at the PEDs.

Validating Data

EMIS team members, who visit a handful of schools to check for consistency, physically verify a small sample of data forms collected from schools. Verifying the validity of data in a fragile environment poses significant challenges. Questions regarding the validity of EMIS data were a concern for donors and MoE officials. As a result, a concerted effort to streamline data verification systems took place. A number of different processes were introduced, including manual and automated systems. However, resource constraints have prevented the EMIS team from verifying a standard sample size of data on an annual basis. Instead, an ad hoc selection of schools is visited throughout the year. Systematic validation of data at provincial and national levels is hampered by the lack of resources.

As relevant departments have taken on ownership of individual data collection processes, increased technical education knowledge has also added a layer of verification, with MoE staff better equipped to spot discrepancies or anomalies. In addition, automated verification systems have been built into the software packages, restricting data entry to relevant formats and within predefined parameters. This has reduced data entry errors. In 2013, the MoE decided to run a thorough assessment of the data quality within the EMIS. The MoE hired an independent consulting firm, the Afghanistan Reliable Technology Services (ARTS), to cross-check and verify the data in the EMIS through a physical verification process in 10 percent of all schools in Afghanistan. The ARTS report found that—despite efforts to institutionalize trend analysis, physical data verification, and data cleaning exercises—clear guidelines and lines of responsibility for these efforts were not in place. As a result, data verification efforts were still taking place in an ad hoc nature. Despite these problems, the report found that, for many of the commonly used indicators, data variation was low to moderate. Certain indicators, however, including permanently absent students, dropout rates, age of students, and availability of books, had larger variation. As such, there remains scope for increasing the accuracy of education data.

Introducing Core Policies

Since 2014, two core policies, namely the "EMIS Strategy 2015–19" and "Information Systems Development Policy" (ISDP), have guided the strategic direction and implementation of the EMIS, ensuring continuous improvements. These policy documents provide a set of guidelines for the development of an efficient and sustainable information management system. In addition, the MoE developed the Information System Development Procedures, which clearly articulate responsibilities and coordination across different MoE programs and departments and with external sources. These procedures have been developed in accordance with the best global practices and in line with Afghanistan's e-government policy. The MoE has also developed the Information System Development Standards to guide software developers in developing software and database applications and in the standards to be used. This ensures effectiveness, accountability, and sustainability of these systems.

The ISDP defines the guidelines for the development of new information systems, including upgrades to existing systems. The document is an implementation guideline for key stakeholders such as project managers, software architects, designers, and developers. It provides a framework for the development of information systems, mandating use of internationally acknowledged methodologies and best practices in the areas of project management and software development, thereby leading to development of high-quality and maintainable information systems.

Looking Ahead

The education data system in Afghanistan continues to evolve. The EMIS team is working on new initiatives to add features and increase accuracy, such as the creation of a unique student identifier (USI). The Student Information Management System is currently in the process of being upgraded and will eventually allow each student to be identified through a USI. This USI would identify students for the duration of their time in education, tracking them from primary all the way through tertiary education. Although plans for the USI system have been developed, implementation is not expected to start until the next phase of the EQUIP project.

The MoE plans to increase the capacity of DEOs and PEDs to access and use data. Central to these plans is increasing Internet connectivity in the DEOs. The National Education Strategy Plan III (NESP III) outlines plans to have 180 DEOs connected to the EMIS by the end of 2017, with a total of 412 DEOs connected by the end of 2020.

Mobile data collection has the possibility to significantly upgrade the capabilities of Afghanistan's system. With connectivity becoming increasingly accessible, mobile data collection is slowly becoming a viable option in the country. As a result, the government has begun working on two different initiatives: a mobile data collection initiative in pilot schools and a mobile school infrastructure management application. In 2013, the Central EMIS Directorate began an experiment in Uruzgan province. The MoE piloted a mobile data collection system in a number of schools. Instead of filling out paper-based school census forms, school principals directly answered questions on mobile phones. The collected data were transmitted directly to the central EMIS directory. Data verification took place with the support of *Shuras*—school management counsels. A data collection application developed in-house by the MoE allowed daily, monthly, and yearly data to be collected from pilot schools. The MoE deemed the pilot to be successful, leading to an effort to develop and streamline the application for future national implementation.

In addition, a mobile-based data collection tool for managing and tracking school infrastructure development is also being piloted. The application allows project managers to collect data, including audio and video, from construction sites. Data for 15 school construction projects are currently being collected through a pilot phase of this project, allowing real-time progress reports on the status of construction projects. This system has the potential to significantly streamline the reporting process, especially for schools being built in remote areas. Box 10.4 shows how the use of mobile phones in a province in Pakistan has enabled real-time access of education data.

The modernization of Afghanistan's EMIS has had fairly significant results. The Central EMIS Directorate has published education statistics every year from 2008 to 2015, with eight years of data currently available through an online platform. Data are collected, analyzed, and disseminated in a timely manner. The types of reported data include enrollment, demographic data, aggregated exam results, school information, infrastructure data, teacher data, and textbook availability. The data are available at the provincial, district, and—to authorized users—school level. The EMIS reports cover general education, Islamic education, technical, teacher training, and literacy programs.

There has been a gradual shift in the use of data from a focus on monitoring and counting to making informed policy decisions. Data are primarily used for

---

Box 10.4 Use of Mobile Phones in Data Collection

Balochistan, a province in Pakistan, experiences safety challenges similar to those in Afghanistan. The Balochistan Department of Education has recently launched a real-time, Android-based school census application. Through the use of mobile phones, authorized users can now access information regarding any of the following aspects in real time:

- School enrollment and attendance
- Teaching and nonteaching staff availability and attendance
- School facilities
- School infrastructure
- Teaching and learning environment
- School visits by education department officials and other stakeholders
- Professional development of teachers
- Use of funds provided to cluster hub schools

Once the basic information (for example, school facilities) has been assessed by external monitors and uploaded, the system does not require additional travel from school authorities because all information can be uploaded locally and accessed from anywhere worldwide through a unique authorization code.

Source: Education Department of Balochistan 2015.

---

monitoring and reporting purposes, including reporting to the United Nations Education, Scientific, and Cultural Organization, international donors, and external stakeholders; but data are increasingly seen as a means to inform education policy decisions. In addition, decentralization of data collection efforts to PEDs has significantly reduced the time required for data to be entered into the system.

Despite significant progress, Afghanistan's education data system still faces many challenges:

- Lack of policies to streamline coordination and sharing of data is leading to significant breakdowns and inefficiencies in coordination between the MoE and other government ministries and bureaus. In the ICT Policy for Afghanistan, the government highlights its commitment to developing an integrated and holistic approach in ICT. In addition, it aims to employ ICT as a tool for effective and transparent governance across all ministries and departments. A number of other ministries are independently developing information management systems, potentially increasing the availability of data that can be incorporated into Afghanistan's EMIS. However, many of these systems are being developed in an isolated manner, possibly leading to fragmented systems across the government that experience significant obstacles in communicating with each other. To address these concerns, the government has launched an Oversight Committee on Management Information System. This committee is tasked with developing consistent definitions and providing guidance and direction on the technical aspects of the development of new information systems. Ensuring the coordination and cooperation between government ministries could prove challenging, but the new committee should help alleviate some of the issues that may arise.

- Sustaining the continuous development of the EMIS is a critical issue, for which the government needs to develop a comprehensive strategic plan. Donor-funded projects have helped establish Afghanistan's EMIS as the core MoE system. However, for its long-term sustainability it is crucial that legal frameworks, strategies, and policies are put in place. Without these, long-term commitment to devoting resources, including human resources and budget, toward the EMIS cannot be guaranteed. Reliance on donor funding carries an inherent risk, and eventually the government will have to finance the system independently. Afghanistan is in the process of developing a five-year strategic plan to streamline the EMIS vision, strategic objectives, and next steps. Once finalized, this plan could significantly improve the enabling environment for Afghanistan's EMIS and ensure its sustainability.

Overall, the case of Afghanistan proves that, even in fragile environments, it is possible to introduce and implement an EMIS. The key aspects were political will, an EMIS vision, and support from the international donor community. Afghanistan's experience sets a model for countries facing similar conflict environments.

References

Education Department of Balochistan. 2015. "Strengthening and Institutionalization of Education Management Information System (EMIS): A Note on the Field Test of Android Based Real Time School Monitoring System at GBMODHS Yazdan Khan." Baolochistan, Pakistan.

Ministry of Education Afghanistan. 2009. *Education Summary Report 1387–88 (2008–2009).* Ministry of Education, Islamic Republic of Afghanistan.

World Bank. 2009. "IDA at Work: Afghanistan—Expanding Access to Quality Education." International Development Association, World Bank, Washington, DC. http://web .worldbank.org/WBSITE/EXTERNAL/PROJECTS/0,,contentMDK:21289161~men uPK:64282137~pagePK:41367~piPK:279616~theSitePK:40941,00.html.

SABER–EMIS Rubric

The SABER–EMIS (Systems Approach for Better Education Results–Education Management Information System) rubric defines each policy lever and indicator. The policy area scores depend on each of the levers and indicators.

Table A.1 Rubric to Benchmark EMIS in Maryland

Policy levers	Indicators	Description of best practices	Scoring			
			Latent	Emerging	Established	Advanced
Policy area 1: Enabling environment		**The system contains crucial components of a comprehensive enabling environment, which addresses related policy elements and enables the functioning of an effective and dynamic system.**	**The system lacks major components of a comprehensive enabling environment.**	**The system contains basic components of a comprehensive enabling environment.**	**The system contains most components of a comprehensive enabling environment.**	**The system contains crucial components of a comprehensive enabling environment.**
1.1 **Legal framework**	Institutionalization of system: the EMIS is institutionalized as an integral part of the education system and the government. Responsibility: Responsibility for collecting, processing, and disseminating education statistics is given to a clearly designated institution or agency. Dynamic framework: The legal framework is dynamic and elastic so that it can adapt to advancements in technology.	An existing legal framework supports a fully functioning EMIS.	A legal framework is not in place.	Basic components of a legal framework or informal mechanisms are in place.	Most elements of a legal framework are in place.	An existing legal framework supports a fully functioning EMIS.

table continues next page

Table A.1 Rubric to Benchmark EMIS in Maryland *(continued)*

Policy levers	Indicators	Description of best practices	Scoring			
			Latent	Emerging	Established	Advanced
	Data supply: The legal framework mandates that schools participate in the EMIS by providing education data.					
	Comprehensive, quality data: The requirement for comprehensive, quality data is clearly specified in the EMIS legal framework.					
	Data sharing and coordination: The legal framework allows for adequate data sharing and coordination among the Ministry of Education and agencies and institutions that require education data.					
	Utilization: The legal framework emphasizes data-driven education policy.					

table continues next page

Table A.1 Rubric to Benchmark EMIS in Maryland *(continued)*

Policy levers	Indicators	Description of best practices	Scoring			
			Latent	*Emerging*	*Established*	*Advanced*
	Budget: The education system budget includes a line item for the EMIS. Confidentiality: The legal framework guarantees that respondents' data are confidential and used for the sole purpose of statistics.					
1.2 **Organizational structure and institutionalized processes**	Organizational structure and institutionalized processes are in place.	The system is institutionalized within the government, has well-defined organizational processes, and has several functionalities beyond statistical reporting.	The system is not specified in policies, and what exists does not have well-defined organizational processes; the EMIS has limited functionalities.	The institutional structure of the system is not clearly specified in policies, it has some organizational processes, and its functionalities are limited.	The institutional structure of the system is defined within the government, and it has defined organizational processes, but its functionalities are limited.	The system is institutionalized within the government, has well-defined organizational processes, and has several functionalities beyond statistical reporting.
1.3 **Human resources**	Personnel: The core tasks of the EMIS are identified, and it is staffed with qualified people.	Qualified staff operate the system, and opportunities are available to improve staff performance and retention.	Minimum standards of qualification are not met for the majority of staff that operate the system, and opportunities are not available to improve staff performance or retention.	Some staff are qualified to operate the system, and limited opportunities are available to improve staff performance and retention.	The majority of staff are qualified to operate the system, and frequent opportunities are available to improve staff performance and retention.	All staff are qualified to operate the system, and well-established opportunities are constantly available to improve staff performance and retention.

table continues next page

Table A.1 Rubric to Benchmark EMIS in Maryland *(continued)*

Policy levers	Indicators	Description of best practices	Scoring			
			Latent	Emerging	Established	Advanced
	Professional development: Professional training is available for EMIS staff.					
1.4 Infrastructural capacity	Data collection: Tools for data collection are available	The system has a well-defined infrastructure to perform data collection, management, and dissemination functions in an integral manner	The system lacks a well-defined infrastructure.	The system has a basic or incomplete infrastructure.	The system has an infrastructure that allows it to perform some of its functions in an integral manner.	The system has a well-defined infrastructure to fully perform its data collection, management, and dissemination functions in an integral manner.
	Database(s): Databases exist under the umbrella of the data warehouse and have both hardware and software means.					
	Data management system: A system is in place that manages data collection, processing, and reporting.					
	Data dissemination: Data dissemination tools are available and maintained by the agency producing education statistics.					

table continues next page

Table A.1 Rubric to Benchmark EMIS in Maryland (*continued*)

		Description of best practices	Scoring				
Policy levers	Indicators		Latent	Emerging	Established	Advanced	

Policy levers	Indicators	Description of best practices	Latent	Emerging	Established	Advanced
1.5 Budget	Personnel and professional development: The EMIS budget contains a specific budget for EMIS personnel and their professional development. Maintenance: The EMIS budget contains a specific budget for system maintenance and recurrent costs. Reporting: The EMIS budget contains a specific budget for reporting costs. Physical infrastructure: The EMIS budget contains a specific budget for physical infrastructure costs. Efficient use of resources: Processes and procedures are in place to ensure that resources are used efficiently.	The system budget is comprehensive, ensuring that the system is sustainable and efficient.	The system suffers from serious budgetary issues.	The system has a basic or incomplete budget.	The system budget contains the majority of required categories to ensure that most parts of the system are sustainable and efficient.	The system budget is comprehensive, ensuring that the system is sustainable and efficient.

table continues next page

Table A.1 Rubric to Benchmark EMIS in Maryland *(continued)*

Policy levers	Indicators	Description of best practices	Scoring				
			Latent	Emerging	Established	Advanced
1.6 Data-driven culture	Data-driven culture	A data-driven culture prioritizes data as a fundamental element of operations and decision making, both inside and outside of the education system.	The system suffers because there is not a data-driven culture that prioritizes data management and data utilization in decision making.	The system has a data-driven culture that demonstrates a basic appreciation of data and interest in developing better data-utilization practices.	A data-driven culture exists that prioritizes data management and utilization within and beyond the education system.	A data-driven culture exists that prioritizes data management and utilization within and beyond the education system, and evidence of that culture is present in daily interaction and decision making at all levels.
Policy area 2: System soundness		**The processes and structure of the EMIS are sound and support the components of an integrated system.**	**The system lacks processes and structure.**	**The system has basic processes and a structure that do not support the components of an integrated system.**	**The system has some processes and a structure, but they do not fully support the components of an integrated system.**	**The processes and structure of the system are sound and support the components of an integrated system.**
2.1 Data architecture	Data architecture	The data architecture is well defined to ensure full system functionality.	The system's data structure does not have a well-defined data architecture.	The system's data architecture includes some components; however, it is incomplete.	The system's data structure has most elements of the data architecture; however, it has some deficiencies that affect the system's functionality.	The data architecture is well defined to ensure full system functionality.

table continues next page

Table A.1 Rubric to Benchmark EMIS in Maryland *(continued)*

Policy levers		Indicators	Description of best practices	Scoring				
				Latent	Emerging	Established	Advanced	
2.2	**Data coverage**	Administrative data: the EMIS contains administrative data.	The data in the system are comprehensive and cover administrative, financial, human resources, and learning-outcomes data.	The data in the system are far from being comprehensive, and coverage is limited.	The data in the system include some of the data areas.	The data in the system include most, but not all, of the data areas.	The data in the system are comprehensive and cover all data areas.	
		Financial data: the EMIS contains financial data.						
		Human resources data: the EMIS contains human resources data.						
		Learning-outcomes data: the EMIS contains learning-outcomes data.						
2.3	**Data analytics**	Data analytics	Tools and processes are available to perform data analytics at different levels on a regular basis.	Tools and processes are available to perform limited tabulations.	Basic tools and processes are available, but the system is not capable of conducting advanced analytical steps (e.g., predictive models, projections).	Tools and processes are available; however, data analytics are not performed regularly.	Tools and processes are available to perform data analytics at different levels on a regular basis.	

table continues next page

Table A.1 Rubric to Benchmark EMIS in Maryland *(continued)*

Policy levers	Indicators	Description of best practices	Scoring			
			Latent	Emerging	Established	Advanced
2.4 Dynamic system	Quality-assurance measures: The system is dynamic and maintains quality-assurance measures.	The system in place is elastic and easily adaptable to allow for changes and advancements in data needs.	The system in place is not easily adaptable to changes and advancements in data needs, because no quality-assurance standards are used.	The system in place is not easily adaptable and requires significant time and resources to accommodate changes or advancements.	The system in place is easily adaptable, but it remains reasonably complex.	The system in place is elastic and easily adaptable to allow for changes and advancements in data needs.
	Data requirements and considerations: Mechanisms are in place for addressing new and emerging data requirements.					
	System adaptability: the EMIS is elastic and easily adaptable to allow for changes and advancements in data needs.					

table continues next page

Table A.1 Rubric to Benchmark EMIS in Maryland *(continued)*

		Description of best practices	Scoring				
Policy levers	Indicators		Latent	Emerging	Established	Advanced
2.5 Serviceability	Validity across data sources: Information brought together from different data or statistical frameworks in the EMIS is placed within the data warehouse using structural and consistency measures. Integration of noneducation databases into the EMIS: Data from sources collected by agencies outside of the EMIS are integrated into the EMIS data warehouse. Archiving data: Multiple years of data are archived, including source data, metadata, and statistical results.	Services provided by the system are valid across data sources; integrate noneducation databases into the EMIS; and archive data at the service of EMIS clients by ensuring the relevance, consistency, usefulness, and timeliness of its statistics	Serious issues exist related to data validity and consistency.	Inconsistencies exist related to data validity and consistency.	The data are consistent and valid; however, some concerns exist.	Services provided by the system are valid across data sources, integrate noneducation databases into the EMIS, and archive data at the service of EMIS clients by ensuring the relevance, consistency, usefulness, and timeliness of its statistics.

table continues next page

Table A.1 Rubric to Benchmark EMIS in Maryland *(continued)*

Policy levers	Indicators	Description of best practices	Scoring			
			Latent	Emerging	Established	Advanced
	Services to EMIS clients: Services provided by the system to EMIS clients include ensuring the relevance, consistency, usefulness, and timeliness of its statistics.					
Policy area 3: Quality data		The system has the mechanisms required to collect, save, produce, and utilize information, which ensures accuracy, security, and timely, high-quality information for use in decision making.	The system lacks mechanisms to collect, save, or produce timely, high-quality information for decision making.	The system has basic mechanisms to collect, save, and produce timely, quality information; however, its accuracy might be questionable.	The system has most mechanisms in place needed to collect, save, and produce timely, high-quality information for use in decision making; however, some additional measures are needed to ensure accuracy, security, and timely information that can be used for decision making.	The system has the required mechanisms in place to collect, save, produce, and utilize information, which ensures accuracy, security, and timely, high-quality information for use in decision making.

table continues next page

Table A.1 Rubric to Benchmark EMIS in Maryland (continued)

Policy levers	Indicators	Description of best practices	Scoring				
			Latent	Emerging	Established	Advanced
3.1 Methodological soundness	Concepts and definitions: Data fields, records, concepts, indicators, and metadata are defined and documented in official operations manuals along with other national datasets and endorsed by the government. Classification: There are defined education system classifications based on technical guidelines and manuals. Scope: The scope of education statistics is broader than, and not limited to, a small number of indicators (e.g., measurements of enrollment, class size, completion). Basis for recording: Data-recording systems follow internationally accepted standards, guidelines, and good practices.	The methodological basis for producing educational statistics from raw data follows internationally accepted standards, guidelines, and good practices.	The methodological basis for producing educational statistics does not follow internationally accepted standards, guidelines, or good practices.	The methodological basis for producing educational statistics follows the basics of internationally accepted standards, guidelines, and good practices.	The methodological basis for producing educational statistics follows most required internationally accepted standards, guidelines, and good practices.	The methodological basis for producing educational statistics from raw data follows internationally accepted standards, guidelines, and good practices.

table continues next page

Table A.1 Rubric to Benchmark EMIS in Maryland (*continued*)

Policy levers	Indicators	Description of best practices	Scoring				
			Latent	Emerging	Established	Advanced	
3.2 Accuracy and reliability	Source data: Available source data provide an adequate basis for compiling statistics.

Validation of source data: Source data are consistent with the definition, scope, and classification, as well as time of recording, reference periods, and valuation of education statistics.

Statistical techniques: Statistical techniques are used to calculate accurate rates and derived indicators. | Source data and statistical techniques are sound and reliable, and statistical outputs sufficiently portray reality. | Source data and statistical techniques lack soundness and reliability. | Source data and statistical techniques have basic soundness and reliability, but statistical outputs do not portray reality. | Source data and statistical techniques follow most required elements to be sound and reliable, but statistical outputs do not portray reality. | Source data and statistical techniques are sound and reliable, and statistical outputs sufficiently portray reality. | |

table continues next page

Table A.1 Rubric to Benchmark EMIS in Maryland *(continued)*

Policy levers	Indicators	Description of best practices	Scoring				
			Latent	Emerging	Established	Advanced	
3.3 Integrity	Professionalism: EMIS staff exercise their profession with technical independence and without outside interference that could result in the violation of the public trust in EMIS statistics and the EMIS itself. Transparency: Statistical policies and practices are transparent. Ethical standards: Policies and practices in education statistics are guided by ethical standards.	Education statistics contained within the system are guided by principles of integrity.	Education statistics contained within system are not guided by principles of integrity.	Education statistics contained within the system are guided by limited principles of integrity (one of the three principles of professionalism, transparency, and ethical standards).	Education statistics contained within the system are mostly guided by principles of integrity (two of the three principles of professionalism, transparency, and ethical standards).	Education statistics contained within the system are guided by all three principles of integrity: professionalism, transparency, and ethical standards.	
3.4 Periodicity and timeliness	Periodicity: The production of reports and other outputs from the data warehouse occur in accordance with cycles in the education system.	The system produces data and statistics periodically in a timely manner	The system produces data and statistics neither periodically nor in a timely manner.	The system produces some data and statistics periodically and in a timely manner.	The system produces most data and statistics periodically and in a timely manner.	The system produces all data and statistics periodically and in a timely manner.	

table continues next page

Table A.1 Rubric to Benchmark EMIS in Maryland *(continued)*

Policy levers	Indicators	Description of best practices	Scoring			
			Latent	*Emerging*	*Established*	*Advanced*
	Timeliness: Both final statistics and financial statistics are disseminated in a timely manner.					
Policy area 4: Utilization for decision making		**The system is wholly utilized by different users for decision making at different levels of the education system.**	**There are no signs that the EMIS is utilized in decision making by the majority of education stakeholders.**	**The system is used by some education stakeholders, but not for major policy decision making.**	**The system is used by most education stakeholders but is not fully operational in governmental decision making.**	**The system is wholly utilized by different users for decision making at different levels of the education system.**
4.1 Openness	EMIS stakeholders: EMIS primary stakeholders are identified and use the system in accordance with the legal framework. User awareness: Current and potential EMIS users are aware of the EMIS and its outputs.	The system is open to education stakeholders in terms of their awareness and capacity to utilize the system.	The system lacks openness to education stakeholders in terms of their awareness and capacity to utilize the system.	The system is open to some education stakeholders in terms of their awareness and capacity to utilize the system.	The system is open to the majority of education stakeholders in terms of their awareness and capacity to utilize the system.	The system is open to all education stakeholders in terms of their awareness and capacity to utilize the system.

table continues next page

Table A.1 Rubric to Benchmark EMIS in Maryland (*continued*)

Policy levers	Indicators	Description of best practices	Scoring			
			Latent	*Emerging*	*Established*	*Advanced*
	User capacity: EMIS users have the skills to interpret, manipulate, and utilize the data produced by the system to ultimately disseminate findings.					
4.2 Operational use	Utilization in evaluation: Data produced by the EMIS are used to assess the education system. Utilization in governance: Data produced by the EMIS are used for governance purposes. Utilization by schools: Data produced by the EMIS are used by schools.	Data produced by the system are used in practice by the main education stakeholders.	Data produced by the system are not used in practice by education stakeholders.	Data produced by the system are used in practice by some education stakeholders.	Data produced by the system are used in practice by the majority of education stakeholders.	Data produced by the system are used in practice by the main education stakeholders.

table continues next page

Table A.1 Rubric to Benchmark EMIS in Maryland *(continued)*

Policy levers	Indicators	Description of best practices	Scoring			
			Latent	Emerging	Established	Advanced
	Utilization by clients: Data produced by the EMIS are used by clients (including parents, communities, and other actors). Utilization by government: The system is able to produce summative indicators (derived variables) to monitor the education system.					
4.3 Accessibility	Understandable data: Data are presented in a manner that is easily digestible.	Education statistics are presented in an understandable manner and are widely disseminated using clear platforms for utilization; assistance is available to users.	The system suffers from serious accessibility issues.	The system has major accessibility issues.	The system has minor accessibility issues.	Education statistics are presented in an understandable manner and are widely disseminated using a clear platform for utilization; assistance is available to users.

table continues next page

Table A.1 Rubric to Benchmark EMIS in Maryland (continued)

Policy levers	Indicators	Description of best practices	Scoring			
			Latent	Emerging	Established	Advanced
	Widely disseminated data: Education statistics are disseminated beyond the Ministry of Education and education statistics-producing agency to other EMIS stakeholders. Platforms for utilization: Platforms are standardized across the EMIS and are customizable to user needs. User support: Assistance is available to EMIS users upon request to help them access the data.					
4.4 Effectiveness in disseminating findings	Dissemination strategy: The national government has an information-dissemination strategy in place. Dissemination effectiveness: Dissemination of EMIS statistics is effective.	Dissemination of education statistics via an EMIS is strategic and effective.	Dissemination is neither strategic nor effective.	Dissemination is reasonably strategic, but ineffective.	A dissemination plan has been implemented; however, room exists for improvement (for full effectiveness in relation to strategic engagement).	The dissemination of education statistics via an EMIS is strategic and effective.

Sample School Census

This section provides an illustration of a school census survey that is being used in Liberia for its data collection process. The school census form is self-explanatory: it contains basic information on school demographics, student enrollments by age and sex and at different levels of the education system. It also includes information on teachers and their qualifications, along with data on school inputs. Data on school expenditure and sources of funding are also included. This survey is representative of the school census forms that are used in many countries.

A. SCHOOL PROFILE

Questionnaire ID number	
A1. EMIS Code Write the full EMIS code number.	
A2. School Name Write the full name of the school.	

A3. Location Write the name of your school's county and district. Then write the name of your school's village, town and/or city, and tick whether your school is in a rural or urban area.	**A3. County**		
	A3b. Education District ·		
	A3c. Other Village, town, and/or city		
	A3d. Rural or Urban	☐ Rural	☐ Urban

| **A4. School Contact** Write the school's primary contact phone number and e-mail address. | **A4a. Mobile number** | |
| | **A4b. E-mail address** | |

| **A5. WAEC code [Secondary Only]** Write the West African Examinations Council (WAEC) Code for grades 9 and 12 | **A5a. Grade 9** | |
| | **A5b. Grade 12** | |

B. SCHOOL PARTICULARS

B1. Type of school Tick <u>ONE</u> Answer.	☐1. Public ☐2. Private ☐3. Mission/religious group ☐4. Community ☐5. Other

B2. Level of school Tick what is applicable.

☐Early Childhood Education	☐Primary (Lower Basic) (Grades 1–6)	☐ Junior Secondary (Upper Basic) (Grades 7–9)	☐Senior Secondary (Grades 10–12)
☐Accelerated Learning Program	☐Alternative Basic Education	☐ Technical and Vocational Education and Training	

B3. Year of establishment Write the YEAR your school was founded.	YYYY

B4. Access to School from Main Road (*)

	Dry Season						Wet Season					
	< 1 Minute	< 15 Minutes	Between 15 and 30 Minutes	Between 30 Min. and 1 Hour	Between 1 and 2 Hours	> 2 Hours	Not Applicable/ Not Accessible	< 1 Minute	< 15 Minutes	Between 15 and 30 Min.	Between 30 Min. and 1 Hour	Between 1 and 2 Hours	> 2 Hours	Not Applicable/ Not Accessible
Foot												
Motor Cycle												
Car												
Boat/Canoe												

(*) Tick one applicable box per means of transport for the dry season and one applicable box during the wet season.

Sections C and D concern only the EARLY CHILDHOOD EDUCATION school level.

C. EARLY CHILDHOOD EDUCATION STUDENTS

C1. Which session does your school operate for Early Childhood Education? *Tick what is applicable.*	☐ Morning	☐ Afternoon	☐ Evening

C2. School hours Write your ECE levels starting and ending time.	C2a. Starting time	⬜ ⬜ : ⬜ ⬜
	C2b. Ending time	⬜ ⬜ : ⬜ ⬜

C3. Enrolled students *For each level of ECE that your school teaches, write the TOTAL NUMBER of male and female STUDENTS, then the number of those students who are Repeaters and the number of students with disability.*

		Total Students	Repeaters	Blind	Deaf	Other Physical Handicap
					Students with Disability	
Nursery I (ABC I)	M					
	F					
Nursery II (ABC II)	M					
	F					
Kindergarten I	M					
	F					
Kindergarten II	M					
	F					
Total	M					
	F					

C4. Enrolled students by level, age and gender *Write the TOTAL NUMBER of STUDENTS at in ECE by grade, age, and gender. Be sure to write the totals in the total column and row.*

		Total Students	≤2	3	4	5	6	7	8	> 8
							Age			
Nursery I (ABC I)	M									
	F									
Nursery II (ABC II)	M									
	F									
Kindergarten I	M									
	F									
Kindergarten II	M									
	F									
Total	M									
	F									

D. EARLY CHILDHOOD EDUCATION OPERATIONS AND STUDENTS

D1. Classrooms Write the **NUMBER OF CLASSROOMS** (rooms used for instruction; **excludes office, staff room, and storage**) by construction type.

Solid Built with cement blocks	Semi-solid Built largely with mud blocks	Makeshift Temporary made of materials, such as mat and sticks	Partitioned Rooms divided into parts as classrooms	Open-air /under the tree	Other Any other space used as a classroom

D2. Classroom furniture totals Write the number of items of furniture at your school for each type.

D2a. Write the number	Chairs	Desks	Benches	Chalkboards

Sections E, F, and G concern only the PRIMARY (LOWER BASIC) school level.

E. PRIMARY (LOWER BASIC) SCHOOL OPERATIONS AND STUDENTS

E1. Which session does your Primary (Lower Basic) school operate? Tick what is applicable.	☐Morning	☐Afternoon	☐Evening

E2. School hours Write your Primary (Lower Basic) school's starting and ending time.	E2a. Starting time	
	E2b. Ending time	

E3. Enrolled students *For each grade that your school teaches, write the total number of SECTIONS (sections are the number of classes within each grade level), then write the TOTAL NUMBER of male and female STUDENTS, the number of those students who are Repeaters and the number of students with disability. New entrants (students entering grade 1 for the first time) and new entrants with ECE need be reported only for Grade 1.*

	(1) Sections		(2) Total Students	(3) Repeaters	(4) New Entrants	(5) New Entrants with ECE	(6) Blind	(7) Deaf	(8) Other Physical Handicap
							Students with Disability		
Grade 1		M							
		F							
Grade 2		M							
		F							
Grade 3		M							
		F							
Grade 4		M							
		F							
Grade 5		M							
		F							
Grade 6		M							
		F							
Total		**M**							
		F							

E4. New Entrants to Grade 1. *Copy the number of new entrants to grade 1 and new entrants with ECE from question E3 (4) & (5), then enter the number of those students by age.*

		Total NE	<6	6	7	8	9	10	11	12	13	14	15	>15
								Age						
E4a. New Entrants	M													
	F													
E4b. New Entrants With ECE	M													
	F													

E5. Enrolled students by grade, age and gender *Write the TOTAL NUMBER of STUDENTS at your school by grade, age, and gender. Be sure to write the totals in the total column and row.*

		Total	< 6	6	7	8	9	10	11	12	13	14	15	>15
								Age						
Grade 1	M													
	F													
Grade 2	M													
	F													
Grade 3	M													
	F													
Grade 4	M													
	F													
Grade 5	M													
	F													
Grade 6	M													
	F													
Total	**M**													
	F													

F. PRIMARY (LOWER BASIC) SCHOOL CURRICULUM AND INSTRUCTION

F1. National curriculum	F1a. Does your school use the **national curriculum?** Tick one answer	☐ Yes ☐No
	F1b. How many copies of the **national curriculum** do you have? Write the number.	

F2a. Textbooks Write the number of textbooks (include only those that are usable) by grade and subject.

Textbooks	Gr. 1	Gr. 2	Gr. 3	Gr. 4	Gr. 5	Gr. 6	Total
Language arts English, literature, foreign languages							
Mathematics Arithmetic, algebra, trigonometry, etc.							
Sciences General science, physical science, biology, chemistry, physics							
Social studies Civics, history, geography							
Other Any other textbooks that are not included in the list above							

	Language arts	Mathematics	Sciences	Social studies	Other
F2b. Write the total number of textbooks that follow the national curriculum for each subject?	_____	_____	_____	_____	_____
F2c. How often do your students use the textbooks in the classroom?	☐ Everyday ☐ 2-3 days a week ☐ Never	☐ Everyday ☐ 2-3 days a week ☐ Never	☐ Everyday ☐ 2-3 days a week ☐ Never	☐ Everyday ☐ 2-3 days a week ☐ Never	☐ Everyday ☐ 2-3 days a week ☐ Never
F2d. Do you have a safe location to store the textbooks?				☐ Yes ☐ No	

G. PRIMARY (LOWER BASIC) SCHOOL INPUT

G1. Classroom Write the **NUMBER OF CLASSROOMS** (rooms used for instruction, **excludes office, staff room and storage**) by construction type.

Solid Built with cement blocks	**Semi-solid** Built largely with mud blocks	**Makeshift** Temporary made of materials, such as mat and sticks	**Partitioned** Rooms divided into parts as classrooms	**Open-air /under the tree**	**Other** Any other space used as a classroom

G2. Classroom furniture totals Write the number of items of furniture at your school for each type.

G2a. Write the number	Chairs	Desks	Benches	Chalkboards

H, I, J Concern only the JUNIOR AND SENIOR SECONDARY school level

H. JUNIOR AND SENIOR SECONDARY SCHOOL OPERATIONS AND STUDENTS

H1. Which session does your secondary school operate? Tick what is applicable.	☐ Morning ☐ Afternoon ☐ Evening

H2a. School hours Write your junior secondary school's starting and ending time.	**Starting time** HH : MM	**Ending time** HH : MM
H2b. School hours Write your senior secondary school's starting and ending time.	**Starting time** HH : MM	**Ending time** HH : MM

H3. Enrolled students *For each grade that your school teaches, write the total number of SECTIONS (sections are the number of classes within each grade level), then write the TOTAL NUMBER of male and female STUDENTS, the number of those students who are Repeaters, and the number of students with disability. Intakes into grade 7 need to be reported only for Grade 7 (students entering grade 7 for the first time).*

						Students with Disability		
	(1) Sections	(2) Total Students	(3) Repeaters	(4) Intakes into grade 7	(5) Blind	(6) Deaf	(7) Other Physical Handicap
Grade 7		M F						
Grade 8		M F						
Grade 9		M F						
Grade 10		M F						
Grade 11		M F						
Grade 12		M F						
Total		M F						

H4. Intakes into Grade 7. *Copy the total intakes into grade 7 from H3 (4), then enter the number of those students by age.*

Intakes into Grade 7		< 12	12	13	14	15	16	17	18	19	20	>20
							Age					
Intakes	M											
	F											

H5. Enrolled students by grade, age and gender *Write the TOTAL NUMBER of STUDENTS at your school by grade, age, and gender. Be sure to write the totals in the total column and row.*

		Total	< 12	12	13	14	15	16	17	18	19	20	>20
								Age					
Grade 7	M												
	F												
Grade 8	M												
	F												
Grade 9	M												
	F												
Total	**M**												
	F												

H6. Enrolled students by grade, age and gender *Write the TOTAL NUMBER of STUDENTS at your school by grade, age, and gender. Be sure to write the totals in the total column and row.*

		Total	< 12	12	13	14	15	16	17	18	19	20	>20
								Age					
Grade 10	M												
	F												
Grade 11	M												
	F												
Grade 12	M												
	F												
Total	**M**												
	F												

I. JUNIOR AND SENIOR SECONDARY SCHOOL CURRICULUM AND INSTRUCTION

I1. National curriculum	**I1a.** Does your school use the **national curriculum?** Tick one answer.	☐ Yes ☐No
	I1b. How many copies of the **national curriculum** do you have? Write the number.	

I2. WAEC& WASSCE Syllabus	**I2a.** Does your school use the **WAEC syllabus?** Tick one answer.	☐ Yes ☐No
	I2b. How many copies of the **WAEC syllabus** do you have? Write the number.	
	I2c. Does your school use the **WASSCE syllabus?** Tick one answer.	☐ Yes ☐No
	I2d. How many copies of the **WASSCE syllabus** do you have? Write the number.	

I3a. Textbooks Write the number of textbooks (include only those that are usable) by grade and subject.

Textbooks	Gr. 7	Gr. 8	Gr. 9	Gr. 10	Gr. 11	Gr. 12	Total
Language arts English, literature, foreign languages							
Mathematics Arithmetic, algebra, trigonometry, etc.							
Sciences General science, physical education, biology, chemistry, physics							
Social studies Civics, history, geography							
Other Any other textbooks that are not included in the lists above							

	Language arts	Mathematics	Sciences	Social studies	Other
I3b. Write the total number of textbooks that follow the national curriculum for each subject?					
	Language arts	Mathematics	Sciences	Social studies	Other
I3c. How often do your students use the textbooks in the classroom?	☐ Everyday ☐2-3 days a week ☐ Never	☐ Everyday ☐2-3 days a week ☐ Never	☐ Everyday ☐2-3 days a week ☐ Never	☐ Everyday ☐2-3 days a week ☐ Never	☐ Everyday ☐2-3 days a week ☐ Never
I3d. Do you have a safe location to store the textbooks?			☐ Yes ☐No		

I4. Student Performance Write the total number of students who have passed or failed the WAEC tests scores in grade 9 and grade 12 by subject and grade. (Use the results that are available as of October 2015. These will most likely be the 2014 results.

L. ALTERNATIVE EDUCATION CURRICULUM AND INSTRUCTION

L1. National curriculum	L1a. Does your school use the **national curriculum?** Tick <u>one</u> answer	☐ Yes ☐No
	L1b. How many copies of the **national curriculum** do you have? Write the number.	

L2a. Textbooks. Write the number of textbooks (include only those that are usable) by level and subject

Textbooks	LEVEL I	LEVEL II	LEVEL II	TOTAL
Language arts English, literature, foreign languages				
Mathematics Arithmetic, algebra, trigonometry, etc.				
Sciences General science, physical education, biology, chemistry, physics				
Social studies Civics, history, geography				
Other Any other textbooks that are not included in the lists above				

	Language arts	Mathematics	Sciences	Social studies	Other
L2b. Write the total number of textbooks that follow the national curriculum for each subject?	_____	_____	_____	_____	_____
L2c. How often do your students use the textbooks in the classroom?	☐ Everyday ☐2-3 days a week ☐ Never	☐ Everyday ☐2-3 days a week ☐ Never	☐ Everyday ☐2-3 days a week ☐ Never	☐ Everyday ☐2-3 days a week ☐ Never	☐ Everyday ☐2-3 days a week ☐ Never
L2d. Do you have a safe location to store the textbooks?				☐ Yes ☐No	

M. ALTERNATIVE EDUCATION PROGRAM INPUT

M1. Classrooms Write the **NUMBER OF CLASSROOMS** (rooms used for instruction, **excludes office, staff room and storage**) by construction type

Solid Built with cement blocks	**Semi-solid** Built largely with mud blocks	**Makeshift** Temporary made of materials, such as mat and sticks	**Partitioned** Rooms divided into parts as classrooms	**Open-air /under the tree**	**Other** Any other space used as a classroom

M2. Classroom furniture totals Write the number of items of furniture at your school for each type.				
	Chairs	**Desks**	**Benches**	**Chalkboards**
M2a. Write the Number				

N, O, P Concern only TECHNICAL AND VOCATIONAL EDUCATION AND TRAINING level

N. TECHNICAL AND VOCATIONAL EDUCATION AND TRAINING OPERATIONS

N1. Which session does your TVET operate? Tick what is applicable.	☐ Morning ☐ Afternoon ☐Evening

N2. School hour Write your TVET School's starting and ending time.	**N2a. Starting time**	
	N2b. Ending time	

N3. Minimal age requirement What is the minimal entrance age required for admission to the TVET center?	_____years

N4. TVET Provider: Name the provider for your program	☐ Government	☐ Other: Specify_____

O. TECHNICAL & VOCATIONAL EDUCATION CURRICULUM, INSTRUCTION & LEARNERS

O1. TEXTBOOKS What textbooks/instruction manuals do your TVET programs have? **Tick what is applicable.**	☐Accounting	☐Agriculture	☐Architectural Drafting	☐Auto-Mechanic
	☐Building Trades	☐Business Education	☐Carpentry	☐Computer Science
	☐Electricity	☐Electronics/ICT	☐Home Arts	☐Hospitality Science
	☐Interior Decoration	☐Metal Work	☐Pastry	☐Plumbing
	☐Soap-Making	☐Tailoring	☐Type & Dye	☐Wood-Work

O2. GENERAL SKILLS TAUGHT What skills do your TVET programs teach? *Tick what is applicable.*	☐Literacy (read and write)	☐Numeracy	☐Entrepreneurship
	☐Life skills *HIV/AIDS, hygiene, etc.*	☐IT skills	☐Other

O3. SERVICES OFFERED What services do your TVET programs offer? *Tick what is applicable.*	☐Access to micro credit	☐Apprenticeship *More than 2 months and with specific training focus*	☐Entrepreneurship training/follow-up
	☐Job promotion activities	☐Toolkit and equipment/starter kit	☐Internship *Less than 2 months in business*
	☐Job counseling	☐Other	

O4. Learner Information Circle the minimuml level of education a learner must have to be admitted to each of your programs? Then write the TOTAL NUMBER of LEARNERS presently enrolled in your program, by gender AND the TOTAL NUMBER of LEARNERS that completed your program in 2014, by gender.

Program	Minimum Requirement Circle one answer 1. No prior education needed 2. Completed Grade 6 (or equivalent) 3. Completed Grade 9 (or equivalent) 4. Completed Grade 12 (or equivalent)				Total Enrollment (2015)		Completers from 2014	
					M	F	M	F
Accounting	1	2	3	4				
Agriculture	1	2	3	4				
Architectural Drafting	1	2	3	4				
Auto-Mechanic	1	2	3	4				
Building Trades	1	2	3	4				
Business Education	1	2	3	4				
Carpentry	1	2	3	4				
Computer Science	1	2	3	4				
Electricity	1	2	3	4				
Electronics/ICT	1	2	3	4				
Home Arts	1	2	3	4				
Hospitality Science	1	2	3	4				
Interior Decoration	1	2	3	4				
Metal Work	1	2	3	4				
Pastry	1	2	3	4				
Plumbing	1	2	3	4				
Soap-Making	1	2	3	4				
Tailoring	1	2	3	4				
Type & Dye	1	2	3	4				
Wood-Work	1	2	3	4				
Other	1	2	3	4				
Total								

P. VOCATIONAL AND SPECIAL EDUCATION SCHOOL INPUT

P1. Classrooms Write the **NUMBER OF CLASSROOMS** (rooms used for instruction; **excludes office, staff room and storage**) by construction type.

Solid Built with cement blocks	Semi-solid Built largely with mud blocks	Makeshift Temporary made of materials, such as mat and sticks	Partitioned Rooms divided into parts as classrooms	Open-air /under the tree	Other Any other space used as a classroom

P2. Classroom furniture totals Write the number of items of furniture at your school for each type and tick those shared between sessions

	Chairs	Desks	Benches	Chalkboards
P2a. Write the number				

The remaining Sections Q and R concern ECE, PRIMARY (LOWER BASIC), JUNIOR AND SENIOR SECONDARY, ABE, ALP AND TVET schools.

Q. SCHOOL INFRASTUCTURE

Q1. School Building From *what materials are your school constructed?*	☐Solid Built with cement blocks and steel ☐Make-Shift Temporary made of materials such as mats and sticks	☐ Semi Solid Built largely with mud blocks ☐ Open Air /Under a Tree ☐ Other

Q2a. School Library Is there a school library?	☐ Yes (Answer Q2b to Q2e ☐ No (Move on to Q3)

Q2b. Is there a librarian or staff member looking after the books?	☐Yes ☐ No	**Q2c.** Reading space for how many students	____ Students
Q2d. Number of books in the library	_____books	**Q2e.** Number of library shelves	____Shelves

Q3. Other facilities: Which of the following do your school have? Tick what is applicable.						
Q3a. Cell phone/mobile coverage	☐Yes			☐No		

Q3b. Fence or surrounding walls	☐Yes		☐Needs repair		☐No	

Q3c. Drinking water	☐Pipe born water	☐Hand pump	☐Well	☐Creek	☐Facility needs repair	☐None

Q3d. Latrine or toilet facility	☐Yes		☐Needs repair		☐No	

Q3e. Tick the group(s) of people for whom the latrine facility is available.	☐1. Boys only ☐2. Girls only ☐3. Boys and girls combined ☐4. Male staff only ☐5. Female staff only ☐6. Male and female staff combined

Q3f. Which of the following facilities are available at your school?	☐ Auditorium ☐ Health Clinic ☐ Principal's office ☐ School Farm	☐ Staff room/office ☐ Hand Washing Facility ☐ School Garden ☐ Computer lab	☐ Functioning generator ☐ Regular Fuel for generator ☐ Sports/Playground ☐ Science lab	☐ Storage ☐Cafeteria ☐Local electricity grid ☐National electricity grid

R. SCHOOL SUPPORT

R1. School finance does your school receive grants from the following entities? If YES, tick YES and specify the amount of grant (in Liberian Dollars) from each of the sources. If NO, tick NO and move on.

Grant source	Yes/No?	Amount (LD$)
R1a. Central government (MOE)	☐Yes ☐ No	
R1b. Local (county/district) government	☐Yes ☐ No	
R1c. Private group/individual	☐Yes ☐ No	
R1d. Mission/Religious group	☐Yes ☐ No	
R1e. Community	☐Yes ☐ No	
R1f. International/domestic NGO/agencies	☐Yes ☐ No	

R2. Donor support does your school receive support from the following **donors**? If yes, then tick the corresponding level for which you receive support.

Donor	ECE	Prim.	Sec.	Alt Ed.	TVET
R2a. UNICEF	☐	☐	☐	☐	☐
R2b. USAID	☐	☐	☐	☐	☐
R2c. Global Partnership for Education (GPE)	☐	☐	☐	☐	☐
R2d. Other Specify:_____	☐	☐	☐	☐	☐
R2e. Other Specify:_____	☐	☐	☐	☐	☐
R2f. Other Specify:_____	☐	☐	☐	☐	☐

R3. School materials Does your school receive school materials from the government or an organization? If YES tick YES and specify the source. If NO, tick NO and move on.

Type of Support	Yes/No	If Yes, by whom	
R3a. Books	☐Yes ☐ No	☐Government	☐Other: Specify_____
R3b. Furniture	☐Yes ☐ No	☐Government	☐Other: Specify_____
R3c. Food/school feeding	☐Yes ☐ No	☐Government	☐Other: Specify_____
R3d. School supplies (stationery etc.)	☐Yes ☐ No	☐Government	☐Other: Specify_____
R3e. Training (for teachers, PTA, etc.)	☐Yes ☐ No	☐Government	☐Other: Specify_____
R3f. Science lab equipment	☐Yes ☐ No	☐Government	☐Other: Specify_____

S. MANAGEMENT AND TEACHING STAFF

S1. Parent-Teacher association (PTA)	S1a. Is there a **functioning PTA?**	☐ Yes ☐No	
	S1b. How many times does it meet in a year? Tick <u>one</u> answer.	☐1. Once ☐3. Three times ☐5. Zero	☐2. Twice ☐4. Four or more times
	S1c. Chairpersons name		
	S1d. Chairpersons telephone/mobile number		

S2. School Management Committee	S2a. Is there a **functioning School Management Committee?**	☐ Yes ☐ No	
	S2b. How many times does it meet in a year? Tick <u>one</u> answer.	☐1. Once ☐3. Three times ☐5. Zero	☐2. Twice ☐4. Four or more times

S3. Staff Complete the following information about each of your school's staff (teachers or trainers who deliver instruction in classrooms and non-teaching staff). Complete the information for teachers or trainers (staff that deliver instruction in classrooms) first and then staff who do not deliver classroom instruction. Be sure to write the total counts of staff by gender at the bottom of the table.

No	Surname	Given name	Sex Circle one	Year of birth YYYY	Payroll No. 11 digits	Current Position Circle what is applicable	Level(s) Teaching Circle what is Applicable	Professional Qualification Circle one answer	Academic qualification Circle one answer	Subject(s) Teaching* Circle what is applicable	Years in position Write the number of years the staff member has held that position	Source of salary Circle one answer
						CODE BANK						
						1. Principal 2. Vice Principal 3. Registrar 4. Custodian 5. Teacher /Trainer 6. Other	1. ECE 2. Primary (Lower Basic) 3. Junior Secondary (Upper Basic) 4. Senior Secondary 5. ALP 6. ABE 7.TVET 8. No teaching	1. No teaching certificate 2. Pre-service C Certificate 3. In-service C Certificate 4. Pre-service B Certificate 5. In-service B Certificate 6. AA Certificate 7. BSc. Education 8. MS. Education or higher 9. TVET Certification from an accredited institution	1. Did not complete secondary school 2. Completed Secondary School 3. Any Bachelor's degree 4. Any Master's degree or above	1. Language arts 2. Mathematics 3. Sciences 4. Social studies 5. Other		1. Gov. 2. Private Inst. (firms religious bodies, NGO) 3. Household (fam, comm..) 4. volunteer
Ex.	Bryant	Charles	M F	1984	01-23-456-7890	1 2 3 4 5 6	1 2 3 4 5 6 7 8	1 2 3 4 5 6 7 8 9	1 2 3 4	1 2 3 4 5	5	1 2 3 4
1.			M F			1 2 3 4 5 6	1 2 3 4 5 6 7 8	1 2 3 4 5 6 7 8 9	1 2 3 4	1 2 3 4 5		1 2 3 4
2.			M F			1 2 3 4 5 6	1 2 3 4 5 6 7 8	1 2 3 4 5 6 7 8 9	1 2 3 4	1 2 3 4 5		1 2 3 4
3.			M F			1 2 3 4 5 6	1 2 3 4 5 6 7 8	1 2 3 4 5 6 7 8 9	1 2 3 4	1 2 3 4 5		1 2 3 4
4.			M F			1 2 3 4 5 6	1 2 3 4 5 6 7 8	1 2 3 4 5 6 7 8 9	1 2 3 4	1 2 3 4 5		1 2 3 4
5.			M F			1 2 3 4 5 6	1 2 3 4 5 6 7 8	1 2 3 4 5 6 7 8 9	1 2 3 4	1 2 3 4 5		1 2 3 4
6.			M F			1 2 3 4 5 6	1 2 3 4 5 6 7 8	1 2 3 4 5 6 7 8 9	1 2 3 4	1 2 3 4 5		1 2 3 4
7.			M F			1 2 3 4 5 6	1 2 3 4 5 6 7 8	1 2 3 4 5 6 7 8 9	1 2 3 4	1 2 3 4 5		1 2 3 4
8.			M F			1 2 3 4 5 6	1 2 3 4 5 6 7 8	1 2 3 4 5 6 7 8 9	1 2 3 4	1 2 3 4 5		1 2 3 4
9.			M F			1 2 3 4 5 6	1 2 3 4 5 6 7 8	1 2 3 4 5 6 7 8 9	1 2 3 4	1 2 3 4 5		1 2 3 4
10.			M F			1 2 3 4 5 6	1 2 3 4 5 6 7 8	1 2 3 4 5 6 7 8 9	1 2 3 4	1 2 3 4 5		1 2 3 4
11.			M F			1 2 3 4 5 6	1 2 3 4 5 6 7 8	1 2 3 4 5 6 7 8 9	1 2 3 4	1 2 3 4 5		1 2 3 4
12.			M F			1 2 3 4 5 6	1 2 3 4 5 6 7 8	1 2 3 4 5 6 7 8 9	1 2 3 4	1 2 3 4 5		1 2 3 4
13.			M F			1 2 3 4 5 6	1 2 3 4 5 6 7 8	1 2 3 4 5 6 7 8 9	1 2 3 4	1 2 3 4 5		1 2 3 4
14.			M F			1 2 3 4 5 6	1 2 3 4 5 6 7 8	1 2 3 4 5 6 7 8 9	1 2 3 4	1 2 3 4 5		1 2 3 4
15.			M F			1 2 3 4 5 6	1 2 3 4 5 6 7 8	1 2 3 4 5 6 7 8 9	1 2 3 4	1 2 3 4 5		1 2 3 4
16.			M F			1 2 3 4 5 6	1 2 3 4 5 6 7 8	1 2 3 4 5 6 7 8 9	1 2 3 4	1 2 3 4 5		1 2 3 4
17.			M F			1 2 3 4 5 6	1 2 3 4 5 6 7 8	1 2 3 4 5 6 7 8 9	1 2 3 4	1 2 3 4 5		1 2 3 4
18.			M F			1 2 3 4 5 6	1 2 3 4 5 6 7 8	1 2 3 4 5 6 7 8 9	1 2 3 4	1 2 3 4 5		1 2 3 4
19.			M F			1 2 3 4 5 6	1 2 3 4 5 6 7 8	1 2 3 4 5 6 7 8 9	1 2 3 4	1 2 3 4 5		1 2 3 4
20.			M F			1 2 3 4 5 6	1 2 3 4 5 6 7 8	1 2 3 4 5 6 7 8 9	1 2 3 4	1 2 3 4 5		1 2 3 4
21.			M F			1 2 3 4 5 6	1 2 3 4 5 6 7 8	1 2 3 4 5 6 7 8 9	1 2 3 4	1 2 3 4 5		1 2 3 4
22.			M F			1 2 3 4 5 6	1 2 3 4 5 6 7 8	1 2 3 4 5 6 7 8 9	1 2 3 4	1 2 3 4 5		1 2 3 4
23.			M F			1 2 3 4 5 6	1 2 3 4 5 6 7 8	1 2 3 4 5 6 7 8 9	1 2 3 4	1 2 3 4 5		1 2 3 4
24.			M F			1 2 3 4 5 6	1 2 3 4 5 6 7 8	1 2 3 4 5 6 7 8 9	1 2 3 4	1 2 3 4 5		1 2 3 4
25.			M F			1 2 3 4 5 6	1 2 3 4 5 6 7 8	1 2 3 4 5 6 7 8 9	1 2 3 4	1 2 3 4 5		1 2 3 4

*Subject 1 = **Language arts:** English, literature, foreign languages
    2 = **Mathematics:** Arithmetic, algebra, trigonometry, etc.
    3 = **Sciences:** General science, physical education, biology, chemistry
    4 = **Social studies:** Civics, history, geography
    5 = **Other:** Any other subjects that are not included in the lists above

T. SUMMARY COUNTS

T1. EARLY CHILDHOOD EDUCATION SUMMARY COUNTS

Total Students (See **Section C4**)			Classrooms (**Section D1**)			Total Teachers (**See Section S3**) ECE Teachers only		
Male	Female	Total	Solid	Semi-solid	Total	Male	Female	Total

T2. PRIMARY (LOWER BASIC) STUDENTS SUMMARY COUNTS

Total Students (See **Section E5**)			Classrooms (**Section G1**)			Total Teachers (See **Section S3**) Primary (Lower Basic) Teachers only		
Male	Female	Total	Solid	Semi-solid	Total	Male	Female	Total

T3. JUNIOR SECONDARY SCHOOL SUMMARY COUNTS

Total Students (See **Section H5**)			Classrooms (**Section J1**)			Total Teachers (See **Section S3**) Junior Secondary Teachers only		
Male	Female	Total	Solid	Semi-solid	Total	Male	Female	Total

T4. SENIOR SECONDARY SCHOOL SUMMARY COUNTS

Total Students (See **Section H6**)			Classrooms (**Section J2**)			Total Teachers (See **Section S3**) Senior Secondary Teachers only		
Male	Female	Total	Solid	Semi-solid	Total	Male	Female	Total

T5. ALTERNATIVE EDUCATION SUMMARY COUNTS

Total Students (See **Section K5**)			Classrooms (**Section M1**)			Total Teachers (See **Section S3**) Alternative Education Teachers only		
Male	Female	Total	Solid	Semi-solid	Total	Male	Female	Total

T6. TECHNICAL AND VOCATIONAL EDUCATION SUMMARY COUNTS

Total Learners (See **Section O4**)			Classrooms (**Section P1**)			Total Trainers (See **Section S3**) TVET Trainers only		
Male	Female	Total	Solid	Semi-solid	Total	Male	Female	Total

U. QUESTIONNAIRE TRACKING CERTIFICATION

U1. Filled out by SCHOOL PRINCIPAL By signing the document, I certify that the questionnaire has been completed and that all data contained herein is correct and accurate to the best of my knowledge. I also confirm that I understand that the information herein will be checked by county and district officials, which may require random monitoring visits.	**Name** FULL NAME	
	Signature	
	Date	DD/MM/YY
U2. Filled out by DISTRICT EDUCATION OFFICER By signing this document, I certify that I have checked the questionnaire and that all data contained herein is correct and accurate to the best of my knowledge.	**Name** FULL NAME	
	Signature	
	Date	DD/MM/YY
U3. Filled out by COUNTY EDUCATION OFFICER By signing this document, I certify that I have checked the questionnaire and that all data contained herein is correct and accurate to the best of my knowledge.	**Name** FULL NAME	
	Signature	
	Date	DD/MM/YY
U4. Filled out by MINISTRY OF EDUCATION (MOE) OFFICER By signing this document, I certify that I have completed the data entry for this form on the data specified and that I have brought to the attention of my supervisors any inconsistencies I have found in the questionnaire while entering the data.	**Name** FULL NAME	
	Signature	
	Date	DD/MM/YY

Structure of a Request for Proposals

The following section provides an example of the request for proposals (RFP) documents by Howard County Public Schools System in the state of Maryland, United States.

1 GENERAL
    1.1   SCOPE OF CONTRACT
    1.2   PURPOSE
    1.3   BACKGROUND
    1.4   SUBMITTAL QUALIFICATIONS
2 OFFEROR INSTRUCTIONS
    2.1   SCHEDULE OF PROCUREMENTS EVENTS
    2.2   PRE-SUBMISSION CONFERENCE
    2.3   DEADLINE FOR SUBMISSION RESPONSES
    2.4   RIGHT TO AMEND, MODIFY AND WITHDRAW
    2.5   WRITTEN QUESTIONS AND OFFICIAL ANSWER
    2.6   ISSUING OFFICE
    2.7   CLARIFICATIONS AND AGENDA
    2.8   OPEN RECORDS
    2.9   TIME
    2.10   COPIES
    2.11   LATE PROPOSALS
    2.12   PERIOD THAT PROPOSALS REMAIN VALID
    2.13   OBLIGATIONS OF HCPSS
    2.14   OFFEROR OBLIGATIONS
    2.15   ORAL PRESENTATION
    2.16   MULTIPLE/ALTERNATIVE PROPOSALS
    2.17   PROPOSAL ACCEPTANCE
    2.18   OPENING PROCEDURES
    2.19   ERRORS IN PROPOSALS

Environmental Benefits Statement

The World Bank Group is committed to reducing its environmental footprint. In support of this commitment, we leverage electronic publishing options and print-on-demand technology, which is located in regional hubs worldwide. Together, these initiatives enable print runs to be lowered and shipping distances decreased, resulting in reduced paper consumption, chemical use, greenhouse gas emissions, and waste.

We follow the recommended standards for paper use set by the Green Press Initiative. The majority of our books are printed on Forest Stewardship Council (FSC)–certified paper, with nearly all containing 50–100 percent recycled content. The recycled fiber in our book paper is either unbleached or bleached using totally chlorine-free (TCF), processed chlorine–free (PCF), or enhanced elemental chlorine–free (EECF) processes.

More information about the Bank's environmental philosophy can be found at http://www.worldbank.org/corporateresponsibility.